THE
ORVIS
FLY-TYING GUIDE

OTHER BOOKS BY TOM ROSENBAUER

The Orvis Fly-Fishing Guide

The Orvis Guide to Reading Trout Streams

The Orvis Streamside Guide to Approach and Presentation

The Orvis Streamside Guide to Leaders, Knots, and Tippets

The Orvis Streamside Guide to Trout Foods and Their Imitations

The Orvis Fly-Tying Manual

The Orvis Guide to Prospecting for Trout

Casting Illusions

THE ORVIS
FLY-TYING GUIDE

Completely Revised and Updated

TOM ROSENBAUER
ILLUSTRATIONS BY ROD WALINCHUS
TYING PHOTOGRAPHS BY TOM ROSENBAUER

LYONS PRESS

Guilford, CT

LYONS
PRESS

An imprint of The Rowman & Littlefield
Publishing Group, Inc.
4501 Forbes Blvd., Ste. 200
Lanham, MD 20706
www.rowman.com

Distributed by NATIONAL BOOK NETWORK

British Library Cataloguing in Publication Information
available

Library of Congress Cataloging-in-Publication Data

Names: Rosenbauer, Tom, author.
Title: The Orvis fly-tying guide / Tom Rosenbauer ; illustrations
  by Rod Walinchus ; tying photographs by Tom Rosenbauer.
Description: Guilford, CT : Lyons Press, [2019] | Includes
  index.
Identifiers: LCCN 2019001058 (print) | LCCN 2019003098
  (ebook) | ISBN 9781493025824 (ebook) | ISBN
  9781493025817 (paperback) | ISBN 9781493025824 (ebook)
Subjects: LCSH: Fly tying—Handbooks, manuals, etc.
Classification: LCC SH451 (ebook) | LCC SH451 .R6184 2019
  (print) | DDC 688.7/9124—dc23
LC record available at https://lccn.loc.gov/2019001058

ISBN 978-1-4930-2581-7 (paperback)
ISBN 978-1-4930-2582-4 (e-book)

Printed in the United States of America

CONTENTS

ACKNOWLEDGMENTS

To all the fishing buddies who have generously shared ideas and patterns over the years: Aaron Adams, Luca Adelfio, Tyler Atkins, Tony Biski, Jon Brett, Sean Brillon, Bill Bullock, Aron Cascone, Monroe Coleman, Shawn Combs, the late Rick Eck, Brett Ference, Cooper Gilkes, the late Kevin Gregory, Steve Herter, John Herzer, Sean Kersting, Pete Kutzer, Jim Lepage, Del Mazza, Jim McFadyean, Galen Mercer, Dave Perkins, Perk Perkins, Bill Reed, Ed Schroeder, John Shaner, the late Tony Stetzko, Tim Sullivan, Greg Vincent, Wayne Walts, Chad Walz, and Rick Wollum.

To the people in the business who have patiently answered my questions about patterns and materials: Don Barnes of Regal Engineering, Martin Bawden of Flymen Fishing Company, Otto Beck, Bill Black, Lee Christianson, Joe Dion, Dana Dodge of Fulling Mill Flies, Pat Dunlap of Cascade Crest, Tim Flagler of Tightline Productions, Jesse Haller, John Harder, John Juracek, Steve Kenerk, T. L. Lauerman of Wapsi, Craig Mathews, Tom McMillen, Angelo Musiani, Art Scheck, Tom Schmeucker of Wapsi, Kevin Sloan, Barry Unwin, Frank Vadala, Marcos Vergara of Hareline Dubbin, and Tom Whiting of Whiting Farms. Special thanks to Carl Coleman for giving me a start in commercial tying and putting his trust in a fourteen-year-old tier. I still use many of the techniques that Carl taught me fifty years ago.

Special thanks to Tim and Joan Flagler of Tightline Productions for sharing some of their top-secret methods of lighting fly tying for photography and for all of the inspiration and new tips they have given me through their videos.

Finally, thank you to my wife, Robin, and son, Brett, for the many hours they have allowed me absent from family time, secreted away in my fly-tying/writing/photography loft.

PART I

THE BASICS

I'm willing to bet my first attempt at fly tying fifty years ago was more pathetic than yours was or will be. I had sent away for a kit from Herter's. The only instructions in the kit were for the Fanwing Royal Coachman, one of the most difficult patterns in the history of fly tying. I hacked my way through the fly and, having read somewhere that dry flies had to be dipped in some kind of potion to make them float, promptly dipped the entire fly in head cement. This should have made the fly immortal, like an ancient insect preserved in amber, but I was so frustrated I threw it in the trash.

I have tried to remember what those early days were like so you won't begin in the same fashion. I don't think I've ever forgotten what it's like to be faced with a pile of strange materials and unusual tools, because I've taught fly tying all my adult life—at Trout Unlimited meetings, impromptu neighborhood "tie and lie sessions," at kids' cancer hospitals, in special wards for disturbed teenagers, and to coworkers at Orvis on lunch hours. One of my favorite classes was during my college years at SUNY Syracuse Environmental Science and Forestry School, where I'd spend Saturday mornings at Vad's Sport Shop, earning beer and textbook money teaching classic Catskill dry flies to a bunch of guys three times my age.

There were only two or three fly-tying instruction books available when I first started tying. At any one time, they might all be out of print, and if the local library didn't have one, you were out of luck. No Lyons Press to keep them in print. No Amazon to find them. No YouTube videos. Now there are hundreds of fly-tying books in print, and I would not even attempt to count the internet videos available to everyone.

With all that free information online, why do we need another fly-tying book, or in this case, a major revision of a book that has been around for years? I do feel that some of us still learn better from books, studying photographs in detail and taking our time, instead of constantly hitting the pause button or, worse yet, sitting through a windy introduction to a video on how the originator invented the fly. Sometimes you just want to get on with it. I also feel it's convenient and efficient to find hundreds of proven fly patterns in one place, ready to access instantly instead of turning on a computer, parsing search terms, and staring at a screen.

On the other hand, there are many skills that are difficult to learn in a book but that a video can teach you in seconds. I'll demonstrate how to accomplish a whip finish in step-by-step photographs in this book because I feel obligated to, but I would be the first to suggest that you either take a basic fly-tying class or watch a video if you don't get the whip finish in a few minutes of studying my photographs. I feel books and videos complement each other in a magical way that was never available to tiers in the past.

This book is divided into three parts: The first part teaches you the basics of tying flies, assuming you have never faced a fly-tying vise and the only tying you've done is lacing your shoes or maybe attaching a fly to your leader. The second part shows how to tie some popular and effective flies. The third part of the book offers the recipes for every fly in the 2018 Orvis fly offering, plus many others. Once you master the basic patterns in Part II of this book, you can move on to the world of fly tying by finding the ones in the pattern index you want to try. I've marked each fly in the pattern index with a difficulty level so you don't get frustrated attempting patterns beyond your skills. If you are just starting out, I recommend you begin by reading Part I, then skim over all the step-by-step patterns so you see what's involved. Make a note on patterns you want to tie or things that aren't clear—another pattern might present the technique in a slightly different manner. Then start with one of the basic patterns like the Woolly Bugger. Tie one pattern until you feel comfortable with the techniques; only then should you move on to another.

How fast should you progress, and how much time should you devote to tying? Some people pick up fly tying instantly, while others struggle. It has little to do with patience or finger dexterity. Del Mazza, perhaps one of the best dry-fly tiers I've ever met, has fingers like spare ribs and less patience than a Labrador retriever.

Your first flies will catch fish, because fish are far less picky about style than fishing buddies. Try to plan at least 30 minutes for each tying session. It might be 30 minutes a night, 30 minutes a week, or 30 minutes a month. These will be some of the most relaxing, therapeutic half-hours you'll ever spend, and they'll add a new dimension to your fishing. One of my greatest pleasures is to start a fishing trip with a small box of new patterns I've created, just waiting to be sampled by eager fish. I hope my book will bring this satisfaction into your life too.

CHAPTER 1

GETTING STARTED

A PLACE TO PARK IT

The ideal place to tie flies is a room of your own, such as an office or a spare bedroom, with plenty of shelf space for books and materials. Natural light is wonderful for fly tying, so having a big window next to you or behind you is ideal. Make sure the door can be closed tightly: Sharp dubbing needles and scissors are attractive to small children, and both cats and dogs seem to enjoy chewing on expensive hackle capes more than anything else you own. You should have a broad, clean worktable and a chair that lets you sit hunched over a vise without back pain.

Barring this ideal location, you can use a temporary spot on a kitchen or dining-room table if you are well organized and all of your gear is portable. In this case, get a pedestal vise, and store all of your materials and tools in boxes that can be moved easily from one room to another.

There is no right height for a fly-tying vise. Some people like to look down on the fly and therefore set the vise so that it is at chest level. I like mine higher, about chin level, but you should experiment to find the height that works best for you, accounting for any vision problems and preventing strain on your muscles. Adjusting the height is easier with a clamp vise, as the jaws can be moved up or down on the stem. If you have a pedestal vise, you'll have to find a table that brings the vise to a comfortable height. Your chair should be centered on the vise, and it should be close enough to let you see every turn of thread in detail.

STORAGE

The best primary storage containers for all fly-tying materials are Ziploc bags. They are perfect for any material that contains feathers, skin, or hair, because carpet beetles and moths can't get inside sealed bags. Carpet beetles are the number-one destroyer of fly-tying materials. Learn to recognize these small insects by the red band in the middle of their bodies. If you find any in your fly-tying area, inspect anything that they might have gotten into (look also for sawdust-like material in the bottom of a bag, which means larvae have been chewing there), and then remove any bags that may have been infested. Throw them outside in the trash or keep them in Ziploc bags under quarantine forever if they are rare or you can't bear parting with them. The material might still have eggs in it, though, and should remain suspect as long as you keep it. Freezing, microwaving, or washing these infested materials are not reliable ways to kill larvae and eggs. Sealing them with moth crystals may work, and it is what we used to do, but I am not comfortable suggesting you douse stuff you will be waving under your nose with paradichlorobenzene or naphtha.

Keeping the door to your tying room closed and making sure the window screens are tight will prevent most problems before they start. However, sometimes bugs come in materials you have purchased. Tanned hides don't have bugs, but other materials like wing quills and feathers and bucktails can't be tanned. To be safe, keep new natural materials in quarantine for a year before you mix them in with other natural materials.

Even though bugs are not a problem with synthetics, tinsels, and other man-made materials, Ziploc bags still make great organizers because loose stuff stays put. Most materials already come in these bags; you can then put smaller bagged materials inside bigger bags. Label all of your bags with a permanent marker to avoid rooting through each bag.

Plastic shoeboxes with tight lids make perfect storage devices. They stack, are usually clear, and keep bugs and pets out of your stuff. Label each box on three sides and on top with a waterproof marker—even when the boxes are stacked in a closet, you'll always know where to find a white bucktail when you need it. Drawers made for nails and screws are great for storing hooks, threads, tinsels, and

The best way I have found to store materials is to organize them in Ziploc bags, stored in plastic storage boxes. It keeps like items together and prevents insects from damaging natural materials.

By organizing your materials in plastic storage boxes, you can stack them neatly in a closet or in a corner.

other man-made materials, but they are not so good for animal products, because they aren't airtight. Big tackle boxes are also useful, but they don't stack.

There are portable tying benches on the market that open up into a big storage area underneath. If you tie in various rooms in your house, you can move your materials and work surface in a single trip.

Eventually you might want to invest in a big roll-top desk. These are great for fly tying, especially if you tie in an area that is used by the rest of the family. The top can be rolled down to keep your messy work area away from prying hands and paws, and you can stop in the middle of a bunch of flies and walk away without worrying.

LIGHTING

You need a lot of light to tie flies, and the older you get the more light you'll need. Trust me—good lighting makes a huge difference in the quality of your flies. The best indoor setup is to have natural light from a window coming from

one side and light from a strong lamp on the other. Of course this only works during the day, and you will probably do a lot of your tying in the evening.

Your working light should come from overhead but be angled slightly so the shadow from your hands working on the fly does not fall directly onto the hook. Any lamp will work in a pinch, but the best lights are LED desk lamps. They contain multiple bulbs that are extremely bright but use little electricity and give off almost no heat. The best ones hide the bulbs behind a translucent panel that distributes the light evenly and reduces shadows, like a soft box on a studio photography light. Most are wonderfully flexible, so you can adjust your lighting to any angle. Nearly all of them also have a switch that allows you to adjust the color of the lighting, from a pale white to a warm evening glow. They are light enough for travel or for moving around the house with ease, the bulbs are nearly unbreakable, and they are happily inexpensive. You can even get rechargeable ones for travel or models that charge in the USB port of a laptop.

My advice is to buy two lamps. Use one directly overhead for your main light, and then use a second for moving around to eliminate shadows on your work. Depending on the pattern you're tying, that secondary light can be moved off to one side or the other to lessen the shadow your fingers cast as you work. I recommend you just turn the lamps to their brightest setting since you can never have too much light. I also recommend that you set the tone of the light to about halfway between the cold white setting and the warmest one, which will give you the closest match to natural daylight (or play with your lamps during the day to figure out which setting is closest to natural light). Just make sure that you get one that extends at least 15 inches above your work surface, because if the light is too close, you'll hit it with your hand when winding with a bobbin. And if you really want to get serious, you can buy an expensive LED drafting lamp, which will throw even more light on your work area. These need a table edge for clamping, so make sure your work surface has a wide and substantial edge.

MAGNIFICATION

About 20 years ago, the quality of my flies started slipping, and I figured I had lost my touch. It took me a couple of years to realize I was losing my near vision with age, because I could still read just fine. Fly tying requires close focus, and if you can't manage naturally, you'll need mechanical aids.

If you are under thirty-five years old, you can probably skip this section. But for most of us, magnification of some type is as critical as good light. Even if you wear bifocals, the magnifiers in your glasses were designed for reading, not for attaching a size 24 hackle to a light-wire hook with 10/0 thread. In addition, trying to use bifocals or progressives when tying flies requires you to cock your head up at an uncomfortable angle, increasing strain on your neck. The maximum magnification you can get in standard reading glasses is about three diopters. Going to glasses with a four- or even five-diopter magnification will improve the quality of your flies and reduce frustration.

You can get half-glasses in this range in some fly shops and catalogs. You can also buy clip-on magnifiers that attach to regular prescription glasses. One of the best devices for improving your close-up vision is a visor with magnifiers that you can flip out of the way when not needed. The one I like has two levels of flip-down magnification plus a loupe for very close work. It even has tiny flashlights on each side of the head for directing a portable light source.

Rolltop desks make great fly-tying spaces. This is my desk in all of its glorious disorganization. Note the two LED desk lamps, which are an inexpensive way to get very bright light on your working area.

You may also see big magnifying loupes mounted on a flexible gooseneck. Adjusting to these can be difficult, though, as they tend to get in the way when you're winding materials around the hook. I have never been able to get comfortable using a magnifying glass in front of my vise, and I'd advise you to fix the source of your magnification closer to your eyes with some type of glasses.

There is another answer for those of you who are extremely nearsighted. I have been cursed with poor vision since birth and can barely negotiate my own living room without glasses or contact lenses. However, years ago I heard someone with the same vision problem talk about being blessed for fly tying. People who are nearsighted can focus at a very close distance, and this guy said he could tie the most incredible flies by taking off his contacts or glasses. I tried it. Without corrective lenses, I focus at between three and four inches, like having built-in magnifiers. But because I also suffer from astigmatism, there was still some blur. So I measured the distance between my eyes and my tying vise, and the next time I had an eye examination I asked my optometrist to write me a prescription

for exactly that distance. Then I sought out the cheapest pair of frames I could find and ordered a pair of glasses with that prescription, strictly for tying flies. I don't tie like this in public because it looks stupid and the frames are dorky, and when I'm home alone it looks like I am kissing an Elk Hair Caddis. But I can see every turn of thread with utmost clarity.

CLAMPING THE HOOK

For most patterns, you should place the hook in the vise by clamping it at the bottom of the bend. This gives you more working room. With a spring-tension vise, merely pull on the clamp until the jaws open up enough to accept the hook. Release the clamp, and the hook will be secure. With a screw-adjustment vise, open the jaws enough to accept the hook and tighten the knurled knob firmly until it is hand-tight. With a cam-operated vise, it's a little trickier. Somewhere on the vise, either a knurled knob or a set

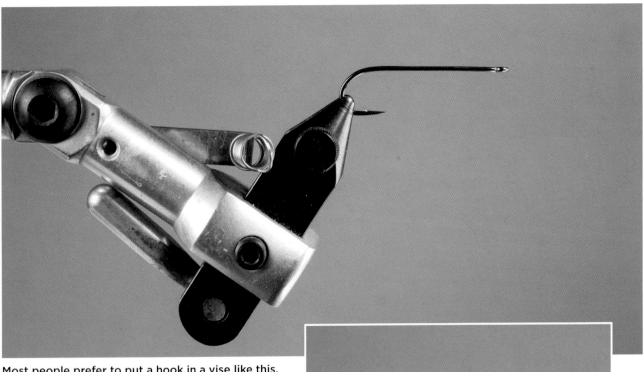

Most people prefer to put a hook in a vise like this. Yes, the point is exposed, but it gives you better working room around the bend of the hook.

When you get a tiny hook like this in a vise, you can see why the point needs to be exposed. You would never have enough working room if the hook was seated lower in the vise jaws.

screw on the stem preadjusts the jaw opening. With the cam lever up, open the jaws to about one-and-a-half times the diameter of the hook wire, and then depress the cam lever. The cam should move to a fully closed position with some resistance and not snap back. If it won't close fully under hand pressure, remove the hook and open the jaws a small amount. If the cam closes fully but the hook wiggles up and down in the vise when you pull on it, remove the hook and tighten the jaws a hair. A well-designed vise will hold a hook so well that you can bend the hook without moving it.

It's important to place the hook properly in the jaws. If the hook is too far back into the jaws, you will have trouble closing them, and the jaws can even snap under pressure. If the hook is too close to the narrow end of the jaws it can be shot out of the jaws like a bullet, with dangerous consequences. With most vises, the hook should be set about a quarter inch into the jaws for hooks bigger than size 6 and half that for hooks down to size 16. For the smallest hooks, it's safe to place them almost to the end of the jaws, so you'll get more working room.

THREADING THE BOBBIN

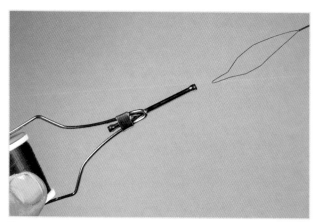

1. Run a wire bobbin threader (or a floss threader from the drugstore) down the tube of the bobbin.

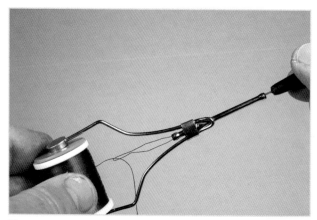

3. Run about four inches of thread through the loop.

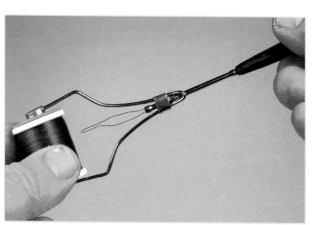

2. Push it through the tube enough that you can get the thread inside the loop.

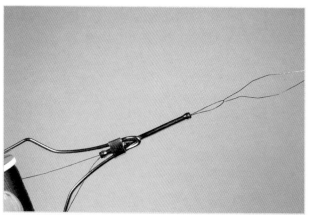

4. Pull the bobbin threader back through the tube. Check the tension on your spool. When you pull on the thread, it should rotate the spool under moderate pressure. If the tension is too loose, remove the thread spool from the bobbin and bend the legs of the bobbin inward. If it's too tight, spread the legs.

ATTACHING THREAD TO A HOOK

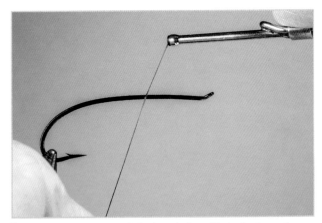

1. Assuming you are right-handed, pull six inches of thread from the bobbin, and cross the thread in front of the near side of the hook, holding the bobbin in your right hand above the hook and holding the tag end of the thread in your left hand.

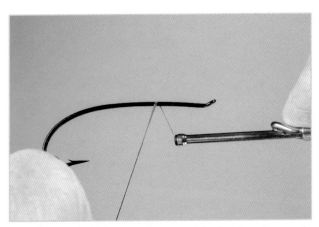

2. Bring the bobbin over the top of the hook and around the far side to the bottom of the hook.

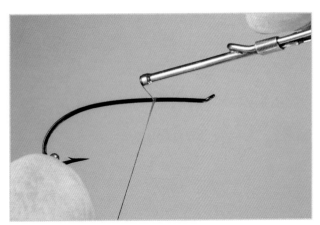

3. By pushing the bobbin to the left, wind the thread from the bobbin one wrap over the tag end of the thread.

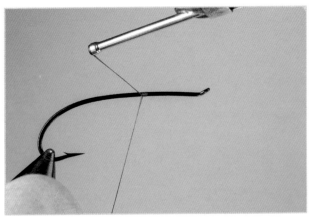

4. Make four more wraps over the tag end of the thread. Keep pushing your left hand to the right and your right hand to the left. Keep tension on both ends, and work the thread coming from the bobbin to the left with each turn of thread. You should now be able to release the loose thread in your left hand and put pressure on the thread coming from the bobbin without the thread slipping off the hook. If it slips, start over with more tension, and make a few more wraps.

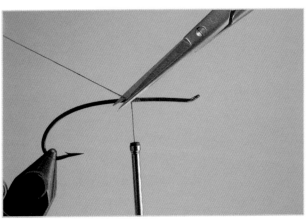

5. Snip the loose end of the thread close to the hook. Pull on the bobbin enough to feed thread from the spool. (Also, if you leave a long enough tag end to wrap around your finger, you may be able to just snap the tag end and break it without even using your scissors.) The thread should be secure and not unwind or spin around the hook. If it does, unwrap and start again.

WINDING THE THREAD

You should always wind away from you, as you did when starting the thread. Experiment with winding thread along the hook shank. Cradle the bobbin in your hand, with your index finger just below the tube and your thumb on the spool. The bobbin tube merely rotates around the shank as you wind. For almost all tying, you should keep about one inch of distance between the end of the bobbin tube and the hook. When the tube gets too close, spin the spool with your thumb to release more thread. If you have to back up, just wind thread back onto the spool by rolling your thumb in the opposite direction. If the bobbin tube is too close to the hook, you'll have trouble maneuvering the bobbin; if it's too far away, you'll lose control.

When you get close to the point of the hook, you'll have to weave in and out to keep the thread from catching on the point and getting nicked. Even though you are weaving, still guide the thread in one direction only—either toward or away from the bend.

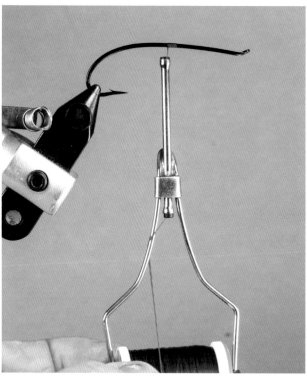

This bobbin is too close to the hook. You won't have enough working room.

This bobbin is a bit too far away from the hook. If the thread is any longer than this, you'll lose control and may also knock the bobbin into lights you have hanging over the vise.

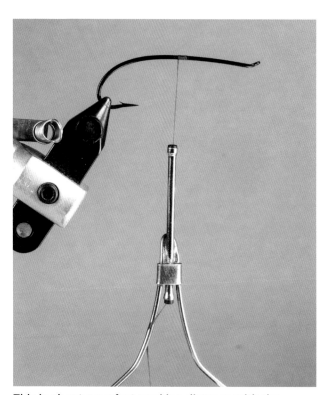

This is about a perfect working distance with the bobbin.

THREAD TENSION

Every turn of thread should be made under tension. Think about each turn as you make it. Haphazard winds make sloppy flies that fall apart. When you are advancing the thread from one part of the shank to another, you should be pulling at about half the breaking strength of the thread. When tying in materials, you may need to put almost eighty percent of the breaking strength into your winds. You get extra tension by locking your thumb on the spool.

A great exercise is to attach the thread to a hook, make a few winds, and pull on the bobbin, locking the spool with your thumb, until the thread breaks. Clean the thread off the hook and try it again. After repeating this a few times you'll know how much tension you can use.

TWISTING AND FLATTENING THREAD

Most fly-tying thread comes wrapped around the spool with a moderate twist. To be honest with you, for most tying I never worry about the twist in the thread, perhaps because I use the finest thread I can get away with. However, the twists in the thread can be manipulated for certain steps.

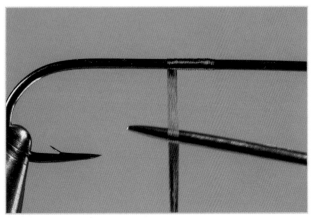

This thread has been flattened by giving the bobbin a counterclockwise spin. It gives you smooth wraps but takes up more room on the hook shank.

When you don't want any bulk on the hook shank, or if you need to wind a smooth base, such as when binding down materials that will be covered by tinsel or floss, you can unwind or flatten the thread by giving your bobbin a good counterclockwise spin (looking down on the bobbin from above). You'll see the twists go out of the thread, and it will flatten close to the hook shank. Flatten thread for smooth underbodies, for binding down bulky materials, and for a smooth head on a streamer or saltwater fly. You may have to untwist thread in several steps if you are winding over a large hook.

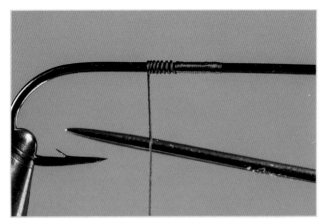

Here the thread has been twisted by spinning the bobbin clockwise. It gives you a narrow diameter where you want precise placement. You can see the difference between these wraps and the flattened wraps to the right.

Twisted thread adds bulk and gives you very precise placement of materials. Spin the bobbin in a clockwise direction (as viewed from above) until the thread twists into a tiny rope. Use twisted thread for building up bulk when raising dry-fly wings upright, when tying in loose materials like hair, or when placing tails at the bend of the hook.

ATTACHING MATERIALS TO THE HOOK

Attaching materials to the hook requires precise tension. More than anything else, thread tension distinguishes an experienced tier from an advanced tier, and like all things worth the trouble, it takes practice. You may watch a professional tier wind around the hook so fast that the bobbin blurs, but you can bet that each turn of thread has carefully controlled tension.

Almost all materials are attached to the upper side of the hook shank, so most techniques work to force the material to stay on top of the hook This is not easy when your thread is rolling around to the far side. Don't ever just "tie something to the hook"; it will end up everyplace except where you want it.

THE FINGER ON FAR SIDE

This technique is the easiest and is used for materials that are not stiff and do not consist of a loose bundle. Typical uses for this technique include tying yarn, chenille, floss, tinsel, and other body materials to the hook.

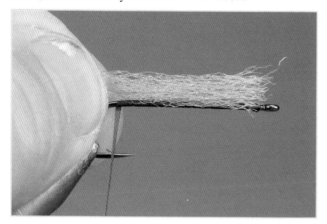

1. Start by placing the material you want to attach either directly on top of the shank or perhaps just slightly on the near upper side. Both ends of the material should lie parallel to the shank. Your thumb and forefinger should be holding the material right at the tie-in point, with your forefinger rolled slightly to the far side of the hook.

2. Loosen your thumb and forefinger, and bring a loose loop of thread over the top of the material and around the hook. When the bobbin is below the hook, pull straight down while pinching your forefinger to the far side of the hook.

3. Loosen up tension slightly, and repeat the process three times, putting more tension on each successive wrap. In general, when attaching materials, you apply little tension on three-quarters of each wrap and only apply firm tension in one direction. For placing materials on top of the hook, the normal scenario, pressure can be applied either straight up or down. When you want materials to lie along either side of the shank, as when making split tails, apply pressure horizontally, parallel to your work surface.

4. Advance the thread along the shank of the hook, always working away from the tie-in point. After three or four wraps, you should be able to release the material without it rolling around the hook. If you wrap back over the tie-in point, you add sloppy bulk and take the chance of moving the material you so carefully placed on top of the hook. Once you have wrapped the material in place, trim the butt ends on top of the hook shank, keeping the scissors parallel to the shank and on top of it. This keeps you from inadvertently cutting your thread.

THE FORTY-FIVE DEGREE ROLL

This is the best way to attach stiffer materials like hackle stems, tails, and synthetic materials such as vinyl ribbing.

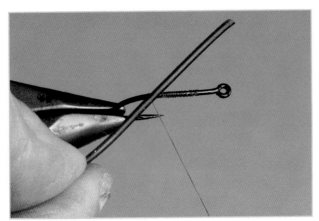

1. Start with the material on top of the hook shank, with the material to be bound in horizontally at a 45-degree angle. The end of the material to be bound under should be pointing away from you and to your right. The end of the material that will not bind under should face toward you.

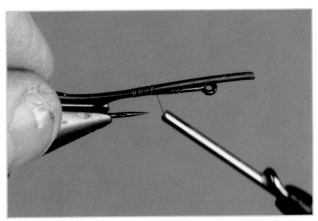

3. In subsequent turns, advance the thread to the right, away from your initial tie-in point with each wrap. Unlike the last method, no wraps should overlap so the foundation formed by the bound-in material is very smooth.

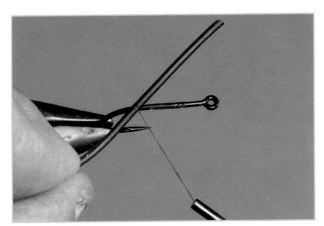

2. Bring the thread loosely over the top of the material, gradually rotating the material so that it is parallel to the shank of the hook. Put some moderate downward tension on the material after the bobbin is under the hook.

THE PINCH

This is the best way to attach materials that consist of a bundle of fibers—hair, feather fibers, or wing quills.

1. Place the material directly on top of the shank, pinching it with the tips of your thumb and forefinger directly over the tie-in spot.

2. It's usually best to spin the thread into a tight rope for the first part of this method, to ensure that you get precise placement. Spinning the thread in this way also helps it jump back toward your fingers.

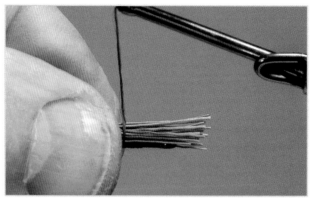

3. Rock your thumb and forefinger slightly so that pressure is on the first knuckle. This opens up a spot over the tie-in place but still keeps the material in place. Keep pressure on the sides of the hook shank. Take one loose turn of thread over the tie-in spot, and work the thread back into the space between your thumb and forefinger.

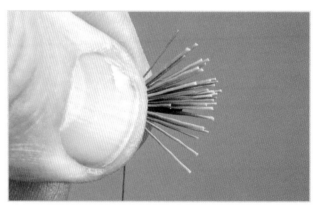

4. Bring the thread all the way around the hook to a point underneath the tie-in spot. Rock your fingers back over the tie-in spot so that the thread you have just wound is covered up and pinched between your fingertips. Pinch the thread and the material together, keeping pressure on the sides of the shank. Pull the thread straight down with firm tension, about eighty percent of its breaking strength. You can also experiment with bringing the thread over the top of the material, under the hook, and back up again, tightening with an upward instead of downward pull. Don't tighten horizontally unless you want the material bound to the sides of the shank. Open up your fingers, and take another wrap, pulling straight down in the same manner. Repeat once or twice more for a total of three to four wraps. Ensure that the material has not rolled to the far side. If it has, try to roll it back in place with your fingers, or unwrap and start over.

5. The material should now be firmly lashed to the top of the hook shank only.

6. Trim the butt ends of the material at a slight angle.

7. Now untwist the thread and bind the butts of the material under with smooth wraps, moving away from the part of the material that you do not want bound to the hook. Hold the material in place as you make these wraps to ensure that it does not roll around the shank. If you have to start over, it's best to cut a new piece or bundle of material, as you will have already put a permanent crimp in the first clump.

THE GRAVITY DROP WITH UPWARD PULL

This method is mainly used to attach wide, flat, delicate materials on top of the hook, such as wing cases and shellbacks on nymphs, and grasshopper and caddis quill wings. It keeps them flat on top of the hook without crushing the fibers together.

1. Pull the material straight forward, usually over the eye of the hook.

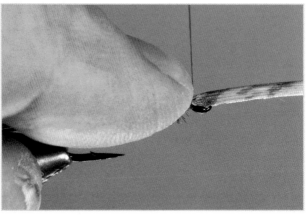

3. Make a third wrap, then pull the bobbin straight up above the tie-in point while pushing straight down with your index finger to keep the material from rolling as you apply pressure.

2. Place a loose loop of thread over the material. Bring the bobbin around and back down below the shank, and just let it drop of its own accord. Make another wrap in the same fashion. Inspect your work, and if the material rolled too far over the far side of the hook, tweak it back by rolling it toward you.

4. Start advancing the thread down over the part of the material you will be binding under, using an upward pull for the next couple of turns and then returning to a standard downward pull as you get farther away from the tie-in point.

WINDING MATERIALS AND TYING OFF

Winding materials around a hook comes almost instinctively, and I'm always surprised how quickly most beginners grasp the concept of switching the material from one hand to the other. In contrast, many people have trouble tying off a material under the thread; they merely wrap thread up against the material to be secured rather than crossing it with the thread. Here are the basics:

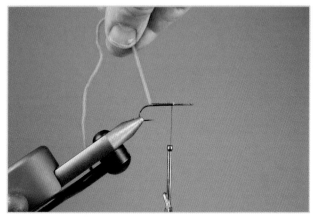

1. Begin by holding the material to be wrapped with your right hand. Wind it away from you, around the back side of the shank.

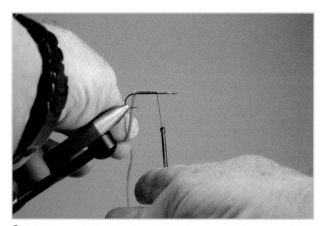

2. Underneath the hook, switch the material to your left hand while your right hand passes around the bobbin. Otherwise, you'll be knocking the bobbin out of control with every revolution.

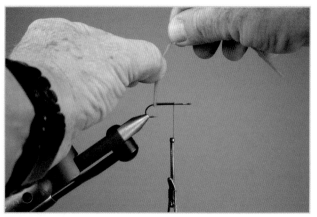

3. Switch back quickly to your right hand, and make another three-quarters of a wrap before using the left hand again.

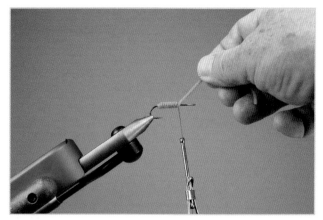

4. After you have made enough wraps and want to secure the material to the hook, hold the material above the hook with your right hand.

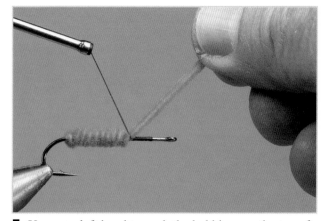

5. Use your left hand to push the bobbin over the top of the hook, making sure you cross over the material to be bound under.

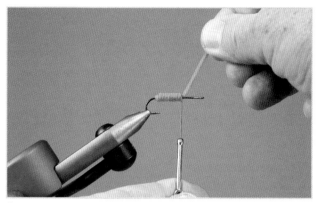

6. After the bobbin is three-quarters of the way around the shank, release it, and let it fall under the shank so it hangs suspended by its weight. Now bring your left hand back to the near side to put downward pressure on the bobbin to help secure the material. Repeat the process at least three times or until the material is secure.

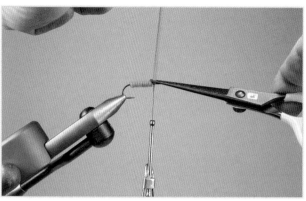

7. Let the bobbin hang below the shank, and trim the material above the shank. This keeps you from accidentally cutting the thread.

THE HALF HITCH

I don't use the half hitch much, but I probably should. It's a great way to keep tension on the thread quickly if you need to cut your thread or otherwise loosen tension on the bobbin, and it keeps the thread from unraveling.

Half hitches are useful both in the middle of a pattern if you have to remove the hook from the vise to trim a hair body and at the end of a fly when finishing the head. Making a half hitch is quick, and you don't need an extra tool. Although you can buy a half-hitch tool or use the blunt end of your dubbing needle, a tool only works at the head of a fly, and by making a half hitch by hand, you can place one anywhere along the hook shank you desire. Some people even finish the head of a fly with a series of half hitches, but I don't recommend that course. A whip finish is far more secure and less likely to come apart.

2. Pull up with the bobbin while rotating your fingers toward you, forming an X with the thread.

1. To begin, pull about four inches of thread from your bobbin. Place two fingers (usually index and middle finger) against the thread, fingernails facing you.

3. Using your fingers to manipulate the thread, place that X on the shank where you wish to place the whip finish. Make sure the loop that you have formed goes over the eye of the hook.

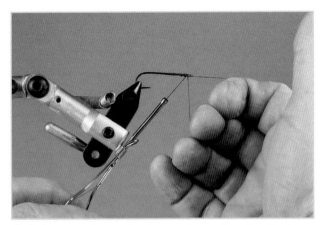

4. Bring your fingers back toward you, keeping the loop tight.

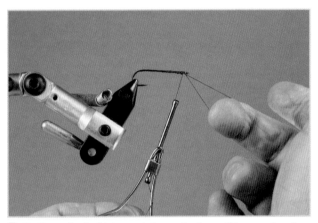

5. Pull on the bobbin to tighten the loop. You can let the loop slip off your fingers and guide it in place with your thumb and forefinger . . .

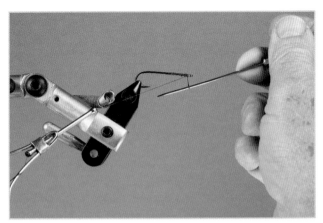

6. . . . but I like to use a dubbing needle or the point of a closed pair of scissors to guide it more precisely. Now you can release pressure on your bobbin, and your wraps will stay in place without unwinding. Trim the tag end of the thread.

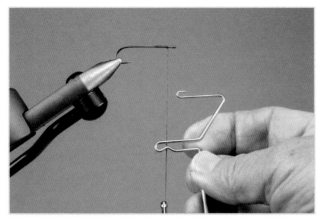

1. Start with three inches of thread between the hook and bobbin. Hold the whip-finish tool in your right hand with your thumb on the near side of the handle, the lower loop of wire (the one with the notch) off to the left, and the open end of the hook at the top, pointing to the right. Brace your index finger against the far side of the open loop, and brace your last three fingers on the far side of the handle. Hold the tool parallel to the thread, and raise the bobbin to a horizontal position, pressing the notch of the lower loop against the thread. Do not let the tool rotate.

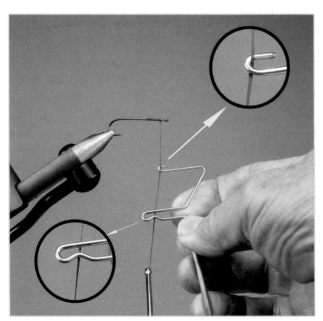

2. Catch the thread in the hook at the top by swiveling the top of the tool slightly to the left and then back. Keep tension on the bobbin so the thread does not slip out of the lower notch. Keep your fingers in place so the tool does not rotate.

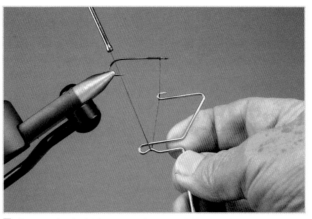

3. Move the bobbin up and toward the hook.

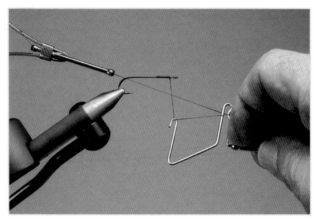

4. Release your forefinger. The upper end of the tool will rotate and flip sides. The thread will cross over itself, forming an X. The most common problem at this point is keeping the thread securely on the hook and in the notch. If you wait until the bobbin is higher than the tool to release your forefinger, you can keep better control. Keep moving the bobbin up and toward the hook while pulling the handle toward you. Place the point where the thread crosses against the hook shank in the exact spot you want to place the whip finish. Bring the tool above the hook while letting it rotate freely. You'll notice there is now a place where the thread crosses itself on the far side, making a triangle.

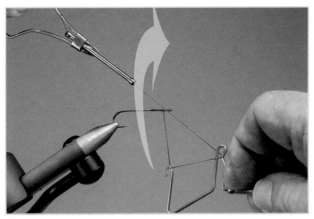

5. Rotate the tool around the hook, using the angle of the bobbin tube to keep the thread crossing point against the hook shank.

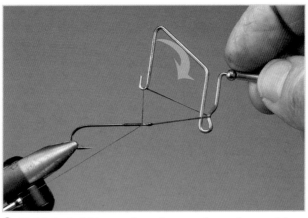

6. Hold the bobbin steady and rotate the tool smoothly around the eye of the hook. Make sure you clear the eye as the thread goes around. Repeat for five complete revolutions. Finish your last wrap under the hook.

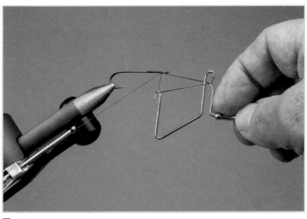

7. Push the tool down and to the left while tilting the handle up.

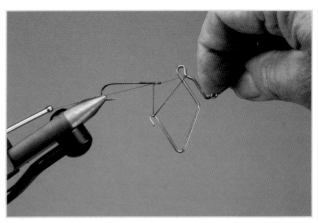

8. Keep pushing until the thread slips out of the lower notch.

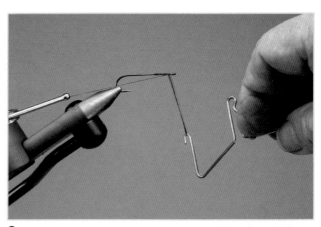

9. Pull up with the bobbin. Follow the thread up with the hook of the whip-finish tool.

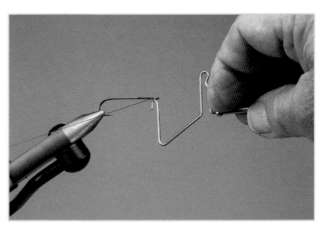

10. Slip the hook out of the loop, and give a couple of short, firm pulls on your bobbin to secure the knot.

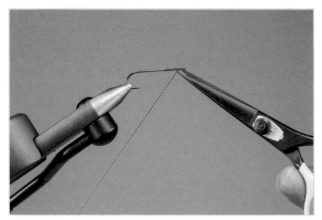

11. Trim the thread carefully, and your whip finish is complete.

THE HAND WHIP FINISH

You can also whip finish with your hand. It's not quite as tight and secure as using the tool, but many tiers use this technique.

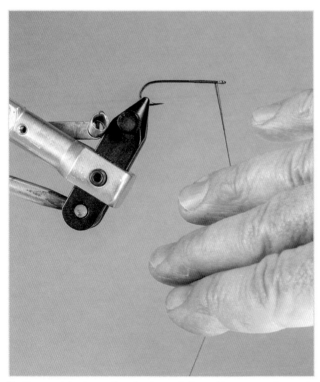

1. Start with about five inches of thread between the end of the bobbin and your hook. Place your middle three fingers against the thread.

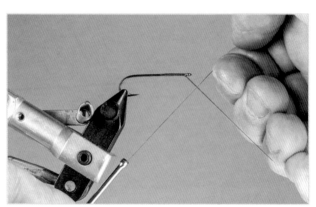

2. Rotate your fingers toward you so that the thread closest to the bobbin crosses the thread on the side facing you.

3. Add pressure with your index finger by moving it away from your middle finger, until the point where the thread crossed itself moves into position on the hook shank where you want the whip finish to go.

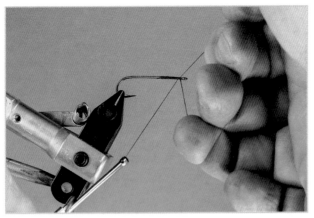

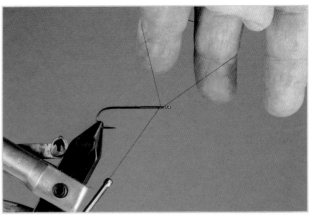

4. Rotate the thread closest to your index finger around the hook shank by twisting your fingers inside the loop. Move the thread closest to your ring finger roughly parallel to the hook shank, and use your index finger to wrap the thread over itself. Make sure you open the loop enough with your fingers so that it clears the eye on each revolution.

6. Slip the thread off your fourth finger, and hold the loop with your middle finger and index finger.

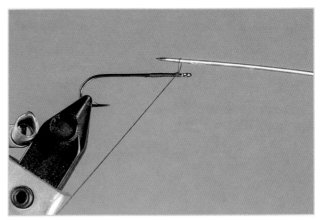

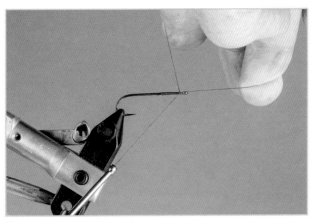

5. Repeat this rotation five times.

7. Slip a dubbing needle into the loop, and draw it tight against the hook. Trim the tag end of the thread.

WHAT TO DO IF THE THREAD BREAKS

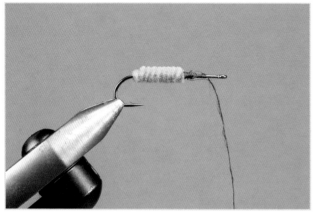

1. Breaking thread in the middle of a fly, or cutting it on the hook point, is part of the game. Everybody does it. It's wise to have a pair of hackle pliers within reach even if you aren't winding hackle, because they're an important part of reattaching thread. If pre-waxed thread breaks, it won't unwind too fast, so you have time to react.

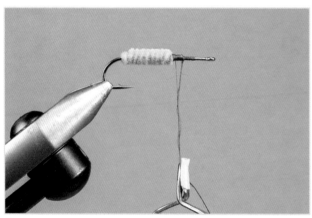

2. Catch the loose end of thread still attached to the fly, clamp a pair of hackle pliers to it, and let the pliers hang below the hook just like a bobbin. The weight of the hackle pliers will keep the thread in place while you get your bobbin rethreaded if necessary, as the thread often slips out of the bobbin tube when it breaks.

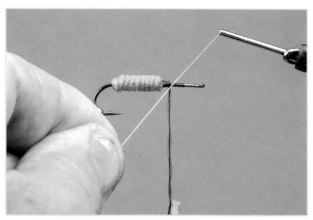

3. Re-thread your bobbin if necessary. Pull six inches of thread from the bobbin tube. Push the hackle pliers slightly to one side and start the new thread right on top of the broken thread, as if you were beginning on a bare shank. (I used green thread for this to show contact between the new wraps and the old ones.)

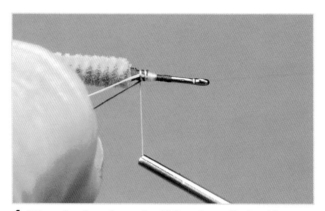

4. Wrap the thread over itself five times. It should now be secure.

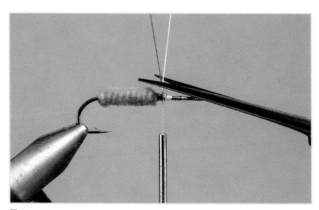

5. Pull both the broken thread and the tag end of the new wrap together on top of the shank. Carefully trim both. It's a good idea to put a small drop of head cement at this point before you continue the fly. You're back in business.

CHAPTER 2

TOOLS

It's possible to tie a fly without tools. It is also possible to ride a bicycle from Maine to California or climb Mount Everest without oxygen. I wouldn't advise taking on any of these for fun. I once tied a bunch of hair-wing salmon flies in a dingy Nova Scotia motel room without a vise or bobbin. I held the hook in my left hand and manipulated materials with the thumb and forefinger of my right hand, while the other three fingers kept tension on the thread. The flies looked terrible and didn't catch any salmon. Good tools are not very expensive, and most will last for decades.

VISE

The vise holds the hook securely so that you can use both hands to manipulate thread and materials. Some will hold everything from a size 28 midge to a size 4/0 tarpon hook. Others specialize in either large or small hooks; some have removable jaws for different size ranges of hooks. Most advertising literature will tell you what size range a vise holds, but if you can't find an answer, assume the vise will hold at least sizes 4 through 20 hooks, which is the range of most trout flies.

Jaw Systems

The most common fly-tying vises use a lever-and-cam system, whereby depressing a lever jams the jaws together around the hook. They all have adjustments so you can change the opening between the jaws and vary the pressure applied when the cam is engaged. You should adjust the jaws so that when the cam is fully engaged, the hook is held so firmly that it will bend first instead of moving in the jaws. If the hook slides up and down in the jaws, open the cam, tighten the jaws slightly, and try again. If you have tightened the jaws so much that you have to force the cam, open the space between the jaws slightly. Forcing jaws, especially over a big saltwater hook, can snap them.

Screw-tightened jaws are also available. With these, you simply tighten a big knob on the end of the jaws until it is hand-tight and the hook is held securely. The disadvantage with this type of vise is that you have to tighten and loosen the screw every time you change hooks, even if they are all the same size.

This cam-operated vise is most likely the first fly-tying vise you would own. It clamps to a table and holds a hook securely. Its basic features keep the cost down.

A third vise design uses an ingenious spring clamp that needs no adjustment, ever. You pull a lever to open the jaws against the spring tension enough to place the hook between the jaws, and when you release the lever, the jaws spring closed around the hook. This vise is fast when tying lots of flies in different sizes and is popular with commercial tiers.

Clamp or Pedestal?

Vises must be secured to a table or other firm surface. One travel vise is built onto a metal ring that goes around a couple of fingers, allowing you to tie anywhere. Another actually comes with a special clamp for attachment to a car steering wheel. Neither of these is particularly handy, unless you're about to start on your coast-to-coast bicycle trip . . .

Most vises are made to attach to a table with either a C-clamp or a movable but weighty pedestal. Many vise designs can be attached either way, and you can usually buy the vise with one type of attachment and purchase the other later. C-clamps are very sturdy and great if you tie fast, if you're tying a lot of big saltwater flies, or if you're working with deer hair and putting a lot of pressure on the fly. However, if not used carefully, these vises can mar the surface of a nice dining room table, and it is sometimes difficult to find a table with the right thickness at the edge for the clamp. Motel nightstands are notorious for not having a wide enough lip for a fly-tying vise.

With a pedestal, you can move your vise from one table to another in seconds, and you can tie on any surface, regardless of whether it has a lip or not. You can tie on a picnic bench, in your den, or on the kitchen table. The disadvantage of pedestal bases is that they are heavy if you take your stuff on a trip, and you are stuck with one jaw height above the table, because the stem of the vise does not raise and lower as it does with a C-clamp vise. Beware, however, if you take your tying vise when traveling by airplane. Tools over seven inches long are not allowed in carry-on luggage, and many fly-tying vises approach that length. A tool is a tool to most TSA officials: I tried to eliminate extra weight in my checked bag once and had to do some fast talking with lots of polite smiles to keep a TSA official from confiscating my vise. Even just putting the pedestal in your carry-on can cause problems. Although it's a lot of weight to add to your checked bag, a big piece of solid metal like that lights up their x-ray machines and almost guarantees a hand inspection of your luggage, requiring a convincing explanation of why you want to carry such a big hunk of metal onto an airplane.

Rotary or Not?

Vises can be made with stationary or rotary jaws. There is no advantage to stationary jaws other than cost, because a rotary vise can be made stationary simply by tightening the rotating feature until it does not move. With a stationary vise, if you want to look at the bottom or far side of the fly, you must either remove the fly from the jaws and remount it upside down, loosen the stem and flip the vise from right-handed to left-handed, or crane your neck around to the far side of the vise. With a rotary vise, the jaws can rotate 360 degrees without removing the hook from the jaws. A set screw controlled by a knob or Allen wrench tightens or loosens the rotation of the jaws. By experimenting with this adjustment, you can come up with an amount of tension that keeps the vise stationary throughout most tying operations yet allows you to rotate the jaws and look at the far side or bottom of the fly (or to actually place materials at these hard-to-reach points).

There are certain operations in fly tying that lend themselves to true rotary tying as well. In rotary tying, the bobbin is placed out of the way, in a thread cradle. You grab the material you want to wind and rotate the jaws while feeding the material to the proper place on the hook. Not only is this faster, it lets you see where the material is going at every angle.

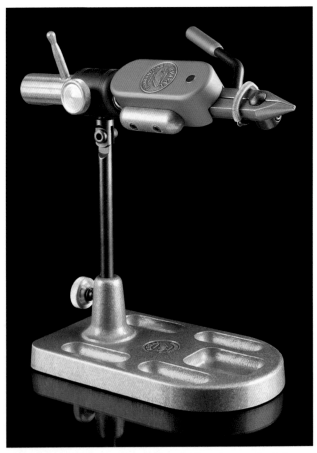

This high-end vise, a Regal Revolution, is a pedestal model that can be used on any surface, regardless of the width of the table edge. The angle of the vise can be adjusted to a traditional 45-degree angle or placed flat as it is here for rotary tying. Note the material clip on the vise (the spring attached to the barrel). Although expensive, a vise like this will last a lifetime or more.

Let's say you are tying a fly on which the entire hook shank must be covered with two layers of tinsel. In traditional winding, you bind one end of the tinsel in place, then wrap it around the hook by reaching over to the far side of the hook with one hand, picking it up with the other hand, and then catching it again with the first hand. You can't just wrap the material around the hook with one hand, because the bobbin gets in the way. Nor can you see how the material is lying on the far side of the hook or underneath it.

In rotary tying, the bobbin is placed out of the way in a bobbin cradle, and the tinsel is held in one hand while the other hand rotates the vise jaws. You can see exactly where each turn of tinsel is placed, eliminating any sloppy gaps or overlaps. When winding hackle, you also get smooth, even wraps. Some people find it an annoyance to switch from stationary to rotary tying, but if you tie lots of flies on which much wrapping is necessary, rotary tying can be a fun and productive option.

Vise Recommendations

My recommendation is to get a C-clamp, stationary vise for your first vise. They are inexpensive, durable, and simple. You can get a decent one for under $50 and a great one for around $100. If you want to upgrade, advance to a pedestal, rotary vise. For this, you should expect to pay a minimum of $150 and as much as $400 for a beautifully machined tool with lots of adjustments, material clips, parachute tools, and other bells and whistles.

SCISSORS

Your scissors should be fine and sharp enough to cut a single hackle fiber or a few strands of marabou without pulling the fibers. Fine points are essential for precision work, such as when you need to clip off a hackle tip without cutting your thread or leaving too much waste material sticking in the hook eye. You'll find straight blades more useful than curved. Finger handles should be wide and comfortable. Some tiers, particularly professionals, tie with the scissors around their fingers all the time, slipping the scissors up and down their fingers as needed. Don't feel bad if you can't get used to doing this—I have been tying for fifty years, and I have never gotten used to keeping scissors on my fingers.

Most tiers like at least two pairs of scissors: one fine pair for delicate work and a heavier pair for cutting hair, tinsel, and large clumps of feathers like marabou. If you stick to one pair, get fine-tipped scissors, and use the heavier inside edge for cutting hair and wire. Tiny serrations on scissors help the blades grab materials. They are an advantage even on fine-tipped scissors and essential on heavier hair scissors.

You'll find that fly-tying shops and catalogs sell the best scissors. I am a scissors freak and own more than twenty pairs. I've bought expensive manicure scissors that cost three times as much as fly-tying scissors, and they don't work as well. Fly-tying scissors come from surgical-supply manufacturers, but suppliers modify these tools specifically for tying.

Scissors are your most important tool. I probably own 20 pairs of them, but at the very least you need a pair with heavier blades for cutting hair and synthetics, and a fine-tipped pair for trimming delicate hackles and other small materials.

BOBBINS AND BOBBIN THREADERS

The best modern bobbins consist of a narrow tube attached to a set of wire legs, which hold the spool of thread or other material in place with plastic or metal balls or discs. The tube helps you place thread where stubby fingers won't go. The bobbin holds the spool and keeps tension on the thread while you tie so that your hands are free to prepare materials. Some of the tubes are polished metal, others are ceramic or metal lined with ceramic insert, which will last a lifetime of tying. Tying thread is often coated with wax, and bobbins with flared ends don't plug up with wax as easily.

If you get a bobbin that has rough edges on the tube that cuts your thread, send it back for a refund immediately. This never happens with the more expensive models but will occasionally happen with budget-priced bobbins.

Because many of the threads we use today are pre-waxed, the bobbin tube gets plugged, and you cannot always suck the thread through the tube. Get a bobbin threader, which is a simple piece of bent wire soldered to a handle. The wire is soft enough not to score the inside of the bobbin tube. If you're on a budget, floss threaders from a drugstore work too.

HACKLE PLIERS

Hackle pliers are used to hold hackles and other delicate materials, and to position them with a precision not easily obtained with stubby fingers. They can also be used to spin dubbing in a loop or to temporarily hold thread if it breaks in the middle of a fly.

Hackle pliers are simple positive-locking clamps. Squeezing the sides opens the jaws, and releasing them tightens the jaws on the material. They should hold a material firmly enough so that it does not slip out under tension and must not have sharp edges that might cut the material.

Basic hackle pliers, sometimes known as "English style," are the best all-around choice. The best ones have wide side plates that make the pliers easy to squeeze, and one side of the jaws is covered with soft plastic or rubber. This helps the pliers to grip delicate feathers without cutting or breaking them.

A smaller pair of hackle pliers is handy for winding hackles smaller than size 20 or for winding delicate feathers such as peacock herl, single strands of ostrich, or pheasant-tail fibers.

Most pliers have a wide loop at one end for slipping around your finger. This way, a hackle can be wound

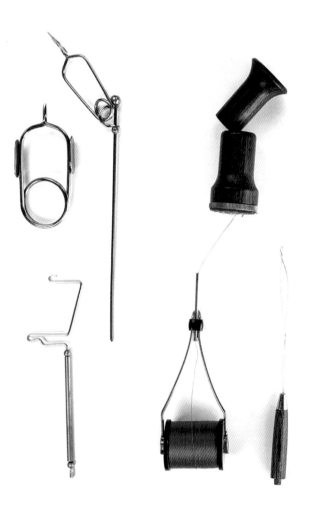

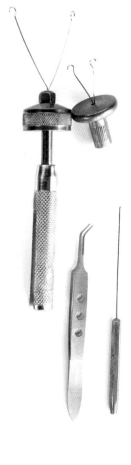

Other tools you will find useful. Clockwise from upper left: Two types of hackle pliers for holding hackles and other delicate materials, a stacker for evening the ends of hairs, two styles of dubbing spinners for spinning fur in a loop, dubbing needle or bodkin for teasing out tiny fibers, small forceps, a bobbin threader, a bobbin for holding thread, and a whip-finish tool.

smoothly around the hook without having to let go of the pliers, except for a brief moment when you pass the pliers around the bobbin. Some tiers say you get better control by just holding the pliers by your thumb and forefinger and switching hands when winding around the hook, but I think you can get equal control by placing the loop over a finger.

One special design consists of a tiny pair of hackle pliers attached to a stem that allows the pliers to rotate freely, both horizontally and vertically. They are great for all-purpose work and especially handy for tricky procedures like winding parachute hackles.

Large or long hackles can also be wound with your fingers. Big saltwater hackles and dry-fly saddle hackles longer than three inches can be handled nicely without pliers, but you may be limited by the dexterity of your fingers.

DUBBING NEEDLE

A dubbing needle is simply a needle attached to a handle. Avoid dubbing needles with round handles, because they can roll off the tying table. I have a habit of involuntarily catching materials that fall off the table between my thighs and have impaled myself more than once on a sharp dubbing needle! Use a dubbing needle to pick out dubbing to make it look fuzzier and to fold wing cases on nymphs. You can also use one to apply head cement to the fly, either in the middle or after you have whip finished the head. You can also use this tool to pick stray fibers out of the hook eye or to make minute adjustments to materials. Some people use the sharp point of their scissors for these procedures, but scissors aren't as precise, and sometimes the thread gets cut involuntarily.

WHIP FINISHER

You must use a knot to finish the fly so the head does not unwind. Some flies also require that you tie off the thread in the middle of a pattern; for example, when you're putting epoxy on the body of a fly before you put it back in the vise to attach a wing. Some tiers recommend using several half hitches, but I don't: They are bulky and nowhere near as secure as a whip finish. The whip finish is a knot that winds the thread over itself about five turns—like the nail knot used to attach a leader to a fly line, or when you pull the thread under the wrap when winding a guide onto a rod.

Whip finishes can be done by hand or with a handy whip-finishing tool invented by Frank Matarelli. The tool makes a tighter, neater knot, and it can place the knot in tricky places, such as at the head of a tiny midge or under a parachute hackle. It is by far the hardest tool to use in fly tying; even so, it can be mastered in a half-hour of diligent practice. Nothing seems to be more satisfying for a novice

fly tier than to learn how to use this tool, and once the technique is mastered, it's a crowd-pleaser for non-tiers to watch.

STACKER

This tool is used to even the ends of many kinds of hairs, so the fine tips line up flush before the bunch is tied in. You can do this by hand, pulling small bunches out and repositioning them, but it takes a long time, and the results are never as neat as with a stacker. The basic type consists of a brass tube with a stainless-steel or aluminum base. You place a bunch of hair in the end of the tube, fine ends first, and tap the stacker on the table. When you slide the tube out of the base, the ends of the hairs will be perfectly even. Really clever stackers have clear or open bases so you can see exactly when the hairs are lined up. For most flies, the medium size is fine, but if you do a lot of work with big streamers, you may want to get a large size to accommodate wide bunches of hair.

OTHER TOOLS

Dubbing Spinner

You can use your hackle pliers to spin fur in a loop, but a dubbing spinner is faster and more fun. The basic type consists of a pair of small hooks to catch the loop, plus a heavy brass weight that you start spinning with your fingers and allow to continue spinning by its momentum. Another model mounts the weight on a shaft with ball bearings, and after spinning the loop, you can use the shaft to wind the spun fur around the hook.

Material Clip

Many but not all vise models come with these. A material clip holds materials that you've tied in but might not wind until you complete other steps. The clip, usually a spring of some sort, attaches to your vise and holds stuff out of the way, acting as a third hand.

Rotating Drier

If you tie epoxy flies or big streamers with glossy heads and don't use quick-setting UV epoxy, this motorized tool gives the finished product a perfectly smooth finish. You place the flies in a piece of foam attached to a battery-operated motorized shaft on a slow governor and let them rotate from a few minutes to overnight, depending on how long it takes the finish to cure. Without this tool, you have

If you work with slow-drying epoxy (as opposed to UV-cure epoxy) it is handy to have a rotating drier like this.

to rotate the flies by hand or in a rotary vise as they dry to keep the epoxy from running to one side.

Hackle Gauge

This is a tool with a small post that you fan a hackle around. It is marked with the correct hackle size for each hook size. I don't use this tool because I fan hackles around the hook as I am tying, but these gauges are very popular.

Hackle Guards

This is another tool I don't use but which is popular nonetheless. Hackle guards are cone-shaped pieces of metal or plastic that keep you from catching hackles in the thread when you finish the head of a fly. I think you can do just as good a job with your fingers, even on tiny flies.

Tweezers or Forceps

These are almost essential but not quite. Tweezers or fine-tipped forceps should be fine enough to pluck a single hackle fiber that has gone astray. They are useful for picking up hooks or small materials. Mine are usually downstairs in the kitchen, where we use them to remove ticks from pets, and I don't miss them very much.

Dubbing Teaser

This can be anything from a piece of male Velcro glued onto a pencil to a fine wire brush to a miniature plastic rake. It is used to brush dubbing under the thorax of a nymph or between the ribs on the abdomen of a fly.

Wing Burners

Elegant wings for dry flies can be made by placing a hackle feather inside a brass tool that is cut to the shape of a mayfly, caddisfly, or stonefly wing, then burning the outside of the feather away with a butane lighter. You can accomplish something similar with certain synthetic materials. The practice is not as common today as it was twenty years ago, but these tools do make gorgeous realistic wings.

Hair Packer

When spinning deer hair, you can pack the bunches of hair relatively tightly with your fingernail, but if you plan on spending much time making deer hair bass bugs of big streamers with deer hair heads, a hair packer can make your tying go much easier. This is simply a heavy piece of metal with a slot in it that helps you place a lot of pressure right along the hook shank so that the bunches of hair you tie in are tightly packed against each other.

Double-Edge Razor Blades

Use these to trim deer-hair bodies. Carefully break a blade in half and put some electrician's tape on the broken end to make it easier to hold. It's also handy for scraping head cement off your dubbing needle. Single-edge blades are fine for scraping the dubbing needle but not sharp enough for trimming deer hair.

Needle-Nose Pliers

Pliers are useful if you like barbless hooks, as you can debarb each fly as you tie it. They also come in handy for opening stuck bottles of head cement or caps on tubes of superglue.

Tiny Wire Cutters

Instead of using your fly-tying scissors for cutting wire used for ribbing, bodies, or tandem flies, use wire cutters intended for electronics or hobbies. You can ruin the fine blades of fly-tying scissors by cutting wire with them.

Moustache Comb or Carding Tool

Many of the long synthetic hairs used to tie big pike or saltwater flies benefit from a good combing. It helps blend the fibers and fluff them up before trimming. A small dog comb, a carding tool used for wool, or a wire-bristled pet brush is very useful if you plan on tying this kind of fly.

Post-Its and Pencil

Keep a Post-It pad handy for writing down materials you realize you need as you are tying. They are also great as disposable mixing areas for epoxy or paints.

Trash Can

Make sure you have a trash can unless you live alone. You can buy handy wire trash-bag frames that fit on the edge of a table right under your work area. I just use a plastic trash can on one side or the other, and sometimes I actually hit it. Needless to say, I keep a small vacuum cleaner close at hand.

Household items from the hardware store or other sources you will find useful. From left: a carding comb or pet slicker brush for combing out synthetic fibers, a pet comb for the same purpose, a pencil for writing down materials you need, sticky notes for taking notes and for mixing epoxy, single-edge razor blades for trimming deer hair, small pliers for flattening materials, small wire cutters for cutting wire and monofilament, and a lighter for singeing the ends of certain materials.

Plastic, Stackable Boxes

Plastic shoeboxes or the bigger styles are wonderful for storing materials. They are airtight enough to keep out beetles and moths and can be stacked in the corner of a room or in a closet. They keep out most cats and dogs, although not ferrets. A heavy rubber band around the outside will discourage even ferrets, however.

Lighter

A lighter is essential if you burn wings or tie extended bodies with Vernille or Ultra Chenille, as you taper this material by singeing the ends.

Tippet Material

You can make weed guards with heavier monofilament, and I like to use 4X tippet when I need a strong, clear rib on a fly.

CHAPTER 3

MATERIALS

Just about anything you find in a craft or fabric store, dead alongside the road, growing on your pet, or pulled from the lint screen of your dryer can be used to tie flies. (I am not kidding; when I was a teenager, an older guy I fished with had a fantastic nymph pattern dubbed from dryer-screen lint). If you stick with this hobby, you will own the most eclectic closet in the neighborhood.

BEWARE OF FREE MATERIALS

I often get questions about using road-killed mammals or birds for fly tying. It seems such a waste to let good materials rot on the roadside, but usually it's a bad idea.

First of all, collecting these materials is usually illegal. In most states, it's illegal to even touch any road-killed animal without a game warden present. Also, with the exception of invasive birds like pigeons or starlings, it is illegal to collect feathers from songbirds—even if they are dead. Also, bringing dead mammal skins or bird feathers into your house invites insect pests that can damage the other natural materials in your collection. The hairs and furs you buy in a fly shop are already tanned, removing the fats and oils that attract insect pests. Roadkills, or sections of hide you might get from a hunter are often dirty, greasy, and harboring insects. I'd steer clear of this stuff unless you know a taxidermist who is willing to tan the hides for you.

Feathers from game birds, however, both upland birds and waterfowl, are OK to keep and can save you money. You can even get feathers that you won't be able to find in

You may be tempted to bring home road kills for tying materials but it is often not a good idea. It is illegal in certain states, animal hides are often dirty and greasy, and you can also introduce beetles and moths that can ruin your other materials. Hairs and furs you buy from a fly shop are cleaned and tanned and much safer. Feathers plucked from legally hunted game birds, on the other hand, don't pose the same problems.

most fly shops. Grouse, quail, pheasant, turkey, woodcock, snipe, and all waterfowl feathers are very useful, and if you hunt or have a friend who hunts, just pluck the feathers from the hide and put them in a carefully labeled Ziploc bag. Keep them separate from other stuff, just in case they contain some arthropod hitchhikers.

A NOTE ON SUBSTITUTIONS

There is nothing more annoying than getting all excited about tying a new pattern, only to find that the inventor of the fly specifies hair from the tail of a winter-killed ermine. Or just as bad is a pattern that calls for a synthetic material that is either no longer available or only sold by a small fly shop in Tasmania. Don't go crazy about trying to obtain these exotic materials—substitute. Maybe the tier calling for the ermine tail is a trapper and happened to have a bunch of tails at his tying desk. And maybe the tier with the Tasmanian synthetic picked up the material when she was on vacation and again just had it handy. Get a picture of the pattern in question, and then find something in your collection that looks close. I am sure the fish won't care. Admittedly, some materials do offer a special property, and maybe you won't be able to find an acceptable substitute that will give your fly the same look. But in most cases, not even another fly tier will know you slipped in a substitute.

Here are the basic materials sold in fly shops and catalogs today, with which you can tie ninety percent of all the flies you see. Which ones do you need? Only the materials for the patterns you want to tie right now. A material that might be unusual on most tiers' tables could be the most essential one in your collection if the recipe for your favorite pattern calls for it.

FEATHERS

Wing Quills

Wing quills are used for many parts of flies, mostly trout and salmon flies. Sections of wing quills make durable and lifelike wing cases on nymphs. Traditional wet-fly wings have been made from duck and goose wing quill sections for centuries. Delicate and effective (but not very durable) wings on dry flies have been made from duck quills for more than a hundred years. More durable materials like hair, synthetics, and turkey flats (body feathers) have replaced duck wing quills on most flies these days.

DUCK

Duck wing quills are usually light gray, almost translucent, and fragile once sections are removed from the center stem. These days, they are used most often for wing cases on nymphs, but forty years ago, half the wings on the dry and wet flies in your box would have been made from duck quills. The ones you'll probably see most often are mallard wings, which have the biggest and best quills, but don't pass up other duck wings if you see them for sale or shoot your own. Black-duck wings have nice dark gray quills, and smaller ducks like wood duck and teal have light, almost transparent quills.

Buy a pair of wings, because if you tie wet- or dry-fly wings from these, you will need to match a primary quill from the right and left wings to get the curve of the quill sections to oppose each other.

TURKEY

Two kinds of turkey wing quills are sold for fly tying: domestic white ones, which are usually dyed bright colors for salmon flies, and speckled or oak mottled turkey. The speckled feather is one of the most useful feathers in fly tying and an essential ingredient in many nymph patterns, the March Brown wet fly, many grasshopper patterns, and the famous Muddler Minnow streamer. Wild-turkey secondary feathers are almost as good. If you have a hunter save you some, make sure you ask for the secondary feathers, which are the ones behind the primary flight feathers on the front of the wing. The primary feathers are too stiff to be useful in fly tying. If you are making Muddler Minnows or wet flies, you'll need matched pairs of quills; if you're tying nymphs or grasshoppers, pairs aren't necessary.

GOOSE

Domestic white-goose secondary wing feathers, dyed bright colors, can be used interchangeably with dyed turkey. Wild Canada goose wing quills, medium to dark gray in color, make nice wing cases and bodies on nymphs.

BIOTS

Biots are stiff fibers from the short side of a primary feather. The ones you see most often are from goose or turkey wing quills, but any large feather will have biots long enough to make a quill body on a fly. Many modern midge and emerger patterns call for bodies wound with a single biot, which gives the fly a segmented look with fuzzy "gills" at each segment. Biots are also used for tails and wing pads on some nymphs, and white ones are an essential part of the famous Prince Nymph.

Common feathers used in tying trout flies. From left: duck wing quills for making wings and wing cases, mottled turkey quill for wing cases and grasshopper wings, mallard flank feather (top) for wings and tails and nymph legs, wood duck flank (bottom) for wings and tails and nymph legs, and a mallard flank dyed to imitate wood duck.

Duck Flank Feathers

Duck flank feathers are used for the wings on many famous wet and dry flies, such as the Light Cahill. These "Catskill style" flies, once the mainstay of a dry-fly angler's fly box, are not as commonly used today, as duck feathers have been replaced by hair and synthetics in most patterns. But many anglers (myself included) still love to tie and fish these tiny bits of fly-fishing history, considering wood duck a staple on the fly-tying bench. The delicate speckles on wood duck, mallard, teal, and merganser feathers also make perfect legs and tails on nymphs. Commonly, you will see mallard for sale, and also mallard feathers dyed a dark yellow to imitate wood duck, which is more expensive and harder to find. If you do see natural wood duck flank for sale, snap it up: No other duck feather has such insect-like markings. Although not commonly sold in fly shops, flank feathers from teal, widgeon, pintail, and hooded merganser also have wonderfully fine-barred flank feathers. Be kind to your local duck hunter, and you might be able to trade a dozen flies for a whole pile of material.

CDC

CDC stands for cul de canard, which in French means something like "butt of the duck." The feathers actually come from the dorsal part of a duck's hind end, and surround the oily preen-gland feathers. These wispy feathers are extremely popular, after American and British tiers discovered French patterns that had been used with deadly success on continental chalk streams for decades.

It is commonly thought that the feathers are prized because they will float a dry fly without needing fly dressing. However, European anglers credit the feather's killing properties to its lifelike behavior on the water—the feather is so delicate that a fly tied with CDC seems to develop a life of its own on the current. The great floating properties of flies tied with CDC probably owe more to the feather's ability to hold tiny pockets of air than to its oil content, as most feathers we buy for tying have already been washed and processed.

But it is not just the floating properties of CDC that make it valuable. Some heavily weighted nymphs, which have no need of CDC's floating properties, still use it. Apparently the tiny wispy fibers move freely in the current and are thus just as lifelike in a sinking fly as a floating fly.

CDC can be bought in bigger feathers for flies size 8 to 16, or in what is called "oiler puffs" for tiny patterns. It is most useful in natural gray, but some tiers like to use white because it shows up better on the water. You can also get it dyed in many different shades. It is a wonderfully easy feather to use, even for a novice.

Pheasant Tail

Cock ring neck pheasant tail feathers are one of the four basic food groups on my fly-tying bench. There is something about this feather, when wound as a body on small dries and nymphs, that fools trout time after time. Pheasant tail is also used for tails and wing cases on many other nymph patterns. Make sure you get cock, not hen, tail feathers, if you are asking a hunter friend for them. Also, the bigger the feather, the wider the rusty brown edges. The plain, undyed feather is most commonly used, but you can also buy them dyed olive, brown, black, and other insect-like colors.

Soft Game Bird Feathers

The most common game bird feathers for sale are Hungarian partridge feathers, which is fortunate because they are also some of the most useful. One small Hungarian partridge skin will give you hundreds of feathers for hackles on wet flies and legs and wing cases on nymphs. If you hunt or know a bird hunter, breast feathers from quail, pheasant, ruffed grouse, snipe, woodcock, and nearly every other game bird will also give you beautifully speckled hackles.

PEACOCK

Peacock is a staple fly-tying material. Bodies on dry flies and nymphs are made from strands of the tail feather. Strands can be stripped of their flue to make the most buggy quill bodies you will ever see. Peacock herl is used on salmon and steelhead flies, and even to create a dark median or dorsal stripe on saltwater patterns. Most commonly, you will use the eyed tail feathers, and the best ones

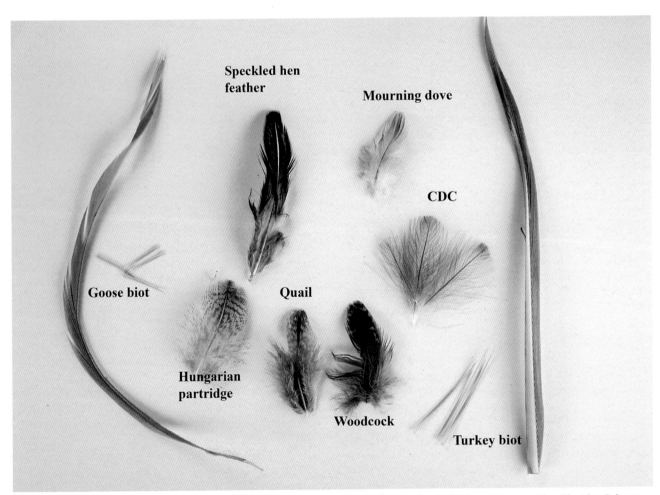

Some other useful feathers. Goose biots are used for tails and legs of nymphs and wing cases on flies like the Prince Nymph. Soft feathers from game birds like Hungarian partridge, quail, woodcock, and mourning dove are used for soft hackle wet flies and legs and tails on nymphs. The speckled hen feather is a mottled feather from a chicken that can be used in place of game bird feathers. CDC is a soft, wispy feather used for wings and hackle on both dry and wet flies, and especially in emergers. Turkey biots are longer than goose biots and are often used to make bodies on flies.

More useful feathers for tying trout flies. At the upper left is a turkey flat, used to make wings on dry flies. Bottom left are two marabou feathers, one dyed purple and one dyed with stripes. Marabou has great action in the water. Next is a cock pheasant tail feather. Its fibers are essential for nymph bodies, legs, and tails. Peacock eye is used to wind bodies and can also be stripped to make thin quill bodies. On the far right is ostrich herl, which makes fuzzy bodies and gills on nymphs.

are tails whose individual herls are covered with heavy, dense flue. You can also buy strung herl, which is fine for winding bodies but does not include the eyed strands that are used for quill bodies. A few patterns call for peacock sword feathers, which are from the side of the tail and don't have the distinctive eye.

MARABOU

Marabou is a soft, downy feather from under the wing of a domestic white turkey. You can buy this feather dyed nearly every color imaginable, in the plain-vanilla variety or with black bars across the feather to imitate baitfish with vertical stripes. Besides being an essential item in the costume of every Las Vegas showgirl, these feathers make lifelike wings on everything from trout streamers to bass bugs. The feather, which is like CDC except much bigger and coarser, wiggles when pulled through the water with a movement that looks just like a minnow or maybe a pork rind. The deadly Woolly Bugger is tied with marabou.

TURKEY FLATS

Turkey flats are breast feathers from a domestic white turkey. They are usually dyed muted colors like tan or dun gray. These feathers are used primarily for wings on parachute and thorax dry flies. Wings made from turkey flats are durable and are lighter than hair wings, so they are great for delicate or small patterns.

OSTRICH

Bunches of ostrich herl can be used as a tail to tie a Woolly Bugger, but most often individual herls are wound around the hook to simulate the feathery gills of aquatic larvae. It has an action similar to that of marabou in the water.

HACKLES

The world of fly-tying hackles has changed dramatically since I first started tying. Then, you had two choices: You either bought small necks from India free-range, semi-wild chickens used for household food, which were imported in huge quantities, or if you were lucky, you found a domestic chicken neck that was raised especially for fly tying, usually by a famous tier who only grew fifty to a hundred capes a year. Now, most hackles you see are domestic capes raised especially for fly tying, and the quality is nothing short of a revelation to older tiers. Forty years ago, a tier would have given his best bamboo rod for a run-of-the-mill cape from the rack of one of today's fly shops. It's ironic that as the supply of quality hackle has increased in the past few decades, a great many highly effective dry flies that use no hackle at all have been developed. Nearly half the dry flies in my box now have no hackle.

Neck Hackles

Inexpensive, imported (Indian) capes are still available, but they are virtually useless for fly tying. As the demand for capes from India decreased, Americans stopped going to India in search of the best quality, and importers no longer grade them. If you dress poppers, small streamers, or smaller saltwater flies, you might find a use for Indian capes, but the same feathers can be obtained from the top of a domestic cape. The lowest-grade domestic cape is still far better for tying dry flies than the best imported one, and it will have three times as many usable feathers. I would urge you not to buy imported capes when you first start tying, as they are harder to wind, and you'll only get discouraged about tying dry flies.

A decent domestic hackle cape will tie from fifty to several hundred flies in each size, depending on the size and quality of the cape. They are usually graded 1, 2, or 3; sometimes gold, silver, and bronze. The more expensive capes will have better feathers overall and a complete range of sizes, from size 10 down to size 28. Most of the grade 4 capes, called "tier's grade," are sold to commercial fly-tying operations, but if you ever see any for sale, snap them up. These capes are usually just smaller than average or are missing a size, but they are well worth their price.

All hackles contain some web. You'll most often see it at the bottom of a feather, and it will extend up the center of the feather in a triangle. Unlike the shiny, translucent hackle fibers at the top of the feather, webby fibers are fuzzy and opaque and will not support a dry fly on the surface because they are too weak. Hen hackles are all web; good dry-fly hackles will show web only at the base of the feather and next to the stern in the lower quarter of the feather. Hackles with web that tapers to less than one-sixth of the length of the individual fibers can be used for dry flies.

When buying neck hackle, look for shiny, fluffy capes, as the shine indicates stiff hackles and the fluff indicates a high quantity of feathers. Look for hackles that have barbs or fibers the same length all the way up the stem. Feathers that have a smaller amount of web along the center stem will have more usable hackle. Not all capes have an equal distribution in hackle sizes. If you tie mainly sizes 14 and 16 flies, pick a cape that seems to have a higher density in the bigger sizes. You usually pay more for a cape that has many tiny feathers that will tie sizes 24 and 26 flies, but most of us don't use those sizes often.

Comparison of chicken neck hackles. On the left is a hen hackle, used for wings on flies, legs on nymphs, and wings on dry and wet flies. Next is an Indian dry fly feather, from a smaller Indian cape. To the left of this is a domestic neck hackle, much longer and typically higher quality than Indian hackle. On the right is a spade hackle from the side of a cape, with long, stiff fibers used for tails.

Natural-colored dry fly capes. From left: black, blue dun, grizzly, brown, and cream.

Hackle capes come in many natural and dyed colors, but for ninety-five percent of all dry-fly patterns you will need only a brown, grizzly (barred black-and-white), cream or light ginger, and blue dun. Get a medium blue dun to start; eventually you will want to buy a dark and light dun, as most insect wings and legs are some shade of gray. Natural blue dun has a special mystique, supposedly due to minute flecks of different colors in the hackle, but it is an unusual color in chickens, and the quality of the hackle is typically not as good as brown, grizzly, or cream. Dyed dun necks start as cream, and the hackles are much denser and stiffer.

Natural colors used in fly tying include the following shades. (White, cream, or grizzly hackles can be dyed any shade, from bright red to chartreuse to purple. The most brightly dyed feathers are most often used for streamers and saltwater flies.)

White: Pure white with no tinge of brown. Very few dry flies call for pure white, so most of these end up dyed to other colors.

Cream: White with a slight yellowish-tan tinge.

Light ginger: Slightly more of a golden cast than cream.

Dark ginger: Also called light brown, it is a golden-brown shade.

Brown: Medium brown.

Coachman brown: A deep, dark brown. It's a hard color to obtain naturally in good quality, and cream capes are often dyed to get this color.

Furnace: A dark-brown hackle with a black center along the stem.

Badger: A cream to light ginger hackle with a black center along the stem.

Grizzly: A white feather with black bars, also known as Plymouth Rock. Those with heavy dark barring are most desirable.

Ginger grizzly: A cream or light ginger hackle with black bars.

Dun grizzly: A blue dun color with black or brown bars. Can be used anywhere a pattern calls for blue dun, and the speckling gives the resulting fly a most insect-like appearance.

Cree: A hackle with black, brown, and white bars. Quite rare, but good ones allow you to tie a fly like the Adams, which requires both brown and grizzly hackle, with one type of feather.

Light blue dun: A pale, almost transparent gray. Blue dun hackles of any shade in natural colors are hard to obtain, so most you find will be cream capes dyed gray.

Medium blue dun: A medium-flat gray shade.

Dark blue dun: A dark-gray, almost black color. Highly prized is the bronze blue dun, a dark dun hackle with tints of brown.

Black: Hard to obtain by breeding, so most are brown capes dyed black.

Hackle capes have uses other than to provide dry-fly hackles. At the side of each cape are short feathers with very stiff fibers. Called spade hackles, these are used to get the stiff tails needed for dry flies. The bigger hackles at the top of a cape can be stripped of all their fibers and wound around hooks to make durable and lifelike bodies on dry flies and nymphs. The bigger hackles about halfway up the cape make great streamer wings, and the biggest hackles at the top of the cape can be used for large saltwater flies.

Some of these are capes from our domestic food industry, but they are also raised specifically for fly tying. They typically start as white or grizzly feathers but are most often dyed. We used to call them "junk" capes, but with the explosion in saltwater fly tying, a cape with really big feathers for tarpon flies can be as hard to find as a Grade 1 dry-fly cape. These big feathers can also be purchased packaged, usually sold as "strung neck hackle" because the feathers are tied together at the base on a long string to keep them together in a package and for ease of use at the tying bench.

Hen Hackles

Hen capes and saddles (from the back of a chicken rather than the neck) are used for wet flies, streamers, and saltwater patterns. Small hen feathers also make superb wings for dry flies. They are almost 100 percent web, so a wet fly or nymph hackled with a hen feather will have lifelike action in the water. Hen hackles dyed bright colors are also used as substitutes for exotic feathers such as Indian crow or blue chatterer on full-dress Atlantic salmon flies. Hen saddle hackles are excellent for legs and wing cases on nymphs, and you can find mottled hen saddles that look exactly like partridge hackle—except they are more durable and easier to wind.

Saddle Hackles

Saddle hackles from a rooster, taken from the upper back of the bird, can either be purchased loose in packages or on the skin. They once were used only for streamer, bass, and saltwater patterns, but thanks to recent advances in the genetics of fly-tying hackle, you can buy superb dry-fly saddles as well. The advantage of using saddles for dry flies is that they wind easier, and you can tie a fly with a single hackle, because the feathers are so much longer than neck hackles. Actually, you can tie up to a half-dozen dry flies with a single feather if it is a good one. When you buy a dry-fly saddle, you usually get only two sizes of feathers—in other words, some saddles will tie size 10 and 12 flies, another might tie 14 and 16. This is fine if you can pick out the saddles in a fly shop, but if you buy them through the mail, you cannot specify the size you want. However, saddles can also be purchased already sized and packaged in packs of about fifteen feathers (which will tie a hundred flies).

Hackle capes: on the left is a domestic saddle cape, full of long, skinny feathers for tying streamers and dry flies. In the middle is an Indian cape, with shorter feathers and usually fewer feathers. This is the kind of cape often included with fly-tying kits. On the right is a domestic dry-fly cape, raised especially for fly tying. These capes have a full range of sizes and the feathers are long.

Saddles for saltwater flies and streamers come either on the skin or strung and packaged. These are wider feathers with heavier stems and more web than the dry-fly variety, and so they are less expensive. You want a wider profile for baitfish imitations, and the heavier, stiffer stem keeps the wing from fouling around the bend of the hook when cast. These feathers can be bought in a wide range of natural and dyed colors.

Schlappen and Cocktails

These are wide, webby feathers from the rear end of a chicken. Use these when you need a long, wide profile, particularly for imitations of bigger species of saltwater baitfish. You can also wind them around the shank of larger flies when you want a wide, webby collar on a fly. They come in natural white or dyed colors.

Saddle hackles: from left, a thin dry-fly hackle that will tie three or four flies with a single feather. The purple feather is a thin saddle for tying streamers with a long, skinny shape, often sold loose in a pack. The green saddle is a wider, webbier feather with a thicker stem, often used for wider streamers and tarpon flies. The blue one is called schlappen, used for very large wings or wound around the head of a fly for a large, opaque profile.

HAIR

When I first started tying, hair was infrequent on dry-fly patterns, being pretty much restricted to Wulffs or big Western stonefly patterns like the Sofa Pillow. Now, we use as much hair as we do hackle on our dry flies, even the tiny ones. It pays to have a number of different types of hair on your tying table, as size and texture of hair can be critical to the way your fly looks and acts on the water.

White-Tailed Deer Belly Hair

Hair from the belly of larger deer flares dramatically when thread is tightened over it. Many bunches are lashed to the hook and then trimmed with scissors or a razor blade to sculpt the fly. This hair is long, coarse, and hollow, which makes it flare and holds air to keep the fly afloat. You can buy this hair in natural gray/brown or dyed just about any color you can find in a box of Crayolas—after all, it is used for bass flies as well.

White-Tailed Deer Back and Face Hair

This hair is harder to find, but if you tie small hair-wing caddis flies or Comparaduns, the finer deer hair will work better than elk. It is sometimes sold as "Comparadun Hair." It is finer and shorter than deer belly hair and flares about

All deer hair is not created equal. On the left is fine, even hair best for wings on dry flies like Comparaduns. Top right is coarser hair used to make deer hair heads on flies like the Muddler Minnow. Bottom right is very coarse belly hair, often dyed, to make bass bugs and mouse flies.

Common hairs used for wings on flies. On the left is a natural bucktail. Next is a dyed bucktail. Squirrel tail is a soft, barred hair used for smaller flies. Calf tail is used for wings on saltwater flies and dry flies. On the right is a piece of calf body hair, used for wings on parachute flies and divided wing dry flies.

half as much, so you can tie in a wing that will keep its shape yet still flare enough to give the fly a robust profile. If you deer hunt or know someone who does, the best hair is from Southern climates or from bow-killed deer earlier in the season. As the season progresses, hair in Northern deer develops long, crinkly black tips that act as solar collectors for heat stored farther down the hollow chamber of the hair. These black tips make the hair harder to even up in a stacker, and the finished fly does not have as clean a profile.

Coastal Deer

Coastal deer is a fly-tying name for black tailed or mule deer that live in the more moderate climate of the Pacific Northwest. Coastal deer can be used interchangeably with white-tailed deer back or face hair, but most tiers consider it inferior to fine white tail hair when tying Comparaduns.

Bucktail

These are tails from white-tailed deer. You can use bucktail for streamer wings, saltwater flies, dry-fly wings and tails, bass-fly wings, steelhead-fly wings, and salmon-fly wings. Unlike deer body hair, bucktail flares little, so you can use

it in places where you want the durability of deer but a narrower profile. Most of the usable part of a bucktail is on the half of the tail toward the tip. As you get near the base of the tail, the hair flares when you tie it in. The best bucktails are those with fine, crinkly hair. The bigger the tail, the better, especially if you tie saltwater flies. A natural bucktail will give you both brown and white hair. Bucktails can be purchased in many dyed colors as well.

Elk

Elk body hair flares less than deer hair of a similar diameter, but is coarser and stiffer. It is used most often for wings of caddis, grasshopper, and stonefly dry flies—as well as many of those big attractor dry flies that imitate who-knows-what. Bull elk is light-colored and coarse, and it works well on caddis dry flies and smaller stonefly imitations. Cow elk is finer and longer-fibered than bull elk and can come in both light and dark shades. It is best for bigger flies. Calf or yearling elk is much like cow elk but slightly finer—a favorite of many tiers. Because elk body hair flares slightly when compressed with thread, it forms a neat caddis- or stonefly-like wing profile without getting out of control. Sometimes you will see elk hocks or mane

You should choose elk hair based on the pattern you are tying. Bull elk on the upper right is coarse with light tips and is best for wings on flies like the Elk Wing Caddis or Humpy. Cow elk, on the bottom, is longer and darker and used for wings on large dry flies. Calf or yearling elk, at the upper left, is used for lighter wings on larger dry flies.

Some less commonly used hairs. On the left is moose body hair, typically used for stiff tails on dry flies. To the right of this is moose mane, which comes in light and dark hairs and can be wound on the body of fly to get a striped effect. Next is antelope, which flares easily and is useful for small hair-bodied flies. On the right in caribou, which is slightly finer than antelope but has similar characteristics.

for sale. These hairs do not flare at all and are used for tails and antennae.

Antelope

Antelope have coarse but very hollow hair that is useful only for spinning bodies, as the ends are usually broken. It is soft and does not hold up as well as deer hair, but it is easy to flare for spun-hair bodies or heads on sculpin imitations.

Caribou

Caribou hair is also soft and hollow but much finer than antelope. If you can find caribou with clean, unbroken tips, it makes superb tiny parachute and Comparadun wings. Because this hair compresses well, there is no bulk where the wing is bound to the shank, and small patterns tied with it look as slim as natural insects. Caribou comes in natural dark gray, light gray, and almost pure white—great for tiny parachutes that you can see in broken water.

Moose

Moose hair is strong and coarse, and it does not flare. It is sometimes used for wings but is more often used for tails on large dry flies. Because moose body hair comes in both dark brown and white, you can tie on one of each and wind them together to get a realistic, segmented body.

Squirrel Tail

Squirrel tail is a soft, barred hair that you can use for streamers, salmon flies, and saltwater flies. It's easy to use and has nice action in the water. Spiky dubbing that looks like rough hare's ear can also be obtained from the base of the tail. Look for clean, straight, fluffy tails. You can use both gray and fox squirrels, and tails from the little red squirrel are sometimes used for Canadian salmon patterns.

Arctic Fox

Use Arctic fox for streamer flies, saltwater patterns, and mixed hair-wing Atlantic salmon patterns. If you substitute Arctic fox tail for bucktail, your fly will "breathe" in the water much like one tied with marabou. Arctic fox Zonker strips include fur still on the hide and can be wound around the shank of the hook like hackle. The hair is longer than rabbit so it is great for larger flies. Dubbing obtained from the base of the tail or in packages is one of the softest and easiest furs to use, and it makes tight, slim bodies. You can purchase tails, Zonker strips, and fur in natural white or many dyed colors.

Calf Body

Calf body hair is short, fine, and solid, and it does not flare at all. Its main use is in Wulff and parachute wings, because it makes very neat, well defined wings. Calf body hair also is extremely durable and stacks instantly. It is most commonly used in pure white, but natural black and brown are also available. You'll sometimes find it dyed, most often to a blue-dun color to imitate mayfly wings.

Calf Tail

You can use calf tail for wings on parachutes and other dry flies, and some tiers think this crinkly hair is better, since it does not hold water as easily as calf body, and so water absorbed by the wing can be flicked off with a single false cast. The downside of calf tail is that it does not stack as easily, and the resulting wing is not as clearly defined, which might look more like an insect wing but is not as appealing to fly tiers. Take your pick.

Calf tails make wonderful streamer wings, are especially easy to use on smaller patterns, and are essential to many bonefish flies. They come in natural white, tan, and brown, and the white ones are easily dyed. When picking calf tails, try to find those with long, relatively straight hair all the way to the tip of the tail. Calf tail with a natural curve is almost impossible to use.

FURS AND DUBBINGS

Pre-Blended Furs

The pleasure of mixing furs to make dubbing blends is becoming a lost art. Being privy to the sale of fly-tying materials for the past forty years, I have seen sales of such items as muskrat and mink fur dwindle to a trickle. In contrast, sales of pre-mixed dubbing blends, with their convenience and easy storage, have taken over. You can buy anything from authentic hare's ear to combinations of synthetics like Antron with a binder of rabbit fur, perhaps with some Lite Brite mixed in for extra sparkle. It's handy to buy a set of dubbing blends, because you always have the perfect shade of fur for a Pale Morning Dun Spinner on hand, in just the right color, with no added labor. The natural fur blends like beaver and possum are easier to dub and are better, I feel, for dry flies, because the fibers are finer and easily hold air bubbles and fly floatant. Most synthetic dubbings are coarser, but have more sparkle, and are better for nymphs. Some dubbing blends combine both natural furs and synthetics, which are great for any kind of fly.

You can make your own pre-blended fur in custom colors by taking any number of colors or types of furs and synthetics and mixing them in a coffee grinder. This mixes and chops all the fibers so they are easier to dub. You can also

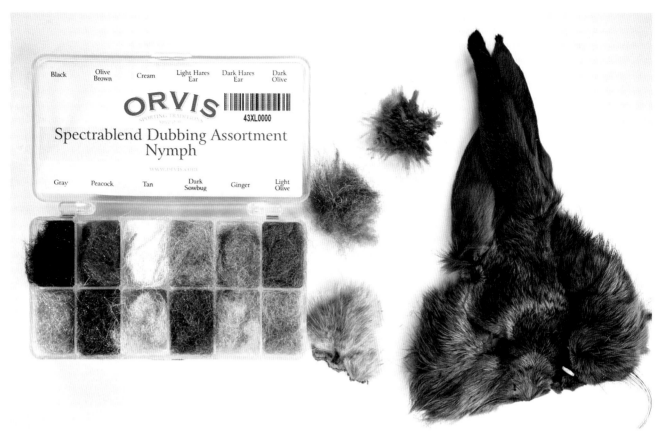

You can buy pre-blended dubbing in sets or in individual bags. Or you can chop and mix it yourself. The furs in the center are, from top to bottom, beaver, Australian possum, and muskrat. On the right is a hare's mask, an essential dubbing material for nymphs.

"felt" your dubbing blends by adding the blend to a bowl of soapy water, draining and rinsing the fur in a colander, and letting it dry on a piece of paper. The idea is to get all the fibers going in different directions, as unidirectional fibers don't hold well to waxed thread when spun between your fingers.

I feel compelled to mention some furs, in case you decide to mix your own dubbings. I still do, and I find it one of the most satisfying aspects of fly tying. It's a creative process that takes absolutely no skill, yet the finished product is exactly what you want. How many elements of our lives are so simple and satisfying?

You can tie with fur from any animal, from a road-killed woodchuck to a snippet from the household cat. When I was a kid, I trapped and skinned a mole because there was a pattern I wanted to tie that called for mole fur. It had the most disgusting smell, and I still cringe when I think about it.

Hare's-Ear Fur

You cannot replace fur from the ears of an English hare with any synthetic, and even the hare's-ear blends on the market don't have enough of the short, spiky hairs for my taste. Hare's ear is one of those magical fly-tying materials that seems to make any fly pattern better. It may be

the earthy, impressionistic colors you blend together, or it may be how the resulting fuzzy body imitates the tiny struggles of an emerging fly. I would advise you to mix all your hare's-ear fur at once, because it takes a few minutes and is quite messy. You can put the fur from a pair of ears into a Ziploc bag and use it whenever you tie. You can buy natural hare's ears in natural gray/brown or dyed to insect-like colors. The most useful dyed color is olive.

Muskrat Fur

The Adams is the most popular dry fly ever invented and, in my opinion, it should only be tied with muskrat fur. Muskrat is a silky, translucent fur, rich in natural oils that keep muskrats warm and dry—and your Adams floating high! It's inexpensive, especially if you know a local trapper. One skin will last a lifetime.

Fox Fur

It's not easy to find red fox fur these days, but it's well worth the effort. Nothing dubs as nicely as fox fur, and the cream belly fur is the ideal body material for the famous Light Cahill dry fly. If you can find a moth-eaten old fur stole at a garage sale, you'll be in heaven. The fur from

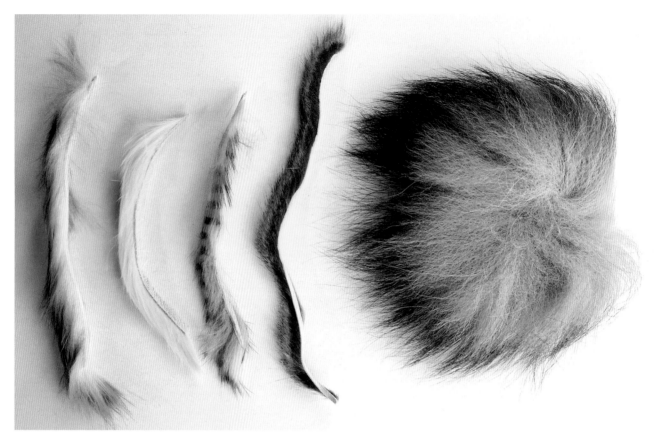

Furs used for wings and collars on streamers. From left: a natural tan rabbit Zonker strip, a dyed chartreuse Zonker strip, an orange barred Zonker strip, a natural pine squirrel Zonker strip, and a patch of arctic fox fur.

an Arctic fox is almost as fine, with the advantage that the white fur can be dyed any color.

Rabbit

Rabbit fur is almost as fine and easy to work with as fox. You can often find entire hides at a very reasonable price, or you can just snip some fur off the Zonker strips you use for streamers.

Zonker Strips

These are narrow strips of rabbit hide, cut with the grain of the fur and still on the tanned skin. Zonker strips are lashed down over the top of a hook to create the famous streamer pattern known as—you guessed it—the Zonker. There are also sculpin imitations and saltwater flies that use the same technique.

Another type of strip, called crosscut rabbit, is cut across the grain of the fur and is wound like hackle to produce the wiggliest fly you'll ever see. The Tarpon Bunny is one pattern that uses this material.

Australian Possum

Australian possum is a wonderful fur that comes in a dizzying array of natural colors, everything from light cream to rust to dark gray. It dubs nicely and has a natural translucence. Many pre-blended dubbings use Australian possum as a binder.

SYNTHETIC MATERIALS

Floss

Floss is a smooth, shiny, threadlike material, wound around the hook to make a glossy body. Although salmon-fly tiers like to use traditional silk floss, most other tiers use the more durable and affordable rayon variety. Floss absorbs water quickly and is best used on wet-fly and streamer bodies. The famous Royal Wulff, however, calls for a floss body, and I defer to tradition on that pattern and a few others. You could just as easily get the red band in the middle of a Royal Wulff with dubbed red fur or some more durable plastic material, but most tiers don't—some patterns just shouldn't be messed with.

The top row is tinsel (oval, gold Mylar, and pearlescent) and the bottom row is floss.

Chenille is a quick and easy way to make a body on a fly. From left is standard cotton chenille, Ultra-Chenille, Estaz or Cactus Chenille, and a variegated chenille that combines the standard cotton fibers with sparkly Mylar strips.

Chenille

Chenille is a soft material wound around a thread core. It is durable and easy to work with, especially for the beginner. Two kinds are available: traditional chenille, which is fairly loose in texture, and Ultra Chenille or Vernille, a tight, fuzzy, finer variety. Both will work for bodies on streamers and wet flies, but the traditional kind is used most often. Vernille is an essential component of the deadly San Juan Worm, and you can also use it for extended bodies on caddis and midge imitations. In these types of flies, you can singe the rough end of the material with a butane lighter to give it a realistic taper.

You can also make chenille by incorporating strands of tinsel or strands of colored Mylar around a thread core; these are sold under such names like Cactus Chenille or Estaz. Some types of chenille incorporate very long fibers for making larger saltwater and streamer flies, often incorporating flashy fibers.

TINSEL AND WIRE

Flat Metallic Tinsel

Metallic or "French" tinsel is a thin metal tape coated with silver or gold. When wound around a hook, it forms a shiny, even body. It is used for wet, streamer, salmon, steelhead, and saltwater flies and can be used to make a whole body or as a rib to give the fly a segmented look. It can be purchased in various sizes, in gold or silver.

Mylar Tinsel

Mylar tinsel is a modern development, typically gold on one side and silver on the other, so you don't have to worry about buying more than one color. Mylar stretches slightly, so it is easier to use than metallic tinsel, and it won't tarnish with age. Its one disadvantage is that it can be cut easily by sharp fish teeth, but you can prevent this by applying head cement or epoxy to the finished body before tying on the wings and hackle. Pearlescent and holographic Mylar, which gives the finished fly the appearance of air bubbles or the translucence of a baitfish, is also available.

Mylar Tubing

Mylar tubing is tinsel woven into a round cord, usually over a thread core. You cut the tubing to length, slip the thread out of the center, and slip the tubing over the hook. This produces an outrageously realistic imitation of a baitfish, and a durable fly to boot. The tubing comes in gold, silver, black, and in various pearlescent shades.

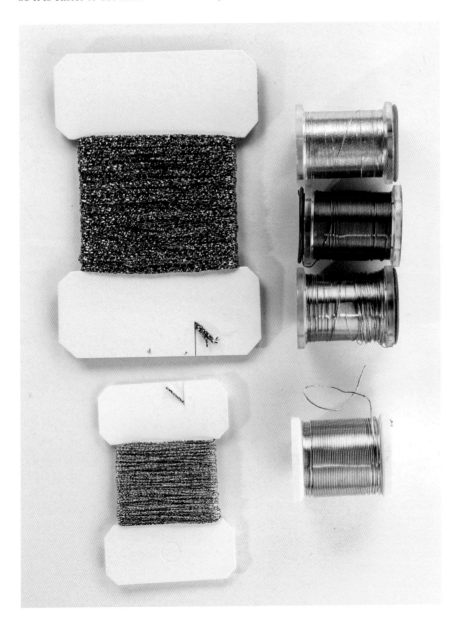

Wire and braid used for winding bodies. On the left are two types of Diamond Braid. At the upper left is three colors of wire for bodies and ribs. Bottom left is soft-non-toxic wire used to add weight under the body of a fly.

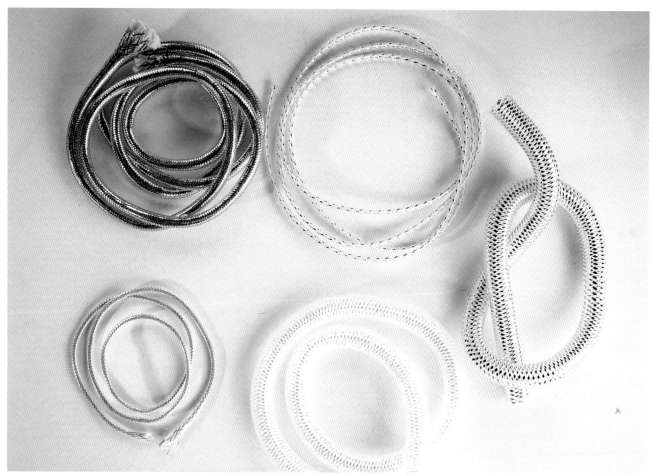

Tubing used for fly bodies. On top, from left to right: standard silver Mylar tinsel, clear tubing with a baitfish pattern woven in, and flexible silver tubing. Bottom row is thin pearlescent Mylar tubing and flexible pearlescent tubing.

Also available is a flexible tubing that can be stretched, shaped, or rolled back onto itself (like rolling a sock). This material is used to make bodies for baitfish, shrimp, and crab imitations.

Oval and Embossed Tinsels

Oval tinsel is fine tinsel wound around a thread core to produce an oval shape. It produces a softer, subtler glitter when used as a rib on trout flies and can be used over almost any type of body material, including flat tinsel. You can wind it all by itself as a body, although few patterns call for this technique.

Embossed tinsel is flat tinsel with a pattern embossed onto its surface. When wound as a body, which some Atlantic salmon patterns still call for, the effect is a shiny body with many facets.

Flat Braid

Flat braid is wound like tinsel, but it is often used to construct entire bodies instead of just ribbing. It makes a slightly thicker body with a scale-like pattern. Although

it is hollow, it acts more like thread or yarn than tubing. You'll find various types in both metallic and pearlescent varieties.

Wire

You can use fine metallic wire on small flies as a rib to give them segmentation and flash and to reinforce delicate materials, such as pheasant tail and peacock herl. You can also wind it by itself to form a thin, segmented body. A few nymphs are actually tied by using very fine wire in a bobbin, which weights the fly slightly and gives the finished product a sparkly, translucent effect. The very finest diameters of wire are used for ribbing, but bigger diameters are available for constructing entire bodies out of wire. It's supremely durable, never loses its color, and comes in a wide variety of shades.

Weighting Wire

To lead or not to lead—nymphs and streamers often need additional weight to get them down to the fish. Traditionally, you'd wind soft wire lead over the hook before the thread was started, and you'd tie the fly over the wire. Using lead weight to flies is still legal in most parts of North America, but it has become illegal in some states and national parks, as well as in the UK. I don't use lead on my flies anymore because I don't want any chance, however remote, of one of my flies ending up in the stomach of a loon or merganser. There are non-toxic alternatives to lead wire that are better for weighting flies: using unweighted flies and putting tungsten putty on the leader, using tungsten or brass beads in the dressing of the fly, using soft non-toxic tin wire instead of lead, or winding an underbody of flexible tungsten sheet. Orvis does not sell lead wire for fly tying, nor do we sell any finished flies tied with lead.

YARNS

Natural Yarns

Yarn is almost always used for bodies, although the tails on a few wet flies and streamers call for short stubs of yarn. Wool yarn is inexpensive and can be purchased on cards at tackle shops or in bulk at stores that sell knitting supplies. Wool yarn is monochromatic and thus not very effective in imitating the subtle colors of insects, but it forms a quick and durable body on many colorful streamer patterns. Another natural yarn you'll see is angora yarn, often sold as "leech yarn." It is very fuzzy, with many long fibers sticking out, and is used for leech patterns and some saltwater flies. Yarn is typically made up of several strands. You can use it as is for bigger flies, or you can unwind the single strands for smaller flies.

Synthetic Yarns

The most common and useful types of synthetic yarns are used for wings and trailing shucks on trout flies rather than for bodies. Antron yarn and Z-Lon are the most common types, made from nylon with what are called tri-lobal fibers. These fibers, flat on three sides instead of round, hold tiny air bubbles to their surfaces (they were originally developed for stain-resistant carpets) and imitate a hatching insect well. Antron is slightly softer and finer in diameter, and Z-Lon is a bit coarser, offering a crinkly texture. Also, Z-Lon does not matt as much as Antron because of its thicker, stiffer fibers, so it is more commonly used for trailing shucks on dry flies and emergers. These yarns can be obtained in many colors, with the most useful being gray, white, tan, and brown. You can wind bodies with these yarns, but the effect is not particularly useful or interesting.

Sparkle yarn, used for bodies on large nymphs, streamers, and saltwater flies, is also known as Aunt Lydia's Rug Yarn. Del Brown's deadly Permit Fly uses segments of

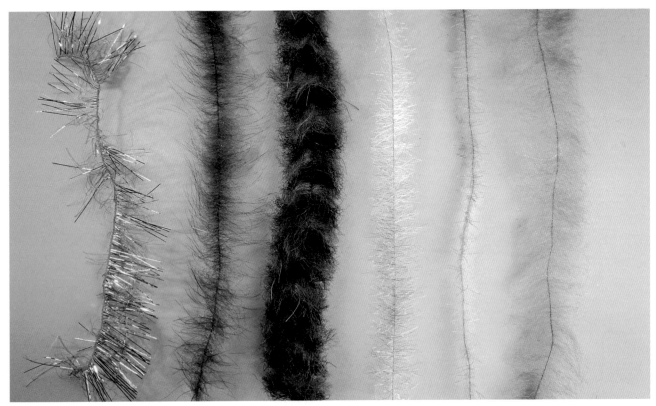

Brushes make it easy to create wide, flowing bodies on large flies. From left to right: flashy Mylar woven around a cotton core, natural fur with a wire core, heavy synthetic fibers combined with tiny rubber legs, pearl Mylar on a wire core, thin synthetic fur combined with tiny rubber legs for smaller flies, and wider synthetic fibers for bigger flies.

sparkle yarn tied across the hook, which are then combed and trimmed to a flat, crab-like shape.

A third type of yarn is used for wings on dry flies, especially parachute flies, and you can often find it sold under the name Para Post. It is a polyester treated with a water-resistant coating that is durable and much easier to work with than natural materials like calf body hair. EP Fiber is another type of polyester yarn that is used in many different fly patterns. It is lightweight, sheds water quickly, is easy to handle, and ties in very securely. It's used for wings and collars on saltwater flies and streamers and wings on dry flies and emergers. One style, called Trigger Point Fiber, is treated with a hydrophobic coating to make it float better when used in dry flies.

Polypropylene yarn is also useful for parachute and spinner wings on flies. It might seem like the perfect yarn for dry flies, because it has a specific gravity of .9, lighter than water, and so it floats naturally, but just because it has a low specific gravity does not mean it is effective when tying dry flies. Floating qualities depend more on the size and shape of a fiber and how well it repels water than on if it bobs back to the surface after being drowned.

Bug Yarn

Bug yarn is a soft nylon fiber you can use to make egg flies. When you tie in a large clump of this fiber and trim it quickly with a sharp pair of scissors, the yarn falls around the hook in an egg shape that looks exactly like a pom-pom—but it's permanently attached to the hook, and you can include multiple colors of yarn to get a realistic egg spot or a marbled color. Bug yarn is also useful for parachute posts, where you'll want a short, wide post of a bright color to act as a visual aid on the water.

Brushes

Brushes are natural or synthetic fibers wound around a wire core. They consist of natural furs like fox, synthetic fibers like Craft Fur, or a combination of soft fibers and flashy tinsel strands. Some even have rubber legs incorporated into them. They make it easy to produce large-diameter, flowing bodies on streamers, saltwater flies, steelhead flies, and bass bugs.

··

BEADS AND EYES

Brass and Tungsten Beads

Nymphs and streamers tied with brass beads are some of the most effective subsurface flies ever developed. Beads add more weight to a fly than you'd achieve with a lead

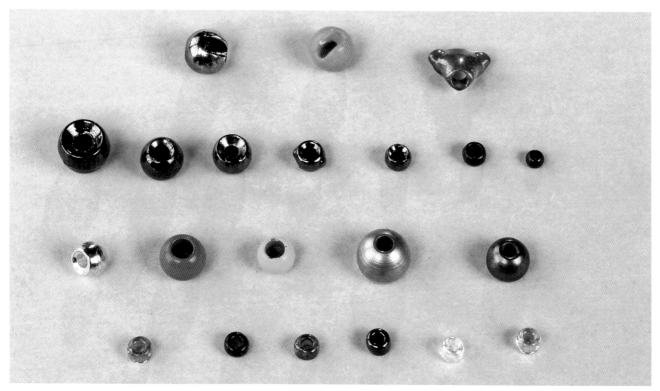

Beads add flash and weight to nymphs and streamers. On the top row are two slotted beads for using with jig hooks, plus a shaped tungsten bead for imitating the shape of a mayfly head. The second row shows the size range available in tungsten beads. The third row shows the colors of paint or plating that can be applied to brass or tungsten beads. On the bottom row are tiny glass beads used for the heads and bodies on smaller flies.

underbody, and they add a sparkle to the head that may imitate the air bubble around an emerging nymph. All of the popular nymph, streamer, and even wet-fly patterns are now tied with versions with bead heads. Simply slip the bead onto the hook before attaching the thread, and then either whip finish the fly just behind the bead or carry the thread forward and apply a hackle or wing case over the bead.

Beads made for fly tying have holes with wide and narrow ends. The wide end threads easier over the point of the hook, while the narrow end keeps the bead from slipping over the hook eye.

Consider using brass beads when you intend to fish a fly in relatively shallow water. Tungsten beads, which are heavier than lead, can add a massive amount of weight to a tiny fly and will get a caddis pupa to the bottom of a deep, fast run in a hurry. Some tiers tie double-bead flies, and if you do this with tungsten flies, make sure you wear a hat, as a tungsten fly on a forward cast can sting harder than a shot from a pellet gun.

The most common beads are brass, but both brass and tungsten beads can be purchased silver, black, or copper plated, or in bright painted colors. They come in various diameters for different hook sizes.

Slotted beads, usually made from tungsten, have a central hole with a slot in one end. The slot makes it easy to place a heavy bead at the head of fly tied on a jig hook, and ensures that the bead slips properly over the bent eye on a jig hook.

Bead diameter in inches	Bead diameter in millimeters	Appropriate hook sizes (depending on exact shape of hook bend)
1/16	1.5	20-24
5/64	2	18-20
3/32	2.5	16-18
7/64	3	14-16
1/8	3.5	12-14
5/32	4	8-12
3/16	4.6	8-10
7/32	5.6	4-6
1/4	6.4	2

This bead chart should help you decide which beads you need for any given hook size. Some beads slide easier onto the hook than others, and with some hooks, you might need to pinch the barb before getting the bead to slip on the shank—it all depends on the exact shape of the hook. Some places size them in millimeters and others in inches, so I provided both measurements here.

Cones

Cones, made from either brass or tungsten, can be used on streamers and saltwater flies. Like beads, they pack a lot of weight and add sparkle.

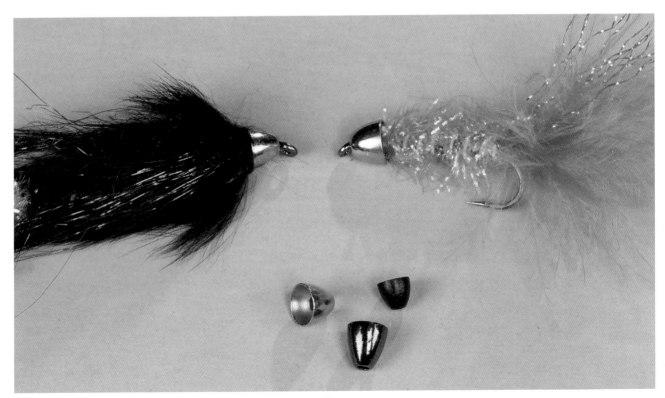

Cones add weight and sparkle to the heads of streamer flies.

Skulls and shanks. Skulls build up the head of a fly and add weight. Shanks allow the tying of an articulated fly without the need to use two hooks in a single fly.

Masks

Masks are versions of cones that add a realistic, baitfish-style head to a fly. One style is made from clear plastic, which acts to build up a large head on a fly without requiring numerous coats of epoxy. Recessed slots in the side of the mask accept realistic eyes, which will give a baitfish imitation a durable head that suspends in the water column—important for flies that should be fished closer to the surface. Another style of mask is made from metal in a flattened shape to imitate the head of a sculpin (a common baitfish in trout streams). It adds a lot of weight to a fly, as well as a realistic shape.

Glass Beads

Glass beads from the craft industry are mainly used for tying nymphs. They don't add as much weight as brass or tungsten, but they give flies a deep, transparent sparkle. You can make bodies by threading a series of glass beads onto the hook, or you can use a single bead for a head. All sizes are available, from tiny sizes that won't crowd a size 24 midge larva, to beads suitable for large streamers. You can buy them in craft stores or packaged for fly tiers.

Bead-Chain Eyes

Bead chain can be cut into pairs and attached to the head of a fly with a figure-eight wrap. This gives a lifelike effect to flies, and adds just a moderate amount of weight. Bead chain is the essential ingredient on most popular bonefish flies. You can get it at a hardware store or buy it from a tackle shop. But before you go off and save yourself a few bucks at the hardware store, you should know the stuff you buy at a fly shop is sometimes pre-cut into pairs, saving you a lot of time, and it is also made from stainless steel. Most hardware store bead chain is not stainless, and so it rusts and corrodes easily.

Dumbbell Eyes

This is the main ingredient of the deadly Clouser Deep Minnow and its variations, which is without question the most useful saltwater fly ever developed. Dumbbell eyes of solid metal add much more weight than bead-chain. Attach them to the front of the hook with a figure-eight wrap, and you can sink a fly quickly, giving it a jigging action when retrieving it. Some dumbbell eyes are made of plated lead, but you already know my feelings about lead. The best ones are made from plated brass and don't tarnish in salt water.

Plastic Eyes

When you want a pair of bug eyes on a fly but don't want weight, plastic eyes are useful. They are used for everything from adult damselfly imitations to crab flies to slow-sinking bonefish flies. They can be purchased as plastic dumbbell shapes or as plastic bead chain.

Stick-On Eyes

Stick-on eyes are flat decals that are pre-cut and attached to paper with a sticky back so they can be stuck to the sides of epoxied heads or popper bodies.

3-D eyes look like doll or taxidermy eyes—which they are. The best ones for tying flies come on an

You can vary the sink rate of your flies by using different eyes. On the left are solid metal dumbell eyes, which add the most weight. In the center are bead chain eyes for just a moderate amount of weight and less splash when a fly enters the water. On the right are plastic eyes for floating flies or sinking flies used in very shallow water.

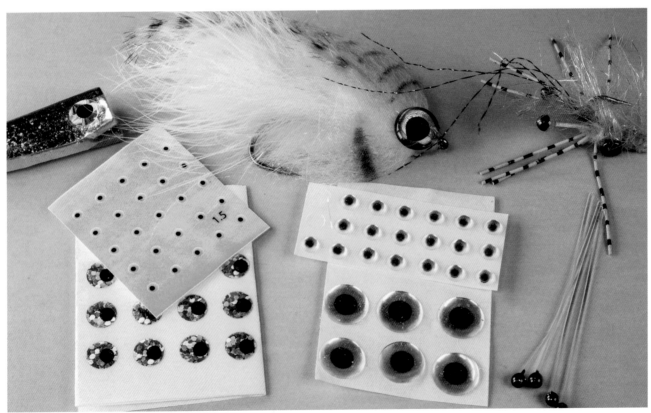

Eyes used to add realism to flies. On the left are flat stick-on eyes, in the middle are 3-D eyes with some depth, and on the right are pre-made eyes for crabs and shrimp.

adhesive-backed strip. You simply pluck them off the paper, and stick them on the head of your fly with epoxy or head cement. Some of them have a holographic treatment that adds further depth and realism. One style of brass dumb-bells has recessed ends so that you can stick a glass eye on each end for a fly that looks real enough to swim in your goldfish bowl.

SYNTHETIC HAIRS

There is nothing more confusing than the array of synthetic wing materials for making saltwater, steelhead, bass, and streamer flies. Scores of different brands and styles within those brands make it impossible to keep up. I'm in the fly-fishing industry, with a number of friends who produce fly-tying materials for a living, and I still get confused. In order to help you navigate all these fibers, I've divided them up into three broad categories based on the kind of fiber used to make them, which will hopefully help you get a handle on it, and also choose an appropriate substitute when you can't find a particular brand.

Nylon Hair

Nylon hair is used on many saltwater, bass, and pike flies for two reasons: one, it is often impossible to find feathers or natural hairs long enough to tie an eight-inch fly, and two, nylon hair is durable and holds up to the sharp teeth of bluefish and barracuda far better than bucktail or hackles. Scores of brands and types are available today, with names like Super Hair, Ultra Hair, and Diamond Hair. You can buy it in fine and coarse deniers, in straight and crinkly, in every color known to baitfish and some that aren't, and even with strands of tinsel mixed in. It's easy to use, can be cut to length, and does not require the preparation and grading that bucktail and feathers do. Nylon hair is often quite translucent, and the diameter of the fiber used for wings on flies is thicker than other synthetic fibers. To get a large profile, you often have to use a lot of it, which weighs down a fly. Also, nylon does not shed water as easily as other fibers, thus making a fly hard to cast, so it is best for patterns that require a skinny profile.

Acrylic Hair

Acrylic hair is very fine and absorbs water quickly, so use it on flies that need a quick sink rate, like bonefish flies. It

There is a dizzying selection of artificial hairs available to fly tiers. From left to right: Flash Blend (a mixture of flashy Mylar and synthetic fibers), DNA Fiber (a very fine, kinked nylon), Craft Fur (a fine acyrlic), Fishair (fine nylon), Kinky Fibre, Ultra Hair (a more coarse nylon), and EP Fiber (a fine polyester). These are just a few and new ones are introduced every year.

is very lifelike, has a natural taper, and is sometimes hard to distinguish from natural fur. Acrylic, with its fine fibers, also breathes well in the water, so it has an enticing wiggle when used on small baitfish or shrimp imitations. It is commonly called Polar Fibre, Craft Fur, Silky Fibers, or Faux Fox (because its fine diameters look like natural fox fur).

Polyester/Polypropylene Hair

Polyester and polypropylene fibers look similar and offer similar properties when used for wings on large flies. Flies tied with these fibers produce big profiles in the water and are commonly used to make wide baitfish patterns like imitations of mullet, menhaden, sunfish, or shad (although by using less fiber you can also make skinnier flies). The big advantage is that even though you can build up a large fly with it, the resulting pattern is lightweight and sheds water with a single back cast. Thus, these are the favorite materials for the very biggest baitfish imitations. EP Fiber, developed by the innovative tier Enrico Puglisi, is the most common brand. These fibers are also available treated with a permanent waterproofing compound for tying floating baitfish or trout dry-fly wings.

FLASHY SYNTHETIC WING MATERIALS

This category of fly-tying materials has boomed along with saltwater fly tying. Flashy synthetic wing materials are simply various kinds of Mylar tinsel cut very fine and sold in packaged hanks. Flashabou is one type that is straight and very shiny. Krystal Flash is a twisted fiber that reflects tiny points of light, which change as the fibers change position, thus creating an impression of fish scales and movement. Angel Hair gives off a translucent, prismatic effect, and holographic tinsel creates a rainbow of depth and colors you wouldn't think possible of something not plugged into a light socket. Besides using these materials "straight" as wings, you can mix them with bucktail or synthetic hairs. They are also very useful on trout flies: Tiny midge-pupa bodies, for example, can be wound with a single strand, and legs, wings, and tails on nymphs take on a whole new sparkle. A few fibers can even be used in dry-fly wings or as legs on beetle imitations.

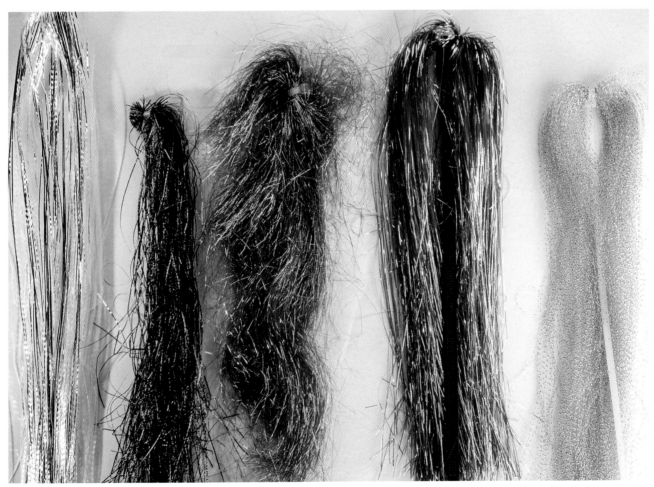

Materials added to fly wings to add flash. From left to right: Mirror Flash, Gliss 'N Glow, Angel Hair, Flashabou, and Krystal Flash.

MISCELLANEOUS SYNTHETIC MATERIALS

Popper Bodies

Most tiers don't get into making their own popper bodies, which involves shaping a piece of cork, gluing it onto a special hook, priming the body, and then painting it. Luckily, you can buy pre-made popper blanks, painted and unpainted, made from cork, foam, or molded urethane. Then it's a simple matter of painting if necessary, adding rubber legs through the body with a heavy needle, and tying hackles or bucktail behind the body.

Foam

Special fly-tying foam is dense, closed-cell foam that compresses without tearing when wound with tying thread. You'll use it mainly for terrestrial imitations and large dry flies. You can buy it in flat sheets for tying beetles or grasshopper and stonefly bodies, or in round cylinders in various sizes for making extended bodies on damselfly imitations, to mention just a few uses. A wing case on an emerger, tied

with a slip of foam, will keep just the head of the fly above water—a very realistic attitude. Foam folded over a hook and glued in place makes a great floating baitfish imitation like the famous Crease Fly. Foam comes in all different colors and thicknesses, and can be cut to shape with your scissors or can be punched out with a premade tool.

Thin Skin

Thin Skin is a plastic sheet used for wing cases on nymphs or for winding bodies on making overlays. It comes in a wide variety of colors and is cut to shape with scissors. Although it is durable, many tiers cover it with a layer of epoxy or head cement to give it more durability and a three-dimensional look.

Swiss Straw

Swiss Straw is a synthetic raffia with a crinkly, translucent look. It absorbs water easily, and you can use it on wing

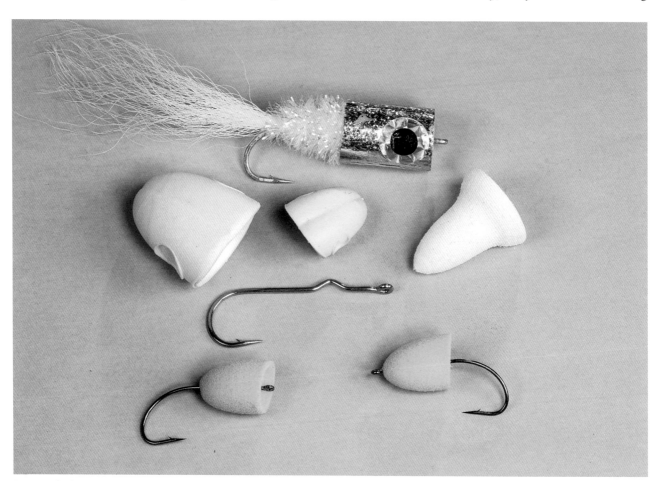

Pre-made foam bodies can be glued to hooks to make poppers. They are usually glued to special kink-shanked hooks to help hold the foam to the hook without rotating. At the bottom you can see how the same body can be made into a noisy popper or a more subtle slider by just reversing its direction on the hook.

You can get very creative with foam sheets and tubes, making fly bodies that float all day long without the use of dry-fly preparations.

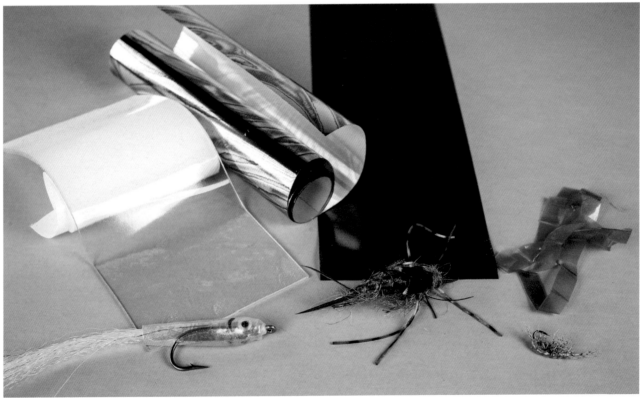

Synthetic body materials, from left to right. Sili Skin or Gummi Body is folded over a hook to create a translucent, soft shape. One type uses a foil sheet that transfers patterns to the skin. Thin Skin is a flexible synthetic used in wing cases and overlays. On the right are latex strips, also used for wing cases and overlays.

Flexible, lifelike legs are made from silicone or rubber and are available in many colors and patterns.

cases on nymphs and as a shellback or overlay on crustacean patterns.

Sili Skin

Sili Skin, also known as Gummi Body, is a clear silicone sheet with adhesive on either one or both sides. It can be folded over itself over a hook to produce a minnow body, but it can also be wrapped over the shank to create nymph abdomens. If you use the type with adhesive on both sides, a foil decal is pressed against the outside of the body to obtain metallic or pearlescent effects.

Rubber Legs

Use rubber legs as nymph and dry-fly legs, on saltwater crab and shrimp imitations, and on bass flies. Many big Rocky Mountain attractor dries use them. Also available are rubber legs with bands painted on them to give an impression of speckling and movement. These legs, usually known as Tentacle Legs, are popular on nymphs, streamers, and saltwater flies.

Silicone Legs

Used in the same places as rubber legs, silicone legs offer the same wiggly movement in the water but are translucent and more durable, because rubber legs break down if exposed to sunlight for long periods. Silicone legs come in a wider variety of colors than rubber legs and in both solid and specked colors. Some incorporate flecks of flashy material.

Spanflex

Spanflex or Flexi Floss is a flat, flexible material used to make bodies and legs. It is translucent and quite effective wound as a body, and when used for legs, it gives a slightly different look than the silicone of rubber legs.

Nylon and Vinyl Tubing and Strips

These synthetics are used for bodies on nymphs and saltwater flies. They are stretchy and translucent, and they come in a wide variety of colors and sizes. One type, known

Some of the synthetics used in fly tying. From left to right: Two diameters of flexible tubing used for bodies, Fibetts used for tails on dry flies, and Swiss Straw used for overlays and wing cases on nymphs.

as Larva Lace, is round and hollow, and it can either be slipped over the shank of the hook or wound like tinsel. V-Rib is flat on one side with a rounded hump on the other so the segmented effect of the body is accentuated. To form bodies with a lot of depth, wind clear or translucent V-Rib over tinsel; as a bonus, bodies made from these materials are nearly indestructible.

Woven Synthetic Wings

Woven synthetic wings are realistic imitations of insect wings made from light, woven materials or polypropylene, which is lighter than water. They sometimes come pre-cut, or you can cut or burn your own to shape. You may even see artificial wings printed with veins to imitate the naturals. These are typically fad materials that never seem

to catch on, possibly because the stiffer wings made from these have to be perfectly matched or they will twist your leader into a Slinky.

Fibetts

Fibetts are a PET material (a class of polyester), very fine and tapered, used to make tails on dry flies. They are much easier to prepare than spade hackle fibers for tails. However, they are more slippery than hackle when you tie them in and are thus a bit trickier to use. They are not as stiff as real hackle fibers, but they are handy, and not all hackle capes have decent spade hackles. Fibetts come in clear, gray, and tan—all the colors you need for tails. They can also be speckled with a permanent marker.

CHAPTER 4

HOOKS, THREADS, AND CEMENTS

HOOKS

I have seen modern hook factories in Japan and Singapore. Even though machines form the point, barb, bend, and eye in one long assembly line, hook making is almost a cottage industry that entails a lot of attention and labor, especially in the tempering and sharpening processes. Hooks made for fly tying are of the highest quality and are as carefully made as giant tuna hooks, where thousands of dollars can be riding on a single piece of wire.

Yes, you can tie flies on plain old bait hooks, just like you can tie materials on a hook with sewing thread. But if you spend a little more, you'll get superb hooks designed especially for fly tying, properly tempered and needle-sharp right from the box. Unless you make a careless cast and knick the point of a hook or a fly rusts in your book, you may never have to sharpen a trout fly tied on a premium hook. In the past, anglers almost always had to sharpen saltwater hooks prior to use because the points were not as strong and sharp as they should have been right from the box. However, today you can fish even the largest hooks with confidence and without sharpening, although you should always check after snags or after a battle with a big fish. (Saltwater hooks, because of their bigger wire diameter, must be razor sharp to penetrate the tough mouth of a tarpon or bluefish.)

PARTS OF A HOOK

Hooks start at the point, the part a fish likes least. The barb is a tiny, raised part of the wire that prevents a hook from slipping back out of the fish's mouth. The bend is the place where the wire is bent to create the shape of, well, a hook. The shank is the long, straight segment of the hook where you place materials when tying a fly. The eye is the little ring at the front end of the hook where you tie your tippet. In my fly-tying directions, when I refer to the front of the hook, I mean the part closest to the eye, and the back or rear is toward the bend. So if I say to "wind forward," I mean towards the eye, and if I say "at the rear of the fly," I mean the part closest to the bend.

BUYING HOOKS

The hook is the most expensive part of a fly. At around 30 cents each for the best quality trout hooks and almost three times that for chemically sharpened saltwater hooks, a little thought should go into the hooks you buy. Fortunately, it's easy, and most packaging or catalogs will tell you the best uses for each style of hook.

If you don't know brands, how can you tell a high-quality hook? Look at the eye first. It should be fully closed, and the place where the final end of the wire was cut should blend into the shank with no sharp edges to cut your leader. The well-finished hook will be a light bronze color. If it's too dark, the hook has probably been coated with too much bronzing, which makes the point dull. The best hooks have needle-points and are sharp 360 degrees around. Needle-points are chemically sharpened, which means the entire hook is dipped in a corrosive bath, and the material removed from the point makes it sharper all around. Less expensive hooks have points that are machine-cut, and cannot be chemically sharpened. Also, some of their strength is sacrificed because material is removed at the sides of the point in the process.

Look for short points rather than long, thin ones, because thin points aren't as strong. Finally, a small, low barb is generally better because it not only penetrates easier but allows you to release your catch easier. Low barbs mean that there has been less cutting into the wire behind the point: The deeper the cut when the barb is made, the weaker the point.

Hooks can be made barbless before tying materials to them by pinching the barb with a pair of flat-jawed (not serrated) forceps or pliers. Forceps made especially for fly tying have this feature, and you can even buy a special de-barbing tool for fly tying. Sometimes you break a hook pinching the barb—better to do it before you tie a fly than after you develop an emotional attachment to the finished product.

HOOK TERMINOLOGY

Hook terminology is not standardized, although it is consistent enough for fly tying—after all, it's only a hobby. Hooks are sized according to their gap or gape, the shortest distance between the point and the shank. This is pretty consistent. The smaller the hook size, the bigger the fly,

until you get to size 1; then the hooks progress through 1/0, 2/0, 3/0, 4/0, and 5/0 in increasing order of size. A 4/0 hook is about the largest size used in tying flies; 28 is the smallest.

However, shank length can vary, and it is this variation as much as anything that can give a fly pattern its character and personality. A 1X-long size 10 hook means a hook with the shank length of a size 9. (Although we use mainly even-sized hooks, odd sizes do exist.) A 3X-long size 10 would have the shank length of a size 7 hook. A stonefly nymph on a regular-shank size 10 hook looks foreshortened and cramped; the same fly on a 3X-long size 10 looks perfect. Short hooks in 1X and 2X do exist, but they are not used as often, except for specialized nymphs.

Wire diameter is treated in a similar fashion, but differences among manufacturers vary greatly. Hypothetically, a 1X-fine size 10 hook has the wire diameter of a size 11 standard hook. But wire standardization is supposed to come along the same year as campaign-finance reform, so I'd advise you to look for dry-fly hooks that say "extra-fine wire" or are just labeled as dry-fly hooks. If a hook is labeled as a nymph or streamer hook and the package doesn't say anything else, it is probably regular-weight wire, which is fine. I'd recommend nymph or streamer hooks labeled "heavy" or "2X stout" if you fish for Atlantic salmon or steelhead with small wets and nymphs, or if you expect to be fishing for trout over twenty inches long

To help dry flies float in the surface film, dry-fly hooks are made from finer wire than hooks designed for nymphs and streamers. They are made from high-carbon steel and then coated with a lacquer finish to resist rust. Very large trout, when caught on heavier tippets, can actually straighten a dry-fly hook so some tiers, when tying dry flies for big trout, use nymph or streamer hooks for their superior strength. The flies may not float as well but you have a better chance of landing a trophy.

with heavy tippets. A regular or fine-wire hook fished on a 2X tippet might bend into an arrow when attached to a heavy trout in fast water.

Hooks can be made with straight or "ring" eyes, turned-up eyes, or turned-down eyes. Because eyes on fly-tying hooks are almost always tapered, you'll see designations like "TUTE" for "turned-up tapered eye." Turned-down eyes are more traditional for trout flies, and about three-quarters of hooks used for trout flies have them. Flies tied with parachute hackle are difficult to finish when tied on up-eye or ring-eye hooks, so use down-eye hooks when tying these patterns.

You'll find turned-up eyes on salmon flies because they accept the Turle knot better (an older knot that always gives a perfectly straight pull, which makes a wet fly swim straighter but is not as strong as a clinch knot, Orvis Knot, or non-slip mono loop). We used to believe that hooks with turned-up eyes gave a bigger "bite" when using small flies, but this is just not the case. The best small hooks for hooking fish I have ever used are the Bigeye hooks tied on ring eyes.

I like ring-eyed hooks and think they give a finished fly a classy look. I also believe they are better at hooking and holding fish, and studies done on the physics of fish hooks seem to support this. Saltwater flies are always tied on ring-eye hooks, which may be due to habit and tradition, although perhaps also because of their strength.

Beyond these guidelines, choose a hook that looks good to you, or is recommended in the pattern description. All of them, if they are sharp, will do a fine job of hooking and holding fish.

SOME BASIC HOOK RECOMMENDATIONS

Dry-Fly Hooks

You can get by most of the time with a standard dry-fly hook, with extra-fine wire and a regular-length shank. The sizes you will use most often are 12, 14, 16, 18, and 20. In sizes smaller than 16, you may want to try the Bigeye hook style. They are made with an oversized eye that adds insignificant weight to the fly but allows easy threading of tiny tippets. One other style that comes in handy is a 2X-long dry fly. The proportions of spent spinners look better on this length, and they are perfect for tying smaller grasshopper and adult stonefly imitations.

Wet-Fly and Nymph Hooks

With wet-fly and nymph hooks, you have a wider range of options. Traditionally, wet flies are tied on standard-length or 1X-short hooks, while nymphs are tied on 1X-, 2X-, and 3X-long styles. Additionally, nymph hooks come as curved styles, where you can tie a little farther down the bend and get a fly that looks naturally curled while drifting in the currents. Shrimp/caddis or worm/caddis hooks have short shanks, helping you get the proportions of a freshwater scud or caddis pupa right. You can also buy a special bead head hook, with an oversized eye to keep the bead from slipping off the hook and a slightly curled bend.

If you want to limit your styles, I'd get some 2X-long nymph hooks in sizes 8 through 18 and some shrimp/caddis hooks in sizes 12 through 16. These two will get you through most nymph patterns with the right look. Some tiers just use dry-fly hooks, especially Bigeye hooks, when tying nymphs smaller than size 18 because tiny nymph hooks are hard to find.

Streamer Hooks

Unless you tie long-shanked flies for trolling or want to tie presentation patterns for framing, just buy 4X-long streamer hooks in sizes 4, 6, 8, and 10. These will tie perfect Muddlers, Zonkers, traditional streamers and bucktails, and Woolly Buggers. You can use longer-shanked streamer hooks, like 6X-long hooks, to tie older patterns, but they are not good fish-holders. The longer shank gives the fish more leverage, making the hooking and fish-holding properties of these hooks less than ideal.

Salmon and Steelhead Hooks

Salmon and steelhead hooks are traditionally made from heavy wire that has been japanned (a process that blackens the wire), with looped, turned-up eyes. Supposedly, the turned-up eye makes a salmon fly swim more provocatively in the water. Use double hooks in very fast water to help stabilize the fly and show the salmon the fly's side profile. (If you went through all the trouble of tying a full-dress salmon fly, you wouldn't want a fish looking at its bottom, would you?) Regular bronzed trout-fly hooks work great for catching Atlantic salmon, and steelhead can be caught on stainless saltwater hooks. But if you are going to tie flies for these species, with their rich history, you could at least acknowledge this history by tying some flies on traditional up-eye hooks. They add a lot of elegance.

Bass-Fly Hooks

Tie subsurface bass flies on large streamer hooks with 3X- or 4X-long shanks. Poppers are tied on a special kink-shank hook to keep the cork or plastic bodies from twisting on the hook once they are glued. You can tie deer-hair bugs on large wet-fly hooks (but never dry-fly hooks, as they aren't strong enough to pull a largemouth out of the weeds!). However, most are tied on special "stinger" hooks, which are strong and light and have a wide gape so the deer-hair body does not get in the way when a bass inhales it.

Saltwater fish like this bluefish might be landed on the same hooks you use for trout, but there is a good chance a light trout hook would break or bend under the pressure of playing saltwater fish, which pull harder than most freshwater fish—and they are also typically larger. Also, salt water can rust and corrode hooks not specially treated for salt water, which is why hooks for these species are either made from stainless steel or plated with nickel, zinc, or tin to resist corrosion.

HOOK STYLE	DESCRIPTION	USE	ORVIS	DAIICHI	TIEMCO	MUSTAD	HOOK SHAPE
Dry	Extra-fine dry fly	Sparse dry flies and emergers	1523	1180	5210	R30NP	
Dry	Barbless dry fly	All dry flies	N/A	1190	900BL	R50XNP	
Dry	2X-long dry	Terrestrial dry flies, spent spinners, stonefly dries	1638	1280	5212	R43NP	
Dry	Bigeye dry fly, straight eye	size 16-26 dry flies; oversize eye allows easy threading to tippet	4641	1110	N/A	N/A	
Dry	Bigeye dry fly, down eye	size 16-26 dry flies; oversize eye allows easy threading to tippet and down-eye makes finishing parachute flies easier	4864	1100	N/A	N/A	
Dry	Tactical dry fly	Barbless hook with long point; used where a small fly is desired but with a bigger hook size for more security in playing fish	2BCH	N/A	N/A	N/A	
Dry	Klinkhammer	Used in the famous Klinkhammer flies, or any pattern where the rear part of the fly is suspended in the water while the front part floats	8A00	D1160	N/A	N/A	
Wet/ nymph	Heavy wet/ nymph hook	Traditional wet flies, soft hackles, and short-bodied nymphs; sinks fly well and will hold heavy fish without bending	1641	1530	3761	S80NP	
Wet/ nymph	Short-shank curved nymph	Caddis nymphs, midge larvae, and pupae; worm flies, freshwater shrimp imitations	1639	J220	2457	C49SNP	
Wet/ nymph	Scud hook	Scud and sow bug imitations or any other wet flies where a short, curved shank is desired	62KC	D1120	2457	C068NP	
Egg hook	Trout/steelhead egg	Egg patterns	76AR	D1520	105	C67SNP	
Wet/ nymph	Tactical Czech nymph	Barbless hook with long point; used where a curved shape is desired in the fly	1P0R	N/A	N/A	N/A	

HOOK STYLE	DESCRIPTION	USE	ORVIS	DAIICHI	TIEMCO	MUSTAD	HOOK SHAPE
Wet/ nymph	Tactical wide gape	Barbless hook with long point; used where a small fly is desired but with a bigger hook size for more security in playing fish	1P13	N/A	N/A	N/A	
Wet/ nymph	Tactical jig hook	Barbless hook with long point; used with a slotted bead to create a fly that always rides upside-down and thus snags less on the bottom	1P2A	N/A	403BLJ	N/A	
Wet/ nymph	Curved nymph	Long-shank nymphs and big stonefly dries; gives the finished fly a more lifelike, curled shape	1510	1270	200R	C53SNP	
Wet/ nymph	Heavy wet/ nymph hook	Traditional wet flies and shorter-bodied nymphs; sinks fly well and will hold up to very large fish without bending	1641	1530	3761	S80NP	
Wet/ nymph	Traditional 2X-long nymph hook	Standard mayfly nymphs	1524	1710	5262	D1560 R73NP	
Wet/ nymph	Bead head hook	Bead head flies (beads slip easily over bend and are held in place by oversize eyes)	1221	N/A	N/A	D1260	
Nymph/ streamer	3X-long nymph/ streamer	Muddler Minnows, smaller streamers, stonefly nymphs	1526	1720	947BL	R74NP	
Streamer	4X-long streamer	Bulkier broader streamer patterns, like sculpins, Zonkers, and Matukas	8808	2220	9395	R75NP	
Streamer	6X-long streamer	Slimmer, skinny streamer patterns like Gray Ghost and other traditional northeastern streamers, trolling streamers	1511	2340	300	3665A	
Bass	Bass bug	Deer-hair bass bugs, streamers	90CC	2720	8089	C52SNP	
Streamer	Straight eye streamer	Streamers where a straight eye is desired for appearance or for fishing with a loop knot	0167	D1750	9395	R75SNP	
Streamer, bass	60-degree jig hook	Larger flies where it is desired the fly ride hook-point-up	2BCJ	D4630	N/A	N/A	
Pike	Pike and muskie hook	Large, long flies used for pike and muskie	13KE	D2461	9394	N/A	

HOOK STYLE	DESCRIPTION	USE	ORVIS	DAIICHI	TIEMCO	MUSTAD	HOOK SHAPE
Steelhead	Intruder hook	Articulated flies where a trailing hook is desired	8A04	D2557	N/A	N/A	
Salmon	Salmon dry-fly hook	Steelhead and Atlantic salmon dry flies	N/A	2421	7989	N/A	
Salmon	Salmon wet-fly hook	Steelhead and Atlantic salmon wet flies	1645	2441	7999	SL53UNP	
Salmon	Double salmon wet-fly hook	Atlantic salmon double-hook wet flies	N/A	7131	N/A	N/A	
Saltwater	Pre-sharpened stainless hook	Tough-mouthed saltwater species, less likely to need sharpening out of the box	9034	2546	SOOS	S71SNP	
Saltwater	Standard stainless hook	All saltwater flies	4E4E	N/A	N/A	34007	
Saltwater	3X-long stainless	Longer, skinnier saltwater flies like sand-eel imitations	4E4G	N/A	911S (4X-long)	34011	

HOOK STYLE	DESCRIPTION	USE	GAMAKATSU				HOOK SHAPE
Saltwater	Black finish saltwater hook	Bonefish or other smaller saltwater species where a shiny hook is not desirable	SL45	N/A	N/A	N/A	
Saltwater	Slim wide gape saltwater hook	Tin plated hook with slimmer profile for quicker hooking	SL12S	N/A	N/A	N/A	
Saltwater	Standard wide gape saltwater	Tin-plated high-carbon hook for small to medium-sized saltwater species	SC15	N/A	N/A	N/A	
Saltwater	Extra strong wide gape saltwater	Tin plated, sharp but very stout wire for large tarpon, sharks, billfish	SC17	N/A	N/A	N/A	

Saltwater Hooks

Saltwater flies should all be tied on stainless or tin-plated hooks. Because of the corrosive nature of salt water, flies tied on regular freshwater hooks rust quickly, ruining the fly. Additionally, hooks advertised as saltwater models use stronger and heavier gauges of steel, which is important because fish caught in salt water are typically much larger and stronger than those caught in fresh water. These bigger, heavier hooks can also be used on patterns for pike or muskie, and even some of the largest trout streamers use saltwater hooks because of their strength and sharpness.

Tactical Hooks

Whether or not you agree with the concept of competitive fly fishing for trout, its growth has spawned a style of hook designed for efficiency, and many non-competitive anglers have embraced these hooks. These typically short-shanked hooks lack barbs and have a long but strong point. The short shank will allow you to tie a smaller pattern on a bigger hook to improve hooking and holding. The barbless point allows you to release a fish quicker and with less injury, and the longer, often curved point holds fish better even if you develop slack in your line.

Jig Hooks

Some patterns call for special hooks designed like the jig hooks used in conventional fishing lures. In a weighted nymph or streamer, these hooks always ride point-up so the fly is less likely to snag on the bottom.

Shanks

When tying a long, articulated fly, it's often good not to have a hook at the front part of the fly. Flies with multiple hooks are more likely to snag or foul and can even be dangerous when you're trying to land a large fish that is still struggling. By making a straight piece of wire with an eye in it and just having a loop on the other end that can be joined to multiple shanks or a regular hook, it's possible to tie very long flies that still retain a hook at the back end.

A NOTE ON HOOK STYLES

Don't get hung up because you can't find the exact hook called for in a fly recipe. The array of fly-tying hooks available today is dizzying and often confusing. The following chart shows most basic fly-tying hooks and their uses. I have referenced four popular hook brands so you can substitute where a dressing calls for a particular brand and model.

THREADS

Until the middle of the twentieth century, all fly-tying thread was silk. Silk fibers were twisted into a thread, and it was great stuff because it is much stronger than cotton.

However, silk rots and loses strength quickly. In the 1960s, flat nylon thread for fly tying was developed, and fly tying has been better and easier since. Now we also tie

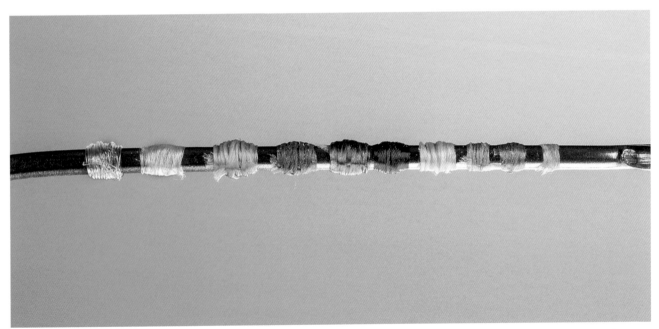

All of these threads were started with five turns, then five turns were added, followed by a five-turn whip finish. You can see the difference in bulk on the hook shank. From left to right: clear monofilament, gel-spun polyester, size G, size 3/0, 210 denier, 140 denier, 6/0, 8/0, 70 denier, and 10/0.

Threads come in a wide variety of colors and diameters.

with polyester thread, nylon monofilament, and gel-spun polyester.

Thread Sizes

Thread is measured on a scale based on diameter that dates back to silk days. The sizes used in fly tying are A, G, 3/0, 6/0, 8/0, and 10/0, with A being the heaviest. This imperfect system has no absolute measurements; it merely gives you a relative size. Another system is the denier scale, which is the weight in grams of 9,000 meters of thread. But this is merely a measurement of weight, not diameter. As denier gets larger, the thread is thicker, and most tiers are comfortable with the idea that 70 denier is about equivalent to 6/0, and 140 denier is comparable to 3/0. Also, because threads can be flattened or twisted, changing the diameter of a thread in the middle of a fly, neither of these systems is perfect.

Size A is hardly ever used today because the smaller threads are so strong that 3/0 is acceptable for even the biggest saltwater flies. You might use sizes 3/0 and G when the material you're tying in needs a lot of pressure, such as when you're tying in large clumps of hair. It is also handy when you need to cover a long stretch of hook shank and don't care about bulk, such as when tying saltwater and bass flies. Heavier thread also helps you build a big head more easily, again mainly for saltwater flies. You can use

6/0 for streamers, big nymphs, and for most saltwater flies, as long as you aren't working with large bundles of hair. Size 8/0 is now the standard for trout flies in sizes 8 to 16, and 10/0 is best for the smallest patterns. Use the smallest diameter you can without breaking the thread, because six turns with 6/0 will hold materials on the hook far better than three turns of 3/0.

Thread Materials

Most fly-tying threads are made from many tiny filaments that are given only a light twist and not twisted into a rope as in sewing thread. This is a huge advantage in fly tying, because by spinning your bobbin, you can either flatten the thread for ultra-smooth wraps or introduce a twist for precise placement of materials.

Pre-waxed thread makes tying easier. It will keep the thread from fraying, and it won't go spiraling out of control if you loosen up accidentally on your tension. You can even dub softer materials to pre-waxed thread without adding additional wax. If you have thread that is not pre-waxed, you can gently melt a bit of soft wax, and rub it onto the spool of thread.

Nylon or polyester? Nylon stretches more, which some tiers feel squeezes materials onto the hook better. Polyester does not stretch as much, and usually pops without warning if you push it too far. But polyester is marginally stronger and lasts longer than nylon. Polyester also has a slightly rougher finish, which aids in gripping materials to the hook. Polyester is also much better in the smaller sizes. Both are very good threads, but you have probably guessed my preference.

GSP thread, or gel-spun polyester, is thin and very strong. It is slipperier than nylon or polyester, but in flies where you need to put a lot of pressure on materials and don't want to build up bulk, it works well. It is also tough to cut with scissors, so I find it annoying and reserve it only for giant pike flies and bass bugs.

One other thread, monofilament thread, looks just like fine tippet material. It is tough to control because the round, slippery thread goes all over the place. Its one use is with epoxy flies; in spots where materials are lashed to the hook before glue is added, the clear thread disappears after the epoxy is dry. Monofilament thread is also used in smaller trout nymphs tied with plastic tubing such as Larva Lace, as it blends well with these translucent materials.

Thread Colors

You can tie almost any fly with either of two thread colors, black or white. Tie dark flies with black thread and light flies with white. Most times the thread never shows at the tiny head of the fly, and it's doubtful it ever makes a difference on trout flies. When tying trout flies with thinly dubbed bodies, however, the thread can show through when the fly is wet. The same hue of thread as the body material blends with the dubbing, or a contrasting color can give the fly a lifelike translucence. The great fly tier and author Darrel Martin has an innovative approach: he ties all of his flies with white thread and tints the thread with a permanent marker to get the color he wants. This way, he can change thread colors several times in the same pattern.

Some saltwater flies call for heads of bright red, pink, or green thread; here the thread color does become an essential part of the pattern, because the heads on saltwater flies are so large.

· ·

CEMENTS

Head Cement

Head cement is a clear lacquer placed at the head of a fly with the dubbing needle after the whip-finish knot is tied. Some tiers say a tight whip finish makes head cement unnecessary, but I have experimented with leaving it off, and my heads tend to fall apart easier if not coated with cement. Head cement also soaks into the hackles of a dry fly, stiffening and strengthening the exposed stems. You can also use head cement in the middle of a fly to strengthen places where certain slippery materials like hairs are tied in.

You can buy head cement in a thick consistency, called "high gloss cement," which makes a nice glossy head on saltwater flies and streamers. It is also available in a thinner, "deep-penetrating" formula. This is best for intermediate steps like strengthening quill bodies or protecting tinsel bodies, and for the heads of dry flies, where you don't want to add bulk to the fly. Both are usually just the same cement with different amounts of solvent or head-cement thinner. You can buy head cement thinner and cut the stuff to any consistency you want.

You can also find water-based head cements, which can be thinned with water but are waterproof once dry. These don't seem to be as strong as solvent-based cements, but they are easier on your respiratory system in confined areas.

Flexible Cements

Standard head cement is hard and stiff once it dries. Certain materials, especially wing quills used for wing cases on nymphs or wings on grasshopper flies, tend to split when you tie them in, and so they are best reinforced with a flexible cement before you tie with them. You can also use vinyl cement for this purpose. You must treat the feather first and then let it dry, usually for thirty minutes, before using it. One popular flexible cement called Softex is great for larger flies. It can be used to stiffen collars on big saltwater flies and streamers, to reinforce bodies made of tubing, or to coat eyes to give them more durability. I have also used Marine Goop for the same purpose. It's a little messy, but with careful application, you can build up a clear, flexible layer on parts of flies.

Spray Fixative

I prefer treating fragile feathers with a spray fixative instead of brushing on flexible cement with a brush or dubbing needle, as the spray is quicker and gives a light but uniform coverage. You can find it in art-supply stores under names like Tufflim or Krylon Krystal Clear, and it is used to spray charcoal or chalk drawings to keep them from smearing. I have also found stuff called Clear Acrylic Sealer in the craft section of discount stores, and it works just as well. Spray this stuff outside, as it has a pretty strong solvent.

Hobby Paints

Model airplane paints in white, black, and yellow are handy for painting eyes on flies. Just make a big dot on each side of the head with yellow or white paint by dipping a nail head or the cut-off end of an old, fine paintbrush. Let it dry, and add a pupil of black with a smaller nail or with the shaft of a paintbrush cut to a narrower diameter. Make sure you put a coat of head cement or epoxy over the eyes after they've dried.

Cements and glues often used in fly tying. On the left is a UV-cure epoxy and UV flashlight, for a quick application of a hard, clear finish. Softex is a flexible cement used for wide applications. In the front are three types of standard head cement—a medium viscosity cement in a handy applicator bottle, deep-penetrating thin viscosity for smaller flies, and a high-gloss, higher viscosity for a glossy buildup. In the back is one type of urethane adhesive for high-strength applications, and a high viscosity cyanoacrylate or super glue for quick strengthening. On the right is a two-part epoxy that dries slower and should be used with a mechanical turner or a rotating vise as it dries.

Epoxy

Clear epoxy is great for painting heads and bodies of saltwater flies. Standard clear epoxy, which comes in varieties ranging from 3-minute to 30-minute, creates a durable finish on a fly head or body. To get an evenly coated head, you must rotate the fly until the epoxy stops running. For the quicker-setting varieties of epoxy, you can either hold the fly in your hand, or you can slowly rotate the hook in a rotary vise. For the longer-setting types, you can buy a small rotisserie device made for fly tying or rod winding. With one of those little machines, you can do dozens of flies at once, placing each one on the big block of foam as you paint the head.

More popular than standard epoxy is the quick-setting UV variety. You apply the epoxy, make sure it is in the right places, and then hit it with a small UV light. The epoxy sets immediately, and you don't need to place it on a rotating device. This is very handy for things like wing cases on nymphs, where you only want a small spot of epoxy and don't want it to run. It's also great for bigger flies. The one drawback of some UV epoxies is that they may leave a greasy, oily finish to the fly. Some are better than others in this respect, but if the finished fly, when dry, still feels greasy or sticky, add a final coat of clear nail polish or head cement. This step is not necessary with standard epoxies,

which is why some tiers still use them despite the added time and effort they require.

Regardless of which epoxy you use, resist the temptation to go with one thick coat. Like most painting jobs, two thinner coats will look much better than one thick glob. Also, even though your flies may feel completely dry, leave finished flies in the sun for a few hours. This final UV finish ensures that any spot you missed will cure properly, and it can also remove the odors that some epoxies leave.

When using epoxy, don't use toothpicks, as color bleeds out of the wood and makes the finished result less than clear. Brushes leave bristles, which are messy to remove, even when the epoxy is wet. The best tool is your dubbing needle, which can be cleaned with acetone before the epoxy has completely hardened.

Super Glue

Some tiers use quick-drying cyanoacrylate glues to reinforce tricky steps in flies. If you do, be careful where it goes, and remember that these glues are stiff and might turn white when dry. The best ones are the more viscous types like Zap-A-Gap. Also, when using these quick-drying glues on flies tied with foam, make sure you use the special ones designated as "foam-safe," or otherwise you will end up with a melted foam fly.

PART II

TYING INSTRUCTIONS

The patterns I show in detail in this chapter were carefully selected to teach nearly any basic skill you'll need in tying flies. I have found that once you've learned how to start your thread and whip finish the head of a fly, it's best to learn by tying specific patterns, not abstract skills. Seeing how all the steps work together to form a neat and durable fly is something you can't learn by practicing skills in a vacuum.

I used a few factors to determine the best patterns to show in a detailed step-by-step sequence:

1. The patterns must be available in a fly shop now and for the next decade or so. Not only does that prove they are popular, but it allows you to buy a sample to compare to your own efforts, or even to unwind (after cutting the head with a razor blade) to see how the fly was put together. Reverse-engineering like this is how many tiers learned in the days before video. For popular patterns, you'll be able to find scores of videos online showing you how to tie them. You'll see many different variations in technique, and one of them might work better for you than the method I show here.

2. They must be effective fish-catchers. Some popular fly patterns sell because they look cool in a fly display case. You can be sure that the patterns you learn here will all be effective when fished with the proper technique.

3. They must demonstrate skills and techniques that can be applied to numerous other patterns you may want to tie. For instance, I could have shown you how to tie a Glo-Bug, a simple and effective egg imitation for trout and steelhead. But that technique is a one-off skill that will only teach you how to tie more Glo-Bugs.

When photographing fly-tying sequences, there is always a temptation to tie them bigger than normal because the shots are easier, but I did not shoot oversized flies for this book. Although proportions are the same, materials behave differently on oversized hooks, and I did not want you to get frustrated because your flies didn't look like the ones in the book. Yours may not right away, but they will in time.

Speaking of sizes, you might wonder whether there are any secrets to tying very small flies, sizes 18 through 28. To start with, keep patterns simple—you'll notice most midge patterns incorporate one or two materials and no tricky techniques. Use 10/0 thread or you'll crowd the hook, especially the eye. Take fewer turns of thread if you can. Use magnification, even if your near-vision is perfect. And develop a light touch so you don't bend the hook or break the thread.

THE GAME PLAN

Don't skip right to the Copper John because you need some for fishing a small stream in North Carolina this weekend. I don't care what kinds of flies you like to fish; start with the Woolly Bugger, and don't move on to another pattern until yours resembles the ones in the photos and you feel comfortable with the techniques. Then you can move on. The Woolly Bugger has worked as a first fly pattern for me in all of the fly-tying classes I have ever taught, and I have yet to find a person who can't tie a decent specimen in 45 minutes. Besides, you want to go fishing right away with one of your own patterns, and the Woolly Bugger will catch nearly every fish that you can chase with a fly rod.

That's why I suggest you learn to tie the patterns in this book by going through them in order. They are not grouped by species but in order of difficulty, so I suggest you follow the sequence below.

Woolly Bugger	Streamer
Clouser Minnow	Saltwater
Frenchie	Nymph
Chernobyl Ant	Dry
Hare's Ear Nymph	Nymph
Copper John	Nymph
Sparkle Dun	Dry
Stimulator	Dry
Cone Head Bunny Muddler	Streamer
Deer Hair Bass Bug	Warmwater
Puglisi Spawning Shrimp	Saltwater
Parachute Adams	Dry

The only time I'd advise you to skip ahead is if you're having problems with a particular technique or if you know you won't be using a specific pattern. Maybe dubbing the Hare's Ear Nymph is driving you nuts, and you're just not getting it. Skip ahead to the dubbing steps on the Sparkle Dun or Stimulator, and see if maybe the text and photos there are just different enough for something to click. If you're still having trouble, examine your materials critically. Did you substitute a dubbing from a packet instead of making your own hare's-ear blend? Some synthetic dubbings, especially those with a lot of sparkle, are more difficult to affix to the thread. Or maybe the only piece of deer hair you own is belly hair, and when you tie it in for a Sparkle Dun wing, it flares all over the place and doesn't look like the picture in the book. In that case, you might go back and read the pattern description and discover that the pattern calls for shorter, finer hair—from a different part of the animal and with totally different behavior when wrapped with thread.

Since I realize you may not have all the materials listed here and can't always run off to a neighborhood fly shop, I've listed the most common substitutes in each pattern description. All of the materials used in these patterns are commonly available, either in basic fly-tying kits or on websites and stores that sell fly-fishing gear. Some materials can also be found in craft stores and the hobby sections of department stores.

The Road Map

You never have to measure anything with a ruler when tying flies. In fact, you seldom want to, because you might be tying a different size than what's shown here, so giving you a measurement would not make sense. All proportions are based on the hook, and all directions are relative to it. Here's the convention I'll use in the pattern descriptions:

HOOKS

The *gape*, or *gap*, is the distance between the point of the hook and the shank.

The shank is the straight part of the hook where most of the tying goes on, between the eye and the bend. It's the most important measuring reference in fly tying, and we often divide it up into imaginary halves, thirds, and quarters. For very small distances, I like to use a subjective but useful measurement, the "thread width." Saying "one-thirty-second of a shank length" would have you going cross-eyed trying to divide a size 14 hook into 32 pieces in your head; it's easier to estimate the distance three or four thread wraps would take.

Back or *back to* means toward the bend.

Forward or *up to* means toward the eye.

Above means above the hook shank.

Below means below the hook shank.

Behind means adjacent to but toward the bend of the hook.

Ahead of means adjacent to but toward the eye of the hook.

FEATHERS AND HAIRS

The *tip* of a feather fiber or hair is always the finer end. These are usually not cut and are left with their natural taper, sticking out of the finished fly to form one of its features.

The *butt* of a feather or hair is the heavier end, the end you've probably just cut from as stem or hide. This is the end that usually gets trimmed and bound under in a finished fly.

PARTS OF A FLY

The names for some parts of flies, particularly nymphs and complicated salmon flies, are not always intuitive. Here are a few basic fly types with their parts labeled.

Shrimp-Type Nymph or Scud

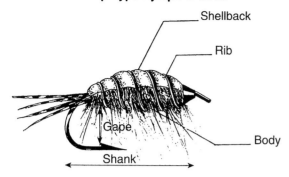

Shellback

Rib

Gape

Shank

Body

Salmon Wet Fly

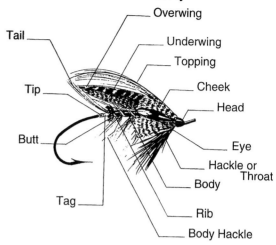

Tail

Overwing

Underwing

Topping

Cheek

Head

Tip

Butt

Eye

Hackle or
Throat

Body

Tag

Rib

Body Hackle

Basic Nymph

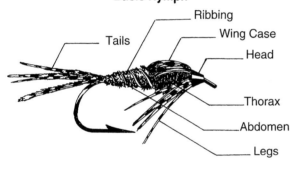

Tails

Ribbing

Wing Case

Head

Thorax

Abdomen

Legs

Streamer

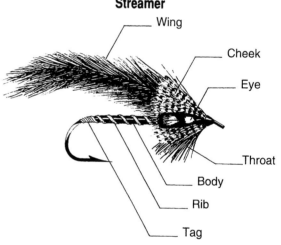

Wing

Cheek

Eye

Throat

Body

Rib

Tag

Basic Dry Fly

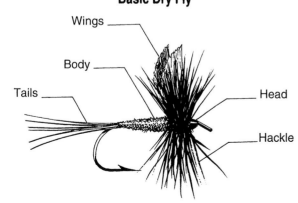

Wings

Body

Tails

Head

Hackle

Saltwater Fly

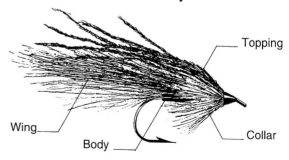

Topping

Wing

Collar

Body

WOOLLY BUGGER

In the late 1960s, a Pennsylvania angler named Russell Blessing took a centuries-old fly pattern called the Woolly Worm and added a marabou tail. This simple addition forever changed fly tying and fly fishing. The Woolly Bugger is not only the fly many people use to catch their first fish—it's also frequently the first fly they attempt when learning to tie. I have yet to find a fish species that can be caught on a fly that will not take a Woolly Bugger, and have caught trout, bonefish, smallmouth and largemouth bass, carp, tarpon, striped bass, bluefish, bluegill, crappie, and probably a half-dozen other species on it.

Blessing tied his original Woolly Bugger in all black because he was trying to imitate a hellgrammite when fishing for smallmouth bass. But it probably looks like a leech, crayfish, crab, sand worm, baitfish, or large stonefly to other fish. Steelhead anglers use them in pink and in all white. The fly has spawned so many variations that if you look at a fly catalog or the streamer section of a shop, you'll notice that many popular patterns are merely embellished versions of the Woolly Bugger in a vast array of colors and materials. The default color for me—and the combination that is most commonly tied and sold—is a black tail and hackle with an olive body. I also like all-black for smallmouths and have had great success with an all-tan version for trout.

Although the Woolly Bugger is a simple, easy-to-tie fly, like any pattern, the material you choose can mean the difference between a fly that just catches fish and one that catches more fish, looks better, lasts longer, and swims better. Woolly Buggers used to be tied with standard cotton chenille, which has inconsistent quality and comes apart easily. Most tiers today use Ultra Chenille (also called Vernille), which looks better and lasts longer than standard chenille, because the outer material is more tightly bonded to the core.

All marabou is not created equal. Look for plumes with dense, fluffy fibers throughout. If you can, avoid using marabou with long, spindly fibers at the end. If that's all you have, combine two or three plumes to get enough bulk to create a tail that wiggles enticingly in the water and still retains some of its shape when wet. Also, be careful of marabou with uneven fibers at the tip and plumes with very thick stems.

Saddle hackle for a Woolly Bugger looks best when it has a slight taper from butt to tip, moderate length, and some web at the base of the feather. This gives the resulting fly more motion in the water. Be careful of saddle hackles that are too short and wide, because you might run out of feather when trying to get to the eye of the hook. These also typically have fibers that look too long on a Woolly Bugger. At the other end of the scale, really slim saddle hackles have fibers that are too short and too stiff, with not enough web to give the hackle a breathing motion in the water.

Woolly Buggers fish best with some weight attached. The one I tied here has a standard non-toxic wire underbody. However, you can put a solid metal bead on the hook before tying to make a bead head bugger, or you can add a metal cone to create a cone head bugger. For very fast and deep water, I will sometimes add both a wire underbody and a set of solid metal dumbbell eyes. It's dangerous to cast, but it sure gets the fly down quickly in the high water of early season.

	Material	Substitutions
Hook	4X-long streamer hook, size 4 through 14	3X-long streamer hook
Weight	Non-toxic wire	Solid metal bead or cone, by themselves or in combination with a wire under-wrap
Thread	Black 6/0 (70 denier)	Any color thread desired
Tail	Black marabou	Any color marabou desired, or a large bunch of ostrich herl
Body	Olive Ultra Chenille	Ultra or standard cotton chenille in any color desired. Sparkle chenille is popular for creating flashier patterns. Peacock herl or dubbing can also be used.
Hackle	Black saddle hackle, palmered (spiraled) over the body	Dyed or natural saddle hackle of any color desired

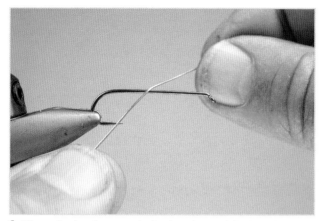

1. Place the hook securely in the vise. While keeping the spool of non-toxic wire in your palm, hold the free end against the shank of the hook, and begin winding it around the shank. You can also just use a loose piece of wire, but you never know exactly how much to use and doing it this way prevents wasting any.

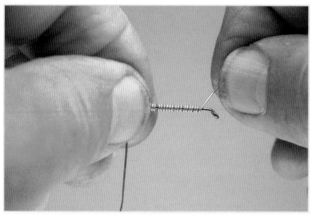

2. Wind forward toward the eye in turns as closely spaced as possible, stopping just short of the eye.

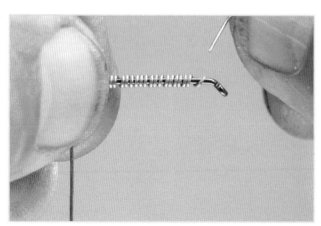

3. Break or cut the forward end of the wire. Break or cut the rear end as well. Try to break it as close to the hook shank as possible.

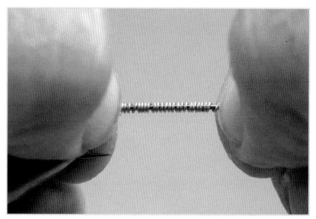

4. Place one thumbnail just behind the hook eye and place your other thumbnail against the rear of the wire. Push them together to eliminate any spaces.

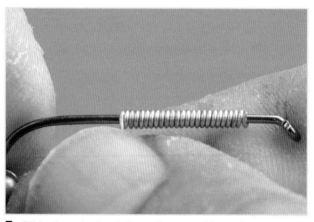

5. Slide the wire back from the eye a bit so that you don't crown the head when you finish the fly. If either end of the wire still sticks out, work them in place with your fingernail.

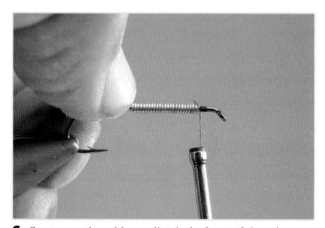

6. Start your thread immediately in front of the wire, holding the rear end of the wire in place with your thumbnail. Form a bump of thread in front of the wire to hold it in place.

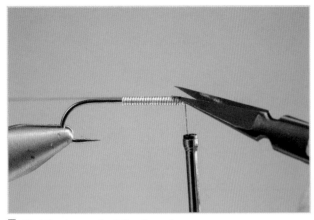

7. Cut the tag end of the thread.

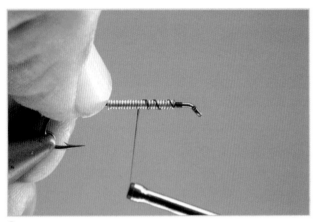

8. Spiral the thread back over the wire, keeping the rear of the wire in place with your thumbnail.

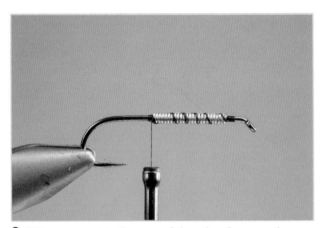

9. When you get to the rear of the wire, form another bump of thread to secure it.

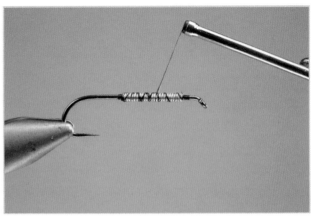

10. Spiral forward and back several times over the wire to further secure it. Some tiers also coat the wire with a thin layer of Super Glue or head cement at this point, but I have found that tight spirals over the wire keep it from rotating later.

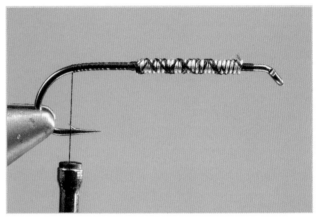

11. Wind the thread back to the beginning of the bend of the hook. When it is in the proper place the thread will hang over the point of the hook barb. This is an important step because if you don't wind back far enough, the marabou tail will foul around the hook bend and ruin the action of the fly.

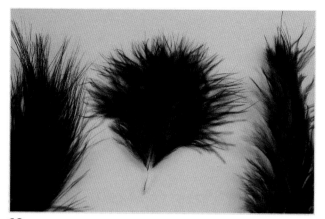

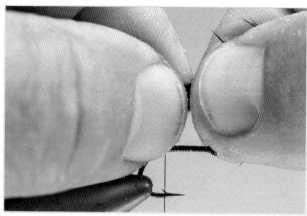

12. Select a marabou feather with full, fluffy, uniform fibers. The feather in the center of this photo is a perfect marabou feather for this fly, and depending on the quality of your pack of marabou, you may have to hunt around to find a decent feather. If you can find marabou like this, you will be able to tie the fly with a single feather. The feather on the left has fibers that are too long and thin and not fluffy enough, but if this is all you have, you can combine two or three feathers by lining up their tips. Any errant fibers that extend beyond the main bunch can also be snapped away with your fingers. Don't trim the ends with your scissors, as you want just a bit of a natural taper to the fibers. The feather on the right has fibers that are too short, and the central stem of the feather is too stiff and won't provide enough action to the fly.

14. Keeping the marabou lined up with the end of your fingers, grasp it in your other fingers in the same place. Most tiers find it helpful to wet the marabou, at least on the portion extending outside of your fingers. It makes the fuzzy marabou much easier to handle. I just stick it in my mouth, but if that creeps you out, wet your fingers with water.

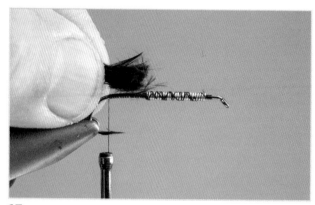

15. Place the ends of your fingers immediately about the tying thread, and trim the butt ends of the marabou so they end at the beginning of the weighting wire.

13. Measure the marabou against the hook shank until it is about one shank length from the ends of your finger to its tips.

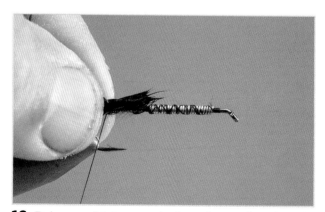

16. Being careful that you don't catch your thread on the hook point, begin to wind thread over the marabou. Make sure that your first turn is right where you left the thread hanging, not forward of this position.

17. Wind forward to the weighting wire. If the marabou ends up a little short of the wire, fill the space in with thread, or if it still extends beyond the wire, trim it back a bit. This helps to make a smooth underbody.

18. Select a saddle hackle that is long but has a bit of web at its base and tapers from butt to tip. The feather in the center is perfect. The feather on the left is too narrow and stiff, and the feather on the right is too wide and short—you might run out of feather if you select one that is too short.

19. Strip the webby ends of the saddle hackle from the stem, but don't cut the stem, as it will give you something to grasp when winding the feather.

20. Hold the saddle hackle by its very tip, and gently stroke the fibers along the stem toward its base until they stick out from the stem.

21. Carefully trim the fibers along the stem for a short distance from its tip, about a dozen fibers down.

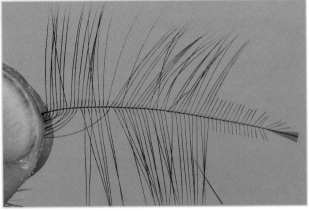

22. Snip the tip of the feather so you are left with a saddle hackle that looks like this.

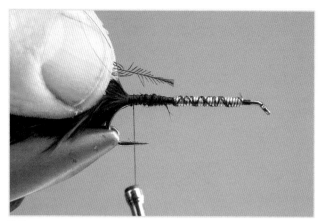

23. Return the thread to the initial marabou tie-in point. Stroke the fibers of the saddle hackle back, and hold them out of the way, exposing just the part of the hackle where you trimmed the fibers. Hold the tip of the saddle hackle above the tie-in point.

24. Wind forward over the tip of the saddle hackle. Those little nubs that you trimmed help secure it better than if you merely tied in the tip without trimming it first. Stop at the rear end of the weighting wire, and trim any remaining saddle hackle tip if it extends beyond this point.

25. Cut a five- to six-inch piece of Ultra Chenille, and hold its end immediately above the place where the weighting wire ends. Begin to tie it in place here.

26. Bind the chenille in place by winding back to the initial marabou tie-in point. If this part seems a bit bigger in diameter than the weighting wire, apply extra tension on the thread to narrow the diameter.

27. Wind the thread all the way forward to the front end of the weighting wire.

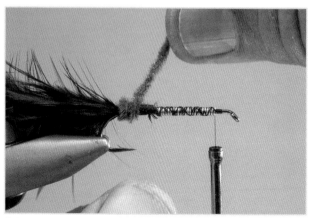

28. Begin winding the chenille immediately over the tie-in point to cover the thread wraps at the bend.

29. Wind the chenille forward in even turns, with each wrap just touching the previous wrap.

30. Wrap the chenille forward so that you end with your last wrap just in front of the weighting wire. Hold the chenille above the hook shank, and tie it in place with three or four very firm wraps of thread.

31. Trim the end of the chenille as close to the hook shank as possible.

32. Take a few more wraps over the end of the chenille to further secure it.

33. Grasp the saddle hackle with your fingers or hackle pliers and begin to wrap forward in smooth spirals. The first turn is the trickiest. Twist the hackle or angle it so that the first turn sweeps the fibers back over the tail. It may take several tries to get the hackle to behave, but by stroking it back with your fingers and by experimenting with angles, you will eventually get it to behave. After the first turn, the rest of them will typically fall in line.

34. As you wind forward, keep stroking the fibers back so they stream back over the body and don't get wound under.

35. Keep winding forward toward the eye.

36. When you get to the spot where you tied off the chenille, hold the hackle above the hook shank, and bind it in place with a half dozen very firm turns.

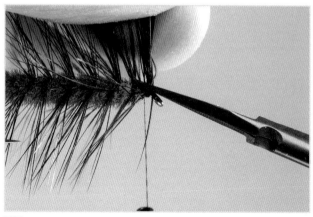

37. Trim the end of the hackle as close to the shank as possible with the point of your scissors.

38. Stroke the hackle fibers back with your fingers, and wind back and forth to form a neat, tight head.

39. Whip finish the head.

40. Trim your thread close.

41. Place a drop or two of head cement on the head only.

42. It's fine, and desirable, if a bit of the cement seeps back into the ends of the chenille and hackle wraps.

CLOUSER MINNOW

It's hard to ignore the Clouser Minnow. Sometimes I try, because the fly is such a cliché—everyone uses it for nearly every species of fish—and I like to experiment with new patterns. But this fly really does work for nearly every species of fish—carp, trout, panfish, striped bass, smallmouth and largemouth bass, and even tarpon. This simple fly was developed by fishing guide Bob Clouser, and its main proponent was the late Lefty Kreh, the most famous fly fisherman of the twentieth century. When Clouser first handed a bunch of flies to Lefty right before a smallmouth bass fishing trip, Lefty looked at the sparse, simple flies and asked, "Are they done yet?" After he returned from a banner day fishing for smallmouths, he simply looked at Clouser and said, "They're done."

Although the Clouser Minnow is a simple pattern, made with bucktail and Krystal Flash, plus a hook and a set of metal dumbbell eyes, there are tricks to tying one properly. The fly should be sparse, and many tiers have a tendency to use too much material. Also the bucktail should be tied in carefully to keep the fly's slim, baitfish shape. It's also important to take bucktail from the top half of the tail if you want that slim profile. Hair toward the base of the tail is coarser, hollower, and flares too much. I do tie Clousers with more bulk for fishing for striped bass in the surf, because I think it helps fish find the fly in frothy water. In that case, you can use hair from the base of the tail. But for most species, the slimmer the better.

Resist the temptation to tie on the dumbbell eyes too casually. There is nothing worse than a Clouser with eyes that spin around to the wrong side of the hook when you're casting. Don't rely on epoxy or head cement at the end of tying to keep the eyes in place. It takes firm, careful winds in the first few steps to make sure the eyes will stay in place.

I tied the version here with olive bucktail for the back, my preferred color for striped bass on the flats. Chartreuse is also common, but really you can use any color combination

	Material	Substitutions
Hook	Standard pre-sharpened saltwater hook, sizes 2/0 through 8	3X-long nymph/Muddler hook for freshwater versions
Thread	White, 3/0 (140 denier)	Black, tan, or red
Eyes	Solid metal dumbbell eyes, plain metal or painted, to achieve desired sink rate	Bead chain eyes for slower sink rate or fish that spook from the splash of heavier eyes
Belly	White bucktail	Any light-toned bucktail to imitate the belly color of baitfish
Flash	Two to four strands of pearl Krystal Flash	Any other flashy material in any color desired
Back	Olive bucktail	Black, brown, gray, or chartreuse

you want, to match baitfish or just the color preferences of the fish you're chasing. For really spooky striped bass on the flats, I often tie this pattern without any flash and with no more than a dozen bucktail hairs for the back and belly. The fly does not look like much, but for spooky fish, I have found this subtle variation is a killer pattern.

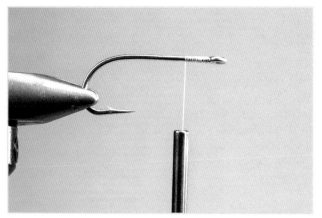

1. Start your thread immediately behind the eye, and wrap back to a point that is about one-third of the hook shank behind the eye.

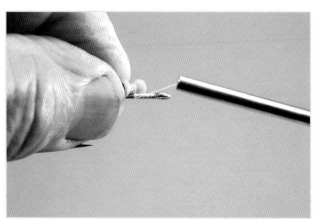

2. Place the eyes on top of the shank. Keep one finger on the eye on the near side, holding it in place, angled slightly back. Take four to six very tight wraps of thread between the eyes, crossing over the eyes from front to rear. Keep tension on the wraps; don't relax the thread.

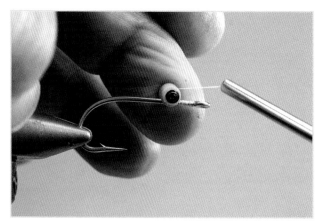

3. Without relaxing tension on the thread, pull the eye on the far side with your finger until the eyes are 90 degrees to the shank, and then make four to six very tight turns of thread in the opposite direction, from rear to front.

4. Repeat steps 2 and 3, making four to six more wraps in each direction.

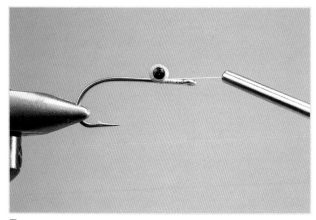

5. Without relaxing tension on the thread, take eight to twelve wraps of thread around the base of the eyes, winding in a horizontal direction. Make sure you apply pressure in all four quadrants to keep firm tension on the base of the eyes.

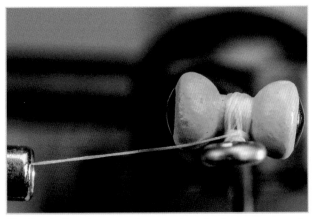

6. Check the eyes to make sure they don't rotate around the shank. If you can wiggle the eyes back and forth, unwrap and start over, using even more tension on the thread. A drop of Super Glue at the base of the eyes is also a good idea, because thread has some stretch and will loosen over time.

9. Hold the bucktail firmly, about three-quarters of the way to the tips. With your other hand, pull toward the base of the bucktail to remove all the fuzz and short fibers at the base of the hair. Repeat this process several times until you can't remove any shorter fibers.

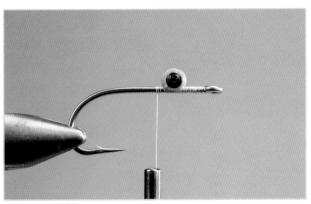

7. Wrap back from the eyes about four turns. If you try to tie the bucktail in too close to the eyes, it will flare, and you will lose the slim baitfish shape.

10. Inspect the tips of the bucktail. If there are any errant hairs that are much longer than the main bunch, gently pull them out.

8. Select a bunch of white bucktail that, when loosely compressed, is about the diameter of a pencil. Pull the bunch of bucktail at an angle from the tail so that the fibers are mostly aligned at the tips. Snip the bucktail at the base, close to the central bone.

11. Measure the white bucktail so that it is about two shank lengths.

12. Transfer the bucktail to your other hand, marking the measured spot with your fingernails so you don't lose your place.

13. Hold the bucktail in this spot over the place where you left the thread hanging. Tie it in with moderate pressure, using a few turns of thread and working toward the eye slightly with each turn. Inspect the hair to make sure it is centered on the shank and not skewed to one side or the other. Wiggle it back into place if it is off-center.

14. Make about four tighter turns to lock the hair in place, moving toward the eye with each subsequent turn.

15. Leave the bucktail sticking over the eyes, and advance the thread to a point just in front of the eyes.

16. Pull the bucktail over the eyes, and lock it in place with four to six very tight turns.

17. Cut the bucktail at a slight angle, sloping toward the eye, using heavy, sharp scissors.

18. Try not to leave any fibers sticking over the eye. Use a pair of finer scissors to trim the hairs if any remain there.

19. Wind forward over the butt ends of the hair to the eye, then return to the point where you first tied in the bucktail.

20. Turn the fly over in the vise, or just rotate the jaws if you have a rotary vise. The hook point should now be on top.

21. Cut two to four strands of Krystal Flash from the hank. Find the middle of the strands and fold them over. I find these are much easier to handle if you wet them, because otherwise static charges make them fly all over the place.

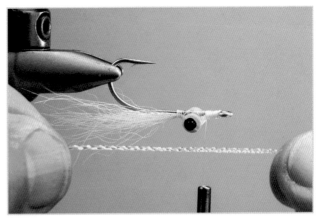

22. Place the strands around your tying thread at the center point where they were folded over.

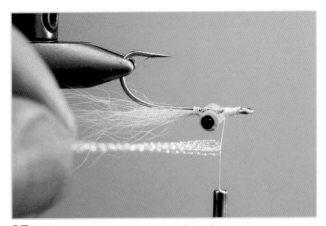

23. Fold the strands over your thread.

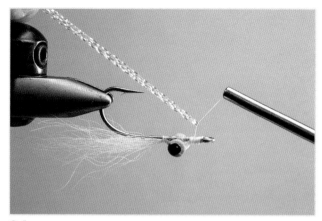

24. Bring your thread up over the hook, and pull the strands down to the shank.

25. Secure them with three or four tight turns of thread, right up against the dumbbell eyes.

26. Carefully trim the ends of the Krystal Flash so they are about 20 percent longer than the white bucktail. Be careful not to trim away any of the bucktail in the process.

27. Select a bunch of olive bucktail, about the same amount as you did for the white, and trim it from the tail, removing the short hairs and pulling away any extra-long hairs. Measure the olive bucktail so it is slightly shorter than the Krystal Flash but a bit longer than the white bucktail belly. These proportions ensure the finished fly will have a nice baitfish-like taper.

28. Move the tying thread three or four turns forward of the dumbbell eyes, and center the olive bucktail between the eyes.

29. Take two turns of thread with moderate pressure, working forward, and then bear down on the hair with firm pressure as you work forward with about five more turns of thread. This will make sure that the bucktail is firmly attached but that it does not flare too much. Stop just behind the hook eye.

30. Trim the bucktail at an angle and further trim any hairs that stick out over the eye with a pair of finer scissors, exactly as you did for the white bucktail.

31. Wind over the head, back and forth, until all spaces are filled and no bucktail shows between turns of thread. (For a very smooth look, you can flatten your thread by spinning the bobbin counterclockwise before making these final winds).

32. Whip finish the head.

33. Apply UV-cure epoxy (or head cement) to the head, allowing just a bit of the glue to seep back into the base of the olive bucktail.

34. Cure the epoxy with a UV light.

35. Turn the fly over and apply epoxy to the base of the white bucktail, starting from the initial thread wraps where the bucktail was first tied in behind the eyes, continuing to the place where the bucktail was pulled over the eyes, and coating the head as well. Let some of the epoxy seep into the winds around the base of the eyes as well. Cure the epoxy. The bucktail may have slipped to one side or the other in tying, but as long as it was initially centered on the shank properly, you can just move it in place with your fingers.

FRENCHIE JIG NYMPH

Even those of us who don't fish in competitions have learned much from anglers who compete nationally and internationally. In these events, the object is to catch as many trout (and grayling in Europe) as possible in a limited amount of time. Under most conditions, fishing nymphs close to the bottom is the most effective way to rack up the numbers. Competitors use simple flies because they lose a lot of them by fishing so close to the bottom. No one wants to lose a dozen flies in a day of fishing if each one takes half an hour to tie. These competitive anglers have proven to the rest of us that subsurface imitations seldom need much adornment because these flies are just as effective—and perhaps more effective—as more complicated flies with more steps.

The Frenchie Jig Nymph was first used by a French angler in competitions, and he was blowing away the competition with his catches. When other anglers finally got a look at his fly box, it was filled with these bugs—merely simplified Bead Head Pheasant Tail Nymphs with fur "hot spots" at the thorax. The bright colors of the hot spots don't imitate anything in nature, yet they seem to increase the effectiveness of the flies, perhaps by drawing a trout's attention.

Another fly-tying innovation from competitive anglers is the use of modified jig hooks, which are designed with the same shape as those used for bass fishing but in smaller sizes for trout fishing. If you place the bead on the hook properly, the fly always rides point-side-up, making it less likely to snag on the bottom when it's fished deep. Invariably, trout are hooked securely in the upper jaw with these hooks. Jig hooks, like all competition hooks (sometimes called tactical hooks) are made barbless with a slightly turned-in point so that while trout are hooked securely, releasing them is also a quick and effortless process—good both for competitive anglers and for those who don't compete but just want to catch lots of trout and release them with minimal handling time.

1. Select a slotted bead appropriate for the hook size. You will notice the slotted bead has a round hole on one side and a slot on the other. Slip the round hole over the hook point, and slide it up over the bend and up to the eye. To get the bead over the bend of the hook, you may need to rotate the bead so the slot allows it to move past the bend. The best position for the slot is to the outside of the hook bend and shank.

2. Bring the bead up to the eye and rotate the bead until it slides all the way down the neck of the jig hook. The correct position for it is for the curved side of the slot facing up and the flat side facing down. This will ensure that the fly rides point-side-up in the water. If the bead

	Material	Substitutions
Hook	Tactical jig, sizes 12-16	2X-long nymph to tie it as a standard nymph
Thread	6/0 orange (70 denier)	Pink or yellow
Tails	Coq de Leon fibers	Brown partridge, wood duck, or grizzly hackle fibers
Body	Natural pheasant tail	Dyed pheasant tail, any color to match color of most common mayfly nymphs
Rib	Copper wire	Gold or silver wire
Hot spot	Orange sparkle dubbing	Pink, yellow, or tan sparkle dubbing

slides down so that it covers the eye, you have chosen a bead that is too big. Go to the next smaller size. If the bead has issues going over the bend of the hook, you've chosen a bead that is too small.

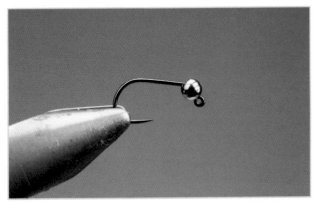

3. This is what proper bead positioning looks like from the side.

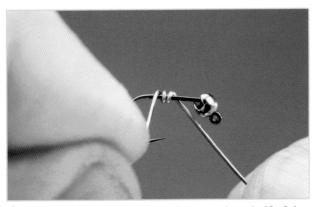

4. Wrap non-toxic weighting wire over about half of the remaining hook shank. Break the wire at both ends, or cut it cleanly with a pair of small wire snips. (If you are left with a little nub or wire sticking out, you can always roll it in place with your fingernail.)

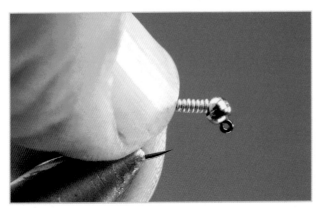

5. Jam the weighting wire up against the bead with your fingernail so that it holds the bead in place. Make sure the slot is positioned properly.

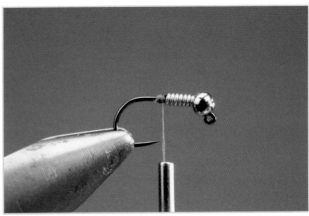

6. Start your tying thread immediately behind the weighting wire and form a small dam of thread to keep the wire up against the bead.

7. Wind the tying thread back and forth over the weighting wire a few times. You don't have to be neat.

8. Wind the thread back to the bend of the hook and just slightly beyond the bend. I like to tie my tails in this position because it makes the tails cock upward a bit when the fly is fished (don't forget it will ride point-side-up), which is the way mayflies typically drift in the current.

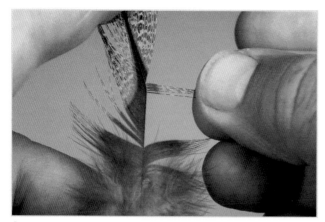

9. From a Coq de Leon feather, isolate about a half dozen fibers on the stem. Line them up perpendicular to the stem and pluck them from the feather with a quick pull. Keep them in your fingertips so they stay lined up. It's easy to manipulate these by pinching the tip of the feather with your middle and index finger, and the butt end of the feather with your thumb and ring finger, then plucking the fibers with the thumb and index finger of your other hand.

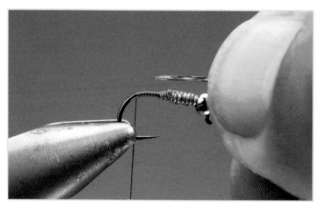

10. Measure the tail fibers against the hook shank. They should be short, about half to three-quarters of a hook shank.

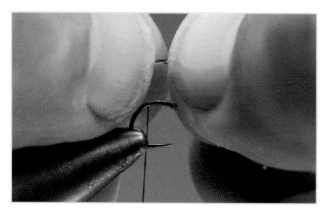

11. Using your fingernail as a guide, transfer the fibers to your other hand, and line up your fingernail with the tie-in point.

12. Angle the fibers with the butts facing slightly toward you and slightly to the near side of the hook shank.

13. Wind over the fibers, allowing the thread to roll them to the top of the hook shank. If they roll too much to the far side, unwind and try again.

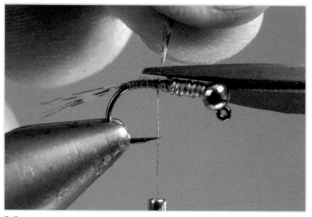

14. Wind the tail fibers almost to the rear end of the weighting wire. Trim the butt ends.

15. Trap the copper wire ribbing against the top of the hook shank with two turns of thread.

16. Gently pull on the wire until the end just about disappears under the thread wraps. (Doing it this way eliminates the need to cut the wire, which saves you a step, eliminates the need to grab your wire cutters, and saves the blades of your scissors in case you're tempted to use them to cut wire.)

17. Wrap back to the base of the tails with tight turns, binding the wire to the top of the hook shank.

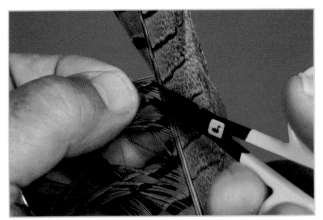

18. Select six to eight pheasant tail fibers. Cut them close to the base of the feather, because some pheasant tails have short fibers that are difficult to wind. Note that some pheasant tails have the long reddish fibers on both sides of the stem and others just on one side. You want the long reddish fibers.

19. Cut the very tips of the pheasant tail fibers to even them up.

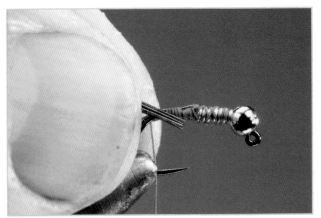

20. Tie in the pheasant tail fibers to the top of the hook shank. Align their tip ends with the end of the weighting wire, slightly to the near side of the hook shank.

21. Wind forward over the pheasant tail fibers to the end of the weighting wire, ensuring that your first turn is just ahead of the tail fibers. Trim any fibers that extend beyond that point, and return your thread to the point where you first tied them in.

22. Wind the pheasant tail fibers forward, pushing them against the thread as you do. The thread will keep them in place so the fibers don't separate.

23. If your pheasant tail fibers are short, grasp them with a pair of hackle pliers. Make sure all the fibers are close together in the hackle pliers. (You can wind them by hand if they are long enough.)

24. Wind in non-overlapping turns to cover the hook shank. Stop just shy of the bead, and tie them off with three tight turns of thread.

25. Spiral the wire over the pheasant tail with about five turns.

26. When you get to the bead, wind the wire a few times over itself for extra security.

27. Snip the wire with your wire cutters (or the very base of your scissors).

28. Bend the tag end of the wire against the hook shank, and take three tight turns of thread over it.

29. Separate a pinch of orange dubbing from the mass of dubbing. Pull it apart so that it is a loose bunch with no lumps. Don't overdo it—you only need a pinch. Wax your thread if you have trouble dubbing. Some dubbings are easier to work with than others. Place the dubbing alongside the thread.

30. With very firm pressure from your thumb and index finger, roll the dubbing against the thread in a single direction.

31. Keep rolling until it is a tight noodle.

32. Wind the dubbing over the exposed thread. You don't need much, just enough to cover the thread wraps. If you have too much, pluck the extra from the thread; if you don't have enough add another tiny pinch.

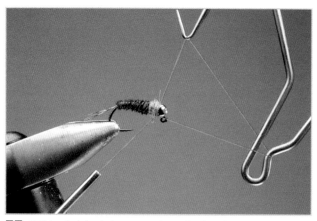

33. Whip finish right up against the bead.

34. Apply a drop of head cement to the whip finish, allowing a bit to soak in under the bead to further secure it.

CHERNOBYL ANT

As you can tell by the name of this fly, it was developed in the 1990s, shortly after the Chernobyl accident in 1986. There were probably large foam attractor flies used for trout before the Chernobyl Ant hit the scene, but it was the first foam fly to receive widespread acceptance, probably because it was the winning fly in the Jackson Hole One-Fly Contest in 1995. This fly was originally developed by Green River guide Emmett Heath, but Rocky Mountain guides soon made their own variations of the fly, and variations on it also were also the top patterns in the 1998, 1999, 2003, and 2005 One-Fly competitions.

The Chernobyl and its variations bring big trout to the surface wherever those trout are accustomed to eating big insects like grasshoppers, stoneflies, cicadas, and crickets. It is also popular in the South America and New Zealand, where large species of beetles are common along trout rivers. Don't rule it out on eastern rivers, either. Eastern anglers who get hung up on a hatch-matching philosophy have no idea how thrilling it is to catch a large trout on a

big foam dry fly. It doesn't imitate anything specific (certainly not any ant I've ever seen), so don't get hung up on the name. Just use it whenever you need a large dry fly that floats all day without being treated with paste or powder.

This pattern only requires two materials: foam and rubber legs. Admittedly, you need a few colors of foam, but the simplicity of this all-synthetic fly belies its deadly allure to trout. Experiment with different colors of foam for the body and back and change the strike indicator tabs if you think another color will be more visible. Try some wild-colored rubber legs, or maybe try adding a wing of polypropylene yarn or EP Fiber. This is the way the Chernobyl Ant is most commonly tied and sold, but you'll see many similar patterns with slightly different materials called by all kinds of wild names.

Large attractor dry flies have become popular, especially for fishing from drift boats on large rivers. Between this pattern and the Stimulator, you'll develop all the skills you need to tie these variations.

	Material	Substitutions
Hook	3X-long nymph, sizes 6-14	2X-long dry fly for smaller flies, 4X-long streamer hook for bigger sizes
Thread	Black, size 3/0 (or 140 denier)	6/0 on flies smaller than size 10. Substitute any color thread you want for different effects
Overlay	Black foam	Any color foam you want
Underbody	Tan foam	Any color foam you want
Legs	Tan speckled Tentacle Legs	Any rubber legs in any color
Indicator tabs	White foam on the rear joint, red foam on the front joint	Bright orange or bright chartreuse would also be great colors in certain light conditions

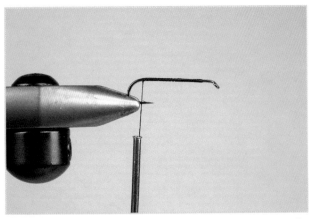

1. Attach the thread to the hook just behind the eye, and wind back to the bend.

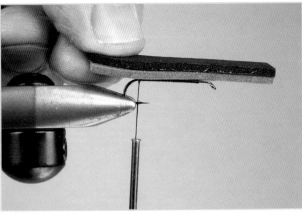

2. Cut a piece of tan foam and a piece of black foam to one hook gape in width and about one-and-a-half times the shank length (or a little longer because you can always trim at the end). Place the black foam over the brown foam, and lay them centered over the hook.

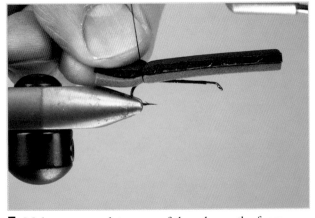

3. Make one complete wrap of thread over the foam.

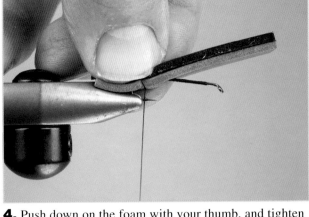

4. Push down on the foam with your thumb, and tighten the wrap, keeping the foam on top of the hook. Hold your index finger on the far side to keep it from rolling.

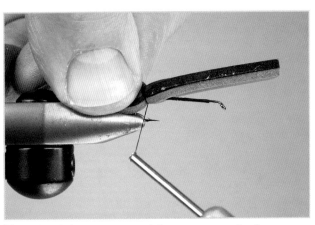

5. Make eight to ten very tight wraps over the foam, making sure it stays on top of the hook.

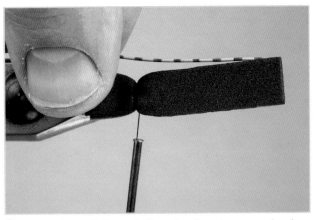

6. Cut a piece of Tentacle Leg that is at least two hook shanks in length, or just tie in one long leg as it comes from the bunch. This will be trimmed anyway. Rotate your vise so that the far side of the hook is pointing up.

7. Tie the leg into the joint you just made with your thread so that the leg is centered between the black and brown pieces of foam. Take only two turns of thread.

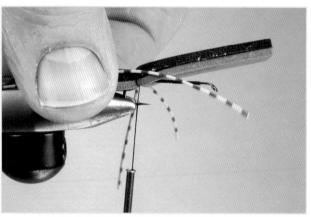

8. Return your vise so that the near side is either facing you or pointing up. (I don't find I need to have it pointing up for the near one, but it really helps with the far leg.) Grab another Tentacle Leg, and hold it against the near side.

9. Tie the leg in with two turns of thread, trapping it against the foam in the spot between the two colors. Tweak both the near and the far legs into place by pulling gently on them.

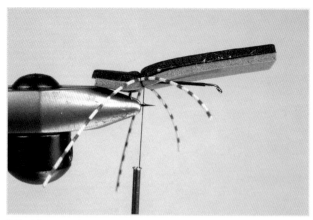

10. Tighten down on the thread, and take a couple more turns to securely place the legs.

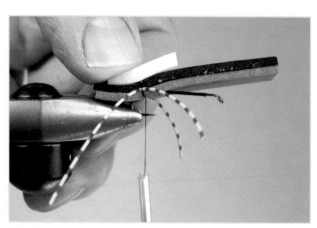

11. Cut a short piece of white foam that is not quite as wide as the body. Place it on top of the joint.

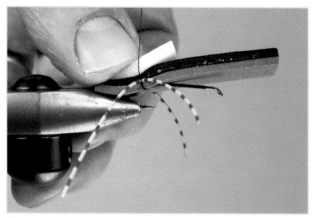

12. Bring the thread around the white foam tab, making sure you clear the legs.

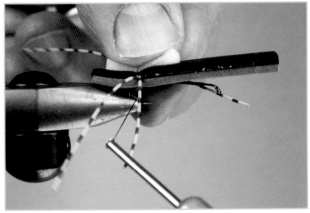

13. Take about three firm turns of thread around the white foam. Press down on it to keep it from rolling.

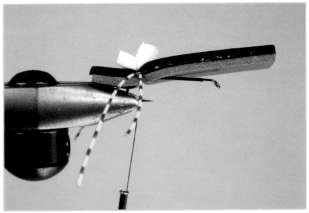

14. Trim both ends of the white tab short—just enough to stick up and act as an indicator.

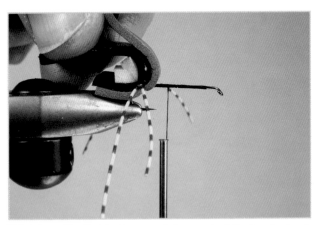

15. Mentally divide the remaining part of the hook shank into three equal parts. Advance your thread to the first third, and pull the foam pieces back.

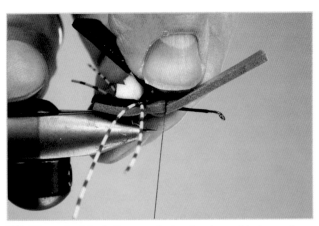

16. Keep the black foam pointing back, and bring only the tan foam forward.

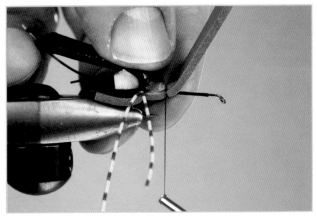

17. Bind the tan foam to the top of the hook shank with a half dozen tight turns of thread.

18. Try to keep the foam centered on the hook shank. Inspect it from the bottom to make sure it's close.

19. Pull both the brown and black foam pieces back, advance the thread to the next third, and tie the tan piece down in the same way.

20. This is what it looks like from the bottom.

21. Advance the thread to just behind the eye and tie in only the tan foam in the same way.

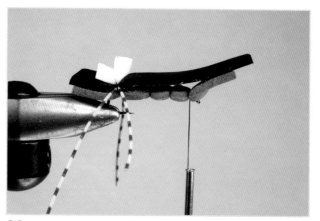

22. Now pull the black foam over the top.

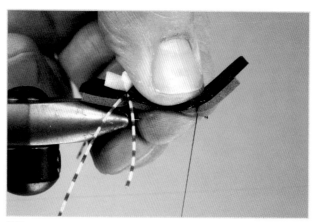

23. Press down on the black foam, and tie it in on top of the tan foam.

24. Tie in a leg on the far side, the same way you did the rear leg.

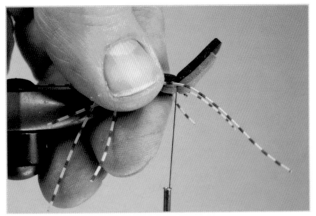

25. Tie in a leg on the near side, as you did with the previous one.

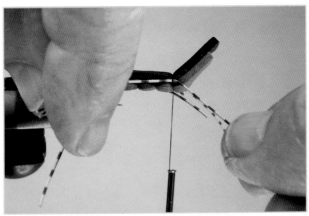

26. Tweak the legs again to make sure they are aligned properly.

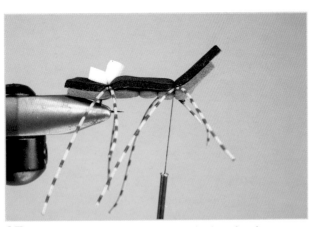

27. Make a few tight turns to lock the legs in place.

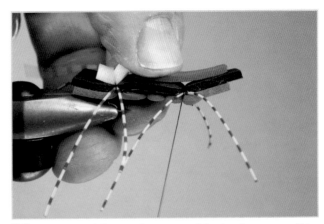

28. Place a red foam tab on top of the hook, as you did with the rear white foam.

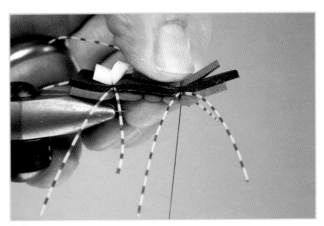

29. Tie in the red foam indicator.

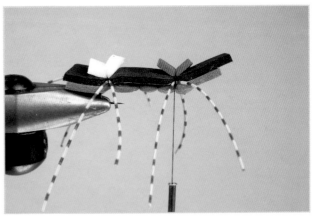

30. Trim the red tab short as you did with the white one.

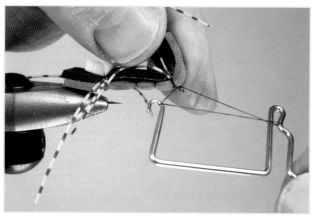

31. Gather the foam and all the legs with the hand that is holding your bobbin, and whip finish under the foam.

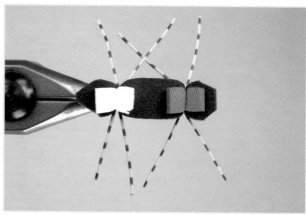

34. Trim the front end of the body to a blunt shape. Trim the rear to a slightly more tapered shape.

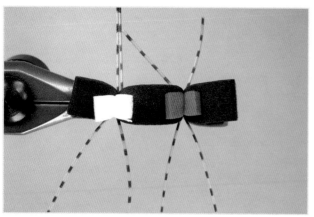

32. Trim all the legs to about a shank length or slightly longer.

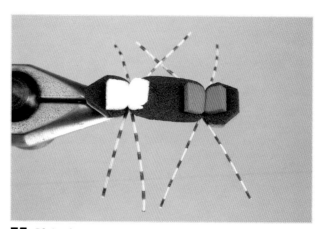

35. If the foam does not stay together in one piece, you can apply a small drop of Super Glue in between the front and rear pieces of foam. I used self-adhesive foam that was sticky on one side so that my foam body parts would stay together.

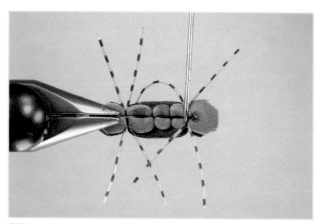

33. Apply thin head cement to all the thread wraps that show on the underside of the body.

HARE'S EAR NYMPH

The Hare's Ear Nymph is one of the oldest artificial nymph patterns. It was likely modified from the old Hare's Ear wet fly in the early days of nymphing, in the first half of the twentieth century. The Hare's Ear wet itself is one of the oldest flies known and was first tied hundreds of years ago.

Today, the popularity of nymphs with metal or glass beads, flashy dubbing, or other bright materials far outweighs the popularity of more traditional, duller styles used prior to the expansion in synthetic materials in the late twentieth century. Still, I find times when fishing a subtler traditional Pheasant Tail or Hare's Ear Nymph is more effective, particularly in heavily fished waters where trout are caught and released frequently on more exuberant patterns. I included this pattern so you could learn techniques that you can use when you want to tie these more traditional styles.

Of course, you can add beads, flashy dubbing, or other adornments to the Hare's Ear Nymph, and you'll see this pattern tied in scores of variations. Go ahead and add them if you wish, but try tying some more somber, traditional variations as well. Regardless of how you dress it up, there is something magic about hare's-ear dubbing—I think because the many spiky fibers add life to the pattern in the water, and also because the different natural shades you get from this dubbing give a more lifelike, impressionistic look to the fly. Natural invertebrates are seldom monotone, exhibiting a mix of shades when alive.

Pre-mixed dubbings sold in bags are wonderfully convenient, but they don't allow the control you get by mixing your own dubbing, and I suspect that it's too expensive and labor intensive for commercial dubbing producers to trim and mix hare's ear in a commercial blend. The ones

you see sold in fly shops are cut with plain rabbit fur or a synthetic fiber. I believe hare's-ear dubbing is unmatched when imitating nymphs with a wide profile of prominent legs and gills, so I urge you to try making some of your own. It's not that difficult, especially if you use an old coffee grinder.

Some people use the loop method for dubbing both the abdomen and thorax of this fly, and then they brush the abdomen and thorax of the fly with a dubbing teaser. I don't do this because I like just the slightly fuzzy body you get with the standard method. By winding the thorax using the loop method, I get a wider, spikier profile that imitates the wide shape of the thorax and gives the impression of legs streaming off both sides of the fly. So, by tying this pattern you'll learn both the standard "noodle" technique of dubbing and the more difficult loop method.

1. Prepare some hare's-ear dubbing. Cut fur from all parts of the ears and the mask (the face of the rabbit below

	Material	Substitutions
Hook	1X-long nymph, sizes 10-18	2X-long nymph, or curved nymph hook
Thread	Black, size 6/0 (or 70 denier)	Substitute any color thread you want.
Weighting wire	Non-toxic wire or lead wire	Leave the weight off if you don't want a fly that sinks quickly. Or add a bead to the head.
Tails	Short bunch of hare's mask fur	Brown hackle fibers
Body	Hare's-ear dubbing dubbed in a noodle	Dubbing made from red squirrel or fox squirrel, combining both underfur and guard hairs. Or just a commercial hare's-ear blend.
Rib	Oval gold tinsel	Flat gold tinsel or copper wire
Thorax	Hare's-ear dubbing dubbed in a loop	Dubbing spun in a loop
Wing case	Duck or goose wing quill segment, natural gray	Gray or black Thin Skin, mottled turkey wing quill segment, or gray Swiss Straw

the ears), being careful to trim the tiny dark hairs on the outside of the ears, which give the dubbing its spiky nature. (You can leave off the white hairs on the inside of the ears and the lighter fur at the very bottom of the mask, unless you want light-colored dubbing.) Trim over a wide bowl so you capture all the fur and guard hairs.

2. Mix the dubbing thoroughly. You can do this by hand by working it back and forth through your fingers, but a better way is to put the fur in an old blade coffee grinder and pulse it quickly a few times until it is well mixed. Alternatively, try filling the bowl with water and a small amount of dish soap, and then swirl everything around until it's mixed. Then rinse the soap in a colander and lay the fur out to dry overnight on a piece of paper towel. On the left is fur cut from the ears. On the right is fur after being pulsed in the grinder twice.

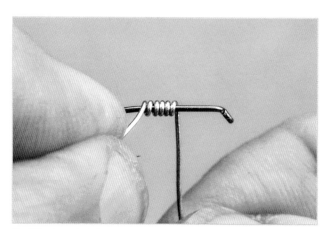

3. Wind weighting wire on the shank of the hook so that it covers about half the hook shank. Leave slightly more room at the rear than at the head.

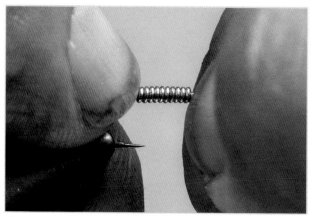

4. Squeeze the wraps together with your fingernails.

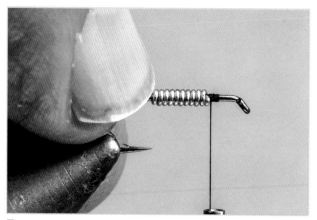

5. Attach the thread just in front of the weighting wire. Build up a slight bump in front of the wraps while holding the rear of the wire in place with your fingernail.

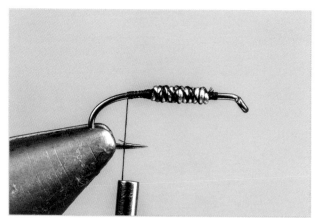

6. While keeping your fingernail tight against the rear of the wire, spiral the thread back to the rear of the wire. Then remove your fingernail and build up a bump of thread behind the wire. Spiral the thread forward to the initial tie-in point, and back to the rear. Wind the thread smoothly back to the point where the bend begins.

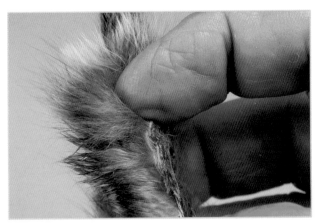

7. Trim a bunch of hare's-ear fur for the tail from the face. Split the mask and ear down the middle so that you can access the fur easily and make dubbing from one half and save the other half for tail material. I have found the best fur for the tail is located just below the ears.

8. Pull a bunch of the fur, about a hook gape in diameter, at a 90-degree angle to the skin so that the ends line up. Snip it in one piece from the skin. Remove any long guard hairs from the bunch.

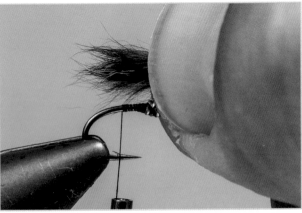

9. Measure the fur on top of the hook shank. You want the tips to extend beyond the bend about one-third of the shank length.

10. Roll the thread over the bunch in one relatively loose turn, keeping a finger on the far side of the hook to keep the tail from rolling around the hook.

11. Wrap forward in smooth, tight turns until the thread is just shy of the weighting wire.

12. Lift the butt ends of the tail straight up and trim it close to the shank. Wrap over the butt ends of the tail until you have a nice smooth transition between the end of the tail and the weighting wire.

13. Align a piece of oval tinsel just even with the end of the weighting wire and wrap back to the tail in smooth, non-overlapping turns. Thread grips oval tinsel very well, so you only need four or five turns to attach it securely.

14. Pull three to four inches of thread from your bobbin. If you have trouble with dubbing, wax the thread, although I find I don't need it for the abdomen. I like to dub the abdomen in about three stages. First, closest to the hook, dub a very thin area about as wide as your fingers. Put a lot of pressure on the dubbing by squeezing as tightly as possible with your thumb and index finger and then rolling it in one direction only.

15. Just below this, add a second pinch of dubbing using slightly more fur. Place it on the hook so that it blends with the end of the first bunch but is slightly larger in diameter. Then add a third bunch just a fraction larger

than the second bunch. (For flies smaller than size 14, you may only need two bunches.)

16. Begin to wind the dubbing, making sure that the first turn of dubbing completely covers the thread wraps at the tail but does not form a lump there.

17. Continue to wrap the dubbing forward with tight turns that just barely overlap. Stop at the middle of hook shank. If you have too much dubbing, unwrap one turn, remove the excess fur, and retighten the fur where you removed it. If you don't have enough fur to reach the middle of the hook shank, add just a pinch.

18. Wrap the oval tinsel forward in even spirals. You will get about three turns.

19. Tie off the tinsel on top of the hook shank with three tight turns of thread.

20. Snip the end of the tinsel. Then take a half dozen more turns to cover the cut end of the tinsel, and form a smooth base for the wing case.

21. Cut a slip of wing quill that is about one hook gape in width. The best place to find wing case material that behaves properly is at the bottom third of a wing quill, just above the lighter-colored fibers that curve sharply. Use your dubbing needle to separate the segments you want, and trim them carefully, so they stay in a single piece.

22. Lay the wing quill segment on top of the hook shank, shiny side up. Make sure that the shinier, thicker area at the base of the wing quill segment is forward of your tie-in point. If you try to tie in the wing case too close to the base of where the segment was attached to the quill, the wing case will collapse like an accordion because of the thicker fibers. (It's OK to have this area forward of the tie-in point, because it will be bound under.)

23. Take a loose turn of thread around the wing case, making sure that this turn is flush with the end of the abdomen. Ensure that the wing case stays on top of the hook shank and is centered. If it is, tighten with an upward pull of your bobbin. Take three more turns in the same fashion.

24. Wrap forward with a half dozen tight turns over the wing case.

25. Lift the butt ends of the wing case, and trim them so they are about even with the end of the weighting wire.

26. Wrap thread over the stubs of the wing case, and taper the point where the end of the weighting wire drops off to the bare shank. (Otherwise when you wind your thorax forward it will be difficult to wrap it smoothly as it makes the abrupt jump.) Return the thread to the end of the abdomen, where you tied in the wing case.

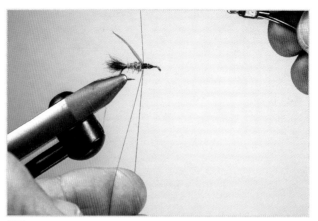

27. Pull seven to eight inches of thread from the bobbin, loop it around your fingers, and wrap over the end of the loop at the hook shank to secure it.

28. Advance the tying thread to just behind the eye while holding the loop with your other hand. Wax both sides of the loop about three-quarters of the way from the hook shank to the end of the loop.

29. Take two to three equal bunches of loose hare's-ear fur, and place them inside the loop, letting the wax hold them in place. You want all the same diameter here, with no taper. Be careful to avoid getting any wax on your fingers, because if you do, it will be impossible to transfer the fur to the loop. Easy does it—resist the urge to use too much dubbing. One finger of your other hand should still be holding the end of the loop.

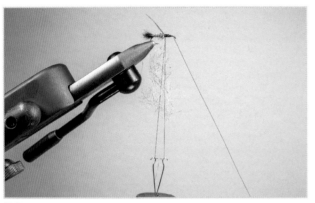

30. Slip the two hooks of a dubbing spinner into the ends of the loop, allowing the loop to close over the fur. At this point you can carefully manipulate the fur so that it is evenly distributed.

31. Pinch the loop just below the fur, and give your dubbing spinner a good twirl. Release pressure where you are holding the loop, and allow the loop to spin the dubbing in place.

32. Keep twirling the spinner and releasing pressure until you have a tight but spiky segment of fur. It is perfectly fine to just keep twirling the dubbing spinner without pinching the loop in place, but I find this method keeps the dubbing spinner from swinging erratically and bumping into my bobbin. (If you use a bobbin cradle, this is the perfect time to use it to keep your bobbin out of the way.)

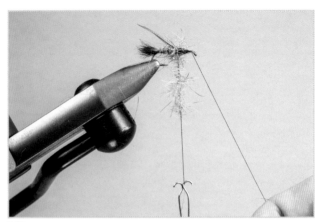

33. Using the dubbing spinner as a handle, take one wrap of dubbing, tight against the wing case but not overlapping it.

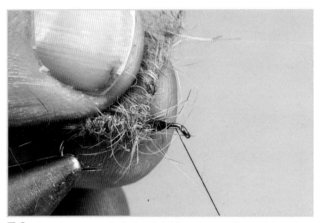

34. Continue to wind the dubbing forward, stroking the fibers backward after each turn.

35. Tie off the dubbing loop in front of the eye with three tight turns of thread. You need to allow enough room to bind it under and tie off the wing case, so don't wind it right up to the eye.

36. Snip the end of the dubbing loop and take about six more turns of thread, forming a smooth base for tying off the wing case.

37. Pull the wing case forward over the eye. Take one loose turn of thread over the quill segment—just use the weight of the bobbin and let gravity apply the pressure. Then tighten with an upward pull. Repeat the process three more times in the same place.

38. Pull up on the ends of the wing case, and trim it close to the hook shank.

39. Wind a smooth, neat head over the ends of the wing case, whip finish, and add a drop of head cement.

40. If you don't think your thorax is wide and fuzzy enough, use a piece of male Velcro attached to a popsicle stick or a dubbing teaser to fuzz out both sides of the thorax.

41. Completed Hare's Ear Nymph, showing good proportions and the proper amount of fuzziness.

COPPER JOHN

The Copper John is one of the most popular nymph patterns in the world, especially for prospecting in faster water when you have no idea what trout may be eating. This pattern is highly visible underwater, has an insect-like shape, and sinks quickly with a combination of a metal bead, weighting wire underbody, and shiny wire over-body. Trout probably take it for a large mayfly nymph, a stonefly nymph, or perhaps a tiny crayfish, but don't worry too much about what it imitates. If you're faced with fast or deep water, the Copper John should be on your short list.

The Copper John was developed by John Barr of Colorado. The original nymph used mottled turkey quill for the wing case and was only tied with standard copper-colored wire. With the development of fly-tying wire in a rainbow of colors by the Wapsi Fly Company (a wholesale developer and distributor of tying materials), anglers began to tie the pattern with red, green, and black wire. Barr initially resisted the wild new colors, but eventually saw their effectiveness. The wing case was later changed to Thin Skin, another Wapsi product that is far more durable than turkey quill and is also available in many colors and patterns. And a strip of Flashabou was added to the wing case to give it extra sparkle and to imitate the split wing case of an emerging nymph. The pattern as tied here is the standard version sold in fly shops, and it is as much staple in those stores as Budweiser is in a corner convenience store.

It is often thought that John Barr "borrowed" the Copper John from artist/guide Bob White, who at about the same time was using a copper-bodied fly as his go-to fly with the Alaskan guides he worked with. But a closer examination of the two patterns shows little similarity beyond the copper body and peacock thorax. Bob's fly used pheasant tail for the tail, legs, and wing case, so although the flies look similar, it's merely a matter of convergent evolution. Neither of these fine anglers has a big ego, and I was lucky enough to be present when they met for the first time. They both had a laugh about the uproar created in the fly-tying community regarding the origin of the pattern.

If you haven't discovered it yet, you will soon find out that fly tiers are a peculiar bunch and can create controversy about almost anything.

1. Before you put the hook in the vise, slip a tungsten bead over the point of the hook. Note that the bead has a smaller diameter hole on one side. That side should face the point as you attach the bead so that the smaller diameter rests up against the eye of the hook. Some

	Material	Substitutions
Hook	2X-long nymph, sizes 10-18	3X-long nymph or curved nymph hook
Thread	Black, size 6/0 (or 70 denier)	Any color thread
Bead	Brass-colored tungsten bead, to match hook size	Copper, black, or silver bead in either tungsten or brass
Weighting wire	Non-toxic wire or lead wire	Leave the weight off if you don't want a fly that sinks quickly
Tails	Brown goose biot	Black or tan goose biot or turkey biot
Body	Copper Ultra Wire	Red, green, and black are other popular wire colors
Wing case	Black Thin Skin with a single strand of pearl Flashabou	Brown or mottled Thin Skin and a single strand of any pearl-colored flashy Mylar
Thorax	Three to five strands of peacock herl	Peacock-colored sparkle dubbing
Legs	Brown Hungarian partridge	Speckled hen feathers, quail feather, or any mottled soft feather

beads have a tough time getting over the barb and bend of the hook. If it is a tight fit, use a pair of forceps to help force the bead over the barb.

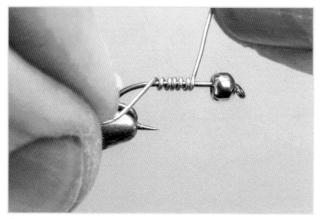

2. Wind the weighting wire over the shank of the hook from about three-quarters of the way to the bend right up to the bead. Break or trim both ends of the wire.

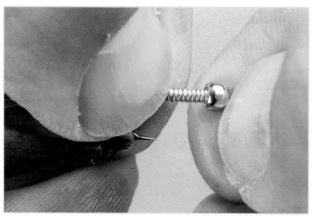

3. Compress the wire into the bead slightly by pushing with your fingernail.

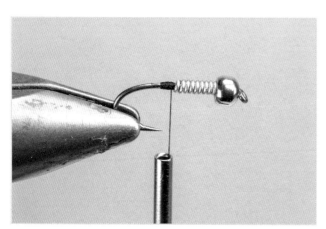

4. Start the thread just behind the weighting wire, and form a small dam of thread up against the weighting wire.

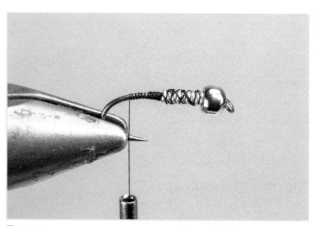

5. Make some cross wraps over the weighting wire. Go back and forth several times. It does not have to be neat. Wind the thread back to where the bend of the hook begins.

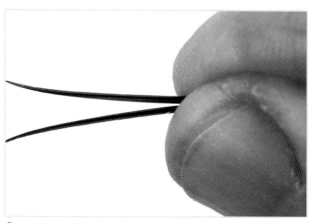

6. Snip two biots from the stem. You will notice they have a slight curve. Grab them with your right thumb and index finger, and arrange them so that the curve of each piece faces out. Line them up by slipping one forward or back until they are even.

7. Hold the tail fibers over the shank until their fine ends stick out about half a shank length beyond the bend. Then transfer them to your other hand, and work them down over the shank until they straddle the shank.

8. Tie them in with a pinch wrap. If they are not aligned on either side of the shank, tweak them into place, or remove them and try again.

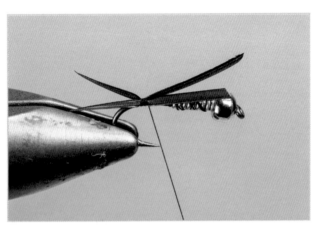

9. Wrap forward in smooth turns until the butt ends almost reach the beginning of the weighting wire.

10. Snip the butt ends. Bind them under, but don't wrap up over the weighting wire.

11. Lay the body wire on the side of the hook shank with the end just touching the end of the weighting wire. Wind back in smooth turns to the tails.

12. Wind forward to about the middle of the shank or just beyond. Now wind back and forth in smooth turns to form a tapered underbody. Don't wind all the way back to the tails when you do this so that you build up the thread in a relatively steep taper. It may help to flatten your thread by spinning the bobbin counterclockwise. End your thread in the middle of the shank.

13. Wind the body wire forward in tight but non-overlapping turns. Be careful that your first turn covers up all the tying thread underneath, then wind forward. Angle the wire back toward the tails so that each turn perfectly abuts the previous turn. Take your time and use firm pressure.

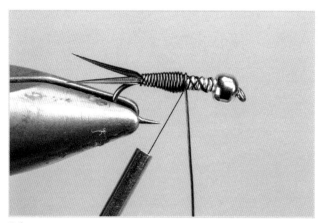

14. When you get to the middle of the shank, hold the wire straight down, and tie it off with three very tight turns.

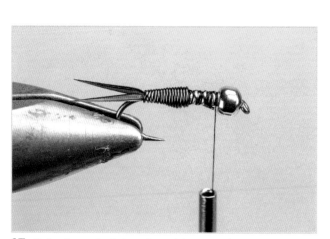

15. Snip the end of the wire with your wire cutters. Make sure you leave enough to bind under but make sure it is not so long that it butts up against the bead. Fold the wire along the shank, and wind forward toward the bead. Some people twist the wire until it breaks, but that never works well for me, and I worry it is not secure enough.

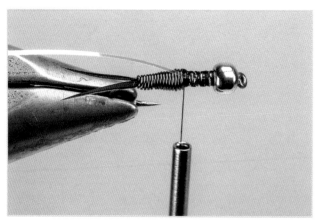

16. Select a single strand of Flashabou, and wind it back directly centered on top of the hook shank until you get to the front end of the wire abdomen.

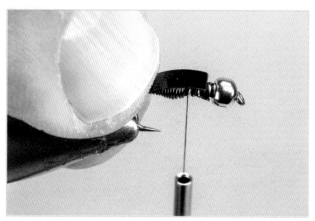

17. Cut a strip of Thin Skin that is about one hook gape in width. Remove the paper backing. Tie the Thin Skin to the top of the shank. Lay it on top of the shank so that it almost extends to the bead.

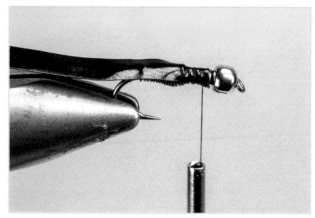

18. Pull straight down as you wind forward to keep it on top of the shank.

19. Select three to five strands of peacock herl from the bottom of an eyed tail. The herl here is thinner so that the thorax does not look too bulky.

20. Snip the fine ends of the herl so that you have nice straight ends.

21. Tie in the herl back to the beginning of the thorax, right up against the wing case materials.

22. Don't advance the thread back to the bead. Rather, wind the herls forward toward the bead, pushing them against the thread as you wind. Herls tend to separate and get out of control when you wind them, and winding up against the thread keeps them all in one bunch.

23. Tie off the herls just shy of the bead with three tight turns of thread. Carefully snip the ends so that they do not extend over the bead.

24. Select a brown mottled Hungarian partridge feather. It should be symmetrical, with about the same length and amount of fibers on each side of the stem. Strip the fuzzy and flimsy fibers from both sides of the feather.

25. Snip the center stem of the feather about halfway from the tip to the bottom of the fibers with your fine scissors.

26. Place the feather on top of the hook shank, colorful side up (the convex side). An equal number of fibers should lie along each side of the thorax and the gap where you snipped the feather should be on top of the shank. The fibers should be about one shank length.

27. Take a couple loose turns of thread around the feather, gathering the fibers to each side.

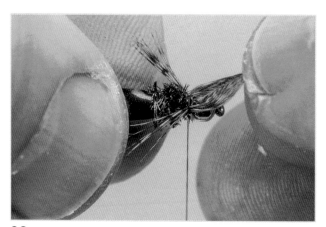

28. Pull gently forward on the stem of the feather, and tweak the fibers so that they fall in place on either side of the hook shank. Just pull the stem forward until the fibers extend to where the tails begin.

29. Now take three tight turns over the fibers to lock them in place. Carefully snip the butt ends of the fibers so that they do not extend over the bead.

30. Fold the Thin Skin forward over the bead. Stretch it tight. The Thin Skin will help keep the partridge fibers separated on each side of the shank. Tie it off with three firm winds. Pull straight down when you bind it in to keep it on top of the hook shank.

31. Carefully trim the Thin Skin so that it does not extend over the bead. You may have to come in at an angle with your fine scissors to trim it properly.

32. Pull the Flashabou over the top of the Thin Skin, making sure it is centered in the middle of the wing case. Tie it off and trim the end.

33. Wrap over the ends of all the materials until they are just covered. Whip finish.

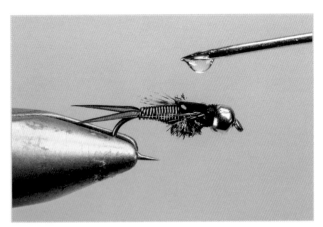

34. Apply a small amount of UV cure epoxy to the wing case and the thread wraps only. Be careful not to get any on the peacock herl or the partridge legs.

35. Cure the epoxy with a UV light.

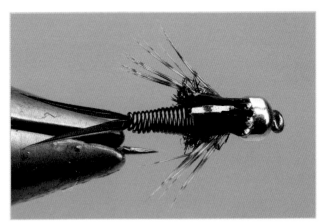

36. Finished Copper John.

PMD SPARKLE DUN

A Sparkle Dun is the go-to fly for many fly fishers during mayfly hatches. It floats well and is easy to see, imitating the stage when a mayfly dun is struggling to free itself from the nymph shuck. This is the most vulnerable stage in a hatching mayfly's life cycle, and trout know it. With this fly you get the visibility of a dry fly combined with the appeal of an emerger.

The Sparkle Dun was developed by Craig Mathews and John Juracek of Blue Ribbon Flies in West Yellowstone, Montana. It's an adaption of a fly called the Comparadun, which is the same fly, except the Z-Lon shuck is replaced with delicate split tails of hackle fibers. Also, the Comparadun was adapted by Al Caucci and the late Bob Nastasi from an old Adirondack pattern called the Haystack, which was tied by the late Fran Betters as a bigger and rougher attractor for use in fast water.

The material used for the wing of this fly makes or breaks it. Hair for Sparkle Duns is specially selected deer hair, and a good piece of it is a treasure. The first thing I do when I visit a fly shop is to go right to the wall where the pieces of deer hair are located and sort through all the packages. If I find a piece of deer hair that looks like prime

The hair on the right is fine, with even tips and short black tips. This is premium hair for a Sparkle Dun. The hair on the left is uneven with long black tips—your Sparkle Duns won't look good or fish as well if you use this hair.

Examples of great hair for Sparkle Duns. The piece on the left is slightly coarse and good for bigger flies, size 10 through 14. The hair in the middle is finer in diameter and best for flies in size 12 through 16. The hair on the right is very fine and is best saved for those little 18s and 20s.

	Material	Substitutions
Hook	Standard dry fly, size 14-20	Bigeye dry fly in smaller sizes
Thread	Yellow 6/0	Any color to match body, 8/0 on smaller sizes
Tail	Brown Z-Lon yarn	Tan Z-Lon or Antron yarn
Body	Fine yellow fur or synthetic dubbing with a tinge of olive or orange	Any color dubbing to match the body of the naturals
Wing	Fine, even textured whitetail deer hair	Two large CDC feathers or hair from the heel of a snowshoe rabbit.

Sparkle Dun hair I buy it. This is often sold as "Compara-dun Hair," so look for that designation. If you tie enough of these flies, you'll find yourself with lots of pieces of it. Some are better for bigger, size 10 and 12 flies. Others make great size 16s and 18s. And if you can find a piece with very fine hair, you can tie them down to a size 20.

Look for a piece of hair where the individual fibers are fine in diameter, the tips are even while on the hide, and the spindly black tips on the hairs are as short as possible. This will tie a nice Sparkle Dun or Comparadun, giving you a solid wing profile without adding a lot of bulk to the body of the fly. Don't worry too much about the color—I don't. The wing is for visibility, and to give an impression of the twitching wings of a mayfly struggling to take off. Better to go for the perfect texture than getting the color just right. I use mostly natural tan deer hair for most light-to-medium-colored mayflies, and I have a few pieces of hair dyed dark gray for darker flies. If the shade is in the ballpark, you're all set.

The body for this fly, and for any dry fly that imitates a mayfly dun or spinner, should be tied from dubbing with a fine texture. The synthetic dubbing sold under names like "Ultrafine" or "Dry Fly Dubbing" is very easy to dub, giving you a tight body with little effort. I am very fond of natural dubbing as well for flies like this. Rabbit or beaver underfur is very fine, and I think it holds air bubbles and fly floatant better, because the fibers are finer than the synthetics. But these furs invariably come with some longer, darker guard hairs in them, which should be plucked from the dubbing before you use it.

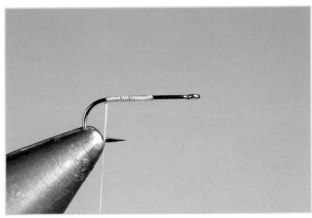

1. Attach your thread to the middle of the hook shank, and wind back to just where the bend begins.

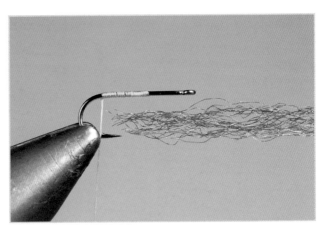

2. Carefully peel apart the Z-Lon yarn until you have a two-inch piece that is about a hook gape in diameter. This will be trimmed and will be enough for a couple flies.

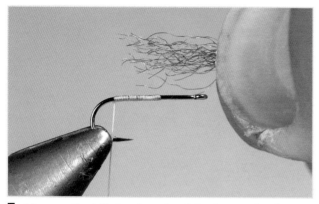

3. Measure the tail shuck so that it is about a shank length or slightly less. The shuck should be sparse and scraggly, so don't overdo it. It is not necessary to trim the back end. You want just the suggestion of a discarded nymph case on the back of the fly.

4. Tie in the shuck by holding it on top of the hook with the front end facing toward you and rolling the thread around it. Keep one finger on the far side of the hook shank so that it stays on top of the shank. If the thread does not roll back over the yarn and wants to roll forward, give your bobbin a counterclockwise spin to make the thread roll back. Your first turn should be relatively loose.

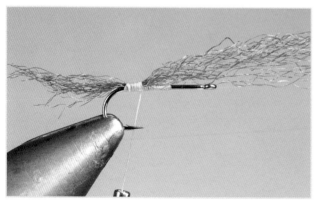

5. Wind forward in smooth even turns. If the yarn does not stay on top of the hook shank, tweak it a bit by rolling it back toward you.

6. Wind forward to about the middle of the hook shank. Trim the yarn in a taper.

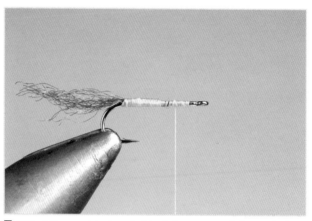

7. Wind forward to just behind the eye, and then wind your thread back to a point that is between one-third and one-quarter of a hook shank behind the eye.

8. Snip a bunch of deer hair from the hide. The bunch should be about twice the hook gape in diameter. It will get slightly smaller after you clean it.

9. Hold the hair by the tips, and clean the fuzz and short hairs from the butt ends. I like to first pull the fuzz from the hair with my fingers, then I flick the hair a few times to help loosen the fuzz. You may want to make a final pass through the butts with a fine comb. Then make a final pass with your fingers. Throughout this process, keep firm pressure on the tips.

10. Place the hairs tip down in a stacker. The hair should fill about half the diameter of the stacker. If the fit is too tight, the hairs will not all fall to the bottom, and if it is too loose, the hairs may not stack evenly. (If you work with hair a lot, you may find the need for at least two sizes of stackers, if not three.)

11. Rap the stacker sharply on a hard surface about five times. Rap it hard enough to push the tips of all the hairs to the bottom but not so hard that the hair jumps back up into the stacker tube. Then twirl the stacker tube to make sure all the hairs touch the bottom. Alternate a few times with sharp raps and short staccato raps.

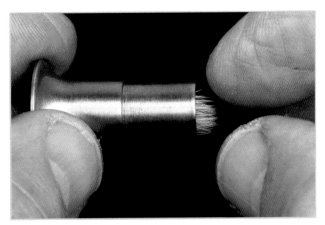

12. Hold the stacker horizontally and carefully remove the tube. Grab the tips of the hair.

13. Measure the wing so that it is one hook shank in length, using the end of your thumbnail as a guide. Then move your thumbnail up to the tie-in point.

14. Attach the wing to the hook shank, tips forward, with a pinch wrap. Take one very tight turn. The hair should roll around the upper half of the hook shank only.

15. Take about four tight turns of thread in the same spot while holding the butt ends of the hair. If the wing rolls to the underside of the hook shank, work it back to the top. Take a couple tight turns winding slightly back toward the tail. Don't let go of the butt ends. (I let go here so you could see the wraps.)

16. Trim the hair at an angle, at about the middle of the hook shank. You probably won't get rid of all the hairs in the first pass.

17. Trim any remaining long hairs. This is where a fine pair of scissors comes in handy. Try to trim so that the taper of the wing butts ends where the trimming of the tail ends, to get one continuous taper.

18. Wind back over the trimmed wing butts to cover all the ends. Fill in any gaps with thread to get a smooth taper. (Many tiers agonize about using too much thread, worrying that the fly won't float properly. But thread weighs very little, and its floating properties have more to do with the way a fly gets pinioned in the surface film due to its materials and construction than with its overall weight.)

19. Advance the thread in front of the wing.

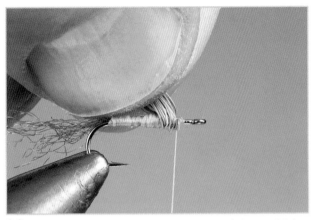

20. Gather all the hairs and pull them straight up. Make sure you get all of them.

21. Build up a tapered dam of thread in front of the wing. Hold the wing upright and make sure the thread builds up immediately in front of the wing but not over it. The amount of thread in front of the wing should be almost as large in diameter as the thread behind the wing.

22. Inspect the wing to make sure it flares 180 degrees around the top of the hook shank.

23. Trim any hairs that stick back toward the tail, and bring your thread over the top of the hook. Then trim any hairs that stick out under the hook.

24. Bring the thread back to the bend, and stroke the wing forward to keep it out of the way when you wind the body.

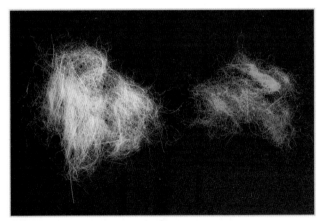

25. If your dubbing is not already pre-mixed to the shade you want, grab two bunches of dubbing in the proportion that looks right to get your desired color. Here I am adding some orange to my yellow dubbing. Tease the fur apart so that it is in loose bunches.

26. Pick up both bunches of fur, and mix them by pulling them apart, recombining and pulling apart again, until they are well mixed. Alternatively, if you are mixing a lot of dubbing, you can place them in an old blade-type coffee grinder and pulse them until they are well mixed. (Coffee snobs tell us these are no good for coffee anyway.) Now is a good time to pluck any longer guard hairs from the dubbing if you are using natural fur.

27. Take just a tiny amount of fuzz, and dub it to the thread close to the body. Just barely get the thread dirty. Slide it up close to the hook. It's your choice whether to wax your thread or not, but most fine dry-fly dubbing goes on the thread well without additional wax.

28. Add more dubbing below this in a slightly bigger diameter, but don't taper the rest of it. You have already built up a taper with your thread, and adding a taper to

the dubbing gives you a body with too much bulk at the forward end.

29. Add dubbing in small amounts rather than putting a big lump on the thread. Use lots of pressure, roll the dubbing in one direction only, and if an area gets too bulky, pull it apart. If an area looks too thin, add just a small amount of fuzz.

30. Wind over the tail until the dubbing starts to wind around the hook. Hold the tails in place as you make your first few wraps.

31. Wind the dubbing forward in smooth, even turns. If it starts to bulk up too much, unwrap a few times, readjust the dubbing or spin it tighter, and resume. If the dubbing is too thin in a spot, overlap slightly.

32. Wind the dubbing to right behind the wing. Make sure you cover all thread wraps.

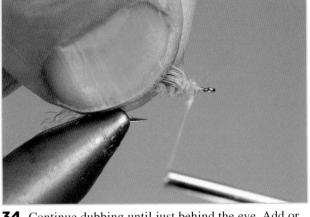

34. Continue dubbing until just behind the eye. Add or remove dubbing as needed. To get a slight taper at the head, just tighten down on your last two turns.

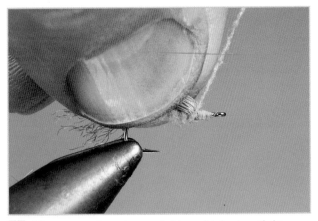

33. Now preen the wing upright, and take two tight turns of dubbing just in front of it.

35. Whip finish, and add a drop of head cement to the thread wraps.

STIMULATOR

The Stimulator is a fly that often begs to come out of my fly box and onto my tippet. When I need a big fly to attract attention, it's often my choice because it floats well, is highly visible, and lands lightly on the water despite its bulk (as opposed to big foam flies whose splat sometimes attracts trout but other times spooks them). The Stimulator is a great fly for a dry dropper rig, hanging a nymph off the hook bend.

Randall Kaufmann originally tied this fly in the 1970s to imitate large stoneflies, and it is deadly when those bugs are on the water. However, also it makes a decent grasshopper imitation, and I have even used it to imitate large emerging mayflies like the giant "Hex" of the Midwest. But don't agonize too much about what it imitates: It is also one of my go-to flies for fishing mountain brook trout streams, where trout don't see many insects at all but grab whatever looks edible. I think this combination of materials just suggests bugginess and movement, and it looks to trout like a big insect struggling on the water.

The pattern as shown here is exactly the way Randall ties it (I am lucky enough to have one of his original flies in my collection). However, tiers use many combinations of colors, from yellow and tan to imitate golden stoneflies to dark brown for the western Skwalas. Some tiers even add rubber legs. Modify this fly as you wish depending on prevalent insect hatches or just in colors you think will be effective. Some tiers like longer hackle on the abdomen than I use here, but I like the shorter hackle in the back and just feel it balances the fly better.

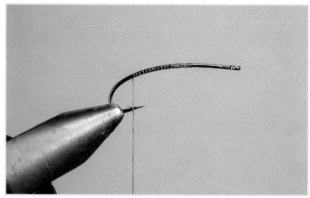

1. Attach the thread to the hook in the middle of the shank. Wind back to where the thread hangs just over the spot where the barb of the hook begins.

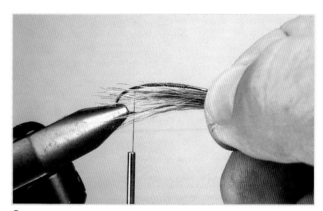

2. Select a bunch of elk hair that is about one hook gape in diameter. (It will be reduced slightly in size after you clean it.)

	Material	Substitutions
Hook	Curved nymph, sizes 6-16	3X-long nymph hook
Thread	Bright orange, 6/0	Yellow, olive, or brown to match body color
Tail	Yearling or cow elk	Bull elk or moose mane
Body	Orange sparkle dubbing	Tan, olive, brown, or black sparkle dubbing
Body hackle	Brown saddle or brown long neck hackle	Grizzly or cream, depending on body color
Rib	Fine gold wire	Fine silver or copper wire
Wing	Yearling or calf elk	Bull elk
Thorax hackle	Grizzly saddle hackle or long neck hackle	Brown or cream
Thorax	Reddish orange sparkle dubbing	Any sparkle dubbing slightly darker than body color

3. Clean the fuzz and shorter hairs at the base of the hair by holding it by the tips in one hand and pulling away with the fingers of your other hand, away from the tips.

4. You can also run a fine-tooth comb through the hairs to help clean them. Make four or five passes to make sure you clean all the shorter stuff out of the bunch.

5. Even the ends of the hair with a stacker. Place the hairs in the stacker tip ends down. Rap the stacker sharply on a table, spin the tube of the stacker to make sure all the hairs fall to the bottom, then rap it again.

6. Hold the stacker horizontally, carefully remove the tube, and grab the evened tips of the hair in your thumb and index finger.

7. Place the hair over the tie-in point so that about one-third shank length extends beyond the tie-in point.

8. Tie the hair to the shank with a pinch wrap. Put just enough pressure on the thread to flare the hair slightly. The amount of pressure you use depends on how hollow the hair is—every piece is different.

9. Wind forward over the hair with moderate pressure, increasing the pressure as you progress forward. Stop at about two-thirds of the way to the eye.

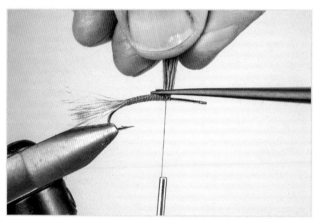

10. Trim the remaining hair. Wind over it to bind down all loose hairs.

11. Prepare a brown hackle that is just about a hook gape in fiber diameter when you flare it around the hook. Strip the webby fibers from the bottom of the feather.

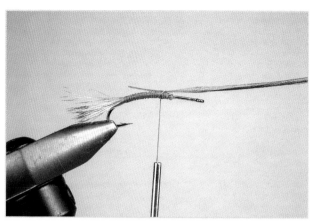

12. Tie in the stem, tip of the hackle facing forward, dull side up. Make three or four turns.

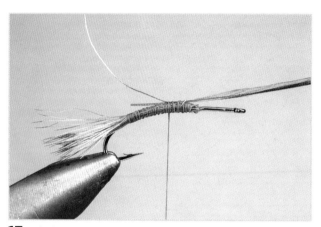

13. Tie in a piece of fine gold wire about three inches long.

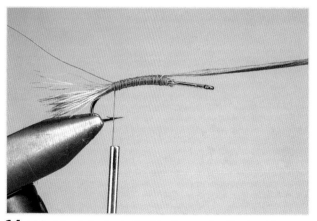

14. Wind back to the tails, binding under the hackle stem and gold wire. The hackle feather should now point over the eye of the hook, and the gold wire should be over the tails, pointing to the back. Place the gold wire in your material clip, or just move it so that it stays out of the way.

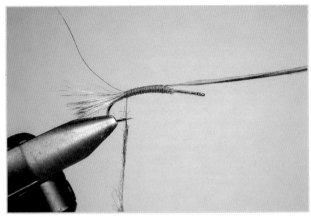

15. Dub about a two-inch length of thread with the orange sparkle dubbing. Taper it slightly so that it is thinnest close to the hook and slightly bigger in diameter as you work down the thread. It helps to do this in three or four steps, and if a spot is too thin, add a bit of dubbing. If a spot is too thick, thin it by pulling the dubbing apart slightly.

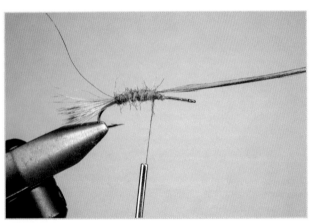

16. Wind the dubbing forward to cover about two-thirds of the hook shank.

17. Grab the brown hackle, and wind it back toward the tail with evenly spaced turns. The shiny side of the hackle should face forward, which makes the hackle fibers sweep backward.

18. You can wind with your fingers if the hackle is long enough, but I would advise using hackle pliers. You can alternate hands as you wind the hackle, but I have found it easier to put my index finger inside the loop of the hackle pliers and just let the pliers rotate around my finger. See what works best for you.

19. When you get to the tail, take two tight turns of the wire around the hackle tip. You can now release the hackle.

20. Wind the wire forward in tight spirals, which will reinforce the hackle and keep it from being cut by the teeth of the large brown trout you will catch on this fly.

21. When you get to the end of the body, take two or three wraps of wire in one spot for security.

22. Tie off the wire, and snip the end with wire cutters or the heavy part of your scissors.

23. Snip the brown hackle tip carefully. Wind the thread forward to the hook eye and back to form a thread base for the wings.

24. Cut a bunch of elk hair about two times the diameter of the bunch you used for the tail. Clean the short hairs and fuzz, as you did with the tails.

25. Stack the hairs to even their ends as you did with the tails.

26. Tie in the wing. It should extend almost to the end of the tail but not quite. Use a pinch wrap, and apply enough pressure to flare the wing slightly.

27. Wind forward with moderate tension, then as you get almost to the eye, apply more tension, enough to flare the hair.

28. Trim the butt ends of the hairs. It will take several snips.

29. When you trim the hairs underneath the shank, hold your bobbin above the shank so that you don't accidentally cut the thread.

30. Wind over the snipped ends of the hair to smooth it out. Return the thread to the base of the wing.

31. Select a grizzly hackle that has fibers slightly longer than the brown body hackle. Flare it over the thorax to check.

32. Tie the grizzly hackle, dull side up, winding the stem forward to the eye. Snip the end of the stem.

33. Dub about two inches of thread with the reddish orange dubbing.

34. Wind back to the wing and then back to the eye.

35. Wind the grizzly hackle through the thorax, with evenly spaced turns.

36. Tie off the grizzly hackle just behind the eye. Snip the end of the hackle carefully.

37. Stroke the hackle back and out of the way, and wind a neat, tight head.

38. Whip finish the head.

39. Apply a drop of head cement to the head.

CONE HEAD BUNNY MUDDLER

I chose the Cone Head Bunny Muddler as an example of a streamer because once you learn to tie it, you'll have the skills to tie various styles of Muddler Minnows and Zonkers, and most of the streamers tied and sold these days build on those skills. It's also a very effective trout and bass fly that has the movement of rabbit fur and rubber legs for action in the water, a deer hair head and collar that create vibrations in the water that seem to attract fish, and the combination of an under-wrapping of weighting wire and a metal cone to get the fly down quickly. The rabbit fur wing not only offers more wiggle in the water than the standard turkey quills used in a Muddler Minnow—it's also vastly more durable.

I have not been able to determine who first tied this fly, but I suspect several tiers probably came up with it in quick succession. We're always combining the attributes of the best patterns, and this hybrid of a Zonker and a Muddler, combined with a cone head, was bound to happen. You can tie this one in almost any color or combination of colors, depending on the preferences of trout and bass in your favorite river. And use whatever color rubber legs you have handy. They are there more for movement than color, so don't agonize if you don't have rubber legs to match the wing and body. The collar and cuffs don't need to match.

Also, it's tough enough to get natural deer hair that is the right length and texture to make a Muddler head without worrying about finding some dyed deer hair with the same qualities. I tie all of mine, regardless of color, with a natural deer hair head and collar, and I find the trout accept it just fine. The hair you use should be a bit finer than that used

	Material	Substitutions
Hook	4X-long streamer, sizes 4-12	3X-long nymph/streamer hook
Thread	3/0 (140 denier), tan, brown, or white	Use thread to match body, but I like tan or white because it is hidden in the deer hair head
Cone	Silver tungsten cone	Gold, copper, or black cone
Weighting wire	Non-toxic wire	Leave it off if you want a slightly lighter fly
Tail	Pearl Krystal Flash	Pearl Flashabou or any flashy pearl-colored synthetic
Wing	Olive Zonker strip	Black, white, brown, or tan Zonker strip
Body	Olive Sparkle Dubbing	Sparkle dubbing to match wing
Throat	Red Flashabou	Red Krystal Flash or any red flashy synthetic
Fins	Brown rubber legs	Black or tan rubber legs
Collar	Natural deer hair	Dyed deer hair to match body

for bass bugs, but coarser than hair used on Comparadun or Sparkle Dun dry flies. Look for a piece of deer hair with nice uniform length; clean, even hairs right up to the tips; and hair length of about 1½ inches long. If the hairs are uniform enough, you can even tie this fly without bothering to stack the hairs.

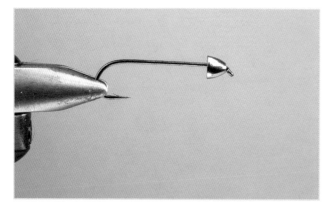

1. Slip a cone onto the hook point, and slide it up to the eye.

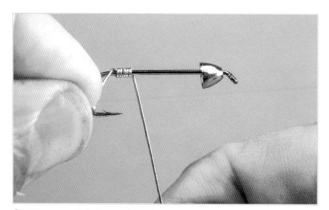

2. Wrap weighting wire along the entire hook shank.

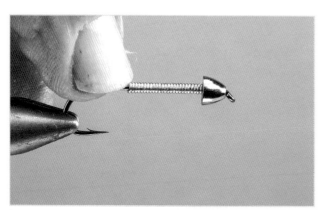

3. Compress the weighting wire so it jams lightly into the cone. Don't push it too hard because that will offset the cone. Push it forward just enough so that it rests up against the inside of the cone. You will be left with a short gap where the tail is tied in.

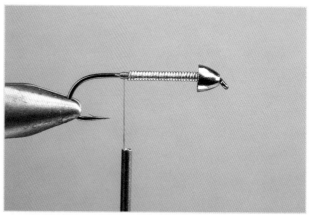

4. Start your thread behind the weighting wire. Wind a bump of thread here.

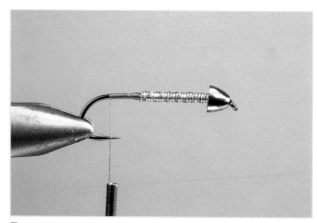

5. Spiral the thread back and forth a few times over the weighting wire. Then wind it back to the bend of the hook.

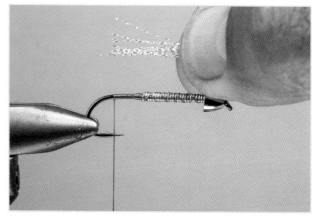

6. Measure a small bunch of Krystal Flash so that it is about three-quarters of a shank length.

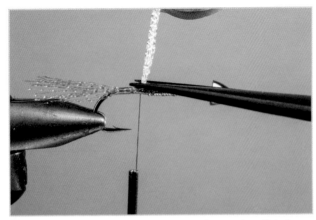

7. Tie in the Krystal Flash, winding forward until it just reaches the weighting wire. Trim the butt ends. Return the thread to the bend.

8. Carefully trim a Zonker strip to a blunt point with just the tips of your scissors. Just cut the hide from the underside, not the fur. (You will notice the fur on a Zonker strip has a natural flow in one direction. Make sure you make this cut at the end of the fur, where it lays flat.

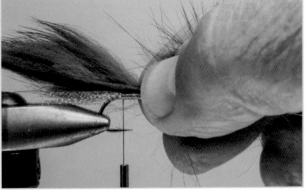

9. Cut the Zonker strip at the other end so that it is about two shank lengths. Lay the strip over the top of the flow, natural flow of the fur to the rear, so that it extends just shy of one shank length beyond the bend. Separate the fur right above the tie-in point with your fingers.

10. Tie in the Zonker strip on top of the hook shank with three tight turns of thread.

11. Push the forward piece of fur back and out of the way. If it does not stay out of the way, make a turn or two of thread right in front of it.

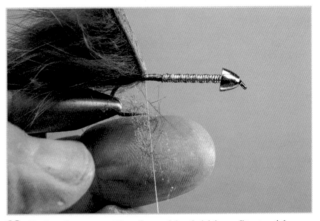

12. Dub a long noodle of sparkle dubbing. Start with a small bunch.

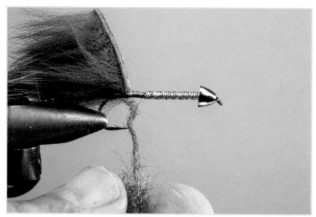

13. Then add a slightly larger diameter of fingertip-sized bunches until you have three to four inches covered. The exact length will depend on the hook size you are using.

14. Wind the dubbing forward to a point about one-eighth inch behind the cone. Add a pinch or two of dubbing if you don't have enough; remove some if you have too much.

15. Pull the Zonker strip tightly over the top of the body, and secure it where the body stops with three or four firm winds. As you did at the tail end, stroke some of the fibers forward to get them out of the way.

16. Trim the end of the strip, and wrap over the butt ends.

17. Turn the fly over in the vise so that it is point-side up.

18. Select about ten strands of red Flashabou. Fold them over your thread, and slide the Flashabou into position just in front of the body. Handling Flashabou is easier if you wet the bunch first.

19. Tie in the Flashabou with a few turns of thread, and trim them. They should extend to just shy of the hook point.

20. Fold two rubber legs over your thread, and work them into place on the hook shank. Take a couple winds of thread over the legs.

21. Manipulate the rubber legs so that the two ends extend along each side of the fly. Wrap back a few turns over them to hold them in place. It may help to turn the hook on its side and hold the rubber legs flush to the side of the body as you do this.

22. Trim the rubber legs so that they are just a bit longer than the Flashabou.

23. Cut a bunch of deer hair that is about the diameter of a pencil.

24. Grab the hair by the tips, and pull any loose hairs, shorter hairs, or fuzz at the base of the hair by pulling on the butt ends with your other fingers.

25. Place the hair in a stacker to even the ends, rap the stacker sharply on the table a half-dozen times, then hold the stacker horizontally and carefully remove the tube, grabbing the deer hair by the tips.

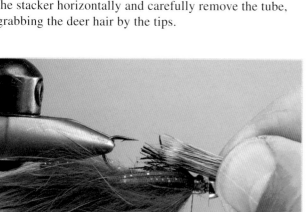

26. Place the deer hair so that it is slightly to your side of the hook shank. The tips should extend about halfway to the hook point.

27. Take one loose turn of thread around the deer hair so that it rolls around the hook shank, covering 180 degrees of the bottom of the hook (the top as you are looking at it now).

28. Take a tighter second turn, beginning to loosen your grip on the hair.

29. Then take a third very tight turn. Release your grip on the tips and let the deer hair roll around the hook shank so that it covers the bottom 180 degrees of the hook. Work it in place with your thumbnail if it does not completely cover the bottom half of the hook.

30. Turn the fly over in the vise, or rotate your vise so that it is now point-side down.

31. Cut another bunch of deer hair, stack it, and line it up on top of the hook shank, slightly to your side of the shank. Make sure the tips line up with the bunch you tied on the underside of the shank.

32. As you did with the first bunch, take a loose turn, a tighter turn, and then a few very tight turns to flare the hair over the top 180 degrees of the shank.

33. Wind the thread forward through the hair about four or five very tight turns. You should feel the hair compress under your thread. Stop when your thread just touches the rear edge of the cone. You will know when you have gone far enough when the hair sticks up at 90 degrees to the hook shank behind the cone.

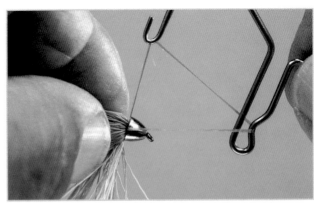

34. Whip finish just at the rear edge of the cone. Pull the hair back to keep it out of the way when you whip finish. When you tighten the whip finish, make sure you pull firmly on the thread to seat the whip finish over the hair that is bunched up against the cone.

35. Using the slope of the cone as a guide, trim the butt ends of the deer hair, being careful that your scissors do not extend over the tips of the hair collar so that you only cut the butt ends of the flared hair. Rotate the vise if you have a rotary vise, or otherwise take the hook out of the vise. Work gradually around the entire perimeter of the cone, making small cuts each time.

36. Take your time, and trim carefully. It will take several passes around the perimeter of the cone until you get all the butt ends flush with the end of the cone. It helps to have a pair of very sharp scissors with serrated blades.

37. Put a small drop of head cement on your dubbing needle, and work the head cement just inside the rear edge of the cone on top, bottom, and sides. This will ensure that the head cement secures both your whip finish and the butt ends of the hair.

38. Completed Conehead Bunny Muddler, showing proper proportions.

DEER HAIR BASS BUG

Deer hair bugs are time-consuming to tie, but to me, they are much more satisfying than just adding rubber legs and feathers to a hard plastic or cork body and painting it. Hard-bodied poppers seem more like building a model airplane than tying a fly. With hair bugs, you're either constructing the whole fly using techniques you have learned tying other patterns, or you'll learn new tricks you can use on trout or saltwater flies.

Deer hair bugs are often more effective at catching bass than hard-bodied flies. They have a different water entry, and when you pull one through the water, all the tiny surfaces and air pockets give the action a different effect. In my experience, they are more effective for smallmouth bass than hard-bodied poppers, perhaps because they behave differently than all the hard-bodied conventional lures bass see every day. An angler with a conventional rod can't duplicate the behavior of a hair bug in the water.

	Material	Substitutions
Hook	Stinger, size 1 through 2/0	Any heavy wire, long-shanked hook
Thread 1	Black 3/0 (140 denier)	Any color thread to match the color of the rear part of the fly
Thread 2	GSP (always off-white)	G size thread or 240 denier (not recommended)
Thread 3	Red 3/0 (140 denier)	Any color thread you want the head to be
Weed guard	20-pound fluorocarbon	Any relatively stiff monofilament, or leave off
Tail	Two full black marabou feathers	Any color marabou, or bucktail
Side tail 1	Two to four pink rubber legs	Any color rubber legs
Side tail 2	Four speckled hen feathers	Four wide saddle hackles
Hackle	Two wide black saddle hackles	Saddle hackles in any color
Body hair	Black, then red, then white deer body hair	Any combination of deer body hair, or a single color for the entire body
Legs	Two or three white rubber legs	Any color of type of rubber legs you want
Eyes	Doll eyes	3-D eyes or any type of raised eye

It's important to use deer belly hair for these bugs. It must be coarse and hollow to flare properly. Look for the coarsest hair you can find, and look for pieces of hair that are clean and even. It will make the preparation of the hair bunches much easier. Most of the trimming can be done with a double-edged razor blade, and don't be economical with the blades. Use one side per bug, or even do your rough-cutting with one side and your fine-tuning with the other. The blade may seem sharp after you've completed one bug, but to make clean cuts, the blade must be from-the-package sharp. I buy inexpensive ones online in lots of a hundred or more.

You can also use a good pair of sharp, serrated scissors. Scissors aren't as efficient for those first big cuts, but they work well for later trimming. Just make sure they are large, with blades at least two inches long, and that the blades have micro-serrations on them, which help grab the deer hair fibers as you cut.

Gel-spun polyester thread (GSP) works much better than other strong fly-tying threads. It's stronger than nylon or standard polyester threads, and it won't cut through the fibers like Kevlar thread. When you spin the deer hair on the hook, put enough pressure on the thread to bend the hook—this is why you need to brace the hook with your other hand as you secure the hair. The tighter you pull, the closer to the shank the thread will be, which ensures that you don't nick the tying thread as you trim the bug.

Don't be slavish about colors or materials for the tail, but do pay close attention to how the materials are applied. You will be spending a good part of a tying session making one of these, and you don't want it to fall apart after a few fish. Because you'll be using a heavy leader fishing for bass, the chances of losing a fly are slim and so you want this fly to last.

This fly also uses a lot of glue, so you may want to have several types on hand. I like UV epoxy to secure the weed guard windings and the head, Zap-A-Gap to secure each bunch of deer hair, and a flexible cement like Softex to stiffen the front face of the bug. But you can substitute standard head cement or any other strong adhesive for each step. Just know that if you don't use Zap-A-Gap or UV-cure epoxy, you may have to wait a bit before you start the next step because some cements take a few minutes to dry.

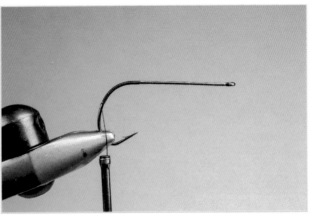

1. Start your black 3/0 thread just above the point of the hook, and wind back halfway down the bend.

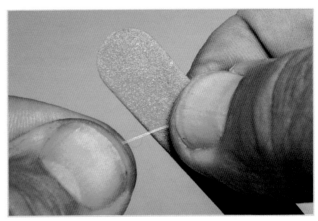

2. Cut a three- to four-inch piece of monofilament. Rough up the last half-inch with a piece of sandpaper, file, or emery board.

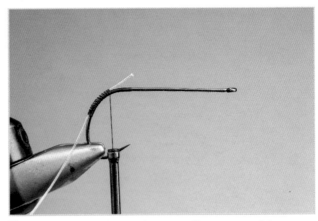

3. Wind the thread over the monofilament, working up the bend. Keep the monofilament on top of the hook by tweaking it back into place with your fingers if it slips to the far side.

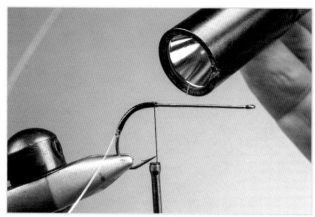

4. Wind to a point over the point of the hook, and cut the end of the monofilament close to the shank. Coat the thread windings with UV epoxy, and cure.

7. Tie the marabou in with three of four tight turns of thread, working slightly forward with each wrap.

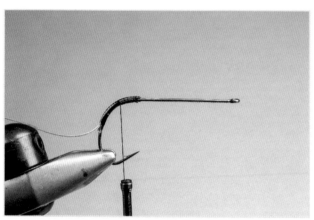

5. Wind the thread back to the point where it hangs over the rear end of the barb.

8. Lift the marabou straight up, and cut it off even with the end of the weed guard.

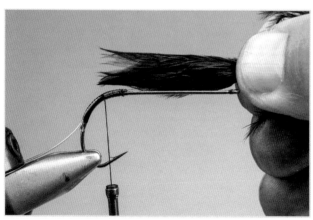

6. Select two wide, fluffy marabou feathers, and line up their tips. Wet the marabou to make it easier to handle. Measure the marabou so that it is about the length of the shank.

9. Wind over the butt ends of the marabou to smooth the base.

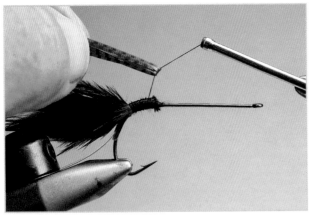

10. Fold the pink rubber legs over your thread, and work them in place on top of the hook shank.

11. Secure them facing backward with a few turns of thread.

12. Pull half of the rubber legs down on each side of the tail, and wind back over them to secure them in place.

13. Trim the rubber legs just a bit longer than the marabou tail.

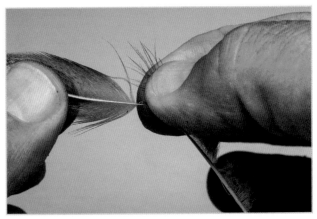

14. Select four spackled hen feathers (sometimes called hen back or hen saddle). From the tips of the feathers to the end of the tail should be equal to the length of the tail. Strip the heavy web from the base of the feathers.

15. Take two feathers and line up their tips. The convex side of one should face the concave face of the other one so their curvature matches. Repeat for the other two feathers.

16. Place one set of feathers on the far side of the hook shank, and tie them in place so they curve outwards.

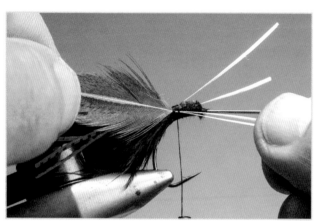

17. Tie the other set on the near side. If they don't flare outward to each side of the hook shank, work them in place with your fingers, or unwind and start over.

18. Once the feathers are in place, wind back over the stems to form a smooth base. Coat the thread winds with UV epoxy.

19. Cure the epoxy.

20. Return the thread to the place where all the winds end. Select two saddle hackles whose fibers are about equal to the gape of the hook. Strip the web from the stems and wind forward over the butt ends to where the thread ends.

21. Wind the saddle hackles forward, either both at the same time or one at a time, depending on which you find easier. Tie the tip ends in place, snip the ends, and wind a few tight turns over them.

22. Whip finish, or make a couple of half hitches. Add a drop of UV epoxy, and cure.

23. This is what the entire arrangement should look like from the top.

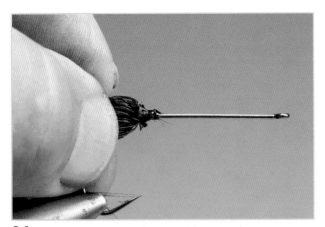

24. Cut a small piece of removable tape, about a half-inch long. Stroke the hackle fibers back with your fingers.

25. Lay the tape around the hackle fibers, and stick it in place, ensuring that the end of the tape does not extend forward of the black thread wraps.

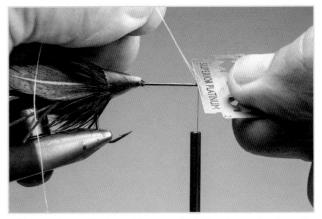

26. Put the GSP thread in your bobbin. Start the thread at the eye of the hook. GSP is difficult to cut with scissors, so you may wish to cut the tag end with a razor blade.

27. Work back to the tail, covering the shank with thread.

28. Cut a hunk of black deer hair from the hide. It should be equal to or slightly larger than the diameter of a pencil. Cut the hair as close to the hide as possible because the closer to the hide, the wider and hollower it is, meaning it will flare best.

29. Clean all the fuzz from the base of the hairs with a comb or your fingers. Fuzz prevents the hair from flaring properly.

30. Cut the tips off the hair so you are left with a bunch of hair that is even at both ends.

31. Grasp the hair in the middle. Lay the hair diagonally across the hook shank. It can be angled toward you or away from you—I like to alternate between these angles on each bunch because it seems to give more uniform bunches. Take one turn of thread loosely around the hair. It should be held securely in your fingers at this point.

32. Take a second turn of thread in exactly the same spot. This one should be slightly tighter, and you should begin to release the deer hair from your fingers.

33. Take a third turn and release the deer hair winding as tight as you can. Brace the tail materials in place with your other hand, as you should be winding tight enough to bend the hook. The hair should now flare 360 degrees around the hook.

34. Continue taking turns of thread in the same spot, four or five turns. Each turn should be as tight as you can make it, and be sure that you apply pressure up, down, away from you, and toward you. If the hair is still spinning around, keep applying tight turns until it almost stops spinning.

35. Push the hair back with your fingers. If it is not distributed equally around the hook shank, you can twist it or work the hairs in place. Inspect the hair from all sides to make sure it is evenly distributed.

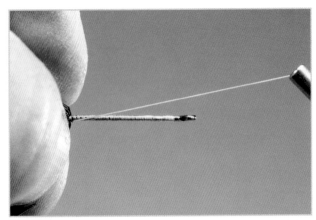

36. Bring the thread forward through the hair, parallel to the hook shank.

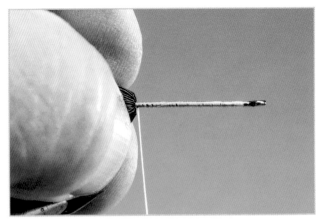

37. Make two tight turns of thread directly in front of the hair.

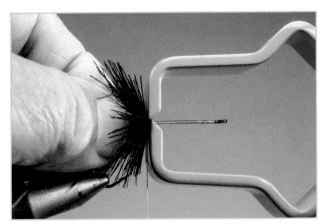

38. With your fingernails or a hair packing tool, keep pressure on the tails while pushing back firmly against the base of the hair.

39. Take two more turns of thread immediately in front of the hair, and add a tiny drop of Zap-A-Gap to the base of the thread.

40. Add a second bunch of black hair the same way you applied the first one. Be careful not to catch any of the hair from the previous turn. You can do this easily by holding back the previous bunch with your fingers while you apply the second bunch. Notice that I angled the hair against the shank opposite of the way I did the first bunch. I think this helps distribute the hair better, as there is always a bias of the way the hair flares from the initial angle. Pack the hair in the same way, and apply another drop of cement.

41. Keep adding bunches of black hair until you reach just shy of the midpoint of the hook. It typically takes about four bunches. If you check to make sure that all the hair is evenly distributed around the hook shank and stands at 90 degrees to it, you will get a nice clean line between the hair colors. The fish could care less though.

42. Prepare a bunch of red deer body hair in the same way you did the black. Spin it the same way, making sure you don't catch any of the black hairs as you spin it.

43. Add a second bunch of red hair.

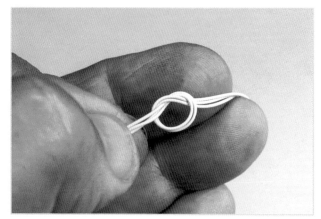

44. Tie the three white legs into an overhand knot. Try to work the knot into the middle.

45. Place the knot over the eye of the hook, and work back to the red hair.

46. Tighten the knot just in front of the hair. Pull it very tight, wind some thread back against it, and apply a drop of Zap-A-Gap.

47. Drape the legs back over the hair to keep them out of the way. You can trim the legs later.

48. Add two more bunches of red deer hair.

49. Switch to white deer hair, and add two or three more bunches. Stop when you have about 1/8 of the shank bare.

50. With sharp serrated scissors, cut the deer hair at the tail to form a vertical line between the shank and the body of the fly. Go around all sides. Trim the front end of the fly in the same way, so you are left with a relatively straight face in the front.

51. Turn the fly over so that it is upside-down in the vise. Pull the rubber legs straight up through the body so that you do not accidentally cut them off. With a new double-edge razor blade, cut from the head to the tail on the bottom of the fly so that you are left with about one-third of the hook gape under the fly.

52. Move the razor blade gently from side to side with a sawing motion, and the hair will cut away cleanly.

53. Pull the rubber legs to one side and trim one side of the fly so that it is also about one-third of the gape in length. It helps to look at the fly head-on when you do this. Pull the rubber legs to the other side, and trim the opposite side of the fly.

54. Now trim the top of the fly. This hair should be left longer. The best proportion for a bass bug is two-thirds of the body above the hook shank and one-third below. Make sure you pull the rubber legs straight down when you cut the top.

55. You will now be left with a rectangular shape.

56. Trim each of the corners on a 45-degree angle to give the fly a more rounded shape. Don't forget to pull the legs out of the way when you make each cut.

57. Trim a bit more to shape the fly into a rough cylinder. Make very small cuts with the razor blade, shaving off just tiny amounts of hair with each cut. If you prefer, you can also use sharp serrated scissors for shaping.

58. Carefully remove the tape that was holding the hackles out of the way. The easiest way to do this is to slip a sharp pair of scissors under the tape, make a tiny slit, and then carefully peel the tape away. Boil some water in a teakettle, and hold the fly in a pair of forceps in the steam for about 10 seconds—be careful the rubber legs don't touch the hot teakettle. Return the fly to the vise—the hackles should be nicely fluffed out, and the deer hair will expand and straighten slightly. Make some final trims of any hair that has expanded and risen up beyond the shape of the fly.

59. Attach the red thread to the shank just behind the eye.

60. Bring the weed guard forward, and take two or three turns of thread over it. Leave it a bit long. Rough up the monofilament just above the hook eye.

61. Pull the weed guard up until it forms a loop under the hook that extends just beyond the hook point. Secure it in place with a dozen very tight turns of thread. Some tiers run the weed guard through the eye and then bend it backward, which is a little more secure. But it takes up quite a bit of space in the eye, and if you plan on using very heavy tippet for bass, you may not have enough room in the eye.

62. Snip the end of the weed guard.

63. Whip finish the head. Coat the thread wraps and the entire face of the fly with UV cure epoxy. Preen the face in place with your fingers to form a flat head that is 90 degrees to the hook shank. Once it looks right, hit the head and the face of the fly with a UV light. The solid face of the fly will give it a better popping action in the water.

64. Turn the fly sideways in the vise. Pick the eyes you want to add. Make a slight divot in the deer hair with fine scissors. Check to make sure the eye will fit into the divot.

65. Fill the divot with a strong, viscous cement like Marine Goop, Liquid Fusion, or arrow fletching cement.

66. Press the eyes into place.

67. You can trim the rubber legs shorter or keep them long as I have here.

PUGLISI SPAWNING SHRIMP

This is one of the more difficult saltwater flies to tie, but I figured I would give you a challenge. If you can tie this one, you can tie almost any saltwater pattern. The main reason I included it is because the Puglisi Spawning Shrimp is such an effective and popular fly. From Christmas Island to Cuba, it's always on the list of recommended flies. It's my go-to bonefish pattern, and I have had trips where I stuck with it for an entire week of fishing. Perk Perkins, the retired CEO of Orvis, is also a big fan of the fly, and he spends over half of every year chasing bonefish. In fact, the people who manage the fly inventory at Orvis call it "Perk's Special Fly," and it is required to always be in stock.

Enrico Puglisi developed this fly for bonefish, but anglers soon found out it is a deadly fly for permit, especially when tied with solid metal eyes. It also catches snook, sea trout, striped bass, triggerfish, and many other species—there are few saltwater fish that won't eat a shrimp. For Cuba, the Bahamas, and the Florida Keys, this fly is typically tied in size 4, but it is also used as large as size 2. For Mexico, Belize, Hawaii, and Christmas Island, it is more often used in size 6 or even size 8, although tying it on a size 8 hook gets a little tricky because there is a lot of stuff to cram on that short shank.

Many guides recommend tying bonefish flies on non-flashy hooks, especially where the fish are heavily pressured. The black seems to be subtler and is less likely to alert the fish that a fly is a fake. I have tied it here on a size 4 Gamakatsu SL45, but for less pressured fish, a brighter, stainless hook is fine. For permit, you probably want to

use a heavier, size 2 or 4 stainless hook because the SL45 wire is slightly thinner—fine for bonefish but I'm not sure I would trust it to a 30-pound permit. Just don't try this fly on a short-shanked saltwater hook, as there is just not enough room.

The unusual way the weed guard is crimped was shown to me by my saltwater fishing buddy Aaron Adams. Bending the legs of the weed guard flat ensures that the hook point does not catch on weeds or coral, but it also exposes the hook point with very little pressure when a fish takes the fly. I have always been suspicious of weed guards, thinking that they often act as fish guards, but this method will protect your hook point without stopping you from hooking a fish.

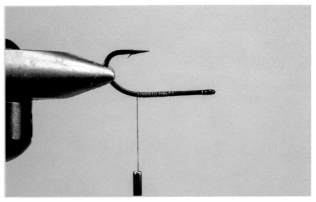

1. Place your hook in the vise upside-down. It's best to angle your vise horizontally if you have a rotary vise, which makes it easier to work on the far side of the hook

	Material	Substitutions
Hook	Gamakatsu SL45 size 2-6	Standard length stainless saltwater hooks
Thread	6/0 orange	Tan, white, olive, or red, depending on shrimp species
Egg sack	Bright orange EP Silky Fibers	Any bright orange yarn
Eyes	Small black shrimp eyes	Tan or white eyes, depending on prevailing shrimp species
Antennae	Black Flashabou and pearl Krystal Flash	Any sparkly flash material in pearl and black
Legs	Brown Sili Legs	Brown, tan, or clear mottled Sili Legs, Tentacle Legs, or fine rubber legs
Carapace	Tan EP Fiber	Tan Craft Fur, or any other fine synthetic hair
Rear body	Pearl Angel Hair, chopped up and dubbed on a loop.	An easier but less durable route is to just dub a pearl sparkle dubbing directly to waxed thread
Front body	Tan EP Shrimp Brush	Tan Foxy Brush or any other brush that is between 1½ and ½ inches wide, depending on the size of the fly
Eyes	Gold bead chain	Solid metal eyes or plastic eyes in any color
Weed guard	20- to 30-pound monofilament	You can just leave the weed guard off if you are feeling brave

when needed. Start your thread in the middle of the hook, and wind back to where the bend just begins.

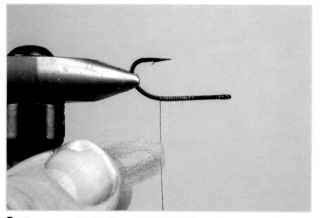

2. Cut a two-inch piece of Silky Fiber about one-eighth-inch diameter or slightly larger. Fold it over the tying thread.

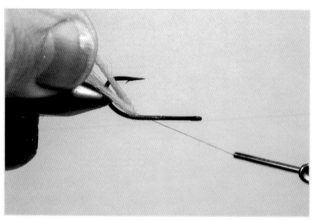

3. Bring the thread to the top of the hook, and slide and manipulate the folded yarn until it sits on top of the hook.

4. Pull one end of the yarn parallel to the near side of the hook, and bind it in place with about three turns of thread.

5. Wind the other end of the yarn forward for about three turns of thread, and fold on back against the far side of the hook shank.

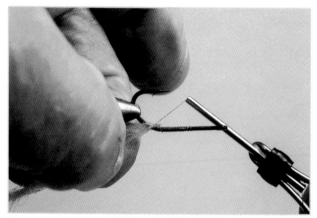

6. Wind the thread back over the yarn so that the yarn is evenly distributed around the hook.

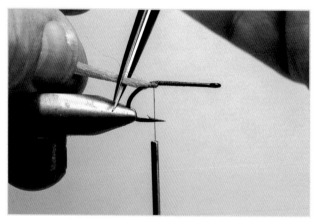

7. Rotate the vise so that the point is now down or remove the hook from the vise, and turn it right-side-up. Trim the yarn so that it extends just slightly beyond the bend.

8. Lay one shrimp eye against the shank so that the eyeball extends just beyond the egg sack. Grab it at the end of the tie-in point with a pair of pliers.

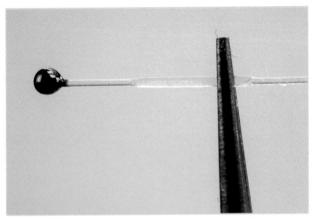

9. Crimp the stem of the eye from the point where you grabbed it, and keep crimping away from the eyeball for about one-half inch.

10. Take the second eye, line it up with the first, and crimp it in the same place.

11. Tie in one eye on the near side of the hook shank, on the near side of the hook (not on top). It may help to rotate the vise jaws so that the rear side of the hook is facing up. Wind toward the eye for a half-dozen turns, and then return the thread to the rear tie-in point.

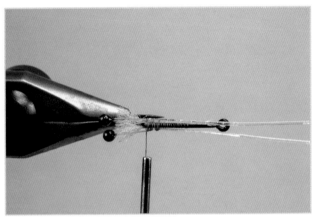

12. Adjust your vise so that the rear side is facing up. Line up the eye, and tie it in, making sure that the stem of the eye is tied in along the far side of the hook shank (which at this point is the upper side).

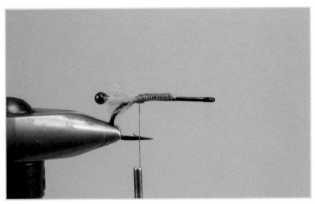

13. Work the eyes into place to that they lie on each side of the egg sack. Wind forward over the stems to the middle of the hook shank with tight turns. Keep adjusting the eyes if necessary. Trim the ends of the stems. Return the thread to that same rear tie-in point.

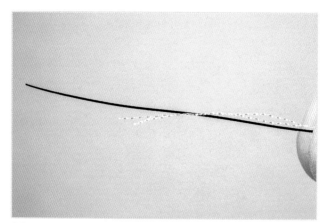

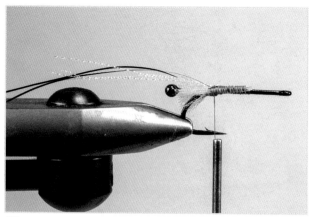

14. Trim two strands of pearl Krystal Flash to about three inches. Add a single strand of black Flashabou that is about four inches long. Line them up so that the black Flashabou extends beyond each end of the Krystal Flash. It makes the strands easier to manipulate if you wet them.

17. Bind the strands down with about three turns of thread.

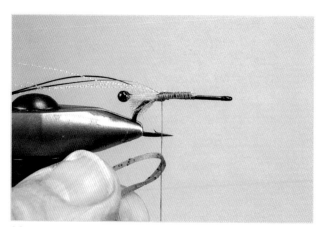

15. Fold the strands over the hook shank at about their midpoint. Don't worry about being too exact—they look more natural slightly staggered but with the black strands about 30 percent longer than the pearl strands.

18. Cut two or three Sili Legs to about four inches long. Fold them over the thread as you did with the flash strands.

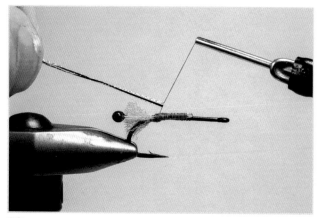

16. Manipulate the strands so that the midpoint is on top of the hook shank and at the rearmost turn of thread.

19. Bind the rubber legs in place as you did with the flash strands. Smooth out the wraps with a few more turns of thread. Again, the legs don't need to be perfectly even. It may be helpful to add a tiny drop of Super Glue to the winds at this point.

20. Cut about a quarter-inch diameter of EP Fiber, approximately two inches in length. Taper both ends by holding the bunch loosely with one hand while very gently teasing out some of the fibers with your other hand. A very light touch helps. If you pulled out any fibers that are much longer than the rest, just pluck them out.

21. Tie in the fibers over that same tie-in point. The part extending over the legs should be slightly shorter than the part extending over the eye. The fibers should extend about one shank length over the legs.

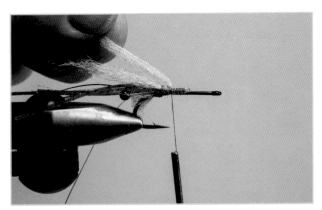

22. Wind forward over the fibers for about four turns. Then fold the forward-facing fibers back over the rear ones. The top fibers should be slightly longer than the bottom ones. If they aren't, unwind and re-adjust them, or trim the fibers and try again. This process is pretty

fiddly, but having the top fibers slightly longer gives the carapace a nice shape.

23. Wind back to the rear tie-in point, binding both bunches of fibers in place. Even up any bumps by winding thread over them to form a smooth underbody.

24. Form a dubbing loop by pulling about two-and-a-half inches of thread from the bobbin, then pulling more thread from the bobbin as you return the thread to the tie-in point.

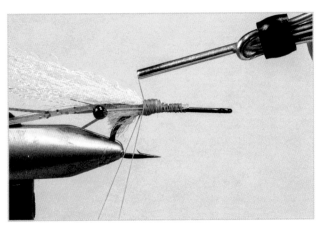

25. Wind back over the place where the loop was formed to bind it in place.

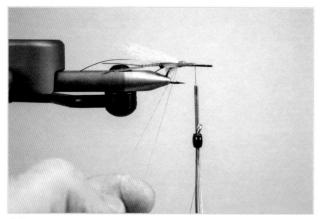

26. Advance the thread to the midpoint of the hook shank.

27. Chop up a small pile of pearl Angel Hair with your scissors. The fibers should be chopped to roughly one-quarter inch.

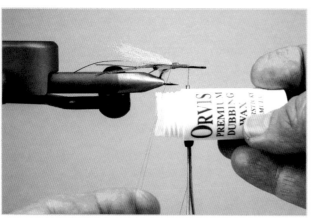

28. Wax both sides of the dubbing loop with a generous amount of wax.

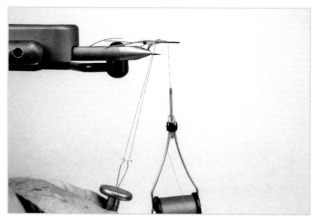

29. Attach a dubbing spinner to the bottom of the loop by hooking each end of the spinner.

30. Arrange the chopped Angel Hair inside the dubbing loop so that it fills about three-quarters of the loop.

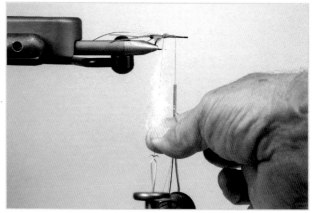

31. Pinch the loop just below the Angel Hair, and spin or twirl the spinner. Slowly open up pressure with your fingers after spinning. This helps to keep the hair from flying off the loop. Continue to spin until the hair is tightly wound around the loop. Pluck any extra-long fibers from the loop.

32. Wind the dubbing forward to the middle of the hook shank. Tie it off with three tight turns of thread.

33. Advance the thread to just behind the eye. Place a set of eyes on top of the shank, and wind diagonally through the eyes with about six turns.

34. Adjust the eyes so they are centered. Make the same number of tight turns on the opposite diagonal. Go back and forth between these diagonals for another round. Once the eyes are in place apply as much pressure as you can to the thread.

35. Wind around the base of the eyes on a horizontal plane to lock the eyes into place. These turns should be as tight as you can make them without breaking the thread. You will need at least ten turns. Apply a drop of Super Glue to the base of the eyes. If you need detailed close-ups of how to apply the eyes, see the pattern description for the Clouser Minnow on pages 85–86.

36. Wind back to the middle of the hook shank. Strip or trim the hairs from about one-eighth inch of a piece of EP Shrimp Dub.

37. Wind the exposed wire of the Shrimp Dub forward to the eyes.

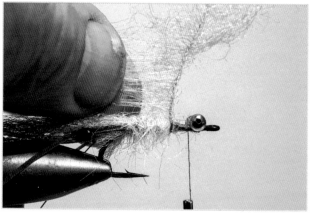

38. Wind the Shrimp Dub forward, stroking the fibers back as you wind so they flow back toward the bend of the hook. Make only three to four turns. You don't want this to be heavily filled in.

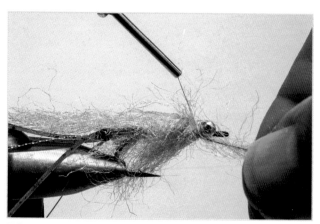

39. Tie the Shrimp Dub off with about four tight turns of thread.

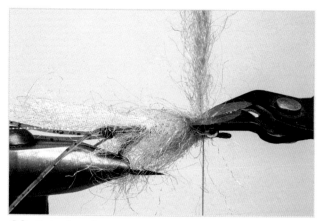

40. Snip the wire of the Shrimp Dub with small wire cutters.

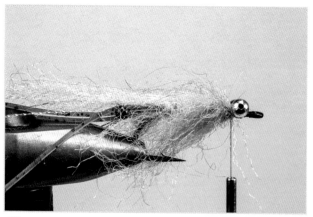

41. Wind over the end of the wire with a few more turns.

42. Cut about a three-inch piece of monofilament. Find the approximate middle, and flatten just a small area with pliers. Fold the monofilament over (it will fold where you crimped it), and angle it over the eye of the hook, loop end up, angling back about 45 degrees toward the hook point. Tie it in with only three turns of thread.

43. Turn the hook over in the vise, and pull the mono until the crimped spot is locked against the hook shank. Bind it in place with a half dozen turns of thread after ensuring that both legs straddle the hook point.

44. Trim the mono so that both legs extend halfway to the bend of the hook.

45. Grab both legs of the mono gently with your pliers just ahead of the hook point, and bend them over flat.

46. With a piece of male Velcro on a stick, a carding comb, or other combing tool, stroke the Shrimp Dub fibers back, pulling out any fibers that are bound under. The fibers should be relatively wispy and flow back toward the hook bend.

47. Whip finish, and apply head cement or UV epoxy to the head and to the wraps between the eyes.

48. The finished fly.

PARACHUTE ADAMS DRY

Based on sales, the Parachute Adams is the most popular fly in the world. It's not a fad (the basic Adams is almost a hundred years old, and the parachute version has been used for at least fifty), and it's not because of some robust marketing program. Any fly that stays around this long has universal appeal that defies analysis, like Beethoven symphonies or chocolate chip cookies. Trout respond to this fly, regardless of prevailing hatches or water conditions. If they are willing to take a dry fly, they'll eagerly accept a Parachute Adams. It's almost like cheating.

I have my theories about this fly. The gray body probably suggests any color to the fish, its neutral shade negating any warning signs that a more definitive color would suggest. The fish can't find fault with it. The mixed brown and grizzly hackle are similarly acceptable, with the added benefit of the barred grizzly hackle suggesting movement, the whirring of wings, the delicate dance of insect legs, or the struggles of an insect trying to shed its nymph shuck. And the white wings are visible to the angler under almost any circumstances. Not only does a visible fly make it easy to see when a trout inhales the fly—it also enables the fly fisher to track the fly's progress, making sure it drifts in the right current lane and is not subjected to drag.

The fly was first tied with wings of calf tail. Calf tail is durable and sheds water reasonably well, but the wing often looks spindly and is thus not as visible on the water. Calf body hair replaces calf tail on most commercial flies, as it can be stacked to even out the ends, and the resulting fly looks better and offers a more distinct wing. But calf body hair, fine textured and uniform, soaks up water easily and thus weighs down the fly and reduces visibility. In addition, tying in enough calf tail or body hair to create a visible wing adds a lot of bulk to the body of the fly, creating a lump in the body that negates a delicate insect shape. I resisted the temptation to use a synthetic for a wing for years, just because the Parachute Adams is such a classic fly, but at last I've given in to modern technology. You can create a large wing profile without bulk, it's easier to tie parachute hackle to a synthetic wing post, the material does not need to be stacked, and you simply trim the wing to shape after tying. Synthetics also shed water better than calf body hair, and they accept fly floatant well.

I learned this method of tying the wing post and winding hackle from Tim Flagler of Tightline Productions, whose videos are the best instructional tools on the internet. The standard method involves winding the hackle down the parachute post and then trying to tie off the hackle over the eye of the hook. It's hard to see what you're doing in this method, and the result is often sloppy, with hackle sticking out over the eye of the hook. Tying the wing and hackle in this unconventional sideways manner ensures that no hackle fibers block the eye of the fly and that the body of the fly is smooth and continuous. It's also easier to wind the hackle down the post from this side view, which is more intuitive for most fly tiers. Whip finishing around the parachute post ensures that the eye of the fly stays clear and is easily threaded with tippet. Once you tie parachutes this way, you'll never go back to the conventional way of winding around the wing from the standard view and tying off the hackle just in front of the eye.

I urge you to try this fly with saddle hackle if you can find the right size. Saddle hackles offer thinner stems, which make it easier to wind two hackles around a parachute post, and they have denser fibers, so you need fewer turns of hackle. With a good domestic saddle hackle, you should be able to tie three or even four flies with a single hackle. Neck hackles work fine, but the resulting fly just does not look as clean. The fish won't care, but you will when you show off your flies to your fishing buddies.

	Material	Substitutions
Hook	Standard dry fly, sizes 10-20	Bigeye hook, sizes 14-20
Thread	Black, 6/0 or 8/0 depending on size	White or gray thread
Tails	Mixed brown and grizzly hackle fibers	Just brown or just grizzly. The fish won't care.
Wing post	White EP Fiber or Para Post	White calf tail or calf body hair
Hackle	One brown and one grizzly hackle	Just grizzly, mixed cream and grizzly, or dun and grizzly
Body	Gray muskrat fur	Natural gray rabbit fur, Australian possum fur, or fine synthetic dubbing

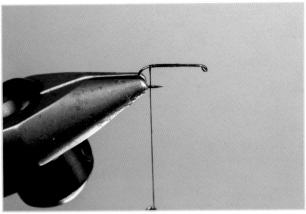

1. Secure a dry fly hook in the vise, start the thread in the middle, and wind smoothly back to the point where the hook bend just starts to slant downward.

2. From a spade hackle, pluck about 10 brown fibers from the feather, pulling them at 90 degrees to the hackle stem and plucking them from the stem in a quick, deliberate movement.

3. Carefully lay these hackle fibers on the edge of a Post-it pad or similar object so that about a third of the fibers extend over the edge.

4. Pluck a similar amount of grizzly hackle fibers. Lay them alongside the brown fibers with their ends even with the ends of the brown fibers. Tweak them with your fingers or a pair of forceps until they are lined up.

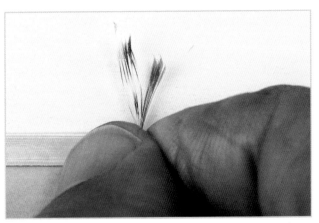

5. Carefully grab all the fibers together in your thumb and index finger.

6. Measure the fibers against the hook shank so that one shank length extends beyond the end of your thumbnail. Transfer the fibers to your other hand if necessary.

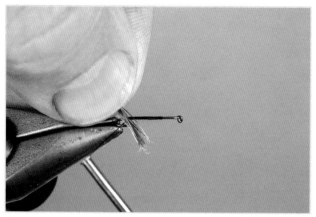

7. Tie the fibers in using the 45-degree roll method.

8. Wind forward halfway to the eye, and trim any fibers that extend beyond this point.

9. Wind the thread forward to a point just shy of the eye. Wind back until the thread hangs at a point that is about one-quarter shank length back from the eye.

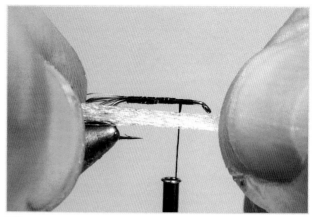

10. Cut a piece of synthetic wing fiber that is about one-third hook gape in diameter when compressed. Two to three inches long is about right (it will be trimmed shorter at the end, but a longer piece makes the wing easier to work with).

11. Tie the wing to the top of the hook shank with the finger on the far side method. Secure with four or five tight turns of thread. Try to keep the turns in the same spot above the hook shank.

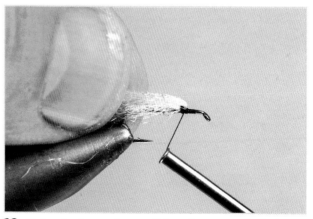

12. Raise the forward part of the wing up, and wind a half dozen turns in front of it. Make these turns tight against the yarn.

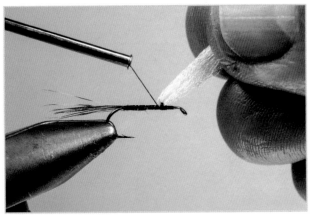

13. Repeat the process and the rear of the wing.

14. Raise both pieces straight up. Wind the thread up around the base of the wing post, extending up on the post a short distance. It helps here to smooth out your thread by spinning the bobbin counterclockwise. Wind back down to the base of the wing.

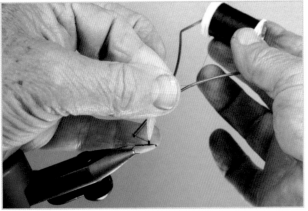

15. I find it easiest to hold the wing with the thumb and index finger of one hand, bringing the bobbin around the wing with the other hand, and then catching the bobbin on the far side with the last three fingers of the hand holding the wing. You can then use them to hand off the bobbin to your free hand.

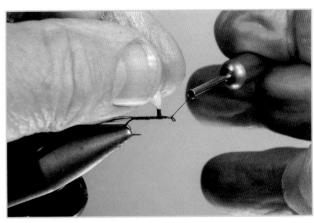

16. Wind forward to just shy of the eye.

17. Prepare a brown and grizzly hackle. Fan the feathers together around the hook to check that the fibers extend from one-and-a-half to two times the gape of the hook. It makes a neater fly if you can find two feathers that have the same fiber length when fanned. These two hackles align perfectly.

18. In this pair of hackles, the brown is shorter than the grizzly, and the finished parachute won't look as neat.

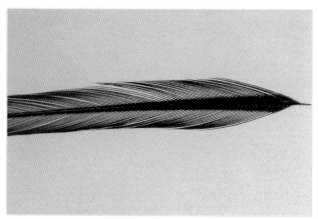

19. Look for the point up on the stem where webby fibers occupy only a small portion at the base of the feather. Strip the webby fibers from the bottom of each feather.

20. Line up both feathers so their stripped fibers align. Estimate how much bare stem will allow you to wind back from the eye and up to the end of the post.

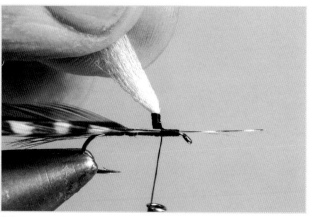

21. Bind the stems to the hook by winding back from the eye to the base of the post.

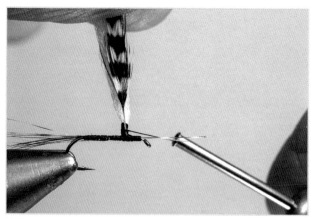

22. Wrap them up around the post until they stick straight up. Hold the wing upright with one hand as you do this.

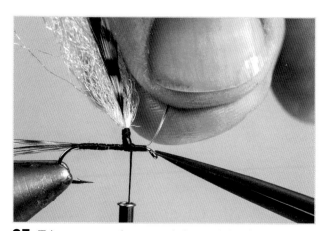

23. Trim any stem that extends beyond the tie-in point.

24. Take the thread back to the initial tie-in point at the tails.

25. Take a tiny amount of dubbing, just a wisp of fuzz, and dub it to the tying thread as close to the hook shank as possible. Scoot this first bunch of dubbing up against the hook shank by pulling it gently upward until it just touches the shank.

26. Take a second, slightly larger diameter bunch of dubbing, and dub it in just below the first bunch. Blend it in so that you start to accomplish a smooth taper. Keep repeating the process with slightly larger bunches until you have a smooth tapered dubbing noodle (about three inches long for a size 14). You can always remove some dubbing if you have too much or add some if you run short.

27. Wind the dubbing forward in tight, adjacent turns, making sure you cover the black thread at the base of the tail, that you have no thread showing between turns, and that no lumps form.

28. When you get to the base of the wing, make sure you sneak the dubbing in tightly at the base of the wing so no black thread shows.

29. Wind up to the eye. At this point, it's necessary to have a thin dubbing noodle. You may want to remove some fur and re-tighten the dubbing, or you may need to add just a wisp more.

30. Wind the dubbing back to the base of the wing. The dubbing should end here. Remove any if you still have more on your thread.

31. Take two horizontal turns of thread around the wing post.

32. Remove the hook from the vise, and reposition it so that it points straight down. If you have a rotary vise, it's helpful to angle your jaws at the horizontal.

33. Apply a small amount of UV-cure epoxy to only the bare thread stem. Be sure none of the epoxy gets on the hackles. Just about a half drop of epoxy should do it. This gives the stem more durability, and the additional stiffness makes it easier to wind the hackles around the base.

34. Cure the epoxy with a UV flashlight.

35. Grab one of the hackles with your fingers if it's long enough or with hackle pliers if desired. Wind toward the wing base. The turns should not overlap and should be evenly spaced. Three to four turns are usually adequate. I like the shiny side of the hackle facing up (toward the end of the wing in this position). I think it looks better, but there is no pragmatic reason not to have the dull side up. You may need to twist or manipulate the hackle slightly to get it to flip over to the side you want. It does not matter which hackle you wind first.

36. Tie off the hackle against the wing post with three tight turns. Make sure that when you secure the hackle, the thread crosses over it. This will happen if you angle the feather slightly away from the wing and keep the thread in line with the hook shank. Wiggle the tying thread slightly as you wind over the hackle to help avoid any fibers getting bound under. When you do this, be careful to angle your thread so that it does not bind under any of the hackle you just wound, and take care not to catch the tails or the eye as you wind.

37. Carefully snip the end of the hackle with the finest-tipped scissors you own.

38. Wind the second feather in the same manner, gently wiggling it side to side to keep from binding down fibers from the previous hackle.

39. Tie off the second feather in the same manner. Trim the end of the hackle in the same way.

40. With a long whip finisher (often called an extended-reach whip finisher), make a whip finish around the base of the wing. Take your time, and try not to catch any hackle fibers. (If you do, they can always be snipped away.) As before, it helps to wiggle the whip finish tool slightly as you do this.

41. Trim any fibers that got bound under and did not stay in line with your fine-pointed scissors.

42. Carefully place a drop of thin head cement at the base of the wing, over the whip finish wraps.

44. If you want to get fancy, you can taper the edges of the wing slightly to a more natural shape.

43. Trim the wing so that it is about one shank length in height.

45. You can see how tying a parachute fly in this manner gives you a clean, tapered body with no hackle to obscure the hook eye.

DRY FLIES

Attractors

21ST CENTURY ADAMS

- **Size:** 12-20.
- **Hook:** Standard dry fly.
- **Thread:** Gray 8/0.
- **Tail:** Four Fibbetts or similar clear synthetic, long and split.
- **Body:** Gray fur.
- **Wing:** Grizzly hen hackles, tied in at tips and snipped.
- **Hackle:** Brown and grizzly mixed.
- **Difficulty:** 3.

ADAMS' PARACHUTE

- **Size:** 14-20.
- **Hook:** Extra-fine dry.
- **Thread:** Black 6/0 or 8/0.
- **Tail:** Brown and grizzly hackle fibers, mixed.
- **Body:** Muskrat fur or gray dubbing.
- **Wing:** White calf tail, upright in a single clump.
- **Hackle:** Brown and grizzly tied parachute style around wing base.
- **Difficulty:** 3.

ADAMS

- **Size:** 10-22.
- **Hook:** Extra-fine dry; Bigeye dry in smaller sizes.
- **Thread:** Black 8/0.
- **Tail:** Brown and grizzly hackle fibers.
- **Body:** Muskrat or medium gray dubbing.
- **Wing:** Grizzly hackle tips, upright and divided.
- **Hackle:** Brown and grizzly, mixed.
- **Difficulty:** 3.

ADAMS' TRUDE

- **Size:** 10-14.
- **Hook:** Extra-fine dry.
- **Thread:** Black 6/0.
- **Tail:** Moose mane.
- **Body:** Gray dubbing.
- **Wing:** White calf tail, down-wing style.
- **Hackle:** Mixed brown and grizzly.
- **Difficulty:** 3.

ADAMS WULFF

- **Size:** 10-16.
- **Hook:** Extra-fine dry.
- **Thread:** Gray 6/0.
- **Tail:** Moose body hair.
- **Body:** Gray fur.
- **Wing:** White calf tail, upright and divided.
- **Hackle:** Mixed brown and grizzly, heavy.
- **Difficulty:** 3.

AUSABLE WULFF

- **Size:** 10-18.
- **Hook:** Extra-fine dry.
- **Thread:** Hot orange 6/0.
- **Tail:** Woodchuck tail fibers or moose body hair.
- **Body:** Bleached Australian possum or other tan fur.
- **Wing:** White calf tail, upright and divided.
- **Hackle:** Brown and grizzly, mixed.
- **Difficulty:** 4.

BEAN'S ORANGE CRUSH

- **Size:** 6-10
- **Hook:** 3X-long nymph.
- **Thread:** Orange 6/0.
- **Body:** Peacock shade synthetic sparkle dubbing.
- **Rib:** Light ginger hackle, palmered through body.
- **Wing:** Two pieces of foam cemented together and laid over body, then secured at bend and at head.
- **Head:** Orange on bottom, tan on top.
- **Legs:** Two Tentacle Legs, secured where foam is lashed down.
- **Indicator:** Two bright yellow tabs of foam tied in where wing is secured.
- **Difficulty:** 3.

BUGMEISTER

- **Size:** 4-14.
- **Color Options:** Peacock, golden, royal.
- **Hook:** 2X-long dry.
- **Thread:** Black 6/0.
- **Tail:** Light elk body hair, stacked.
- **Body:** Peacock herl or Antron/hare dubbing, picked out.
- **Rib:** Fine copper or gold wire.
- **Wing:** Light elk body hair over peacock herl and pearl Krystal Flash.
- **Hackle:** Grizzly or brown, tied parachute style.
- **Thorax:** Peacock herl
- **Wing post:** White calf body hair, Z-Lon, or Antron.
- **Difficulty:** 4.

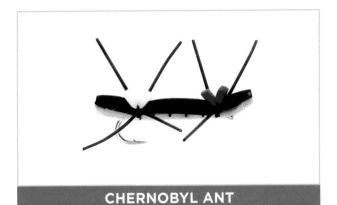

CHERNOBYL ANT

- **Size:** 6-14.
- **Hook:** 3X-long nymph.
- **Thread:** Black 6/0.
- **Body:** Tan foam, left long at tail and over head.
- **Rib:** Tying thread.
- **Wing:** Black foam, laid over tan and secured with glue over head and tail.
- **Legs:** Olive Tentacle Legs, two at each place foam is tied down.
- **Indicator:** Bright red tab of foam at forward tie-in point; white foam at rear tie-in point.
- **Difficulty:** 3.

GRIFFIN'S STIMICATOR FLY

- **Size:** 8-18.
- **Hook:** Curved nymph.
- **Thread:** Orange 6/0.
- **Tail:** Yearling elk.
- **Body:** Orange dubbing.
- **Rib:** Brown hackle palmered through body, followed by fine gold wire.
- **Underwing:** Orange Krystal Flash.
- **Head:** Orange or chartreuse foam bead glued just behind eye.
- **Difficulty:** 3.

HARE'S EAR PARACHUTE

- **Size:** 12-16.
- **Hook:** Extra-fine dry.
- **Thread:** Tan 6/0.
- **Tail:** Natural deer body hair tips.
- **Body:** Rough and full, dubbed with dark hare's-ear dubbing.
- **Wing:** White calf tail, tied as a single post.
- **Hackle:** Grizzly, parachute style.
- **Difficulty:** 3.

HOLO HUMPY

- **Size:** 10-16.
- **Hook:** Standard dry.
- **Thread:** Black 6/0.
- **Tail:** Moose mane.
- **Body:** Flashabou, covered with head cement or thin epoxy.
- **Overbody:** Black foam pulled over the top of body.
- **Wing:** In three parts: fine orange poly yarn over white poly yarn over midge pearl Krystal Flash. Wing extends back over the body, and a short stub is left in front of the hackle.
- **Hackle:** Brown.
- **Legs:** Four Tentacle Legs tied in at wing tie-in point.
- **Difficulty:** 4.
- **Notes:** Popular body colors are lime, purple, red, and orange. EP Fibers or Trigger Point fibers are one type of fine poly yarn.

INDICATOR KLINKHAMMER

▌ **Size:** 12-16.
▌ **Hook:** Sedge.
▌ **Thread:** Tan 8/0.
▌ **Body:** Rusty brown dubbing.
▌ **Thorax:** Peacock-colored synthetic sparkle dubbing.
▌ **Wing:** Yellow and orange Para Post or EP Fiber.
▌ **Hackle:** Grizzly, parachute.
▌ **Difficulty:** 2.

KICKING KLINK

▌ **Size:** 12-16.
▌ **Hook:** Sedge.
▌ **Thread:** To match body color.
▌ **Body:** Thinly dubbed fur.
▌ **Wing:** Clear Antron or poly yarn.
▌ **Hackle:** Brown tied parachute around wing.
▌ **Legs:** Two fine Tentacle Legs on each side.
▌ **Difficulty:** 3.
▌ **Notes:** Popular colors are olive and mahogany, but body can be made in any color to match prevalent insects.

IRRESISTIBLE

▌ **Size:** 10-16.
▌ **Hook:** Extra-fine dry.
▌ **Thread:** Black 6/0.
▌ **Tail:** Brown hackle fibers or mink-tail guard hairs.
▌ **Body:** Spun gray deer hair clipped to shape.
▌ **Wing:** Grizzly hackle tips, upright and divided.
▌ **Hackle:** Brown and grizzly mixed.
▌ **Difficulty:** 4.

KLINKHAMMER

▌ **Size:** 10-16.
▌ **Color Options:** Gray, brown, olive, tan.
▌ **Hook:** Extra-fine dry.
▌ **Thread:** Tan 6/0.
▌ **Wing:** White Antron.
▌ **Hackle:** Brown, parachute style.
▌ **Abdomen:** Dubbed fur.
▌ **Thorax:** Peacock herl.
▌ **Difficulty:** 3.
▌ **Notes:** The body should be started on the bend of the hook to get a curved shape.

MOSQUITO DRY FLY

- **Size:** 12-18.
- **Hook:** Standard dry.
- **Thread:** Black 8/0.
- **Tail:** Grizzly hackle fibers.
- **Body:** One dark and one light piece of moose mane, wound together.
- **Wing:** Grizzly hackle tips.
- **Hackle:** Grizzly.
- **Difficulty:** 2.
- **Notes:** Add thin head cement over the body for durability.

PATRIOT

- **Size:** 12-18.
- **Hook:** Extra-fine dry.
- **Thread:** Brown 6/0.
- **Tail:** Light deer-body hair.
- **Body:** Three strands of smolt-blue Krystal Flash with a mid-band of two or three turns of red floss.
- **Wing:** White Antron yarn, upright and divided.
- **Hackle:** Brown neck hackle.
- **Difficulty:** 3.

PMX

- **Size:** 10-16.
- **Hook:** 3X-long nymph.
- **Thread:** Black 6/0.
- **Tail:** Yearling elk hair.
- **Body:** Red floss rear two-thirds, front third peacock herl.
- **Wing:** Yearling elk.
- **Post:** Large bunch of white Para Post or other poly yarn.
- **Hackle:** Grizzly, parachute.
- **Legs:** Two brown rubber legs on each side.
- **Difficulty:** 3.
- **Notes:** This is the red version. Other body colors include olive and Royal (the Royal also features a small butt of peacock herl in addition to the red floss body and peacock herl thorax).

PURPLE PARACHUTE ADAMS

- **Size:** 12-20.
- **Hook:** Standard dry.
- **Thread:** Black 8/0.
- **Tail:** Mixed grizzly and brown hackle fibers.
- **Body:** Rear two-thirds purple floss, front third purple dubbing.
- **Wing:** White calf tail.
- **Hackle:** Mixed grizzly and brown wound parachute style around wing.
- **Difficulty:** 3.

ROYAL COACHMAN

- **Size:** 12-16.
- **Hook:** Extra-fine dry.
- **Thread:** Black 6/0.
- **Tail:** Golden pheasant tippets or brown hackle fibers.
- **Body:** Peacock herl in two sections with a red floss center band.
- **Wing:** White duck-wing quill segments, upright and divided.
- **Hackle:** Brown.
- **Difficulty:** 4.

ROYAL TRUDE DRY FLY

- **Size:** 10-18.
- **Hook:** Standard dry.
- **Thread:** Black 8/0.
- **Tail:** Golden pheasant tippets.
- **Body:** Rear third peacock herl, middle third red floss, front third peacock herl.
- **Wing:** White calf tail tied down over body.
- **Hackle:** Brown.
- **Difficulty:** 3.

ROYAL HUMPY

- **Size:** 12-18.
- **Hook:** Standard dry.
- **Thread:** Red 6/0.
- **Tail:** Moose mane.
- **Body:** Red floss with elk hair overlay on top.
- **Wing:** White calf tail.
- **Hackle:** Brown.
- **Difficulty:** 3.

ROYAL WULFF

- **Size:** 10-18
- **Hook:** Extra-fine dry.
- **Thread:** Black 6/0.
- **Tail:** Brown bucktail
- **Body:** Red floss flanked front and rear with peacock herl.
- **Wing:** White calf tail or calf body hair, upright and divided.
- **Hackle:** Brown.
- **Difficulty:** 4.

TACTICAL USUAL

- **Size:** 12-22.
- **Hook:** Wide gape tactical.
- **Thread:** Bright orange 8/0.
- **Tail:** Snowshoe rabbit foot tied heavy.
- **Body:** Tan fur or dubbing from snowshoe rabbit foot underfur.
- **Wing:** Snowshoe rabbit foot tied heavy.
- **Difficulty:** 1.
- **Notes:** The wing should be allowed to splay 180 degrees around the top half of the hook to provide stability.

TURCK'S TARANTULA

- **Size:** 8-12.
- **Color Options:** Green, tan, red.
- **Hook:** 2X-long dry.
- **Thread:** Tan 3/0.
- **Tail:** Golden pheasant tippets.
- **Body:** Antron dubbing or floss.
- **Wing:** White or tan calf body hair.
- **Hackle:** Trimmed neck hackle, palmered over body.
- **Collar:** Deer body hair tips.
- **Legs:** Round Living Rubber or Sili Legs, tied in front of the collar.
- **Head:** Spun deer body hair.
- **Difficulty:** 4.

THE DOCULATOR

- **Size:** 12-18.
- **Hook:** Standard dry.
- **Thread:** Brown 6/0.
- **Body:** Strip of yellow foam wound around hook.
- **Rib:** Tying thread.
- **Wing:** Elk hair.
- **Hackle:** Grizzly.
- **Head and Indicator:** Strip of yellow foam.
- **Difficulty:** 3.
- **Notes:** Tie the strip of yellow foam at the eye after wing is attached. Fold it over to the wing tie-in point, and leave a tab sticking out over the back as an indicator. Tie in hackle last, after foam is secured.

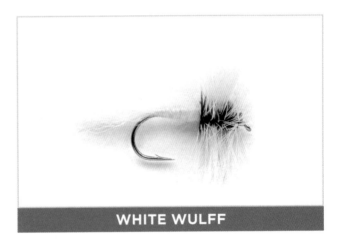

WHITE WULFF

- **Size:** 10-14.
- **Hook:** Extra-fine dry.
- **Thread:** White 6/0.
- **Tail:** White calf tail or mink-tail guard hairs.
- **Body:** White dubbing.
- **Wing:** White calf tail, upright and divided.
- **Hackle:** Badger.
- **Difficulty:** 3.

YELLOW HUMPY

- **Size:** 10-18.
- **Hook:** Extra-fine dry or Bigeye dry.
- **Thread:** Bright yellow 6/0.
- **Tail:** Light elk hair.
- **Body:** Light elk hair pulled over thread underbody.
- **Wing:** Formed from the tips of the elk hair used to make the body, upright and divided.
- **Hackle:** Brown and grizzly mixed.
- **Difficulty:** 4.

CDC CADDIS

- **Size:** 14-18.
- **Hook:** Standard dry.
- **Thread:** Brown 8/0.
- **Body:** Dubbed CDC fibers.
- **Wing:** CDC feather topped with two brown partridge hackles treated with flexible cement for durability.
- **Hackle:** CDC, clipped short after winding.
- **Difficulty:** 2.

Caddis

BLACK CADDIS

- **Size:** 14-20.
- **Hook:** Standard dry.
- **Thread:** Black 8/0.
- **Body:** Tying thread.
- **Rib:** Black hackle palmered over body.
- **Wing:** Black wing quill section with flexible adhesive on underside for durability. Secure over body of fly, and cut into a V-shape.
- **Hackle:** Black.
- **Difficulty:** 2.

DAVY'S SKATING CADDIS

- **Size:** 14-18.
- **Hook:** Standard dry.
- **Thread:** Brown 8/0.
- **Body:** Dubbed fur.
- **Wing:** Yearling elk, split to each side by wing case.
- **Wing Case:** Tan raffia or Thin Skin.
- **Hackle:** Brown partridge on bottom and sides only.
- **Difficulty:** 3.

EC DRY FLY

- **Size:** 14-18.
- **Hook:** Standard dry.
- **Thread:** Tan 8/0.
- **Tail:** Tan Antron or Z-Lon.
- **Body:** Rear half olive fur, front half olive fur.
- **Wing:** Yearling elk slanted back.
- **Hackle:** Light blue dun, wound around butts of wing.
- **Difficulty:** 3.
- **Notes:** After the wing is tied in, leave the butts long. Pull them upright, and post them, then wind the hackle around them. Butts should be trimmed short after hackle is wound.

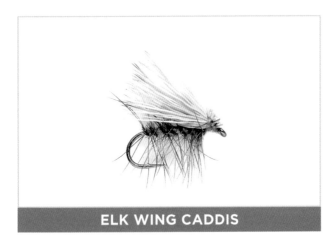

ELK WING CADDIS

- **Size:** 10-18.
- **Color Options:** Olive, tan, gray, black.
- **Hook:** Extra-fine or Bigeye dry.
- **Thread:** Brown 6/0 or 8/0.
- **Body:** Dubbed fur to match color of pattern.
- **Rib:** Copper wire.
- **Wing:** Light elk hair tied on top of the hook, allowing some fibers to extend along sides. The wing butts should extend forward to form head.
- **Hackle:** Brown, gray, or black, palmered over body.
- **Difficulty:** 3.

GODDARD CADDIS

- **Size:** 10-16.
- **Hook:** Extra-fine dry.
- **Thread:** Tan 6/0.
- **Body:** Natural caribou or deer hair, spun and trimmed to shape, leaving longer hairs at bend.
- **Hackle:** Brown.
- **Antennae:** Brown hackle stems.
- **Difficulty:** 3.

HEADLIGHT CADDIS

- **Size:** 14-18.
- **Hook:** 2X-long dry.
- **Thread:** Black 8/0.
- **Body:** Pearlescent tinsel with bright green Ultra Chenille tied over the top and extending slightly beyond the hook bend.
- **Thorax:** Brown fur.
- **Wing:** In three parts: tan Z-Lon at the bottom, a CDC feather over that, and a piece of tan Medallion sheeting over the top. The sheeting is cut in a V-shape to imitate the wing.
- **Post:** White calf body hair.
- **Hackle:** Blue dun wound parachute around wing.
- **Antennae:** Black nylon.
- **Difficulty:** 4.

HENRYVILLE SPECIAL

▎ **Size:** 12-18.
▎ **Hook:** Extra-fine dry.
▎ **Thread:** Olive 6/0 or 8/0.
▎ **Body:** Olive floss.
▎ **Rib:** Undersized grizzly hackle, palmered in an open spiral.
▎ **Wing:** Underwing of wood-duck flank fibers with overwing of gray mallard-wing quill tied flat.
▎ **Hackle:** Brown.
▎ **Difficulty:** 4.

MATHEWS X CADDIS

▎ **Size:** 14-18.
▎ **Color Options:** Tan, olive.
▎ **Hook:** Extra-fine dry.
▎ **Thread:** Tan 6/0.
▎ **Tail:** Z-Lon or Antron.
▎ **Body:** Dubbed fur.
▎ **Wing:** Fine deer hair.
▎ **Head:** Butts of wing hail trimmed.
▎ **Difficulty:** 2.

LOW RIDER CDC

▎ **Size:** 14-18.
▎ **Hook:** Standard dry.
▎ **Thread:** Black 6/0.
▎ **Body:** Brown dubbed fur.
▎ **Wing:** Yearling elk.
▎ **Hackle:** CDC tied on before wing.
▎ **Difficulty:** 2.
▎ **Notes:** Trim the butt ends of the wing but leave them exposed for form a short head.

NBK CADDIS

▎ **Size:** 14-18.
▎ **Hook:** Standard dry.
▎ **Thread:** Black 6/0.
▎ **Body:** Rear extended body of thin brown foam, front one-third brown fur.
▎ **Rib:** Tying thread.
▎ **Wing:** Two CDC feathers over a few strands of pearl Krystal Flash.
▎ **Post:** White Para Post.
▎ **Hackle:** Brown, parachute.
▎ **Difficulty:** 4.
▎ **Notes:** Also tied in tan, black, and olive.

OCTOBER YAK

- **Size:** 6-10
- **Hook:** 3X-long nymph.
- **Thread:** Tan 6/0.
- **Body:** Three layers of foam: tan on the bottom, orange in the middle, and brown on top.
- **Rib:** Tying thread.
- **Wing:** Yearling elk over a few strands of orange Krystal Flash.
- **Thorax:** Brown fur.
- **Hackle:** Brown, tied short over thorax.
- **Head:** Brown foam from top body segment tied up to the eye and pulled back over the thorax.
- **Legs:** Two Tentacle Legs.
- **Difficulty:** 3.
- **Notes:** Although it is tied to imitate the large October fly, it also makes a good adult stonefly imitation.

SLOW-WATER CADDIS

- **Size:** 14-18.
- **Color Options:** Gray, ginger, olive, black, brown.
- **Hook:** Extra-fine dry.
- **Thread:** 8/0 to match body color.
- **Body:** Antron dubbing.
- **Wing:** Two thin hen hackle tips coated with clear spray fixative.
- **Hackle:** Dry-fly hackle to match body color.

- **Thorax:** One or two wraps of the hackle over a dubbing base. Trim the hackle flat on the top and bottom.
- **Difficulty:** 2.
- **Notes:** Diluted cement can be used to coat the wings. It is important that any coating be put on the wings very sparingly.

SPLITSVILLE CADDIS

- **Size:** 14-18.
- **Hook:** Standard dry.
- **Thread:** Black 6/0.
- **Body:** Peacock herl.
- **Wing:** Yearling elk over CDC, split by hackle.
- **Hackle:** Brown, hackle stacker style.
- **Difficulty:** 3.
- **Notes:** The hackle stacker style is made by forming a double loop of tying thread (four strands in total), winding the hackle around the thread loops, and then pulling the thread between the wings.

Damselflies and Dragonflies

FLUTTERING BLUE DAMSEL

- **Size:** 8-12.
- **Hook:** 2X-long dry.
- **Thread:** Black 6/0.
- **Body:** Extended body tied in at thorax. Braided nylon colored with blue and black bands with permanent marker.
- **Thorax:** Blue dubbed fur.
- **Wing:** Yearling elk.
- **Legs:** Two black Sili Legs on each side. One pair facing forward and the other pair laid back along wing and body.
- **Eyes:** Black plastic.
- **Hackle:** Grizzly.
- **Difficulty:** 3.

GIBSON'S DRAGONFLY

- **Size:** 8-12.
- **Hook:** 3X-long nymph.
- **Thread:** Black 6/0.
- **Body:** Long, thin extended body of blue-dyed elk hair.
- **Wing:** Yearling elk tied spent and divided and marked with black permanent marker.
- **Hackle:** Grizzly.
- **Eyes:** Light green plastic eyes.
- **Difficulty:** 4.
- **Notes:** The blue elk hair is pulled over the wings to form a thorax.

Mayflies

AK'S QUILL

- **Size:** 16-22.
- **Color Options:** Red Quill, BWO, Trico, PMD.
- **Hook:** Extra-fine dry.
- **Thread:** Brown, olive, or cream 8/0.
- **Tail:** Spade hackle or Microfibetts to match body color.
- **Body:** Stripped hackle quill.
- **Wing:** Dun, brown, cream, or white hen-hackle tips.
- **Thorax:** Antron dubbing to match body color.
- **Difficulty:** 3.

BLACK GNAT

- **Size:** 12-18.
- **Hook:** Extra-fine dry fly; Bigeye dry in smaller sizes.
- **Thread:** Black 6/0.
- **Tail:** Black hackle fibers.
- **Body:** Black fur.
- **Wing:** Natural mallard quill sections, upright and divided.
- **Hackle:** Black.
- **Difficulty:** 3.

BLUE DUN

- **Size:** 12-20.
- **Hook:** Extra-fine dry; Bigeye dry in smaller sizes.
- **Thread:** Gray 6/0.
- **Tail:** Medium-dun hackle fibers.
- **Body:** Muskrat fur or gray dubbing.
- **Wing:** Mallard-wing quill segments, upright and divided.
- **Hackle:** Medium dun.
- **Difficulty:** 3.

BLUE WINGED OLIVE

- **Size:** 14-22.
- **Hook:** Extra-fine dry.
- **Thread:** Olive 6/0 or 8/0.
- **Tail:** Dark-dun hackle fibers.
- **Body:** Medium olive fur.
- **Wing:** Dark-dun hackle tips.
- **Hackle:** Dark dun.
- **Difficulty:** 3.

BLUE QUILL

- **Size:** 12-18.
- **Hook:** Extra-fine dry.
- **Thread:** White 6/0.
- **Tail:** Blue-dun hackle fibers.
- **Body:** Stripped peacock quill.
- **Wing:** Matched pair of gray mallard primary wing-quill sections, upright and divided.
- **Hackle:** Blue dun.
- **Difficulty:** 4.

BLUE WINGED OLIVE PARACHUTE

- **Size:** 14-20.
- **Hook:** Extra-fine dry.
- **Thread:** Olive 6/0.
- **Tail:** Dark-dun hackle fibers.
- **Body:** Olive-brown dubbing.
- **Wing:** Dark-dun turkey-body feather clump.
- **Hackle:** Dark dun, parachute style.
- **Difficulty:** 3.

BLUE WINGED OLIVE THORAX

- **Size:** 16-24.
- **Hook:** Bigeye dry.
- **Thread:** Olive 6/0 or 8/0.
- **Tail:** Medium-dun hackle fibers, split around small ball of dubbing.
- **Body:** Medium olive dubbing.
- **Wing:** Dark-dun turkey flat.
- **Hackle:** Medium dun, clipped on bottom.
- **Difficulty:** 3.

CANNON'S BUNNY DUN

- **Size:** 16-24.
- **Color Options:** Black, PMD, olive.
- **Hook:** Bigeye dry.
- **Thread:** 6/0 to match body color.
- **Tail:** Dun Microfibetts or hackle fibers, split around small ball of fur.
- **Body:** Dubbed fur to match pattern description.
- **Wing:** Clump of snowshoe-rabbit's-foot guard hairs and underfur.
- **Head:** Body dubbing wound past wing to eye.
- **Difficulty:** 3.

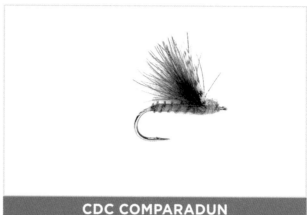

CDC COMPARADUN

- **Size:** 16-20.
- **Color Options:** Sulphur, Hendrickson, olive, brown.
- **Hook:** Bigeye dry, down-eye.
- **Thread:** White 8/0.
- **Tail:** Light-dun Microfibetts, split around small ball of fur, two per side.
- **Wing:** Bunch of natural CDC fibers with a few fibers of wood-duck flank feather mixed in.
- **Abdomen:** Biot quill to match pattern description.
- **Thorax:** Fur dubbing to match pattern description.
- **Difficulty:** 3.

CRIPPLE DUN BWO

- **Size:** 14-20.
- **Hook:** Standard dry.
- **Thread:** Olive 8/0.
- **Tail:** Blue dun hackle fibers.
- **Body:** Olive fur.
- **Wing:** Single burnt or cut wing made from synthetic veined material, spent and on one side only.
- **Hackle:** Blue dun, short.
- **Difficulty:** 2.

DAVE'S OH-SO-ISO

- **Size:** 10-14.
- **Hook:** 2X-long dry.
- **Thread:** Red 6/0.
- **Tail:** Three moose mane fibers.
- **Body:** Dark mahogany-dyed pheasant tail fibers.
- **Wing:** White Para Post.
- **Hackle:** Brown and grizzly mixed, parachute style around wing.
- **Difficulty:** 3.

EASTERN GREEN DRAKE

- **Size:** 8-10.
- **Hook:** 2X-long dry.
- **Thread:** Olive 6/0.
- **Tail:** Brown Microfibetts.
- **Body:** Tannish olive fur.
- **Rib:** Olive floss.
- **Hackle:** Grizzly dyed olive.
- **Legs:** Wood duck, divided style.
- **Difficulty:** 3.

DUN VARIANT

- **Size:** 12-16.
- **Hook:** Standard dry.
- **Thread:** Black 6/0.
- **Tail:** Dark blue dun hackle fibers, long.
- **Body:** Stripped natural brown hackle stem.
- **Hackle:** Dark blue dun, long and full.
- **Difficulty:** 2.
- **Notes:** Apply thin head cement to body for durability.

EXTENDED BODY EASTERN GREEN DRAKE

- **Size:** 8-10.
- **Hook:** 2X-long dry.
- **Thread:** Tan 8/0.
- **Tail:** Peacock sword surrounded by tips of dyed-brown elk from the body.
- **Rib:** Tan 8/0 thread.
- **Wing:** Brown hen hackle three-fourths as long as the shank.
- **Hackle:** Two brown hackles tied full, wrapped over half of the thorax.
- **Abdomen:** Mixture of cream and golden tan Antron dubbing.
- **Thorax:** Cream dubbing.
- **Difficulty:** 4.
- **Notes:** The tail is approximately one-and-a-half times the length of the hook shank.

GRAY FOX

- **Size:** 12-16.
- **Hook:** Extra-fine dry.
- **Thread:** Yellow 6/0.
- **Tail:** Ginger hackle fibers.
- **Body:** Tan fur.
- **Wing:** Gray mallard flank, upright and divided.
- **Hackle:** Ginger and grizzly, mixed.
- **Difficulty:** 3.

HAIRWING WESTERN GREEN DRAKE

- **Size:** 10-12.
- **Hook:** Extra-fine dry.
- **Thread:** Olive 6/0.
- **Tail:** Moose mane.
- **Body:** Light olive dubbing.
- **Rib:** Brown monofilament or heavy thread.
- **Wing:** Deer or elk hair.
- **Hackle:** Olive-dyed grizzly.
- **Difficulty:** 3.

GRAY FOX VARIANT

- **Size:** 10-14.
- **Hook:** Standard dry.
- **Thread:** Yellow 6/0.
- **Tail:** Cream hackle fibers, long.
- **Body:** Stripped cream hackle stem.
- **Hackle:** One cream, one brown, and one grizzly hackle, wound together and tied long and full.
- **Difficulty:** 2.
- **Notes:** Apply thin head cement to body for durability.

HENDRICKSON, DARK

- **Size:** 12-16.
- **Hook:** Extra-fine dry.
- **Thread:** Gray 6/0.
- **Tail:** Dark-dun hackle fibers.
- **Body:** Dark muskrat or dark gray fur.
- **Wing:** Wood-duck flank, upright and divided.
- **Hackle:** Dark dun.
- **Difficulty:** 3.

HENDRICKSON, LIGHT

- **Size:** 12-16.
- **Hook:** Extra-fine dry.
- **Thread:** Tan 6/0.
- **Tail:** Medium-dun hackle fibers.
- **Body:** Pinkish tan fox fur or dubbing.
- **Wing:** Wood-duck flank, upright and divided.
- **Hackle:** Medium dun.
- **Difficulty:** 3.

INDICATOR PARACHUTE (ADAMS)

- **Size:** 12-18.
- **Hook:** Extra-fine dry.
- **Thread:** Black 8/0.
- **Tail:** Dark-dun Microfibetts, splayed.
- **Body:** Adams Gray Antron dubbing blend.
- **Post:** Yellow and red Antron or Z-Lon.
- **Hackle:** Mixed grizzly and brown dry-fly hackle, tied parachute style.
- **Difficulty:** 4.

INDICATOR SPINNER (MAHOGANY)

- **Size:** 14-18.
- **Hook:** Extra-fine dry.
- **Thread:** Brown 6/0.
- **Tail:** Blue dun hackle fibers split in a V.
- **Wing Post:** Yellow and red Antron or Z-Lon (yellow forward).
- **Wing:** White Evett's Spinner Wing.
- **Hackle:** Brown dry-fly hackle tied parachute style.
- **Abdomen:** Mahogany turkey biot.
- **Thorax:** Dark brown Antron dubbing.
- **Difficulty:** 4.

LIGHT CAHILL

- **Size:** 10-20.
- **Hook:** Extra-fine dry.
- **Thread:** Yellow 6/0 or 8/0.
- **Tail:** Cream or light ginger hackle fibers.
- **Body:** Red-fox belly or cream dubbing.
- **Wing:** Wood-duck flank, upright and divided.
- **Hackle:** Cream or light ginger.
- **Difficulty:** 3.

MARCH BROWN

- **Size:** 12-14.
- **Hook:** Extra-fine dry.
- **Thread:** Yellow 6/0.
- **Tail:** Brown hackle fibers.
- **Body:** Fawn fox fur or tan dubbing.
- **Wing:** Darkly speckled wood-duck flank, upright and divided.
- **Hackle:** Brown and grizzly, mixed.
- **Difficulty:** 3.

MCCOY'S AP DRAKE PARACHUTE

- **Size:** 10-14.
- **Hook:** 2X-long dry.
- **Thread:** Magenta 6/0.
- **Tail:** Moose mane, tied in a bunch at end of body with middle fibers snipped out to create a splayed tail.
- **Body:** Dark brown-dyed elk, tied as a long, thin extended body.
- **Rib:** Tying thread.
- **Wing:** White deer hair.
- **Hackle:** Brown and grizzly mixed, tied parachute style.
- **Difficulty:** 4.
- **Notes:** The wing butts are not trimmed and wound under but are left untrimmed to help provide a bigger base for the hackle. They can be cut short after hackle is wound.

PALE MORNING DUN THORAX

- **Size:** 16-22.
- **Hook:** Bigeye dry.
- **Thread:** Yellow 6/0 or 8/0.
- **Tail:** Light dun hackle fibers, split around small ball of dubbing.
- **Body:** Pale yellow dubbing with a touch of pale olive.
- **Wing:** Light dun turkey flat.
- **Hackle:** Light dun, clipped on bottom.
- **Difficulty:** 3.

PARACHUTE PHEASANT TAIL

- **Size:** 12-18.
- **Hook:** Extra-fine dry.
- **Thread:** Orange 6/0.
- **Tail:** Ring-necked pheasant tail fibers.
- **Rib:** Fine copper wire.
- **Wing:** White calf-tail post.
- **Hackle:** Brown, tied parachute style around wing post.
- **Abdomen:** Ring-necked pheasant tail fibers, twisted and wound.
- **Thorax:** Brown dubbing around base of wing.
- **Difficulty:** 4.

QUILL GORDON

- **Size:** 12-16.
- **Hook:** Extra-fine dry.
- **Thread:** Yellow 6/0.
- **Tail:** Medium-dun hackle fibers.
- **Body:** Stripped peacock quill.
- **Wing:** Wood-duck flank, upright and divided.
- **Hackle:** Medium dun.
- **Difficulty:** 3.

REAL MCCOY MUCK BUG HEX

- **Size:** 4-8.
- **Hook:** 3X-long nymph.
- **Thread:** Brown 6/0.
- **Tail:** Pheasant tail fibers.
- **Body:** Yellow-dyed elk hair tied to encircle body. Let the tip ends of the hair extend a bit over the tails to aid in flotation.
- **Rib:** Tying thread and brown and grizzly hackle palmered over body.
- **Wing:** Calf tail slanted forward over hook eye.
- **Hackle:** Brown and grizzly mixed.
- **Difficulty:** 4.

REAL MCCOY FOAM BELLY HEX

- **Size:** 4-8.
- **Hook:** 3X-long nymph.
- **Thread:** Tan 6/0.
- **Tail:** Pheasant tail.
- **Body:** Yellow foam strip wound over shank overlaid with yearling elk. Let the tip ends of the body overlay extend slightly over the tails to help in flotation.
- **Rib:** Tying thread.
- **Thorax:** Yellowish tan dubbed fur.
- **Wing:** White deer hair.
- **Hackle:** Brown and grizzly mixed and tied parachute style.
- **Difficulty:** 4.
- **Notes:** The wing butts are not trimmed and wound under but are left untrimmed to help provide a bigger base for the hackle. They can be cut short after hackle is wound.

RED QUILL

- **Size:** 12-16.
- **Hook:** Extra-fine dry.
- **Thread:** Olive 6/0.
- **Tail:** Medium-dun hackle fibers.
- **Body:** Stripped Coachman-brown hackle quill.
- **Wing:** Wood-duck flank, upright and divided.
- **Hackle:** Medium dun.
- **Difficulty:** 3.
- **Notes:** Strip and soak hackle stems in water prior to using.

RINKER'S CDC WONDER BUG

- **Size:** 12-20.
- **Hook:** Tactical wide gape.
- **Thread:** To match body color.
- **Tail:** Tan Z-Lon.
- **Body:** Dubbed fur to match natural.
- **Wing:** Fine deer hair over CDC, tied back over body.
- **Head:** Trim ends of deer hair short.
- **Difficulty:** 2.
- **Notes:** Can be tied to imitate any emerging mayfly. Common body colors are cream, pinkish tan, yellow, and olive.

SPARKLE DUN

- **Size:** 14-20.
- **Color Options:** Tan, olive, black, Baetis (olive/brown).
- **Hook:** Extra-fine dry or Bigeye dry.
- **Thread:** Tan 8/0.
- **Tail:** Brown Z-Lon tied as trailing shuck.
- **Body:** Dubbed fur the color of pattern description.
- **Wing:** Coastal deer hair tied in single clump and splayed across top 180 degrees of hook.
- **Head:** Body dubbing, continued past wing.
- **Difficulty:** 3.

RS 2

- **Size:** 14-24.
- **Color Options:** Trico (black), gray, olive, PMD (yellowish olive).
- **Hook:** Bigeye dry.
- **Thread:** 8/0 to match body color.
- **Tail:** Clear Microfibetts, splayed.
- **Body:** Fine synthetic dubbing to match pattern color.
- **Wing:** White or natural gray CDC.
- **Difficulty:** 2.

SULPHUR PARACHUTE

- **Size:** 14-20.
- **Hook:** Extra-fine dry.
- **Thread:** Pale yellow 6/0.
- **Tail:** Light-dun hackle fibers.
- **Body:** Pale yellow dubbing.
- **Wing:** Light-dun turkey-body feather clump.
- **Hackle:** Cream, parachute style.
- **Difficulty:** 3.

TACTICAL LEXI'S GET ER DUN

- **Size:** 12-18.
- **Hook:** Tactical wide gape.
- **Thread:** Tan 6/0.
- **Tail:** Coq de Leon fibers.
- **Body:** Rear half stripped peacock quill, front half yellow/olive fur.
- **Wing:** Gray calf body hair.
- **Hackle:** Blue dun tied parachute style around base of wing.
- **Difficulty:** 3

WESTERN CDC SULPHUR

- **Size:** 16-18.
- **Hook:** Extra-fine dry.
- **Thread:** Yellow 8/0.
- **Tail:** Light dun or Sulphur Microfibetts.
- **Body:** Presoaked quill dyed Sulphur orange.
- **Wing:** Yellow CDC plumes.
- **Thorax:** Antron dubbing in cream or Sulphur.
- **Difficulty:** 3.
- **Notes:** This fly is effective tied with either a traditional Sulphur orange body color or when mixed with cream to lighten the color.

Midges

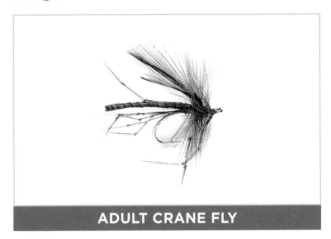

ADULT CRANE FLY

- **Size:** 14-18.
- **Color Options:** Orange, cream.
- **Hook:** Extra-fine dry.
- **Thread:** Cream 8/0.
- **Body:** Antron dubbing to match pattern color.
- **Wing:** Two white neck-hackle tips, splayed over back.
- **Hackle:** Cream, wound parachute style.
- **Post:** Orange Antron or Z-Lon.
- **Legs:** Six fine pheasant fibers, three on each side, knotted.
- **Difficulty:** 3.
- **Notes:** This fly is very effective when skittered.

GRIFFITH' S GNAT

- **Size:** 16-20.
- **Hook:** Bigeye dry.
- **Thread:** Black 8/0.
- **Body:** Peacock herl from base of stem.
- **Rib:** Fine silver wire.
- **Hackle:** Grizzly with fibers the length of hook gape, palmered through body.
- **Difficulty:** 1.

JOSH'S TACTICAL REAPER MIDGE

- ▐ **Size:** 14-18.
- ▐ **Hook:** Tactical wide gape.
- ▐ **Thread:** Gray 8/0.
- ▐ **Body:** Fine holographic tinsel wound over shank.
- ▐ **Wing:** Fine holographic tinsel.
- ▐ **Hackle:** Grizzly.
- ▐ **Difficulty:** 2.

MIDGE

- ▐ **Size:** 20-26.
- ▐ **Color Options:** Gray, black, cream, olive.
- ▐ **Hook:** Bigeye dry.
- ▐ **Thread:** 8/0 to match body color.
- ▐ **Tail:** Hackle fibers to match pattern color.
- ▐ **Body:** Dubbing to match pattern color.
- ▐ **Hackle:** Sparse, to match pattern color.
- ▐ **Difficulty:** 2.

Spinners

ANGEL WING TRICO SPINNER

- ▐ **Size:** 18-24.
- ▐ **Hook:** Bigeye dry.
- ▐ **Thread:** Black 10/0.
- ▐ **Tail:** Microfibetts, split.
- ▐ **Body:** Pale olive fur.
- ▐ **Wing:** Angel Hair tied split and spent.
- ▐ **Thorax:** Black fur.
- ▐ **Difficulty:** 2.
- ▐ **Notes:** Also tied in mahogany in larger sizes to imitate rusty spinners.

HISE'S HEX SPINNER

- ▐ **Size:** 10-12 (main hook).
- ▐ **Hook:** 3X-long nymph hook in sizes 4-8 for rear body, main hook standard dry fly.
- ▐ **Thread:** White 3/0.
- ▐ **Tail:** Moose mane.
- ▐ **Body:** Pale cream elk or deer hair encircling hook.
- ▐ **Rib:** Tying thread and cream hackle palmered through body.
- ▐ **Thorax:** Cream fur.
- ▐ **Thorax Overlay:** White deer hair.
- ▐ **Wing:** Four large tan CDC feathers on each side, tied spent.
- ▐ **Hackle:** Cream.
- ▐ **Difficulty:** 5.

continued

Notes: The body is tied on a separate hook and the bend of this hook is cut with wire cutters after the piece is tied. The extended body is secured with a loop of tying thread or monofilament to the front hook, which comprises the thorax of the fly.

MCCOY'S GRAY DRAKE SPINNER

- **Size:** 10-14.
- **Hook:** 2X-long dry.
- **Thread:** Mahogany 8/0.
- **Tail:** Moose mane.
- **Body:** Gray deer hair encircling hook. Allow the tips to extend slightly over the tails to aid flotation.
- **Rib:** Tying thread.
- **Wing:** Fluorescent orange Para Post.
- **Hackle:** Grizzly, parachute style and trimmed front and rear.
- **Difficulty:** 3.

KRYSTAL SPINNER (RUSTY)

- **Size:** 12-22.
- **Hook:** Standard dry.
- **Thread:** Orange 8/0.
- **Tail:** Pale blue dun hackle fibers or Microfibetts.
- **Body:** Rusty orange turkey biot.
- **Thorax:** Rusty brown dubbing.
- **Wing:** Pearlescent Krystal Flash.
- **Difficulty:** 2.
- **Notes:** Can be tied in other colors to imitate various mayfly spinners.

PERFECT SPINNER (RUSTY)

- **Size:** 12-18.
- **Hook:** Standard dry.
- **Thread:** Orange 8/0.
- **Tail:** Gray Microfibetts.
- **Body:** Rusty orange fur.
- **Wing:** Synthetic veined wings, cut or burned to shape and tied spent.
- **Hackle:** Blue dun, short.
- **Difficulty:** 3.
- **Notes:** Can be tied in other colors to imitate various mayfly spinners.

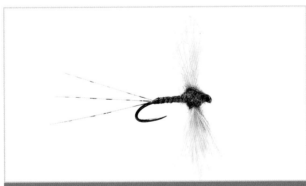

LEXI'S GET ER DUN SPINNER (RUSTY)

- **Size:** 12-22.
- **Hook:** Tactical wide gape in larger sizes; Bigeye dry in smaller sizes.
- **Thread:** Orange 8/0.
- **Tail:** Coq de Leon fibers.
- **Body:** Rusty orange turkey biot.
- **Wing:** Pale blue dun hackle, wound, split, and posted and then tied spent.
- **Thorax:** Rusty brown dubbing.
- **Difficulty:** 3.
- **Notes:** Can be tied in other colors to imitate various mayfly spinners.

REAL MCCOY AP SPINNER

- **Size:** 12-16.
- **Hook:** 2X-long dry.
- **Thread:** Mahogany 8/0.
- **Tail:** Moose mane.
- **Body:** Brown deer hair encircling hook. Allow the tips to extend slightly over the tails to aid flotation.
- **Rib:** Tying thread.
- **Wing:** Fluorescent green Para Post.
- **Hackle:** Grizzly, parachute style and trimmed front and rear.
- **Difficulty:** 3.

SNOWSHOE SPINNER

- **Size:** 12-18.
- **Hook:** Standard dry.
- **Thread:** 8/0 to match body color.
- **Tail:** Microfibetts.
- **Body:** Dubbed fur.
- **Wing:** Snowshoe rabbit's foot hair with a few strands of Angel Hair mixed in.
- **Difficulty:** 2.
- **Notes:** Common colors for the body are tan, rusty, cream, and olive.

RUSTY SPINNER

- **Size:** 12-18.
- **Hook:** Standard dry.
- **Thread:** Orange 8/0.
- **Tail:** Microfibetts, split.
- **Body:** Rusty orange fur.
- **Wing:** Pale blue dun hackle, wound, split, and posted and then tied spent.
- **Thorax:** Rusty orange sparkle dubbing.
- **Difficulty:** 3.

SPLITSVILLE SPINNER

- **Size:** 12-18.
- **Hook:** Standard dry.
- **Thread:** To match body color.
- **Tail:** Microfibetts, split.
- **Body:** Turkey biot.
- **Wing:** Dun Para Post, tied spent and posted.
- **Hackle:** Grizzly tied hackle stacker style.
- **Difficulty:** 3.
- **Notes:** Most common body colors are rusty, olive, and tan. The hackle stacker style is made by forming a double loop of tying thread (four strands in total), winding the hackle around the thread loops, and then pulling the thread between the wings.

BIG SKY SALMON FLY

- **Size:** 4-8.
- **Hook:** 4X-long streamer.
- **Thread:** Orange 3/0.
- **Tail:** Black rubber legs inserted into foam body and glued.
- **Body:** Orange foam cylinder, tied as an extended body. A black lateral line is made with permanent marker. An overlay of black foam that helps form the underwing is secured to the first two segments closest to the thorax but left to hang free above the rest of the body.
- **Rib:** Black segments made with 3/0 tying thread. Each segment is whip-finished in place and finished with head cement.
- **Thorax:** Orange sparkle dubbing.
- **Wing:** Black Krystal Flash underwing over which is yearling elk.
- **Legs:** Two orange and black speckled Tentacle Legs tied in at each side so that two on each side point forward and two on each side point back.
- **Post:** Large piece of bright orange egg yarn.
- **Hackle:** Brown tied parachute around wing post.
- **Head:** Black foam from underwing extended over thorax, split at the eye so that antennae can face forward.
- **Eyes:** Doll eyes glued to side of head.
- **Antennae:** Black rubber legs.
- **Difficulty:** 5.

GEE'S SUPAFLY STONE

- **Size:** 4-10.
- **Hook:** 4X-long nymph.
- **Thread:** Tan 6/0.
- **Tail:** Brown biots glued in between body segments.
- **Body:** Orange sparkle dubbing.
- **Overlay:** Two pieces of foam glued together—tan on bottom and brown on top. Extend over thorax and leave part sticking out over head. Trim head to shape.
- **Wing:** Orange Pearlescent Krystal Flash, then synthetic veined wing material spotted with black permanent marker, with tan EP Fiber on top.
- **Legs:** Brown rubber legs, two strands knotted with one piece cut off beyond leg joint. Three pairs spaced along thorax.
- **Antennae:** Brown rubber legs.
- **Eyes:** Black plastic glued in between foam sections.
- **Difficulty:** 4.

KING'S CDC STONE

- **Size:** 8-14.
- **Hook:** 3X-long nymph.
- **Thread:** Yellow 8/0.
- **Tail:** CDC feather.
- **Body:** Pale orange dubbed fur.
- **Wing:** In three sections tied at stages along the body. Each section consists of three or four CDC feathers. The effect should be of one continuous wing extending on top of the fly.
- **Hackle:** Grizzly, tied parachute and wound around a post made from the butt ends of the final CDC wing.
- **Difficulty:** 3.

LARSON'S LEGEND GOLD STONE

- **Size:** 6-14.
- **Hook:** Curved nymph.
- **Thread:** Yellow 6/0.
- **Tail:** Yellow goose biot flecked with black permanent marker.
- **Body:** Tan foam on top of body, yellow foam underneath.
- **Wing:** Tan synthetic raffia with tan EP Fibers over the top.
- **Legs:** Yellow round rubber legs flecked with black permanent marker, knotted and tied in three separate places along thorax.

- **Head and Wing Case:** Brown foam tied on top of thorax.
- **Antennae:** Yellow Fibbetts flecked with black marker or stiff yellow-dyed grizzly hackle fibers.
- **Eyes:** Dots of black nail polish on each side of head.
- **Difficulty:** 4.

ROGUE FOAM STONE GIANT

- **Most Popular Sizes:** 4-8.
- **Color Options:** Golden, brown, black.
- **Hook:** 2X-long dry.
- **Thread:** 6/0 to match body color.
- **Body:** Round foam body.
- **Rib:** Same as thread.
- **Wing:** Black bucktail over a flat trimmed sheet of packing foam over ten to fifteen strands of pearl Krystal Flash.
- **Legs:** Round Living Rubber or Sili Legs tied on each side of the head.
- **Head:** Deer body hair pulled back so that tips form a collar.
- **Difficulty:** 3.
- **Notes:** The segmentation to the foam body is done on a needle prior to tying the fly.

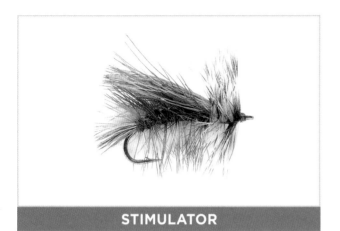

STIMULATOR

- **Size:** 8-16.
- **Color Options:** Olive, yellow, orange.
- **Hook:** Curved nymph.
- **Thread:** Fluorescent fire-orange 6/0.
- **Tail:** Natural elk hair.
- **Rib:** Fine gold wire.
- **Wing:** Bull elk hair.
- **Hackle:** Grizzly, palmered over the thorax.
- **Abdomen:** Dubbing the color of the pattern description, palmered with brown saddle hackle.
- **Thorax:** Dubbing the color of the pattern description.
- **Difficulty:** 2.

YELLOW SALLY

- **Size:** 14-18.
- **Hook:** Extra-fine dry.
- **Thread:** Yellow 6/0.
- **Tail:** Red floss.
- **Body:** Yellow dubbing.
- **Wing:** Elk hair.
- **Hackle:** Cream or yellow.
- **Difficulty:** 2.

Terrestrials

BAILE'S PANTHER CREEK HOPPER

- **Size:** 6-12.
- **Hook:** 3X-long nymph.
- **Thread:** Olive 6/0.
- **Body:** Thin dubbed body of olive dubbed fur, topped with a glued section of olive and yellow foam strips. The foam is secured near the bend with dubbed thread and again secured at the thorax. The olive section is folded over the hook eye to form a head.
- **Wing:** Yearling elk.
- **Legs:** Two brown Sili Legs tied in at each side to form four legs on each side.
- **Forelegs:** Two brown Sili Legs threaded through the olive foam.
- **Eyes:** Dots of black nail polish.
- **Indicator:** Strip of orange foam tied on top of thorax.
- **Difficulty:** 4.

BANK BEETLE DRY

- **Size:** 10-16.
- **Hook:** 2X-long dry.
- **Thread:** Yellow 6/0.
- **Body:** Yellow sparkle dubbing.
- **Overlay:** Black foam tied over the body and left extending over the eye and trimmed to form a head.
- **Legs:** Two round black rubber legs tied in at each side to form four legs total on each side.
- **Indicator:** White foam.
- **Difficulty:** 2.

BEEFCAKE BEETLE

- **Size:** 10-14.
- **Hook:** 3X-long nymph.
- **Thread:** Black 6/0.
- **Underbody:** Iridescent green foam tied on the underside of the hook and black foam tied above the hook, secured with tying thread to form segments.
- **Overbody:** Two strips of thick black foam secured at the middle of the body and at the thorax. They extend over the hook eye and are trimmed to form a head.
- **Legs:** Black Sili Legs tied in at each point the overbody is secured. Tie a knot in the rearmost legs to form leg joints.

- **Indicator:** White foam strip secured at each overbody tie-in point.
- **Antennae:** Black Sili Legs tied in between the two overbody pieces of foam.
- **Difficulty:** 4.

BIG EYE HOPPER

- **Size:** 6-12.
- **Hook:** 4X-long streamer.
- **Thread:** Yellow 6/0.
- **Abdomen:** Three strips of foam, glued together and segmented with about six whip finishes using the tying thread. Cream on the bottom, light orange in the middle, and tan on top. The middle orange piece is left longer than the other two and trimmed to make a tapered abdomen.
- **Thorax:** The same three colors of foam as the abdomen, tied down in the middle of the hook and then just behind the eye. The foam is left extending over the eye and trimmed to form a head.
- **Legs:** Rear legs are two pieces of tan Tentacle Legs knotted together and tied in the middle of the body. Front legs are two single legs of the same material tied in at the forward tie-in point on each side to form four legs.
- **Wing:** Yearling elk over gray poly yarn over pearl Krystal Flash.
- **Indicator:** Red foam tied in at each thorax tie-in point.
- **Eyes:** Small doll eyes glued to the side of the foam head.
- **Difficulty:** 4
- **Notes:** The abdomen section is best tied separately on a needle. The needle is then slipped out, and the entire assembly is tied to the hook.

BUBBA'S HOG CALLER HOPPER

- **Size:** 6-10.
- **Hook:** 3X-long nymph.
- **Thread:** Brown 6/0.
- **Abdomen:** Brown foam sandwiched between pale orange foam, whip finished with tying thread at six places. Tied on a needle first and then lashed to the entire hook. The end is left long over the eye and trimmed to form a head.
- **Thorax/Rear Legs:** Orange foam strips tied along the sides of the body, attached at the two thorax tie-in points. Before tying in, thread the pieces on a needle, and whip finish one orange and black Sili Leg to the end of each leg with bright orange thread. Also make three black dots on each leg with a black permanent marker or black nail polish.
- **Wing:** Yearling elk over about a dozen strands of pearl midge Krystal Flash.
- **Hackle:** Brown wound parachute style around the post.
- **Post:** Orange egg yarn.
- **Indicator:** Yellow foam strip attached at both thorax tie-in points.
- **Legs:** One yellow Sili Leg strand tied in at each side to form two legs on each side.
- **Eyes:** Small doll eyes glued to each side of the head.
- **Difficulty:** 4.

CARTOON HOPPER

- **Size:** 6-10.
- **Hook:** Curved nymph.
- **Thread:** Black 6/0.
- **Body:** Two strips of foam, dark brown on the bottom and orange on top, glued together and attached to the hook in the middle of the shank. Ends are left long over the eye and trimmed to form the head.
- **Legs:** Two tan Tentacle Legs tied in at each side so that two legs on each side extend toward the rear and two point forward.
- **Wing:** White poly yarn over slightly longer bunch of pearl Krystal Flash.
- **Hackle:** Black, wound over a thin thorax of brown sparkle dubbing.
- **Eyes:** Small doll eyes glued to each side of the head.
- **Difficulty:** 3.

DAVE'S CRICKET

- **Size:** 10-12.
- **Hook:** 2X-long dry.
- **Thread:** Black 6/0.
- **Tail:** Black deer hair and dark brown yarn loop.
- **Body:** Dark brown yarn.
- **Rib:** Black hackle palmered through body, trimmed short.
- **Wing:** Black turkey wing quill segment, tied flat over body.

- **Legs:** Pair of black turkey-wing quill fibers, trimmed and knotted.
- **Head:** Spun and clipped black deer hair, formed into a square shape with some fibers left trailing over the wing as a collar.
- **Difficulty:** 4.

- **Body:** Black foam, over which is a full bunch of dark green Krystal Flash. Both are wound under and then pulled over the top of the hook. The foam extends over the eye and is trimmed to form a head.
- **Legs:** Three pieces of stiff black nylon on each side, crimped to form joints.
- **Difficulty:** 2.

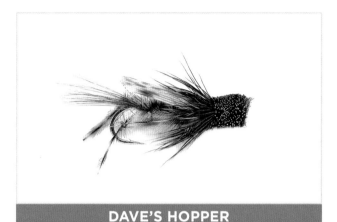

DAVE'S HOPPER

- **Size:** 10-12.
- **Hook:** 3X-long nymph/streamer.
- **Thread:** Yellow 6/0.
- **Tail:** Red deer hair with cream yarn folded over the top.
- **Body:** Cream yarn.
- **Rib:** Brown hackle palmered through body, trimmed short.
- **Wing:** Underwing of yellow deer hair, overwing of mottled turkey quill.
- **Legs:** Trimmed and knotted stems from yellow grizzly hackle.
- **Head:** Deer hair spun and trimmed into square shape. Tips are left untrimmed on top of the back of the head to form a collar.
- **Difficulty:** 4.

FOAM PARK HOPPER

- **Size:** 10-16.
- **Hook:** 2X-long dry.
- **Thread:** Tan 6/0.
- **Body:** Strip of olive foam doubled over and whip finished in four places with tying thread to form a segmented body. Best tied separately on a needle and then attached to the hook one-third shank length back from the eye.
- **Wing:** Tan synthetic veined wing material topped with yearling elk.
- **Thorax:** Tan fur.
- **Legs:** A single orange Sili Leg on each side, forming two legs on each side. The rear leg is knotted to form a joint.
- **Difficulty:** 3.
- **Notes:** Tie in the synthetic veined wing after the body is attached. Then tie in the elk hair facing forward over the eye. Dub the thorax up to the eye and back to the wing tie-in point. Then fold the elk hair back over the thorax. Tie in the legs last at the wing tie-in point.

FLASH BEETLE

- **Size:** 10-16.
- **Hook:** Standard dry.
- **Thread:** Black 6/0.

HARD BODY ANT

- **Size:** 10-18.
- **Color Options:** Brown, black.
- **Hook:** Bigeye dry, straight eye.
- **Thread:** Black 6/0.
- **Body:** Balls of brown or black epoxy at front and rear of hook shank.
- **Hackle:** Black, in middle of shank.
- **Difficulty:** 2.
- **Notes:** The balls are formed by adding paint to the epoxy when it is being mixed and are then applied to the hook. The hook should be rotated until the epoxy balls are dry, then the hackle is applied.

LETORT HOPPER

- **Size:** 10-16.
- **Hook:** 2X-long dry.
- **Thread:** Yellow 6/0.
- **Body:** Pale yellow dubbed fur.
- **Wing:** Section of mottled turkey wing, coated with flexible adhesive and tied flat over the body.
- **Head:** Spun deer hair, with ends left long and extending back over the wing.
- **Difficulty:** 3.

INDICATOR BEETLE

- **Size:** 12-18.
- **Hook:** Standard dry.
- **Thread:** Orange 6/0.
- **Body:** Orange foam, bound under along the hook shank and pulled over the top of the shank. Trim the end to shape to form a head.
- **Legs:** Three orange Tentacle Legs, tied across the hook to leave three legs on each side
- **Difficulty:** 2.

PSYCHO ANT

- **Size:** 10-14.
- **Hook:** 3X-long nymph.
- **Thread:** Black 6/0.
- **Body:** Purple-dyed peacock herl.
- **Overlay:** Black foam pulled over the body.
- **Wing:** White poly yarn and a few strands of pearl Krystal Flash, tied in the middle of the body and left to extend forward and to the rear.
- **Hackle:** Black, trimmed on the bottom.
- **Legs:** One tan and one purple Tentacle Leg, tied in at each side to form four legs on each side.
- **Difficulty:** 3.

Notes: Begin by tying in a foam strip at the front and the rear of the hook shank, leaving them extending forward and back. Wind the herl body, then bring the thread to the middle of the hook and bring both foam strips to the middle to tie them in. Finish the fly at this point, in the middle of the body.

QUICK SIGHT FOAM ANT DRY

- **Size:** 14-18.
- **Hook:** Standard dry.
- **Thread:** Black 6/0.
- **Body:** Black foam tied over the body to form a bulbous abdomen and a smaller head and thorax. A dot of bright orange fabric paint in placed on the back.
- **Legs:** Stiff black nylon or thread stiffened with head cement.
- **Difficulty:** 2.

QUICK SIGHT BEETLE

- **Size:** 12-16.
- **Hook:** Extra-fine dry.
- **Thread:** Black 6/0 or 8/0.
- **Body:** Wide piece of black foam tied over back.
- **Legs:** Three pieces of black, varnished thread straddling the shank to form six legs.
- **Head:** Small piece of foam left untrimmed at head.
- **Indicator:** A dot formed with bright orange fabric glue is painted on top of the foam for visibility.
- **Difficulty:** 2.

REECE'S BEEFCAKE HOPPER

- **Size:** 6-8.
- **Hook:** 3X-long nymph.
- **Thread:** Tan 6/0.
- **Body:** Doubled strip of tan foam, segmented with tying thread. The bottom strip is tied under the hook shank and the top one above it. Trim a head around the eye.
- **Wing:** Brown Thin Skin cut to shape.
- **Rear Legs:** Knot two brown round rubber legs to one Tentacle Leg. Trim the single Tentacle Leg beyond the leg joint and tie in place.
- **Front Legs:** Knotted Tentacle Legs, one on each side to form two legs on each side.
- **Antennae:** Thin yellow Tentacle Legs.
- **Eyes:** Spot of black marker on each side of head.
- **Difficulty:** 3.

ROSENBAUER'S PARACHUTE BEETLE

- **Size:** 12-16.
- **Hook:** Standard dry.
- **Thread:** Black 6/0.
- **Body:** Bright green sparkle dubbing.
- **Overbody:** Black foam, left long in front of eye and trimmed to form a head.
- **Post:** Pink egg yarn.
- **Hackle:** Black wound parachute style around post.
- **Difficulty:** 3.

SKILTON'S QUICK SIGHT ANT

- **Size:** 12-18.
- **Hook:** Standard dry.
- **Thread:** Black 6/0.
- **Body:** Quick Sight pre-made foam body tied to the hook at the forward third.
- **Hackle:** Black.
- **Difficulty:** 1.
- **Notes:** Quick Sight Ant Bodies are foam cylinders with a white spot on the end.

SCHROEDER'S PARACHUTE HOPPER

- **Size:** 8-14.
- **Color Options:** Yellow or olive.
- **Hook:** 2X-long dry.
- **Thread:** Cream 6/0.
- **Body:** Yellow or olive dubbing.
- **Wing:** Mottled turkey quill.
- **Hackle:** Grizzly, parachute style.
- **Legs:** Knotted pheasant-tail fibers.
- **Post:** White calf tail.
- **Difficulty:** 3.

SMITH'S FLYING ANT

- **Size:** 14-18.
- **Hook:** Standard dry.
- **Thread:** Black 6/0.
- **Body:** Brown fur.
- **Wing:** Light gray hackle tips tied in reverse with the butts clipped off.
- **Hackle:** Brown.
- **Difficulty:** 2.

SPLITSVILLE BEETLE

- **Size:** 12-16.
- **Hook:** Standard dry.
- **Thread:** Black 6/0.
- **Body:** Brown sparkle dubbing.
- **Overbody:** Black foam strip tied over the top of the body.
- **Wing:** Gray poly yarn tied spent.
- **Hackle:** Grizzly, tied hackle stacker style over wing base.
- **Difficulty:** 3.
- **Notes:** The hackle stacker style is made by forming a double loop of tying thread (four strands in total), winding the hackle around the thread loops, and then pulling the thread between the wings.

SPLITSVILLE FLYING ANT

- **Size:** 14-18.
- **Hook:** Standard dry.
- **Thread:** Black 6/0.
- **Body:** Rear half rusty brown fur, front half black fur.
- **Wing:** Gray poly yarn tied spent.
- **Hackle:** Grizzly, tied hackle stacker style over wing base.
- **Difficulty:** 3.
- **Notes:** The hackle stacker style is made by forming a double loop of tying thread (four strands in total), winding the hackle around the thread loops, and then pulling the thread between the wings.

TRAVIS PARA-ANT

- **Size:** 12-18.
- **Color Options:** Black, cinnamon.
- **Hook:** Extra-fine dry.
- **Thread:** 8/0 to match body color.
- **Hackle:** To match body, or dyed grizzly to match body color.
- **Abdomen:** Antron dubbing in desired color.
- **Thorax:** To match abdomen.
- **Post:** White or fluorescent-orange Antron.
- **Difficulty:** 3.

XTF HOPPER

- **Size:** 8-12.
- **Hook:** Curved nymph.
- **Thread:** Olive 6/0.
- **Body:** Extended body of pale olive foam, segmented with tying thread and formed on a needle.
- **Wing:** Pink bucktail over a wing cut from tan synthetic wing material.
- **Rear Legs:** Two Tentacle Legs, knotted. One leg is trimmed beyond the joint.
- **Front Legs:** One knotted Tentacle Leg on each side facing to the rear and one set, shorter and not knotted, facing forward.
- **Antennae:** Two Tentacle Legs extending out over eye.
- **Saddle:** Strip of light olive foam, cut to shape and glued over the thorax.
- **Difficulty:** 3.

Caddis

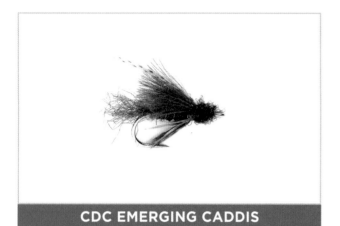

CDC EMERGING CADDIS

- **Size:** 14-20.
- **Color Options:** Cream, olive, brown.
- **Hook:** Extra-fine dry or Bigeye dry.
- **Thread:** 6/0 or 8/0 to match body color.
- **Tail:** Sparse Z-Lon yarn to match body.
- **Body:** Z-Lon or Antron yarn, twisted tightly before winding. Color to match pattern description.
- **Rib:** Fine gold wire.
- **Wing:** A few long wood-duck fibers for antennae, over which is tied sparse Z-Lon yarn, over which is tied a CDC feather.
- **Hackle:** Cream, palmered through thorax area, trimmed on bottom.
- **Head:** Dubbed Antron to match body.
- **Difficulty:** 3.
- **Notes:** Wing colors for cream variation is cream CDC over cream Z-Lon; olive is dark dun CDC over dark dun Z-Lon; brown is dun CDC over brown Z-Lon.

BASTIAN'S FLOATING CADDIS

- **Size:** 14-18.
- **Hook:** Standard dry.
- **Thread:** Tan 8/0.
- **Tail:** Clear Antron shuck.
- **Body:** Tan fur.
- **Rib:** Single piece of pearlescent Krystal Flash.
- **Overlay:** Tan foam.
- **Hackle:** Partridge.
- **Head:** Brown fur.
- **Difficulty:** 3.
- **Notes:** Body can be changed to match color of naturals.

BLACKHURST TACTICAL CDC CADDIS

- **Size:** 14-18.
- **Hook:** Tactical wide gape.
- **Thread:** Brown 8/0.
- **Body:** Hare's-ear fur.
- **Rib:** Brown micro stretch tubing.
- **Wing:** CDC overlaid with fine deer hair.
- **Hackle:** Hare's-ear fur spun in a loop.
- **Difficulty:** 4.
- **Notes:** Body can be changed to match color of naturals.

GRANNOM EMERGER

- **Size:** 12-16.
- **Hook:** Grub or emerger.
- **Thread:** Black 8/0.
- **Body:** Dirty white floss.
- **Rib:** Black micro stretch tubing.
- **Wing:** Small blue dun hackle tips tied in at sides of first thorax segment.
- **Thorax:** In two parts: first part small amount of black fur; second part same fur with wing case of black Thin Skin.
- **Forewing:** Dark CDC tied forward over eye.
- **Difficulty:** 4.

SEDGEHAMMER

- **Size:** 14-18.
- **Hook:** Grub.
- **Thread:** Olive 8/0.
- **Body:** Rough natural dubbing like squirrel or hare's ear.
- **Rib:** Single strand of pearlescent Krystal Flash.
- **Wing:** Light gray poly yarn overlaid with fine deer hair.
- **Head:** Same dubbing as body.
- **Difficulty:** 2.

KING'S TACTICAL HUMPBACK CADDIS

- **Size:** 14-18.
- **Hook:** Tactical wide gape.
- **Thread:** Olive 8/0.
- **Tail:** Olive Antron or Z-Lon.
- **Body:** Olive fur.
- **Wing Case:** CDC, tied in at tail position and pulled over the entire body and secured.
- **Thorax:** Olive fur.
- **Hackle:** Blue dun tied parachute style around stubs of wing case.
- **Difficulty:** 4.
- **Notes:** Can be tied in any color to match naturals. When wing case is pulled forward and secured, leave the wing stubs long, post them like a parachute wing, and wind hackle around them. The wing stubs can be trimmed short after hackle is wound.

SPOTLIGHT EMERGER

- **Size:** 14-16.
- **Hook:** Grub.
- **Thread:** Olive 8/0.
- **Body:** Single layer of pearlescent tinsel.
- **Body Overlay:** Fine olive Vernille, burnt at end and left hanging over bend of hook.
- **Rib:** Fine gold wire.
- **Wing:** Short clear Antron with a few long strands of mallard flank.
- **Legs:** Partridge or brown hen.
- **Thorax:** Olive fur.
- **Post:** White calf body hair.
- **Hackle:** Blue dun tied parachute around wing.
- **Difficulty:** 5.

Mayflies

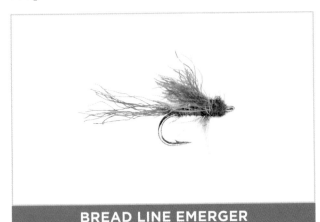

BREAD LINE EMERGER

- **Size:** 12-20.
- **Hook:** Standard dry fly.
- **Thread:** 8/0 to match body color.
- **Tail:** Shuck of brown Z-Lon.
- **Body:** Goose biot to match body of natural.
- **Wing:** Snowshoe rabbit's foot underfur.
- **Hackle:** Short blue dun wound behind wing.
- **Head:** Fur to match body color.
- **Difficulty:** 2.
- **Notes:** Match body and head color to popular naturals. Most common are olive, yellow/olive, tan, or cream.

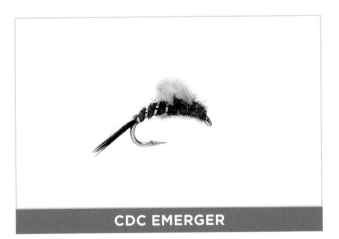

CDC EMERGER

- **Size:** 14-18.
- **Hook:** Tactical wide gape.
- **Thread:** Olive 6/0.
- **Tail:** Olive pheasant tail.
- **Abdomen:** Olive dubbing.
- **Thorax:** Olive dubbing.
- **Rib:** Pearl Flashabou.
- **Wing Case:** CDC feather, tied in and looped over thorax.
- **Difficulty:** 2.
- **Notes:** Also tied in cream.

CDC BUDDING EMERGER

- **Size:** 12-20.
- **Hook:** Scud.
- **Thread:** 8/0 to match body color.
- **Tail:** Sparse brown Z-Lon or Antron.
- **Body:** Tying thread.
- **Rib:** Piece of cream tying thread.
- **Thorax:** Dubbing to match natural.
- **Wing Post:** Small loop of thin white foam.
- **Hackle:** CDC wound parachute around wing post and trimmed short.
- **Difficulty:** 3.

CDC LOOP WING QUILL EMERGER

- **Size:** 12-20.
- **Hook:** Standard dry fly.
- **Thread:** 8/0 to match body color.
- **Tail:** Long sparse Coq de Leon fibers.
- **Body:** Stripped hackle quill to match natural.
- **Wing Case:** CDC feather tied in behind hackle and folded over hackle after it is wound.
- **Hackle:** Cream or blue dun.
- **Difficulty:** 2.
- **Notes:** Choose natural or dyed hackle feathers for body to match natural. Natural brown hackle stem for tan-colored mayflies, dyed yellow or orange for Sulphurs and PMDs, dark olive for olive mayflies.

CDC MAYFLY EMERGER

- **Size:** 12-20.
- **Hook:** Grub.
- **Thread:** 8/0 to match body color.
- **Tail:** Sparse blue dun hackle fibers.
- **Body:** Natural or synthetic dubbing to match color of natural.
- **Wing:** CDC tied slanting 45 degrees over back.
- **Thorax:** Same as body.
- **Difficulty:** 2.
- **Notes:** Most popular colors are tan and cream.

JR'S FLASHBACK EMERGER

- **Size:** 14-20.
- **Hook:** Standard nymph or dry fly.
- **Thread:** Gray 8/0.
- **Tail:** Pheasant tail fibers.
- **Body:** Tying thread.
- **Rib:** Fine silver wire.
- **Wing:** Pheasant tail fibers.
- **Thorax:** Gray fur.
- **Wing Case:** Pearlescent tinsel.
- **Head:** XS pearl glass bead.
- **Difficulty:** 2.

EXTREME EMERGER

- **Size:** 12-20.
- **Hook:** Standard dry fly.
- **Thread:** 8/0 to match body color of natural.
- **Tail:** Long sparse Coq de Leon fibers.
- **Body:** Tying thread.
- **Rib:** Fine gold wire.
- **Wing:** Small loop of pearlescent Diamond Braid.
- **Hackle:** Sparse cream or blue dun.
- **Difficulty:** 2.
- **Notes:** Most popular colors are olive and yellow.

KING'S TACTICAL OUTRIGGER EMERGER

- **Size:** 14-18.
- **Hook:** Tactical wide gape.
- **Thread:** Tan 8/0.
- **Tail:** Sparse shuck of brown Antron.
- **Body:** Tail material twisted and wound.
- **Wing:** Loop of brown Antron tied on each side of thorax.
- **Thorax:** Tannish-pink fur.
- **Hackle:** Blue dun tied hackle stacker style and folded over thorax.
- **Difficulty:** 4.

continued

- **Notes:** The hackle stacker style is made by forming a double loop of tying thread (four strands in total), winding the hackle around the thread loops, and then pulling the thread over the thorax. This pattern is tied to imitate a Hendrickson mayfly, but it can be modified to match the color of any natural.

LEXI'S TACTICAL PARA EMERGER

- **Size:** 12-18.
- **Hook:** Wide gape tactical.
- **Thread:** 8/0 to match body color.
- **Tail:** Gray poly yarn.
- **Body:** Striped peacock quill, natural or dyed to match natural.
- **Wing:** Gray poly yarn tied in as parachute post.
- **Hackle:** Brown or blue dun, tied parachute style around base of wing.
- **Difficulty:** 3.
- **Notes:** Coat the body with thin head cement after tying in for durability.

LOW HANGING FRUIT

- **Size:** 14-18.
- **Hook:** Standard dry fly.
- **Thread:** Cream 8/0.
- **Tail:** Tan Antron, singed at end.
- **Body:** Orange biot.
- **Wing:** Small loops of synthetic veined wing material, tied in on each side of thorax.
- **Thorax:** Cream fur.
- **Post:** Small piece of McFlylon or similar egg yarn.
- **Hackle:** Cream wound parachute style around wing.
- **Difficulty:** 3.
- **Notes:** Keep wing post long until after hackle is wound then trim short. This color variation is for a PMD or Sulphur, but it can be tied in any color variation.

PINO WINE PMD

- **Size:** 14-18.
- **Hook:** Standard dry.
- **Thread:** Pink 8/0.
- **Tail:** Long, split cream hackle fibers.
- **Body:** Tying thread covered with fine monofilament.
- **Hackle:** Cream wound parachute style around wing.
- **Difficulty:** 3.
- **Thorax:** Mixed pale olive and pale dun Antron dubbing.
- **Difficulty:** 3.

ROSENBAUER'S CDC RABBIT'S FOOT EMERGER

▌ **Size:** 14-18.
▌ **Hook:** Scud.
▌ **Thread:** 8/0 to match body color.
▌ **Tail:** Brown Antron yarn.
▌ **Body:** Dubbing to match body of nymph, typically brown or olive.
▌ **Wing:** Hairs from toe of snowshoe rabbit tied 45 degrees over body.
▌ **Legs:** CDC tied on underside of hook.
▌ **Head:** Dubbing to match body of adult mayfly.
▌ **Difficulty:** 2.
▌ **Notes:** Most common head colors are tan, cream, yellow, and olive.

SPLITSVILLE EMERGING DUN

▌ **Size:** 14-18.
▌ **Hook:** Scud.
▌ **Thread:** Yellow 8/0.
▌ **Tail:** Tan Antron.
▌ **Body:** Cream synthetic dubbing.
▌ **Wing:** CDC fiber, slanting forward.
▌ **Hackle:** Blue dun tied hackle stacker style and folded over to split CDC wing fibers.
▌ **Difficulty:** 3.
▌ **Notes:** The hackle stacker style is made by forming a double loop of tying thread (four strands in total), winding the hackle around the thread loops, and then pulling the thread over the thorax. This pattern is tied to imitate a cream mayfly, but it can be modified to match the color of any natural.

SMITH'S CRIPPLED EMERGER (BWO)

▌ **Size:** 14-20.
▌ **Hook:** Scud.
▌ **Thread:** Olive 8/0.
▌ **Tail:** Olive Z-Lon.
▌ **Body:** Olive biot.
▌ **Wing:** Dun hackle tips tied in reverse on each side of thorax.
▌ **Thorax:** Olive fur.
▌ **Hackle:** Blue dun wound through thorax.
▌ **Difficulty:** 3.
▌ **Notes:** To make the wings, tie in hackles by the tips instead of the butts. Snip the hackles just beyond the bound-in fibers to get the proper shape.

TRAVIS HI-VIS BAETIS PARA EMERGER

▌ **Size:** 16-22.
▌ **Hook:** Short-shank curved nymph.
▌ **Thread:** Dark olive 8/0.
▌ **Tail:** Natural wood-duck flank fibers.
▌ **Rib:** Two strands of Gray Ghost Krystal Flash, twisted and spiraled.
▌ **Wing Post:** Strip of yellow dry-cell Fly Foam.
▌ **Hackle:** Light blue dun, undersize, tied parachute style.
▌ **Abdomen:** Dark olive/brown Antron dubbing.

SULPHUR EMERGER

- **Size:** 14-18.
- **Hook:** Swimming nymph.
- **Thread:** Yellow 8/0.
- **Tail:** Pheasant tail fibers.
- **Body:** Pheasant tail fibers.
- **Rib:** Fine copper wire.
- **Wing:** Light gray CDC.
- **Thorax:** Pale yellow dubbing.
- **Hackle:** Cream, tied parachute style around base of wing.
- **Difficulty:** 3.
- **Notes:** This fly is tied "upside-down," with the wing and hackle on the same side of the shank as the hook point.

Midges

I.C.S.I. MIDGE FLY

- **Size:** 18-22.
- **Hook:** Bigeye dry.
- **Thread:** Olive 8/0.
- **Body:** Gray, olive, or black dubbing.
- **Wing:** High-visibility orange yarn.
- **Hackle:** Grizzly, tied parachute style.
- **Difficulty:** 3.

TWIN TERRITORY MIDGE EMERGER

- **Size:** 14-16.
- **Hook:** Wide gape tactical.
- **Thread:** Gray 10/0.
- **Tail:** Two strands of midge pearlescent Krystal Flash.
- **Body:** Stripped peacock quill.
- **Thorax:** Fine peacock herl.
- **Wing Case:** White foam tied over thorax with short stub left over eye of hook.
- **Hackle:** Grizzly.
- **Difficulty:** 3.

NYMPHS

General

BEAD HEAD BRASSIE

- **Size:** 12-18.
- **Hook:** Short-shank curved nymph.
- **Thread:** Black 6/0.
- **Body:** Copper wire.
- **Head:** Peacock herl.
- **Other Materials:** Copper bead between eye of hook and peacock herl.
- **Difficulty:** 1.

BEAD HEAD CRYSTAL SOFT HACKLE

- **Size:** 12-16.
- **Hook:** 2X-long nymph.
- **Thread:** Olive 6/0.
- **Tip:** Small bump of body dubbing.
- **Tail:** Black-dyed pheasant tail encircling tip.
- **Abdomen:** Olive flash dubbing.
- **Thorax:** Peacock herl.
- **Rib:** Gold wire.
- **Legs:** Gray partridge tied as a collar.
- **Bead:** Copper.
- **Difficulty:** 2.

BEAD HEAD FLASHBACK HARE'S EAR

- **Size:** 12-16.
- **Color Options:** Hare's ear, black, olive.
- **Hook:** 2X-long nymph.
- **Thread:** Black 6/0.
- **Tail:** Hare's guard hairs the color of body.
- **Rib:** Oval gold tinsel tied over abdomen.
- **Wing Case:** Pearlescent tinsel tied over top of abdomen.
- **Abdomen:** Natural hare's-ear dubbing, or dyed hare's ear in black or olive. Pearlescent tinsel tied over top.
- **Thorax:** Same as abdomen.
- **Legs:** Dubbing picked out at sides of thorax.
- **Head:** Brass bead between thorax and eye of hook.
- **Difficulty:** 3.

BEAD HEAD FLYMPH

- **Size:** 12-18.
- **Hook:** Curved nymph.
- **Thread:** Tan 6/0.
- **Tail:** Cream hackle fibers.
- **Abdomen:** Cream fur, thin.
- **Thorax:** Hare's-ear dubbing.
- **Rib:** Tying thread.
- **Legs:** Black hen hackle.
- **Bead:** Small brass, tied behind hackle.
- **Difficulty:** 2.

BEAD HEAD PRINCE

- **Size:** 12-18.
- **Hook:** 2X-long nymph.
- **Thread:** Black 6/0.
- **Tail:** Brown goose-quill fibers.
- **Body:** Peacock herl.
- **Rib:** Flat gold tinsel.
- **Legs:** Brown hackle fibers, collar style.
- **Head:** Brass bead.
- **Horns:** White goose-quill fibers (biots).
- **Difficulty:** 2.

BEAD HEAD HARE'S EAR NYMPH

- **Size:** 12-18.
- **Hook:** 2X-long nymph.
- **Thread:** Tan 6/0.
- **Body:** Rough-dubbed hare's ear.
- **Rib:** Gold wire.
- **Wing pads:** Black hackle, tied in by the tips and tied down along half of body.
- **Head:** Gold bead.
- **Difficulty:** 2.

BEAD HEAD RUBBER-LEG CDC PHEASANT TAIL

- **Size:** 12-18.
- **Hook:** Short-shank curved nymph.
- **Thread:** Brown 6/0.
- **Tail:** Pheasant-tail fibers.
- **Hackle:** Dun CDC.
- **Abdomen:** Pheasant-tail fibers, twisted.
- **Thorax:** Peacock herl.
- **Legs:** Black Living Rubber.
- **Head:** Gold bead.
- **Difficulty:** 3.

BEAD HEAD RUBBER LEGGED COPPER JOHN

- **Size:** 12-18.
- **Hook:** 2XL nymph
- **Thread:** Black 6/0.
- **Tail:** Two white round rubber legs.
- **Abdomen:** Black wire.
- **Thorax:** Peacock herl.
- **Wing Case:** Black Thin Skin and a few strands of pearl Flashabou, coated with epoxy.
- **Legs:** Two white round rubber legs on each side.
- **Bead:** Copper.
- **Difficulty:** 3.
- **Notes:** Also tied with copper, red, or green wire.

BEAD HEAD SOFT-HACKLE PHEASANT TAIL

- **Size:** 12-16.
- **Hook:** 2X-long nymph.
- **Thread:** Orange 6/0.
- **Tail:** Pheasant-tail fibers.
- **Rib:** Copper wire.
- **Hackle:** Brown partridge hackle wound as a collar.
- **Abdomen:** Pheasant-tail fibers, twisted and wound.
- **Thorax:** Short section of peacock herl.
- **Head:** Copper bead between hackle and eye of hook.
- **Difficulty:** 3.

BEAD HEAD SOFT-HACKLE HARE'S EAR

- **Size:** 10-16.
- **Hook:** 2X-long nymph.
- **Thread:** Tan 6/0.
- **Tail:** Mottled brown partridge fibers.
- **Body:** Hare's-ear dubbing or Dubbing Brush.
- **Rib:** Oval gold tinsel if body is dubbed; none if Dubbing Brush is used.
- **Hackle:** Brown partridge, wound as a sparse collar.
- **Other Materials:** Brass bead between body and hackle.
- **Difficulty:** 2.

BUBBA'S ELECTRIC PRINCE

- **Size:** 12-18.
- **Hook:** Curved nymph.
- **Thread:** Black 6/0.
- **Tail:** Two brown biots.
- **Abdomen:** Tying thread, built up to a taper.
- **Thorax:** Peacock herl.
- **Rib:** Chartreuse wire.
- **Wing Case:** Two tan biots.
- **Legs:** Two tan Tentacle Legs on each side.
- **Bead:** Brass.
- **Difficulty:** 3.
- **Notes:** The abdomen can also be made with red or copper wire. Coat the abdomen with head cement or epoxy for shine and durability.

COPPER JOHN

- **Size:** 10-18.
- **Color Options:** Red, copper, green.
- **Hook:** 2X-long nymph.
- **Thread:** 6/0 to match body color.
- **Tail:** Two goose biots tied splayed, to match body color.
- **Abdomen:** Colored copper wire over a tapered base of dubbing.
- **Thorax:** Peacock herl with epoxied Flashabou or tinsel shellback.
- **Legs:** Partridge.
- **Head:** Brass, copper, or gold bead.
- **Difficulty:** 2.

CZECH MATE HARE & RED

- **Size:** 12-18.
- **Hook:** Grub.
- **Thread:** Brown 6/0.
- **Abdomen:** Hare's-ear fur.
- **Thorax:** Red dubbing.
- **Rib:** Single strand of pearlescent Flashabou.
- **Overlay:** Brown latex or Thin Skin.
- **Legs:** Thorax picked out.
- **Difficulty:** 1.

CZECH MATE HARE & CREAM

- **Size:** 12-16.
- **Hook Type:** Grub
- **Thread:** Brown 6/0.
- **Abdomen:** Cream fur.
- **Thorax:** Hare's-ear fur.
- **Rib:** Strand of pearlescent Flashabou.
- **Overlay:** Clear latex or Thin Skin over abdomen and thorax.
- **Legs:** Thorax picked out.
- **Difficulty:** 1.

CZECH MATE HARE'S EAR

- **Size:** 12-18.
- **Hook:** Grub.
- **Thread:** Brown 6/0.
- **Abdomen:** Hare's-ear fur.
- **Thorax:** Dark brown fur.
- **Rib:** Single strand of pearlescent Flashabou.
- **Overlay:** Brown latex or Thin Skin.
- **Difficulty:** 1.

CZECH MATE PINKY

- **Size:** 12-18.
- **Hook:** Grub.
- **Thread:** Black 6/0.
- **Abdomen:** Pink fur.
- **Thorax:** Gray fur.
- **Rib:** Red wire.
- **Overlay:** Clear latex or Thin Skin over pearlescent flash tinsel.
- **Difficulty:** 1.

CZECH MATE SPARKLE & ORANGE

- **Size:** 12-18.
- **Hook:** Grub.
- **Thread:** Brown 6/0.
- **Abdomen:** Tan sparkle dubbing.
- **Thorax:** Orange fur.
- **Rib:** Yellow thread.
- **Overlay:** Olive latex or Thin Skin over pearlescent flash tinsel.
- **Difficulty:** 2.
- **Notes:** Color the overlay over the thorax with a dark brown permanent marker (and color the abdomen overlay with an olive marker if you can't find olive latex).

DEPTH CHARGE CZECH-MATE

- **Size:** 14-16.
- **Hook:** Scud.
- **Thread:** Brown 6/0.
- **Abdomen:** Hare's-ear fur.
- **Thorax:** Chartreuse fur hot spot with hare's-ear fur ahead of it.
- **Rib:** Gold wire.
- **Overlay:** Olive Thin Skin or latex.
- **Bead:** Brass.
- **Difficulty:** 2.
- **Notes:** Bury the bead within the body instead of the normal position at the head

GREEN WEENIE

- **Size:** 12-16.
- **Hook:** 2X-long nymph.
- **Thread:** Chartreuse 6/0.
- **Body:** Chartreuse Vernille looped at bend and then wound over shank.
- **Head:** Tying thread built up and epoxied.
- **Difficulty:** 1.

HARE'S EAR

- **Size:** 10-16.
- **Color Options:** Black, olive, natural.
- **Hook:** 2X-long nymph.
- **Thread:** Black 6/0.
- **Tail:** Hare's-mask guard hairs, same color as body.
- **Body:** Hare's-mask dubbing.
- **Rib:** Oval gold tinsel.
- **Wing:** Mallard wing-quill segment tied over thorax.
- **Abdomen:** Hare's-mask dubbing.
- **Thorax:** Hare's-mask dubbing.
- **Legs:** Thorax dubbing picked out at sides.
- **Difficulty:** 2.

IAN'S BRASS ASS

- **Size:** 12-20.
- **Hook:** Grub.
- **Thread:** Black 6/0.
- **Abdomen:** Copper wire.
- **Thorax:** Tying thread.
- **Wing Case:** Black Thin Skin on top with single strand of gold tinsel at each side.
- **Difficulty:** 2.
- **Notes:** Coat the entire fly with epoxy or head cement after tying.

HOLY GRAIL

- **Size:** 12-16.
- **Color Options:** Black, hare's ear, olive.
- **Hook:** Short-shank curved nymph.
- **Thread:** Black, brown, or olive 6/0.
- **Body:** Antron/Hare dubbing.
- **Rib:** Strand of pearl Flashabou.
- **Wing Case:** Peacock herl.
- **Legs:** Partridge tied as beard.
- **Difficulty:** 3.

JOSH'S WHITE LIGHTNING

- **Size:** 12-18.
- **Hook:** Curved nymph.
- **Thread:** White 6/0.
- **Tail:** Pair of white biots.
- **Abdomen:** Orange sparkle dubbing.
- **Thorax:** Peacock herl.
- **Rib:** Gold wire.
- **Overlay:** Yellow Antron yarn with a few strands of pearl midge Flashabou. After securing, pull it back, and leave a small stub to imitate emerging wings.
- **Legs:** White biot tied on each side.
- **Bead:** Brass.
- **Difficulty:** 3.

LE BUG

- **Size:** 12-18.
- **Hook:** Grub.
- **Thread:** Olive 6/0.
- **Abdomen:** Olive fur.
- **Rib:** Copper wire.
- **Thorax:** Peacock herl.
- **Legs:** Gray partridge.
- **Bead:** Brass.
- **Difficulty:** 2.
- **Notes:** Other popular body colors are orange and gray.

LIGHTNING BUG

- **Size:** 12-18.
- **Hook:** Grub.
- **Thread:** Pink 6/0.
- **Tail:** Pink-dyed mallard flank or partridge.
- **Abdomen:** Pearlescent tinsel.
- **Thorax:** Pink fur.
- **Rib:** Copper wire.
- **Bead:** Silver.
- **Difficulty:** 2.
- **Notes:** Also popular in orange.

LEPAGE' S BEAD HEAD HARE'S EAR (NATURAL)

- **Size:** 12-18.
- **Hook:** 2X-long nymph.
- **Thread:** Tan 6/0.
- **Tail:** Hare's-ear guard hairs.
- **Body:** Natural hare's-ear fur.
- **Rib:** Flat gold tinsel.
- **Wing:** Mottled turkey pulled over thorax bead.
- **Thorax:** Copper bead.
- **Difficulty:** 2.

MILLER'S TACTICAL PLUS ONE

- **Size:** 12-18.
- **Hook:** Tactical wide gape.
- **Thread:** Orange 6/0.
- **Tail:** Three pheasant tail fibers.
- **Abdomen:** Thinly dubbed tan translucent dubbing.
- **Thorax:** Tan translucent dubbing.
- **Rib:** Single strand of pearl Krystal Flash.
- **Wing Case:** Brown mottled Thin Skin coated with epoxy.
- **Legs:** Thorax dubbing picked out.
- **Bead:** Silver.
- **Difficulty:** 3.
- **Notes:** The orange thread should show through the abdomen.

MILLER'S TACTICAL VICTIM

- **Size:** 12-16.
- **Hook:** Tactical jig.
- **Thread:** Olive 6/0.
- **Tail:** Pheasant tail.
- **Abdomen:** Tying thread.
- **Thorax:** Orange sparkle dubbing hot spot followed by olive sparkle dubbing.
- **Rib:** Olive wire.
- **Bead:** Black.
- **Difficulty:** 2.

PHLAMIN PHEASANT

- **Size:** 14-18.
- **Hook:** Grub.
- **Thread:** Black 6/0.
- **Tail:** Black-dyed pheasant tail.
- **Abdomen:** Black-dyed pheasant tail.
- **Thorax:** Dark olive sparkle dubbing.
- **Rib:** Single strand of pearl Krystal Flash.
- **Wing Case:** Black Thin Skin coated with head cement or epoxy.
- **Legs:** Black-dyed pheasant tail.
- **Bead:** Red glass.
- **Difficulty:** 3.

OOEY GOOEY GRUB

- **Size:** 6-12.
- **Hook:** Grub.
- **Thread:** White 6/0.
- **Body:** Pearlescent Sili Skin colored on top with dark orange permanent marker and coated with Softex.
- **Difficulty:** 2.

PURPLE HAZE

- **Size:** 14-18.
- **Hook:** Grub.
- **Thread:** Black 6/0.
- **Tail:** Two strands of purple Krystal Flash.
- **Abdomen:** Blueish/purple Krystal Flash.
- **Thorax:** Purple dubbing.
- **Legs:** Black hen hackle wound as a collar.
- **Difficulty:** 3.

RUBBER GRUB NYMPH

- **Size:** 10-16.
- **Hook:** Grub.
- **Thread:** Tan 6/0.
- **Abdomen:** Tan Sili Skin with back colored with brown permanent marker.
- **Thorax:** Peacock sparkle dubbing.
- **Bead:** Silver.
- **Difficulty:** 3.
- **Notes:** Coat the abdomen with Softex after tying.

TACTICAL HOT SPOT NYMPH

- **Size:** 12-16.
- **Hook:** Tactical wide gape.
- **Thread:** Tan 6/0.
- **Tail:** Black hackle fibers.
- **Tip:** Orange thread.
- **Abdomen:** Pheasant tail.
- **Thorax:** Yellow hot spot followed by tan dubbing.
- **Rib:** Copper wire.
- **Bead:** Brass.
- **Difficulty:** 2.

TACTICAL GLISTER GRUB

- **Size:** 12-18.
- **Hook:** Tactical wide gape.
- **Thread:** Olive 6/0.
- **Abdomen:** Chartreuse sparkle dubbing.
- **Thorax:** Dark olive sparkle dubbing.
- **Rib:** 4X monofilament.
- **Overlay:** Clear Thin Skin over abdomen and thorax.
- **Difficulty:** 2.

TACTICAL PURPLE REIGN

- **Size:** 12-16.
- **Hook:** Tactical jig.
- **Thread:** Black 6/0.
- **Tail:** Black biots.
- **Body:** Purple sparkle dubbing.
- **Rib:** Purple wire.
- **Wing Case:** Pair of white biots.
- **Legs:** Black CDC wound as a collar.
- **Bead:** Black slotted tungsten.
- **Difficulty:** 3.

TACTICAL SOFT HACKLE HARE'S EAR JIG

- **Size:** 12-16.
- **Hook:** Tactical jig.
- **Thread:** Orange 6/0.
- **Tail:** Brown hackle.
- **Abdomen:** Hare's-ear fur.
- **Thorax:** Peacock sparkle dubbing.
- **Rib:** Oval gold tinsel.
- **Legs:** Brown partridge wound as a collar.
- **Bead:** Gold slotted tungsten.
- **Difficulty:** 2.

TACTICAL TUNGHEAD FRENCH JIG

- **Size:** 12-16.
- **Hook:** Tactical jig.
- **Thread:** Black 6/0.
- **Tail:** Coq de Leon fibers.
- **Tip:** Red Flashabou.
- **Abdomen:** Olive-dyed pheasant tail.
- **Thorax:** Peacock sparkle dubbing.
- **Rib:** Silver wire.
- **Legs:** Natural CDC wound as a collar.
- **Bead:** Black slotted tungsten.
- **Difficulty:** 2.

TACTICAL SOFT HACKLE PHEASANT TAIL JIG

- **Size:** 12-16.
- **Hook:** Tactical jig.
- **Thread:** Orange 6/0.
- **Tail:** Pheasant tail.
- **Abdomen:** Pheasant tail.
- **Thorax:** Dark brown sparkle dubbing.
- **Rib:** Copper wire.
- **Legs:** Brown partridge wound as a collar.
- **Bead:** Copper slotted tungsten.
- **Difficulty:** 2.

TACTICAL TUNGHEAD PURPLE JIG

- **Size:** 12-16.
- **Hook:** Tactical jig.
- **Thread:** Black 6/0.
- **Tail:** Coq de Leon fibers.
- **Abdomen:** Purple-dyed pheasant tail.
- **Thorax:** Purple sparkle dubbing.
- **Rib:** Silver wire.
- **Legs:** CDC fibers wound as a collar.
- **Bead:** Silver slotted tungsten.
- **Difficulty:** 2.

TACTICAL TUNGHEAD UV NYMPH

- **Size:** 12-16.
- **Hook:** Tactical wide gape.
- **Thread:** Brown 6/0.
- **Tail:** Cream hackle fibers.
- **Abdomen:** UV tinsel.
- **Thorax:** Hare's-ear fur.
- **Rib:** Tying thread.
- **Bead:** Black tungsten.
- **Difficulty:** 2.
- **Notes:** Coat abdomen with epoxy or head cement.

THE FLY FORMERLY KNOWN AS PRINCE

- **Size:** 12-18.
- **Hook:** 2X-long nymph.
- **Thread:** Red 8/0.
- **Tail:** Two brown goose biots, splayed using ball of red thread.
- **Body:** Two to four fibers of peacock herl.
- **Rib:** Flat gold tinsel.
- **Wing:** Two pieces of holographic film cut in the shape of biots.
- **Hackle:** Brown rooster.
- **Head:** Tungsten bead.
- **Difficulty:** 2.

T. H. SOFT HACKLE PUPA

- **Size:** 12-16.
- **Color Options:** Olive, cream, black, tan, brown.
- **Hook:** Bead head.
- **Thread:** 6/0 to match body color.
- **Body:** Medium olive Antron dubbing.
- **Rib:** Fine gold wire.
- **Hackle:** Sharptail grouse or natural partridge.
- **Head:** ⅛-inch black tungsten bead.
- **Difficulty:** 2.

TIM'S CANDY CRANE

- **Size:** 1/0-6.
- **Hook:** Gamakatsu Split Shot/Drop Shot bait hook (substitute curved nymph in sizes 6-10).
- **Thread:** Olive 6/0.
- **Tail:** Olive Spanflex or Flexi Floss.
- **Body:** Underbody made from tan Krystal Flash wound over the hook, coated with epoxy.
- **Overlay:** A few strands of peacock herl and light olive Swiss Straw.
- **Rib:** Olive wire.
- **Difficulty:** 3.
- **Notes:** After the overlay is tied in, apply a second coat of epoxy or clear nail polish over the entire fly.

TROUT MASTER NYMPH

- **Size:** 12-18.
- **Hook:** Curved nymph.
- **Thread:** Tan 6/0.
- **Tail:** Brown partridge.
- **Abdomen:** Hare's-ear fur.
- **Thorax:** Orange translucent dubbing.
- **Rib:** Gold wire.
- **Wing Case:** Brown mottled turkey section.
- **Legs:** Brown partridge.
- **Eyes:** Small black plastic eyes (or burnt and painted monofilament).
- **Difficulty:** 2.
- **Notes:** Can also be tied with pheasant tail for the body, peacock herl for the thorax, and a wing case of pheasant tail.

TUNGHEAD BLOODY MARY

- **Size:** 12-18.
- **Hook:** 2X-long nymph.
- **Thread:** Black 6/0.
- **Tail:** Brown biots.
- **Body:** Red Flexi Floss.
- **Rib:** Peacock herl and gold wire.
- **Legs:** Brown partridge or speckled hen hackle wound as a collar.
- **Bead:** Brass-colored tungsten.
- **Difficulty:** 3.

TUNGHEAD BITCH CREEK

- **Size:** 6-12.
- **Hook:** 2X-long nymph.
- **Thread:** Black 6/0.
- **Tail:** White Living Rubber.
- **Hackle:** Church-window pheasant feather.
- **Abdomen:** Black chenille.
- **Thorax:** Orange chenille.
- **Head:** Black tungsten bead.
- **Difficulty:** 3.

TUNGHEAD BREADCRUST

- **Size:** 12-18.
- **Hook:** 2X-long nymph.
- **Thread:** Black 6/0.
- **Body:** Orange wool or fur.
- **Rib:** Stripped tail quill from ruffed or sharptail grouse.
- **Hackle:** Grizzly hen saddle tied collar style.
- **Head:** Faceted tungsten bead.
- **Difficulty:** 3.
- **Notes:** To get the rough appearance of the body, leave some stubble on the stripped tail quill.

TUNGHEAD DURACELL JIG

- **Size:** 12-16.
- **Hook:** Tactical jig.
- **Thread:** Tan 6/0.
- **Tail:** Coq de Leon fibers.
- **Abdomen:** Purple-tan dubbing.
- **Thorax:** Purple/tan dubbing.
- **Rib:** Red wire.
- **Legs:** CDC wound as a collar.
- **Bead:** Silver slotted tungsten.
- **Difficulty:** 2.

TUNGHEAD HARE'S EAR

- **Size:** 12-16.
- **Hook:** Short-shank curved nymph.
- **Thread:** Black 6/0.
- **Body:** Rough hare's-ear dubbing.
- **Head:** Gold-colored tungsten bead.
- **Difficulty:** 2.

TUNGHEAD FAST WATER PRINCE JIG

- **Size:** 12-16.
- **Hook:** Tactical jig.
- **Thread:** Orange 6/0.
- **Tail:** Brown Spanflex.
- **Body:** Peacock sparkle dubbing.
- **Wing Case:** Two pieces of tan Spanflex.
- **Legs:** Brown CDC tied as a collar.
- **Bead:** Brass-colored slotted tungsten.
- **Difficulty:** 2.

TUNGHEAD PHEASANT TAIL

- **Size:** 10-16.
- **Hook:** Short-shank curved nymph.
- **Thread:** Orange 6/0.
- **Tail:** Ring-necked pheasant tail fibers.
- **Body:** Ring-necked pheasant tail fibers, twisted and wound.
- **Rib:** Copper wire.
- **Head:** Copper-colored tungsten bead.
- **Difficulty:** 2.

TUNGHEAD PHEASANT TAIL JIG

- **Size:** 12-16.
- **Hook:** Tactical jig.
- **Thread:** Brown 6/0.
- **Tail:** Coq de Leon fibers.
- **Abdomen:** Pheasant tail.
- **Thorax:** Peacock sparkle dubbing followed by hare's ear.
- **Rib:** Copper wire.
- **Bead:** Black slotted tungsten.
- **Difficulty:** 2.

TUNGHEAD QUILL JIG

- **Size:** 12-16.
- **Hook:** Tactical jig.
- **Thread:** Tan 6/0.
- **Tail:** Coq de Leon fibers.
- **Abdomen:** Stripped peacock quill coated with head cement.
- **Thorax:** Hare's ear mixed with peacock sparkle dubbing.
- **Bead:** Brass-colored slotted tungsten.
- **Difficulty:** 3.

TUNGHEAD PRINCE

- **Size:** 10-16.
- **Hook:** 2X-long nymph.
- **Thread:** Black 6/0.
- **Tail:** Two brown biots, split.
- **Body:** Peacock herl.
- **Rib:** Flat gold tinsel.
- **Wing:** Two wide white biots, tied flat over body in a narrow V shape.
- **Hackle:** Brown, tied as a collar and pulled under.
- **Head:** Gold-colored tungsten bead.
- **Difficulty:** 3.

TUNGHEAD SOFT HACKLE HARE'S EAR

- **Size:** 10-16.
- **Hook:** 2X-long nymph.
- **Thread:** Tan 6/0.
- **Tail:** Brown hackle fibers.
- **Body:** Hare's-ear dubbing.
- **Rib:** Oval gold tinsel.
- **Hackle:** Mottled brown partridge wound as a collar.
- **Head:** Tungsten bead tied between hackle and eye of hook.
- **Difficulty:** 2.

TUNGHEAD STONEFLY

▌ **Size:** 4-14.
▌ **Color Options:** Peacock, black, yellow.
▌ **Hook:** 3X-long nymph/streamer.
▌ **Thread:** 6/0 to match body color.
▌ **Tail:** Two goose biots, splayed.
▌ **Rib:** Fine copper wire.
▌ **Wing Case:** Mottled turkey, folded twice.
▌ **Hackle:** Sparse saddle or hen hackle to match body, clipped short on the bottom.
▌ **Abdomen:** Antron/hare dubbing.
▌ **Thorax:** Two faceted tungsten beads.
▌ **Difficulty:** 3.
▌ **Notes:** Dub lightly between the two beads in the thorax with the same dubbing used for the abdomen.

WIGGLE HARE'S EAR

▌ **Size:** 10-16.
▌ **Hook:** 2X-long nymph (plus smaller hook for abdomen).
▌ **Thread:** Black 6/0.
▌ **Tail:** Brown hackle fibers.
▌ **Abdomen:** Hare's-ear fur.
▌ **Thorax:** Hare's-ear fur.
▌ **Rib:** Gold wire.
▌ **Wing Case:** Brown mottled turkey wing segment.
▌ **Legs:** Brown hen hackle.
▌ **Difficulty:** 4.
▌ **Notes:** The abdomen is tied on a smaller hook. After it is tied, the hook bend and point are snipped off, and it is tied to the body with a loop of monofilament.

TUNGHEAD ZUG BUG

▌ **Size:** 10-16.
▌ **Hook:** 2X-long nymph.
▌ **Thread:** Red 6/0.
▌ **Tail:** A few peacock-sword fibers.
▌ **Body:** Peacock herl.
▌ **Rib:** Oval silver tinsel.
▌ **Wing Case:** Wood duck (or dyed mallard imitation) tied flat over the body and clipped short.
▌ **Hackle:** Brown, wound and pulled under.
▌ **Head:** Gold-colored tungsten bead.
▌ **Difficulty:** 3.

WIGGLE PHEASANT TAIL

▌ **Size:** 12-16.
▌ **Hook:** 2X-long nymph (plus smaller hook for abdomen).
▌ **Thread:** Black 6/0.
▌ **Tail:** Pheasant tail.
▌ **Abdomen:** Pheasant tail.
▌ **Thorax:** Peacock herl.
▌ **Rib:** Copper wire.
▌ **Wing Case:** Pheasant tail.
▌ **Legs:** Brown hen hackle.

continued

- **Difficulty:** 3.
- **Notes:** The abdomen is tied on a smaller hook. After it is tied, the hook bend and point are snipped off, and it is tied to the body with a loop of monofilament.

Caddis

BEAD HEAD CADDIS PUPA

- **Size:** 12-16.
- **Hook:** Bead head.
- **Thread:** Olive 6/0.
- **Body:** Caddis-green Lite Brite dubbing.
- **Hackle:** Partridge.
- **Head:** ⅛-inch gold bead.
- **Difficulty:** 3.

BEAD HEAD EMERGING SPARKLE CADDIS

- **Size:** 12-16.
- **Hook:** 2 X -long nymph.
- **Thread:** Olive 6/0.
- **Tail:** Section of Antron shuck left hanging over rear.
- **Abdomen:** Olive dubbing with cream Antron-yarn shuck.
- **Thorax:** Peacock her!.
- **Legs:** Brown partridge fibers.
- **Head:** Brass bead.
- **Difficulty:** 4

BEAD HEAD KRYSTAL CADDIS LARVA

- **Size:** 10-16.
- **Color Options:** Olive, cream.
- **Hook:** Short-shank curved nymph.
- **Thread:** Black 8/0.
- **Rib:** Olive or pearl Krystal Flash.
- **Abdomen:** Cream or olive Antron dubbing.
- **Thorax:** Black fur dubbing, short.
- **Head:** Brass bead.
- **Difficulty:** 1.

BEAD HEAD SOFT HACKLE CADDIS PUPA

- **Size:** 14-18.
- **Hook:** 2X-long nymph.
- **Thread:** Olive 6/0.
- **Abdomen:** Olive fur.
- **Thorax:** Olive fur.
- **Wing:** White Antron yarn.
- **Legs:** Brown partridge.
- **Bead:** Brass.
- **Difficulty:** 2.

CZECH MATE CADDIS

- **Size:** 14-18.
- **Hook:** Grub.
- **Thread:** Brown 6/0.
- **Abdomen:** Tan fur.
- **Thorax:** Brown fur.
- **Rib:** Tying thread.
- **Overlay:** Clear latex over abdomen and thorax.
- **Legs:** Thorax fur picked out.
- **Difficulty:** 2.

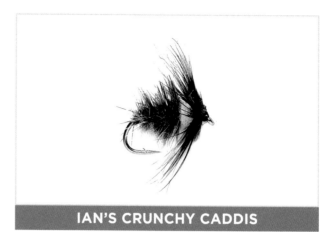

IAN'S CRUNCHY CADDIS

- **Size:** 10-14
- **Hook:** Grub.
- **Thread:** Black 6/0.
- **Abdomen:** Hare's-ear fur.
- **Thorax:** Chartreuse bead.
- **Rib:** Trimmed brown hackle.
- **Legs:** A few turns of black ostrich and a few turns of black hen hackle.
- **Difficulty:** 3.

GRIFFIN'S EURO CANDY CADDIS

- **Size:** 14-16.
- **Hook:** Grub.
- **Thread:** Olive 6/0.
- **Abdomen:** Woven from cream waxed twine and olive stretch body tubing.
- **Thorax:** Peacock sparkle dubbing.
- **Wing Stubs:** Black goose biot.
- **Bead:** Black.
- **Difficulty:** 3.

JAN'S PEARL CADDIS PUPA

- **Size:** 14-18.
- **Hook:** Grub.
- **Thread:** Black 6/0.
- **Abdomen:** Pearl sparkle dubbing, with overlay of tan Antron yarn pulled over the top.
- **Thorax:** Black fur.
- **Legs:** Brown hen hackle tied in at sides.
- **Bead:** Brass.
- **Difficulty:** 2.

LAFONTAINE SPARKLE PUPA

- **Size:** 12-16.
- **Color Options:** Brown/green, brown/yellow.
- **Hook:** Extra-fine dry fly.
- **Thread:** Brown 6/0.
- **Tail:** Brown or tan Antron or Z-Lon yarn, sparse and scraggly.
- **Body:** Brown, yellow, or green dubbing, with Antron or Z-Lon yarn pulled over top and bottom to encase the body in a "bubble."
- **Legs:** Mallard flank.
- **Head:** Brown fur.
- **Difficulty:** 4.

POLISH NYMPH

- **Size:** 12-16.
- **Color Options:** Brown/green, olive/cream.
- **Hook:** Short-shank curved nymph.
- **Thread:** Black 6/0.
- **Tail:** Short bunch of brown or olive saddle or hen-hackle fibers.
- **Body:** Woven floss body with darker color for the back.
- **Wing Case:** Darker floss color, doubled and tied over thorax.
- **Legs:** Stripped hackle tips or stripped peacock herl, crumpled and bent to shape.
- **Head:** Built-up tying thread.
- **Difficulty:** 3.

OLIVER EDWARDS RYACOPHILA LARVA

- **Size:** 10-16.
- **Hook:** Short-shank curved nymph.
- **Thread:** Olive 6/0.
- **Body:** Four-ply Antron yarn.
- **Rib:** Pale green Flashabou or 6X tippet material.
- **Legs:** Partridge dyed yellow/olive.
- **Difficulty:** 4.
- **Notes:** Use only three of the four strands of Antron for the body. Twist the yarn, and wrap forward to the legs. After you have tied in the legs, pull the last piece of Antron over for the back. Finish the fly by adding marking to the first three segments on the body above the legs with a black felt marker.

SHAGGY WIRE CADDIS

- **Size:** 14-18.
- **Hook:** Scud.
- **Thread:** Black 6/0.
- **Abdomen:** Yellowish olive wire, with two strands of peacock herl overlay.
- **Thorax:** Short sections of brown, then black fur.
- **Rib:** Fine gold wire.
- **Difficulty:** 2.

TACTICAL OLIVER EDWARDS HYDROPSYCHE LARVA

- **Size:** 12-16.
- **Hook:** Tactical Czech nymph.
- **Thread:** Cream 6/0.
- **Tail:** Aftershaft feather from the base of a partridge feather.
- **Body:** Cream/gray fur with pheasant tail overlay.
- **Rib:** Fine silver wire.
- **Legs:** Fine black feathers of fibers stripped from a golden pheasant tail.
- **Difficulty:** 2.
- **Notes:** Sometimes this fly is tied with ostrich herl gills spiraled through the body, and some tiers use Thin Skin instead of pheasant tail fibers for the overlay.

THRIFT SHOP CADDIS

- **Size:** 14-18.
- **Hook:** Grub.
- **Thread:** Black 6/0.
- **Abdomen:** Pale olive sparkle dubbing.
- **Thorax:** Tan dubbing.
- **Rib:** Strand of pearl Flashabou.
- **Wing Case:** Black Thin Skin coated with epoxy.
- **Legs:** Brown partridge.
- **Antennae:** Two strands of wood duck flank.
- **Bead:** Black.
- **Difficulty:** 3.

TACTICAL PEEPING CADDIS TUNGHEAD

- **Size:** 14-16.
- **Hook:** Tactical jig.
- **Thread:** Olive 6/0.
- **Tail:** Small stub of furled and burnt Antron yarn, with two strands of pearl Krystal Flash on each side and brown partridge encircling these.
- **Abdomen:** Hare's-ear fur.
- **Rib:** Fine copper wire.
- **Bead:** Black slotted tungsten.
- **Difficulty:** 2.
- **Notes:** The stub of Antron yarn can be tan or green, to match the color of cased caddis larvae.

WITCH DOCTOR

- **Size:** 14-18.
- **Hook:** Grub.
- **Thread:** Tan 6/0.
- **Abdomen:** Peacock-colored sparkle dubbing.
- **Thorax:** Tan fur.
- **Wing:** Short stub of white Antron.
- **Bead:** Brass.
- **Difficulty:** 2.

Crustaceans

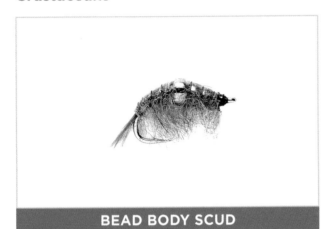

BEAD BODY SCUD

- **Size:** 10-14.
- **Color Options:** Olive, pink, orange.
- **Hook:** Short-shank curved nymph.
- **Thread:** Olive 6/0.
- **Tail:** Mallard dyed olive.
- **Body:** Antron dubbing with gold bead in middle of body.
- **Shellback:** Clear Scud Back.
- **Rib:** Copper wire.
- **Difficulty:** 3.

FLASHBACK SCUD

- **Size:** 12-16.
- **Hook:** Daiichi 1150 short-shank curved nymph.
- **Thread:** Olive 6/0.
- **Body:** Mixed gray/olive synthetic dubbing, rough. Pearlescent Mylar pulled over the top and bound in place with the ribbing.
- **Rib:** Fine monofilament (6X).
- **Difficulty:** 2.
- **Notes:** Pick out dubbing under shank to imitate legs.

EDWARDS' FRESHWATER SHRIMP

- **Size:** 14-18.
- **Hook:** Grub.
- **Thread:** Gray 6/0.
- **Tail:** Gray partridge.
- **Body:** Gray fur palmered with gray partridge.
- **Rib:** Monofilament.
- **Overlay:** Clear Thin Skin.
- **Antennae:** Gray partridge.
- **Difficulty:** 3.
- **Notes:** Spin the tips of about three gray partridge feathers in a dubbing loop, and wrap them through the body to create the legs.

JAN'S STILLWATER SNAIL

- **Size:** 8-16.
- **Hook:** Curved nymph.
- **Thread:** Brown 6/0.
- **Body:** Peacock herl and brown ostrich.
- **Rib:** Fine oval gold tinsel.
- **Legs:** Brown partridge tied as a collar.
- **Difficulty:** 2.

JAN'S TROUT CRAYFISH

- **Size:** 6-10.
- **Hook:** 3X-long nymph.
- **Thread:** Orange 6/0.
- **Tail:** Orange rabbit fur in two bunches.
- **Body:** Orange fur.
- **Overlay:** Clear Thin Skin with black diagonal slashes made with permanent marker.
- **Rib:** Orange-dyed grizzly hackle.
- **Eyes:** Black plastic tied in at bend.
- **Difficulty:** 3.
- **Notes:** Leave a piece of the body material hanging over the eye to imitate the tail.

ROUSE'S J-DUB SOWBUG

- **Size:** 14-16.
- **Hook:** Curved nymph.
- **Thread:** Tan 6/0.
- **Tail:** A few strands of clear nylon.
- **Abdomen:** Tan translucent dubbing picked out at sides.
- **Overlay:** Brown Thin Skin.
- **Rib:** 5X tippet.
- **Difficulty:** 2.

KILLER BUG

- **Size:** 14-18.
- **Hook:** Scud.
- **Thread:** Red 6/0.
- **Body:** Pinkish tan wool tied with a slight taper.
- **Rib:** Fine copper wire.
- **Difficulty:** 1.

TACTICAL DIRTY PINK SHRIMP

- **Size:** 14-18.
- **Hook:** Tactical Czech Nymph.
- **Thread:** Pink 6/0.
- **Body:** Pink translucent dubbing, picked out underneath to imitate legs.
- **Overlay:** Clear or pink Thin Skin.
- **Rib:** Red wire.
- **Difficulty:** 2.
- **Notes:** Paint a tiny black eye on each side of the head.

Damselflies and Dragonflies

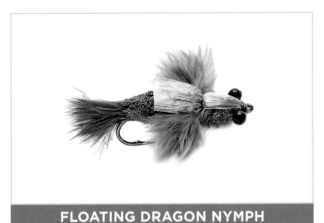

FLOATING DRAGON NYMPH

- **Size:** 8-12.
- **Hook:** 3X-long nymph.
- **Thread:** Olive 3/0.
- **Tail:** Large bunch of olive marabou.
- **Abdomen:** Olive deer hair, spun and trimmed to a wide, flat shape.
- **Thorax:** Olive fur.
- **Wing Case:** Synthetic raffia, olive.
- **Legs:** Large bunch of olive marabou on each side.
- **Eyes:** Black plastic.
- **Difficulty:** 3.

LIVING DAMSEL

- **Size:** 8-14.
- **Hook:** 2X-long nymph.
- **Thread:** Olive 6/0.
- **Tail:** End of marabou extended body.
- **Abdomen:** Extended body made from marabou feather, ribbed with tying thread for shape and durability.
- **Thorax:** Olive fur.
- **Rib:** Oval gold tinsel over front part of thorax.
- **Wing Case:** Pheasant tail.
- **Legs:** Partridge dyed olive.
- **Eyes:** Small metal dumbbell eyes.
- **Difficulty:** 3.
- **Notes:** Make the tail/abdomen assembly by tying on a pin, then slip out the pin and attach it to the hook.

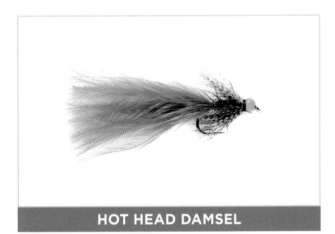

HOT HEAD DAMSEL

- **Size:** 8-14.
- **Hook:** 2X-long nymph.
- **Thread:** Red 6/0.
- **Tail:** Long, pale olive marabou.
- **Body:** Olive fur.
- **Rib:** Copper wire.
- **Legs:** Partridge dyed olive wrapped as a collar.
- **Bead:** Fluorescent chartreuse.
- **Difficulty:** 2.

Egg

MICRO EGG

- **Size:** 20.
- **Color Options:** Peach, flame, chartreuse.
- **Hook:** Heavy wet/nymph hook.
- **Thread:** 8/0 to match body color.
- **Body:** Egg yarn or poly yarn.
- **Difficulty:** 2.
- **Notes:** This fly is tied using standard egg-tying techniques, however only one to two strands of yarn are needed to complete the fly. Another option is to loop-dub the egg and trim to shape.

Mayflies

AMERICAN PHEASANT TAIL

- **Size:** 12-18.
- **Hook:** 2X-long nymph.
- **Thread:** Orange 6/0.
- **Tail:** Pheasant-tail fibers.
- **Rib:** Copper wire.
- **Wing Case:** Pheasant-tail fibers tied over thorax as wing case.
- **Abdomen:** Pheasant-tail fibers.
- **Thorax:** Peacock herl.
- **Legs:** Ends of wing-case fibers tied back on each side and clipped.
- **Difficulty:** 3.

BEAD HEAD AMERICAN PHEASANT TAIL

- **Size:** 12-20.
- **Hook:** 2X-long nymph.
- **Thread:** Orange 6/0.
- **Tail:** Pheasant-tail fibers.
- **Rib:** Fine copper wire.
- **Wing Case:** pheasant-tail fibers.
- **Abdomen:** Twisted and wound pheasant-tail fibers.
- **Thorax:** Peacock herl.
- **Legs:** Ends of wing case pulled to each side after wing case is tied in at head.
- **Difficulty:** 3.
- **Notes:** This fly is tied thicker and fuller than the traditional English Pheasant Tail.

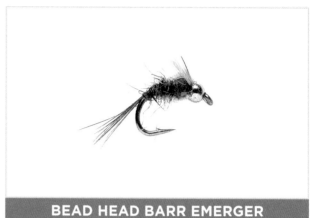

BEAD HEAD BARR EMERGER

- **Size:** 18-22.
- **Color Options:** PMD, BWO.
- **Hook:** Short-shank curved nymph.
- **Thread:** Gray or olive 8/0.
- **Tail:** Stiff brown hackle fibers.
- **Wing Case:** Dun or pale olive hackle fibers.
- **Abdomen:** Olive/brown Superfine Antron dubbing.
- **Thorax:** Blue-dun or pale-olive Superfine Antron dubbing.
- **Head:** Brass or gold bead.
- **Difficulty:** 3.

BEAD HEAD ZUG BUG

- **Size:** 12-18.
- **Hook:** 2X-long nymph.
- **Thread:** Red 6/0.
- **Tail:** Peacock-sword fibers.
- **Body:** Peacock herl.
- **Rib:** Flat silver tinsel.
- **Wing Case:** Natural wood duck side feather tied flat and trimmed to half of body length.
- **Hackle:** Brown, collar style.
- **Head:** Brass bead.
- **Difficulty:** 2.

BLESSING'S LAZY BIOT BWO

- **Size:** 16-20.
- **Hook:** Grub.
- **Thread:** Black 6/0.
- **Tail:** Sparse black Z-Lon.
- **Abdomen:** Olive biot.
- **Thorax:** Olive fur.
- **Rib:** Tying thread.
- **Wing Case:** End of biot pulled over the top of the thorax.
- **Legs:** Sparse black Z-Lon.
- **Difficulty:** 3.
- **Notes:** Coat the abdomen with head cement.

EASTERN GREEN DRAKE NYMPH

- **Size:** 8-10.
- **Hook:** 3X-long nymph/streamer.
- **Thread:** Cream or tan 8/0.
- **Tail:** Light-dun goose biots, splayed.
- **Wing Case:** Bleached badger hackle tips.
- **Extension:** Medium-dun CDC plume.
- **Hackle:** Cream saddle.
- **Abdomen:** Cream or light tan dubbing.
- **Thorax:** To match abdomen.
- **Difficulty:** 3.
- **Notes:** Often this nymph will have a grayish or tannish/olive appearance.

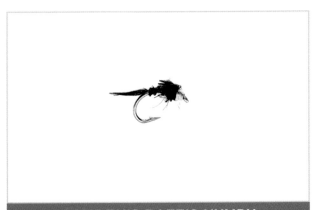

CAMDEN'S BAETIS NYMPH

- **Size:** 16-20.
- **Hook:** Grub.
- **Thread:** Black 8/0.
- **Tail:** Black hackle fibers.
- **Abdomen:** Tying thread.
- **Thorax:** Black fur.
- **Rib:** Black wire.
- **Legs:** Black hackle fibers.
- **Bead:** Pearlescent glass.
- **Difficulty:** 2.

FLASHBACK BAETIS NYMPH

- **Size:** 16-20.
- **Hook:** Grub.
- **Thread:** Olive 8/0.
- **Tail:** Olive-dyed partridge.
- **Abdomen:** Tying thread coated with head cement.
- **Thorax:** Tying thread.
- **Wing Case:** Iridescent tinsel.
- **Legs:** Olive-dyed partridge.
- **Difficulty:** 2.

FLASHBACK BEADHEAD AMERICAN PT

- **Size:** 12-18.
- **Hook:** 2X-long nymph.
- **Thread:** Brown 6/0.
- **Tail:** Pheasant tail.
- **Abdomen:** Pheasant tail.
- **Thorax:** Peacock herl.
- **Rib:** Copper wire.
- **Overlay:** Iridescent tinsel over both abdomen and thorax.
- **Legs:** Brown partridge.
- **Bead:** Brass.
- **Difficulty:** 3.

GG CALLIBAETIS NYMPH

- **Size:** 12-16.
- **Hook:** 3X-long nymph.
- **Thread:** Tan 6/0.
- **Tail:** Tan ostrich herl.
- **Abdomen:** Tan biot.
- **Thorax:** Two turns of tan ostrich followed by tan fur.
- **Wing Case:** Tan Thin Skin.
- **Legs:** Bleached partridge.
- **Bead:** Copper.
- **Difficulty:** 3.

FLASHBACK HARE'S EAR NYMPH

- **Size:** 10-18.
- **Hook:** 2X-long nymph.
- **Thread:** Brown 6/0 or 8/0.
- **Tail:** Natural hare's-mask guard hairs.
- **Rib:** 6X monofilament, over abdomen only.
- **Wing Case:** Continue overlay of pearlescent tinsel over thorax.
- **Abdomen:** Hare's-mask dubbing with an overlay of pearlescent tinsel.
- **Thorax:** Rough, loose hare's-mask fur dubbed on a loop.
- **Legs:** Thorax dubbing picked out at sides.
- **Difficulty:** 2.

HETERO GENIUS NYMPH

- **Size:** 12-16.
- **Hook:** Grub.
- **Thread:** Tan 6/0.
- **Tail:** Pheasant tail.
- **Abdomen:** Rear half pheasant tail, front half copper wire.
- **Thorax:** Peacock sparkle dubbing.
- **Rib:** Copper wire over pheasant tail only.
- **Wing Case:** Pheasant tail.
- **Legs:** Pheasant tail.
- **Bead:** Copper.
- **Difficulty:** 3.

HICKEY'S AUTO EMERGER GLASS

- **Size:** 14-18.
- **Hook:** Grub.
- **Thread:** Olive 6/0.
- **Tail:** Pheasant tail.
- **Abdomen:** Olive pearlescent tinsel or Krystal Flash.
- **Thorax:** Olive fur.
- **Rib:** Copper wire.
- **Wing Case:** Iridescent tinsel.
- **Wing Buds:** Gray CDC clipped short.
- **Bead:** Pearlescent olive glass.
- **Difficulty:** 3.

HIGA'S S.O.S.

- **Size:** 14-18.
- **Hook:** Grub.
- **Thread:** Black 6/0.
- **Tail:** Black-dyed pheasant tail.
- **Abdomen:** Tying thread.
- **Thorax:** Dark purple dubbing.
- **Rib:** Silver wire.
- **Wing Case:** Red Spanflex or Flexi Floss.
- **Legs:** Two strands of black Krystal Flash on each side.
- **Bead:** Silver.
- **Difficulty:** 2.

HICKEY'S AUTO EMERGER TUNGHEAD

- **Size:** 14-18.
- **Hook:** Grub.
- **Thread:** Olive 6/0.
- **Tail:** Pheasant tail.
- **Abdomen:** Olive pearlescent tinsel or Krystal Flash.
- **Thorax:** Olive fur.
- **Rib:** Copper wire.
- **Wing Case:** Iridescent tinsel.
- **Wing Buds:** Gray CDC clipped short.
- **Bead:** Black tungsten.
- **Difficulty:** 3.

HISE'S HEX

- **Size:** 4-8.
- **Hook:** 3X-long nymph.
- **Thread:** Tan 6/0.
- **Tail:** Gray marabou.
- **Abdomen:** Tan Sili Skin colored brown on top with permanent marker.
- **Thorax:** Tan fur.
- **Legs:** Gray marabou tied full around thorax.
- **Eyes:** Black plastic.
- **Difficulty:** 2.

HOT HEAD EURO PHEASANT TAIL

- **Size:** 14-18.
- **Hook:** 2X-long nymph.
- **Thread:** Orange 6/0.
- **Tail:** Pheasant tail.
- **Abdomen:** Pheasant tail.
- **Thorax:** Hare's ear.
- **Rib:** Fine copper wire.
- **Wing Case:** Iridescent tinsel.
- **Bead:** Hot orange.
- **Difficulty:** 2.

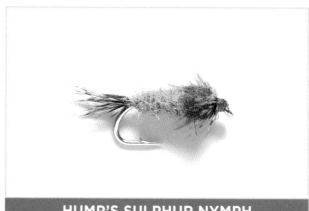

HUMP'S SULPHUR NYMPH

- **Size:** 14-18.
- **Hook:** 2X-long nymph.
- **Thread:** Tan 6/0.
- **Tail:** Brown hackle fibers.
- **Abdomen:** Hare's ear.
- **Thorax:** Dark brown fur.
- **Legs:** Brown hackle fibers tied at sides.
- **Difficulty:** 1.

HUMP'S GREEN DRAKE NYMPH

- **Size:** 6-10.
- **Hook:** 3X-long nymph.
- **Thread:** Tan 6/0.
- **Tail:** Cream hackle fibers.
- **Abdomen:** Cream fur with three sections of gray ostrich herl tied across the shank and trimmed.
- **Thorax:** Cream fur.
- **Wing Case:** Brown mottled turkey.
- **Legs:** Cream hackle wound through thorax.
- **Difficulty:** 3.

OVERBITE BAETIS

- **Size:** 18-22.
- **Hook:** Curved nymph.
- **Thread:** Olive 8/0.
- **Tail:** Pheasant tail.
- **Abdomen:** Olive biot.
- **Thorax:** Peacock sparkle dubbing.
- **Wing Case:** Pheasant tail.
- **Legs:** Pheasant tail.
- **Difficulty:** 3.

PHEASANT TAIL

- **Size:** 10-20.
- **Color Options:** Flashback, natural, olive.
- **Hook:** 2X-long nymph.
- **Thread:** Rusty brown or orange 6/0.
- **Tail:** Natural pheasant-tail fibers.
- **Rib:** Copper wire.
- **Wing:** Pheasant-tail fibers tied over thorax as wing case.
- **Abdomen:** Pheasant-tail fibers.
- **Thorax:** Pheasant-tail fibers.
- **Difficulty:** 2.
- **Notes:** In the Flashback version, the wing case is made from pearl Flashabou or similar iridescent material instead of pheasant-tail fibers.

QUASIMODO PHEASANT TAIL

- **Size:** 14-18.
- **Hook:** Grub.
- **Thread:** Tan 6/0.
- **Tail:** Pheasant tail.
- **Abdomen:** Pheasant tail.
- **Thorax:** Peacock herl.
- **Rib:** Copper wire.
- **Wing Case:** Iridescent tinsel.
- **Legs:** Pheasant tail.
- **Bead:** Brass.
- **Difficulty:** 2.

RED QUILL EMERGER

- **Size:** 12-16.
- **Hook:** 2X-long nymph.
- **Thread:** Orange 6/0.
- **Tail:** Three wood-duck flank fibers.
- **Hackle:** Medium or dark dun hen.
- **Abdomen:** Stripped and soaked red/brown hackle stem, wound over a thin layer of monofilament and coated with head cement.
- **Thorax:** Rust Antron, thinly dubbed.
- **Difficulty:** 2.

TACTICAL TUNGHEAD BIOT NYMPH

- **Size:** 12-16.
- **Hook:** Wide gape tactical.
- **Thread:** Tan 6/0.
- **Tail:** Coq de Leon fibers.
- **Abdomen:** Olive biot.
- **Thorax:** Pale olive sparkle dubbing.
- **Bead:** Brass-colored tungsten.
- **Difficulty:** 3.
- **Notes:** Can also be tied with a rusty brown biot.

TIM'S DRAKE DEL DIABLO

- **Size:** 10-14.
- **Hook:** Grub.
- **Thread:** Brown 6/0.
- **Tail:** Three sections of mottled turkey feather, separated and stiffened with head cement.
- **Abdomen:** Mixed tan and olive yarn, tied in bunches across the hook and trimmed. Two of the tail sections are tied over the top to create an over-body, and one is tied under the hook to make the belly.
- **Thorax:** Mixed olive and tan ostrich.
- **Rib:** Monofilament.
- **Wing Case:** Bright green Thin Skin, over which is a piece of brown Thin Skin, slit so that the green peeks through.
- **Legs:** Knotted brown Sili Legs, three tied in on each side.
- **Eyes:** Black plastic.
- **Difficulty:** 5.

TUNGHEAD HARE'S EAR FLASHBACK

- **Size:** 10-16.
- **Color Options:** Natural, olive.
- **Hook:** 2X-long nymph.
- **Thread:** Black 6/0.
- **Tail:** Guard hairs from a hare's mask, stacked.
- **Body:** Dark hare's-ear dubbing.
- **Rib:** Fine gold wire or tinsel.

- **Wing Case:** Pearl Flashabou.
- **Head:** Faceted tungsten bead.
- **Difficulty:** 3.

TUNGHEAD SKINNY QUILL NYMPH

- **Size:** 12-16.
- **Hook:** Wide gape tactical.
- **Thread:** Olive 6/0.
- **Tail:** Coq de Leon fibers.
- **Abdomen:** Tan biot.
- **Thorax:** Hare's-ear fur.
- **Bead:** Brass-colored tungsten.
- **Difficulty:** 2.

TUNGHEAD SOFT-HACKLE PHEASANT TAIL

- **Size:** 12-16.
- **Hook:** 2X-long nymph.
- **Thread:** Black 6/0.
- **Tail:** Pheasant-tail fibers.
- **Hackle:** One or two wraps of pheasant or partridge hen feather.
- **Abdomen:** Three pheasant-tail feathers twisted with a short section of fine copper wire.
- **Thorax:** Peacock herl.
- **Head:** Faceted tungsten bead.
- **Difficulty:** 2.

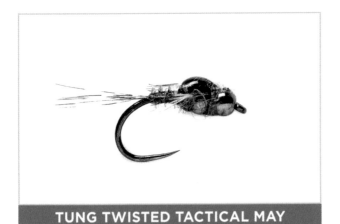

TUNG TWISTED TACTICAL MAY

- **Size:** 12-18.
- **Hook:** Tactical wide gape.
- **Thread:** Olive 8/0.
- **Tail:** Coq de Leon fibers.
- **Abdomen:** Olive biot.
- **Thorax:** Olive fur.
- **Wing Case:** Iridescent tinsel coated with epoxy.
- **Legs:** Coq de Leon.
- **Bead:** Black tungsten (2).
- **Difficulty:** 3.
- **Notes:** One tungsten bead is buried in the thorax under the wing case for extra weight; the other is placed at the head in the standard position.

ZUG BUG

- **Size:** 10-18.
- **Hook:** 2X-long nymph.
- **Thread:** Black 6/0.
- **Tail:** Peacock-sword fibers.
- **Body:** Peacock herl.
- **Rib:** Flat silver tinsel.
- **Wing:** Wood-duck side feather, tied flat over body and trimmed to half of body length.
- **Hackle:** Brown.
- **Difficulty:** 2.

Midges

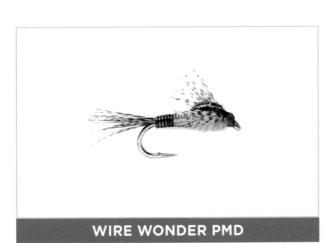

WIRE WONDER PMD

- **Size:** 14-18.
- **Hook:** Grub.
- **Thread:** Orange 6/0.
- **Tail:** Brown partridge.
- **Abdomen:** Fine copper wire.
- **Thorax:** Cream fur.
- **Wing Case:** Iridescent tinsel.
- **Legs:** Brown partridge.
- **Difficulty:** 2.

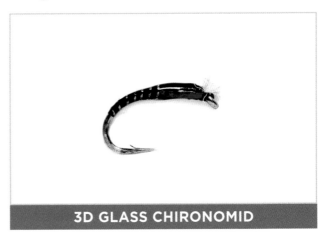

3D GLASS CHIRONOMID

- **Size:** 16-22.
- **Hook:** Grub.
- **Thread:** Red, black, or olive 6/0.
- **Abdomen:** Tying thread.
- **Thorax:** Tying thread built up with a piece of red tinsel or flash tied in at each side.
- **Rib:** Strand of pearl Krystal Flash.
- **Legs:** Small tuft of white Antron facing over eye.
- **Difficulty:** 2.
- **Notes:** The entire fly, except for the tuft of yarn, should be coated in epoxy or head cement.

BIRCHELL'S HATCHING MIDGE

- **Size:** 16-24.
- **Color Options:** Cream, olive, black, gray, red.
- **Hook:** Curved nymph hook.
- **Thread:** 8/0 to match body color.
- **Tail:** Six to eight fibers of Z-Lon or Antron.
- **Wing Post:** White turkey-flat fibers tied short.
- **Hackle:** Grizzly, tied parachute style around the post.
- **Abdomen:** Dyed goose or turkey biot.
- **Thorax:** Peacock herl or ostrich herl.
- **Difficulty:** 3.
- **Notes:** In larger sizes, this is an effective emerging mayfly nymph pattern.

CRYSTAL MIDGE

- **Size:** 16-18.
- **Color Options:** Gray, black, olive.
- **Hook:** Short-shank curved nymph.
- **Thread:** 6/0 to match body color.
- **Rib:** Fine gold or silver wire.
- **Wing:** Pearl Krystal Flash fibers, clipped short.
- **Abdomen:** Two twisted Antron-yam fibers, or buildup of 6/0 thread.
- **Thorax:** Antron dubbing or ostrich herl to match abdomen color.
- **Head:** Clear glass craft bead.
- **Difficulty:** 2.

BRASSIE

- **Size:** 14-20.
- **Hook:** 2X-long nymph.
- **Thread:** Black 8/0.
- **Abdomen:** Fine copper wire.
- **Thorax:** Peacock herl.
- **Difficulty:** 1.

DISCO MIDGE

- **Size:** 16-22.
- **Color Options:** Olive, pearl, red, pink.
- **Hook:** Bigeye dry.
- **Thread:** Cream 8/0 to match pattern color, forms body.
- **Rib:** Pearlescent Krystal Flash.
- **Thorax:** Peacock herl or fur.
- **Difficulty:** 1.

FLEXIFLOSS CHIRONOMID

- **Size:** 16-22.
- **Hook:** Grub.
- **Thread:** Olive 6/0.
- **Abdomen:** Tying thread.
- **Thorax:** Red Flexi Floss.
- **Rib:** Tan Flexi Floss.
- **Wing Case:** Color top of thorax with a brown marker.
- **Legs:** Small tuft of white Antron facing over eye.
- **Difficulty:** 2.
- **Notes:** The entire fly, except for the tuft of yarn, should be coated in epoxy or head cement.

LAZER LARVA

- **Size:** 16-22.
- **Hook:** 2X-long nymph (dry-fly hook in sizes 20-22).
- **Thread:** Olive 8/0.
- **Abdomen:** Tying thread.
- **Rib:** Red wire.
- **Difficulty:** 1.
- **Notes:** Coat fly with head cement or epoxy after tying.

GINNY MIDGE

- **Size:** 16-24.
- **Hook:** Grub.
- **Thread:** White 8/0.
- **Abdomen:** Pearl Midge Krystal Flash.
- **Thorax:** Black fur.
- **Wing Case:** Loop of two strands of Pearl Midge Krystal Flash.
- **Bead:** Clear glass.
- **Difficulty:** 2.

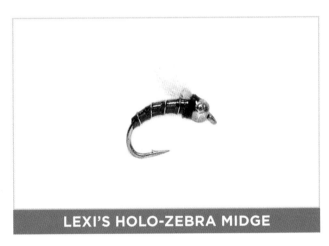

LEXI'S HOLO-ZEBRA MIDGE

- **Size:** 16-22.
- **Hook:** Grub.
- **Thread:** Red 6/0.
- **Abdomen:** Red Krystal Flash ribbed with silver wire.
- **Wing:** Short stub of white Antron yarn.
- **Bead:** Copper.
- **Difficulty:** 2.

MAD BOMBER CHIRONOMID

- **Size:** 16-22.
- **Hook:** Curved nymph.
- **Thread:** Black 6/0.
- **Abdomen:** Tying thread.
- **Rib:** Red and silver wire.
- **Bead:** White.
- **Difficulty:** 2.

M & M MIDGE PUPA

- **Size:** 16-24.
- **Color Options:** Cream, olive, black, gray, red.
- **Hook:** Curved nymph.
- **Thread:** 8/0 to match body color.
- **Wing Case:** White Antron or Z-Lon tied under thorax and pulled back from the eye.
- **Abdomen:** Turkey or goose biot to match pattern color.
- **Thorax:** Peacock or ostrich herl.
- **Difficulty:** 3.

MAGIC MIDGE

- **Size:** 18-22.
- **Hook:** Curved nymph.
- **Thread:** White 8/0.
- **Abdomen:** Tying thread.
- **Thorax:** Black fur.
- **Wing:** Single white biot.
- **Legs:** Black Z-Lon.
- **Difficulty:** 2.

NYMPH-MIDGE WD-40

- **Size:** 18-22.
- **Color Options:** Tan, gray, olive.
- **Hook:** Bigeye dry.
- **Thread:** Olive 8/0.
- **Tail:** Mallard-flank fibers.
- **Wing:** Mallard flank pulled over thorax.
- **Abdomen:** Tying thread.
- **Thorax:** Gray fur.
- **Difficulty:** 1.

STAN'S BEAD HEAD MIRACLE NYMPH

▌ **Size:** 16-22.
▌ **Hook:** 2X-long nymph (dry-fly hook in sizes 20-22).
▌ **Thread:** Black 6/0.
▌ **Body:** White thread or floss.
▌ **Rib:** Copper wire.
▌ **Bead:** Pink glass.
▌ **Difficulty:** 1.

TUNGHEAD ZEBRA MIDGE

▌ **Size:** 16-22.
▌ **Hook:** Grub.
▌ **Thread:** Black 6/0.
▌ **Abdomen:** Tying thread.
▌ **Rib:** Silver wire.
▌ **Bead:** Silver-colored tungsten.
▌ **Difficulty:** 1.

Stoneflies

BEAD HEAD GIANT STONE

▌ **Size:** 6-10.
▌ **Color Options:** Brown, black.
▌ **Hook:** 3X-long nymph/streamer.
▌ **Thread:** Black 6/0.
▌ **Tail:** Black or brown goose biots, tied short in a V.
▌ **Rib:** Black or brown Body Glass.
▌ **Wing Case:** Black or brown Swiss Straw or feather section, folded twice over thorax.
▌ **Abdomen:** Black or brown Antron dubbing.
▌ **Thorax:** Black or brown Antron dubbing, tied rough and picked out.
▌ **Antennae:** Black or brown goose biots tied forward over eye.
▌ **Difficulty:** 4.

BEAD HEAD STONEFLY

▌ **Size:** 4-10.
▌ **Color Options:** Brown, yellow.
▌ **Hook:** 4X-long streamer.
▌ **Thread:** Yellow 6/0.
▌ **Tail:** Yellow goose biot.
▌ **Rib:** Light brown Flexi Floss.
▌ **Wing Case:** Light mottled turkey, folded twice.
▌ **Abdomen:** Brown or pale amber dubbing.
▌ **Thorax:** Same dubbing as abdomen.
▌ **Legs:** Yellow grizzly hackle.
▌ **Head:** Two brass beads.
▌ **Difficulty:** 3.

EDWARDS' LITTLE BLACK STONE

- **Size:** 14-18.
- **Hook:** 3X-long nymph.
- **Thread:** Black 6/0.
- **Tail:** Two pieces of black moose mane.
- **Abdomen:** Thin vinyl strip, black.
- **Thorax:** Black fur.
- **Wing Case:** Three sections of black Thin Skin.
- **Legs:** Three segments of black hackle at each fold of wing case.
- **Antennae:** Two pieces of black moose mane.
- **Difficulty:** 4.

KAUFMANN' S MINI STONEFLY

- **Size:** 10-12.
- **Color Options:** Brown, black.
- **Hook:** 3X-long nymph/streamer.
- **Thread:** Brown or black 6/0.
- **Tail:** One pair turkey biots, splayed.
- **Body:** Antron/hare dubbing.
- **Rib:** Swannundaze.
- **Wing Case:** Dark turkey-tail segment.
- **Legs:** Black Living Rubber.
- **Antennae:** Same as tail.
- **Other Materials:** Gold bead.
- **Difficulty:** 4.

HALFBACK NYMPH

- **Size:** 8-16.
- **Hook:** Curved nymph.
- **Thread:** Black 6/0.
- **Tail:** Pheasant-tail fibers.
- **Rib:** Brown saddle hackle palmered through both abdomen and thorax.
- **Abdomen:** Peacock herl, with a shellback of pheasant-tail fibers over the top.
- **Thorax:** Peacock herl.
- **Difficulty:** 3.

KAUFMANN'S STONE

- **Size:** 2-10.
- **Color Options:** Brown, black.
- **Hook:** Curved nymph.
- **Thread:** Brown 6/0.
- **Tail:** Black or reddish brown goose biots.
- **Rib:** Black or brown transparent Body Glass, V-Rib, or Swannundaze.
- **Wing Case:** Three segments or dark turkey tail, cut or burned to notched shape.
- **Abdomen:** Black or brown dubbing, rough, with translucent synthetic or natural fibers.
- **Thorax:** Same as body.
- **Legs:** Dubbing picked out at thorax.
- **Head:** Same as body.
- **Antennae:** Reddish brown or black goose biots.
- **Difficulty:** 4.

LITTLE YELLOW STONEFLY

- **Size:** 14-18.
- **Hook:** 3X-long nymph.
- **Thread:** Yellow 6/0.
- **Tail:** Two pieces of elk hair.
- **Abdomen:** Thin vinyl strip, yellow.
- **Thorax:** Pale yellow fur.
- **Wing Case:** Three sections of olive Thin Skin.
- **Legs:** Three segments of cream hackle at each fold of wing case.
- **Antennae:** Two pieces of elk hair.
- **Difficulty:** 4.

MONTANA NYMPH

- **Size:** 8-14.
- **Hook:** 3X-long nymph/streamer.
- **Thread:** Black 6/0 or 8/0.
- **Tail:** Black hackle fibers.
- **Wing Case:** Two strands of black chenille pulled over the thorax as wing case.
- **Abdomen:** Black chenille.
- **Thorax:** Yellow chenille, with black saddle hackle palmered through.
- **Difficulty:** 1.

MICRO STONE

- **Size:** 14-18.
- **Hook:** Heavy wet/nymph.
- **Thread:** Brown 6/0.
- **Tail:** Two goose biots, splayed.
- **Wing Case:** Brown hen.
- **Abdomen:** Golden Antron overwrapped with golden turkey biot, marked with black or brown Pantone pen.
- **Thorax:** Golden Antron.
- **Legs:** Brown hen divided under the wing case.
- **Head:** Copper or gold bead.
- **Antennae:** Goose biots to match tail (optional).
- **Difficulty:** 4.

OE STONEFLY NYMPH

- **Size:** 4-14.
- **Hook:** Curved nymph.
- **Thread:** Brown 6/0.
- **Tail:** Brown goose biot.
- **Abdomen:** Brown yarn ribbed with thick black thread, covered by clear Thin Skin or V-Rib. Cover the top of the abdomen with a dark brown marker.
- **Thorax:** Brown fur or yarn.
- **Wing Case:** Dark brown Thin Skin in three sections.
- **Legs:** Brown mottled hen saddle at each wing-pad joint.
- **Antennae:** Brown goose biots.
- **Difficulty:** 4.

PRINCE NYMPH

- **Size:** 8-16.
- **Hook:** 2X-long nymph.
- **Thread:** Brown 6/0.
- **Tail:** Two goose biots, brown, tied in a V.
- **Body:** Peacock herl.
- **Rib:** Oval gold tinsel.
- **Wing:** Two broad white goose biots, tied flat in a V over body.
- **Hackle:** Brown.
- **Difficulty:** 2.

SEXY STONE

- **Size:** 4-12.
- **Hook:** 4X-long nymph.
- **Thread:** Brown 6/0.
- **Tail:** Two brown-speckled Tentacle Legs.
- **Body:** Brown/black variegated chenille.
- **Legs:** Three brown-speckled Tentacle Legs on each side.
- **Antennae:** Two brown-speckled Tentacle Legs.
- **Difficulty:** 2.
- **Notes:** Also known as the Rubber Leg Stone or just "Rubberlegs." Often tied in various shades of brown, amber, and black.

ROSETTA STONE NYMPH

- **Size:** 6-14.
- **Hook:** 4X-long nymph.
- **Thread:** Tan 6/0.
- **Tail:** Ginger goose biot.
- **Abdomen:** Copper Mirage Flashabou or similar.
- **Thorax:** Copper sparkle dubbing.
- **Rib:** Black V-Rib.
- **Wing Case:** Clear Thin Skin in two sections.
- **Legs:** Brown-mottled Sili Legs.
- **Bead:** Gold colored tungsten.
- **Antennae:** Ginger goose biot.
- **Difficulty:** 3.
- **Notes:** Can also be tied in black. All materials in the black version are black, except for the abdomen underbody, which is silver.

TED'S GOLDEN STONE

- **Size:** 8-10.
- **Hook:** 3X-long nymph/streamer.
- **Thread:** Black 6/0.
- **Tail:** Two pieces of 0X mono, mottled with a black Sharpie marker.
- **Body:** Golden Stone Antron/Hare dubbing over flattened plastic form.
- **Rib:** Medium-dun size A monocord or Kevlar.
- **Wing Case:** Fifteen to twenty stripped peacock herl strands highlighted with Sharpie marker.
- **Legs:** Six yellow knotted turkey biots highlighted with Sharpie marker.
- **Eyes:** Melted mono dumbbell.
- **Weight:** Medium non-toxic wire wrapped around or beside the plastic underbody.

TED'S STONE

- **Size:** 4-12.
- **Hook:** 4X-long nymph.
- **Thread:** Olive 6/0.
- **Tail:** Two amber goose biots flecked with black permanent marker.
- **Abdomen:** Cream fur over wire tied to sides of shank to get flat shape.
- **Overlay:** Dark brown turkey tail segment.
- **Thorax:** Cream fur.
- **Rib:** Tying thread.
- **Wing Case:** Same as abdomen overlay without rib.
- **Legs:** Six amber goose biots, knotted and flecked with black permanent marker.
- **Eyes:** Small plastic.
- **Head:** Section of wing case left extended over body.
- **Difficulty:** 4.
- **Notes:** Can be tied in various colors to imitate different types of stoneflies.

TUNGHEAD 20 INCHER

- **Size:** 8-14.
- **Hook:** Curved nymph.
- **Thread:** Black 6/0.
- **Tail:** Brown goose biots.
- **Abdomen:** Peacock herl.
- **Thorax:** Tan fur.
- **Rib:** Fine oval silver tinsel.
- **Wing Case:** Pheasant tail.
- **Legs:** Brown partridge tied in at sides.
- **Bead:** Brass.
- **Difficulty:** 3.

TUNGSTEN NEMEC STONE NYMPH

- **Size:** 4-10.
- **Hook:** 4X-long nymph.
- **Thread:** Tan 6/0.
- **Tail:** Brown turkey biots.
- **Abdomen:** Amber translucent dubbing.
- **Overlay:** Brown turkey biots tied over top of abdomen.
- **Thorax:** Amber translucent dubbing, tied heavy and picked out.
- **Rib:** Copper wire.
- **Wing Case:** Two sections of dark mottled brown Thin Skin, cut to shape.
- **Legs:** Black-speckled tan Sili Legs, two on each side.
- **Antennae:** Two black-speckled tan Sili Legs.
- **Bead:** Copper tungsten.
- **Difficulty:** 3.

Worms

SHAKY WORM

- **Size:** 10-16.
- **Hook:** Scud.
- **Thread:** Red 6/0.
- **Body:** Silicone worm material.
- **Overlay:** Red liquid solder.
- **Difficulty:** 1.
- **Notes:** Tie a thread base and attach worm material with careful wraps. Coat wraps with red liquid solder. Be sure not to use head cement or nail polish, as they will eat through the worm material.

THE WORM

- **Size:** 10-14.
- **Hook:** Tactical Czech nymph.
- **Thread:** Pink 6/0.
- **Abdomen:** Pink silicone worm material.
- **Thorax:** Pink silicone worm material.
- **Bead:** Red-colored brass or tungsten.
- **Difficulty:** 3.
- **Notes:** Slip head on hook. Attach thread. Tie in silicone behind bead. Slip a third of worm material through bead with bobbin threader. Whip finish remaining worm material to abdomen, and leave long. Apply liberal head cement around bead.

TACTICAL TUNG BELLY WORM

- **Size:** 10-14.
- **Hook:** Tactical Czech nymph.
- **Thread:** Pink 6/0.
- **Body:** Pink Vernille or Ultra Chenille, burnt at both ends.
- **Rib:** Tying thread.
- **Bead:** Orange.
- **Difficulty:** 1.
- **Notes:** Slip bead onto hook. Thread Vernille through bead. Attach thread at bend of hook, rib through to center of body and whip finish. Slip bead to center of shank, re-attach thread in front of bead and rib through to eye. Whip finish, and coat underside of hook with head cement to keep bead in place.

TUNGHEAD MEDUSA

- **Size:** 10-16.
- **Hook:** Grub.
- **Thread:** Pink 6/0.
- **Tail:** Short burnt pink Vernille and four longer strands of pink Flexi Floss.
- **Abdomen:** Tying thread with iridescent tinsel for overlay.
- **Rib:** Clear V-Rib.
- **Legs:** Same as tail left extending over eye.
- **Bead:** Gold-colored tungsten.
- **Difficulty:** 3.
- **Notes:** Tail and legs can be tied in at the same time.

VERNILLE SAN JUAN WORM

- **Size:** 8-16.
- **Color Options:** Tan or red.
- **Hook:** Short-shank curved nymph.
- **Thread:** Red 6/0.
- **Body:** Vernille tied in at bend and head, singed at both ends with butane lighter.
- **Difficulty:** 1.

WET FLIES

GOLD RIBBED HARE'S EAR

- **Size:** 10-16.
- **Thread:** Black 6/0.
- **Hook:** Standard wet.
- **Tail:** Guard hairs from hare's mask.
- **Body:** Dubbed fur from hare's mask.
- **Rib:** Oval gold tinsel.
- **Wing:** Mallard wing quills.
- **Hackle:** Guard hairs from hare's mask, tied as a beard only.
- **Difficulty:** 3.

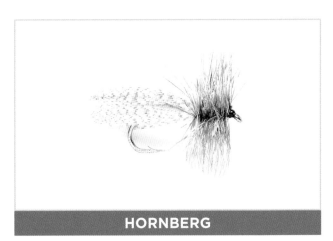

HORNBERG

- **Size:** 10-12.
- **Hook:** 3X-long nymph.
- **Thread:** Black 6/0.
- **Body:** Flat silver tinsel.
- **Wing:** Two yellow hackle tips inside two mallard-flank feathers.
- **Hackle:** Brown and grizzly, mixed.
- **Difficulty:** 2.
- **Notes:** The wing is wide and tied on the side of the shank so that it covers the body.

MARCH BROWN WET

- **Size:** 12-14.
- **Hook:** Heavy wet/nymph.
- **Thread:** Black 6/0.
- **Tail:** Brown partridge.
- **Body:** Fawn fox fur or other tan dubbing.
- **Rib:** Yellow thread or floss.
- **Wing:** Mottled turkey or speckled hen wing-quill segments.
- **Hackle:** Brown partridge, collar style.
- **Difficulty:** 3.

TACTICAL SPIDER HARE & PARTRIDGE

- **Size:** 10-16.
- **Thread:** Black 6/0.
- **Hook:** Tactical wide gape.
- **Body:** Hare's-ear dubbing, sparse and thin.
- **Hackle:** Brown partridge, two turns only.
- **Difficulty:** 2.

SPARKLE SOFT HACKLE

- **Size:** 10-16.
- **Thread:** Tan 6/0.
- **Hook:** Heavy wet fly/nymph.
- **Body:** Rear two-thirds yellow sparkle dubbing, sparse. Front third brown sparkle dubbing.
- **Hackle:** Brown partridge, two turns only.
- **Difficulty:** 2.

WOOLLY WORM

- **Size:** 6-12.
- **Color Options:** Black, brown, olive.
- **Hook:** 3X-long nymph.
- **Thread:** Black 6/0.
- **Tail:** Red hackle fibers.
- **Body:** Black, olive, or brown chenille.
- **Hackle:** Badger or grizzly, palmered over body.
- **Difficulty:** 1.

Articulated

BEEL'S BEARDED WONDER

- **Size:** 6.5 inches.
- **Thread:** Brown 3/0.
- **Front Hook:** Partridge Universal Predator or similar size 1/0.
- **Rear Hook:** Partridge Universal Predator or similar size 1/0.
- **Connector:** Black wire with three purple beads.
- **Rear Tail:** Brown bucktail over white bucktail.
- **Rear Body:** Brown crosscut rabbit wound around shank.
- **Rear Collar:** Brown deer hair and orange Sili Legs on top only.
- **Tail:** Brown wool encircling shank.
- **Body:** Brown crosscut rabbit wound around shank.
- **Wing:** Large bunch of peacock herl tied in middle of body.
- **Top Head:** Brown deer hair, spun and trimmed to shape.
- **Bottom Head:** Tan Laser Dub.
- **Eyes:** White metal eyes with black pupil.
- **Difficulty:** 4.

GRUMPY MUPPET

- **Size:** 3.5 inches
- **Front Hook:** Daiichi 2546 Salt size 1 or similar.
- **Rear Hook:** Daiichi 2546 Salt size 4.
- **Connector:** Silver wire and two olive beads.
- **Rear Tail:** Olive craft fur barred with black permanent marker.
- **Rear Body:** Pearl polar chenille.
- **Body:** Pearl polar chenille.
- **Wing:** Olive craft fur with black permanent marker stripes in two bunches, middle of shank and at front. Two large olive-dyed mallard flank feathers on each side. Two olive Sili Legs on each side.
- **Collar:** Orange, then olive Laser Dub.
- **Eyes:** Large red weighted eyes with black pupils.
- **Difficulty:** 4.

KINKY ZONKER

- **Size:** Size 2-6.
- **Thread:** Black 3/0.
- **Front Hook:** 40 mm shank.
- **Rear Hook:** Gamakatsu B10S size 1/0.
- **Connector:** Connect rear hook directly to shank.
- **Rear Tail:** Black rabbit fur tied over rear body Zonker style.
- **Rear Body:** Black Cactus Chenille.
- **Collar:** Black marabou and olive-mottled marabou.
- **Head:** Black Flash & Slinky on top, Yellow Flash & Slinky on bottom. Trim head, but leave rear fibers long to add to the collar.
- **Eyes:** Pearl eyes, glued to sides of head.
- **Difficulty:** 3.
- **Notes:** Also tied in olive and brown/orange.

LYNCH'S DOUBLE D STREAMER

- **Size:** 7.5 inches.
- **Thread:** White 3/0.
- **Front Hook:** Owner 45-degree down eye (5326) or similar.
- **Rear Hook:** Gamakatsu B10s size 2 or similar.
- **Connector:** Silver wire and two black beads.
- **Rear Body:** Rear half silver Polar Chenille, front half white rabbit.
- **Rear Wing:** Large mallard flank feather tied flat.

- **Body:** White rabbit, then silver Polar Chenille, then white rabbit in front. There is also a single ball glass rattle buried under the body.
- **Wing:** Four mallard flank feathers and silver Holo Flash.
- **Beard:** Tan rabbit fur.
- **Head:** Natural deer hair with collar, trimmed flat on bottom, at a wedge-shaped angle on top and coated with thin UV-cure resin.
- **Eyes:** Prismatic eyes glued to sides of head.
- **Difficulty:** 5.
- **Notes:** Also popular in olive/gold and orange/olive configurations.

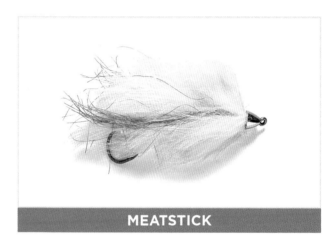

MEATSTICK

- **Size:** 4-6 inches.
- **Thread:** Black 6/0.
- **Front Hook:** 25 mm shank.
- **Rear Hook:** Red bait hook.
- **Connector:** 30-pound backing.
- **Rear Tail:** Pink marabou.
- **Rear Body:** Pink Cactus Chenille on rear half of shank only.
- **Wing:** Black rabbit strip over red Flashabou.
- **Collar:** Black rabbit.
- **Cone:** Silver.
- **Difficulty:** 3.
- **Notes:** Also tied in white.

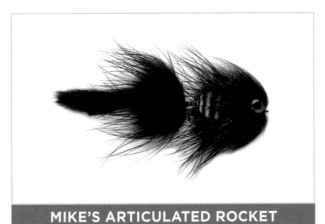

MIKE'S ARTICULATED ROCKET

- **Size:** 4 inches.
- **Thread:** Tan 3/0.
- **Front Hook:** Gamakatsu B10s #1 or similar.
- **Rear Hook:** Gamakatsu B10s #2 or similar.
- **Connector:** Silver wire and two yellow beads.
- **Rear Tail:** Tan Zonker strip.
- **Rear Body:** Olive Cactus Chenille ribbed with yellow saddle hackle.
- **Rear Collar:** Tan marabou.
- **Body:** Olive Cactus Chenille ribbed with yellow saddle hackle.
- **Wing:** Two short hen grizzly hackles tied in at sides.
- **Collar:** Tan marabou, then orange Laser Dub, then tan Laser Dub.
- **Eyes:** Large pearl eyes glued to sides of head.
- **Difficulty:** 4.

MIKE'S MARACEIVER

- **Size:** 5.5 inches.
- **Thread:** White 3/0.
- **Front Hook:** Gamakatsu B10s #1 or similar.
- **Rear Hook:** Gamakatsu B10s #2 or similar.
- **Connector:** Silver wire and two pearl beads.
- **Rear Tail:** Gray marabou and pearl Krinkle Flash.
- **Rear Body:** Pearl Krinkle Flash.
- **Rear Collar:** Gray marabou on top, white marabou on the bottom.

- **Body:** Tying thread.
- **Wing:** Gray marabou and pearl Krinkle Flash on top, white marabou on bottom. Wing should be tied at about the middle of the front hook shank.
- **Collar:** Gray bucktail on top, white bucktail on the bottom. Bucktail should be tied with tips extending over the hook eye, then folded back and secured to form a two-tone head. The head should be coated with epoxy or head cement.
- **Eyes:** Large pearl eyes glued to sides of wing/collar.
- **Difficulty:** 4.
- **Notes:** Fly is also tied in yellow/tan and olive/white, with lighter color on the bottom and darker color on top.

MIKE'S MEAL TICKET

- **Size:** 4 inches.
- **Thread:** Brown 3/0.
- **Front Hook:** Gamakatsu B10s #1 or similar.
- **Rear Hook:** Gamakatsu B10s #2 or similar.
- **Connector:** Silver wire and two tan beads.
- **Rear Tail:** Olive-barred rabbit strip tied over body Zonker-style.
- **Rear Body:** Copper Polar Chenille.
- **Rear Collar:** Orange-barred Sili Legs.
- **Front Tail:** Olive-barred rabbit strip.
- **Body:** Copper Polar Chenille.
- **Collar:** Orange-barred Sili Legs with brown wool on top and tan wool underneath.
- **Eyes:** White metal dumbbell eyes with black pupil.
- **Difficulty:** 3.
- **Notes:** Also tied with tan- or purple-barred rabbit strips.

ROUSE'S POODLE

- **Size:** 3.5 inches.
- **Thread:** 3/0 (140 denier) to match body color.
- **Front Hook:** Gamakatsu B10s #2 or similar.
- **Rear Hook:** Gamakatsu B10s #4 or similar.
- **Connector:** Silver wire and three red beads.
- **Rear Tail:** White bucktail and pearl Krystal Flash.
- **Rear Body:** Pearl Cactus Chenille.
- **Rear Collar:** Pearl Polar Chenille.
- **Front Tail:** White arctic fox and pearl Krystal Flash.
- **Body:** Pearl Cactus Chenille.
- **Collar:** White arctic fox tied to encircle hook, longer on top.
- **Head:** Pearl Cactus Chenille.
- **Eyes:** Yellow metal dumbbell eyes with black pupils.
- **Difficulty:** 3.
- **Notes:** Also tied in olive and black.

SCHMIDT'S JUNKYARD DOG

- **Size:** 5 inches.
- **Thread:** Black 3/0.
- **Front Hook:** Gamakatsu SP11 3L3H #2/0 or similar.
- **Rear Hook:** Gamakatsu B10S #1 or similar.
- **Connector:** Silver wire and two black beads.
- **Rear Tail:** Black marabou.
- **Rear Body:** Black Polar Chenille.

- **Rear Collar:** Black marabou, then black artic fox.
- **Body:** Tying thread.
- **Wing:** Black marabou encircling hook, tied in about one-third shank length back from the eye.
- **Collar:** Black arctic fox hollow-tied around hook.
- **Head:** Black Laser Dub, trimmed in front.
- **Eyes:** Large yellow eyes glued to side of head.
- **Difficulty:** 4.
- **Notes:** To hollow-tie the fox, tie in a bunch on top of the hook with tips facing over the eye. Fold it back and tie in facing back. Repeat on the bottom of the hook. This method gives the fly more bulk at the head.

SCHMIDT'S VIKING MIDGE

- **Size:** 6 inches
- **Thread:** Tan 3/0.
- **Front Hook:** Gamakatsu SB11 #1/0 or similar.
- **Rear Hook:** Gamakatsu B10S #2 or similar.
- **Connector:** Copper wire and single orange bead.
- **Rear Tail:** Pair of tan schlappen feathers and tan marabou.
- **Rear Body:** Copper Polar Chenille.
- **Rear Collar:** Brown rubber legs.
- **Body:** Copper Polar Chenille.
- **Wing:** Tan marabou.
- **Head:** Tan Laser Dub trimmed to shape.
- **Eyes:** Yellow metal eyes with black pupils.
- **Difficulty:** 3.

SCHULTZY'S S3 SCULPIN

- **Size:** 3.5 inches.
- **Thread:** Olive 3/0.
- **Front Hook:** Daiichi 2546 Salt #1 or similar.
- **Rear Hook:** Daiichi 2546 Salt #4.
- **Connector:** 30-pound backing.
- **Tail:** Long strip of mottled olive rabbit.
- **Body:** Olive rabbit strip, wound.
- **Cheeks:** Olive grizzly marabou.
- **Wing:** Olive grizzly saddle hackles plus a half dozen olive barred Sili Legs.
- **Collar:** Olive grizzly schlappen and mallard flank.
- **Flash:** Red Holographic Flashabou and copper Flashabou.
- **Head:** Olive rabbit, spun in dubbing loop.
- **Eyes:** Yellow metallic eyes with black pupils.
- **Difficulty:** 4.
- **Notes:** Sometimes, the rear hook is left off, and just the front hook is used. If the rear hook is used, the long rabbit strip is lashed to it with tying thread.

SCHULTZY'S S4 SCULPIN

- **Size:** 3.5 inches.
- **Thread:** Olive 3/0.
- **Front Hook:** Daiichi 2546 Salt #1 or similar.
- **Rear Hook:** Daiichi 2546 Salt #4.
- **Connector:** 30-pound backing.
- **Rear Tail:** Copper Flashabou.

- **Front Tail:** White arctic fox, with brown grizzly marabou tied on bottom to imitate pectoral fins.
- **Wing:** Long strip of mottled tan rabbit, lashed to end of second hook.
- **Body:** Tan rabbit strip, wound.
- **Topping:** Grizzly saddle hackles plus a half dozen chartreuse barred Sili Legs.
- **Collar:** Brown grizzly marabou and orange Amherst pheasant tail fibers.
- **Flash:** Red Holographic Flashabou and copper Flashabou.
- **Head:** Tan rabbit, spun in dubbing loop.
- **Eyes:** Yellow metallic eyes with black pupils.
- **Difficulty:** 4.

SENYO'S ICED OUT SCULPIN

- **Size:** 4 inches.
- **Thread:** Black 6/0.
- **Front Hook:** 24 mm shank or hook with bend broken off.
- **Rear Hook:** Intruder hook.
- **Connector:** 30-pound backing stiffened with flexible glue.
- **Rear Tail:** Purple Laser Dub.
- **Wing:** Black rabbit strip, lashed to rear hook as well.
- **Collar:** Purple Laser Dub on bottom, black Laser Dub on top. Black Sili Legs on each side.
- **Head:** Trimmed black Laser Dub on top, trimmed orange Laser Dub on bottom.
- **Eyes:** White metal dumbbell eyes with black pupils.
- **Difficulty:** 3.
- **Notes:** Also tied in white and olive.

SWINGIN D

- **Size:** 4-6 inches.
- **Thread:** Brown 3/0.
- **Front Hook:** Daiichi 2546 Salt #1/0 or similar.
- **Rear Hook:** Daiichi 2546 Salt #2 or similar.
- **Connector:** Silver wire and three gray beads.
- **Rear Tail:** White schlappen.
- **Rear Body:** Pearl Polar Chenille, then white rabbit.
- **Rear Wing:** Mallard flank tied flat on top.
- **Body:** White rabbit, then red Polar Chenille.
- **Wing:** Grizzly saddle hackles and pearl Flashabou.
- **Collar:** White marabou.
- **Head:** White foam cone.
- **Difficulty:** 4.
- **Notes:** Also tied in olive and white.

TRASH CAN STREAMER

- **Size:** 4 inches.
- **Thread:** Black 6/0.
- **Front Hook:** 24 mm shank.
- **Rear Hook:** Intruder hook.
- **Connector:** 30-pound backing.
- **Body:** Black Cactus Chenille.
- **Wing:** Black saddle hackles and black rabbit strip.
- **Head:** Black rabbit.
- **Eyes:** Red metal dumbbell eyes with black pupil.
- **Difficulty:** 3.
- **Notes:** Also tied in olive.

Buggers

BEAD HEAD FLASH BUGGER

- **Size:** 4-8.
- **Color Options:** Brown, black, olive.
- **Hook:** 4X-long streamer.
- **Thread:** 6/0 to match body color.
- **Tail:** Marabou to match pattern description.
- **Body:** Lite Brite dubbing to match pattern description.
- **Rib:** Grizzly saddle hackle.
- **Head:** Black brass bead.
- **Difficulty:** 2.

BEAD HEAD WOOLLY BUGGER

- **Size:** 4-10.
- **Color Options:** Olive/brown, black.
- **Hook:** 4X-long streamer.
- **Thread:** Black 6/0.
- **Tail:** Black or olive marabou.
- **Body:** Olive or black chenille.
- **Hackle:** Medium olive or black saddle, palmered through body.
- **Head:** Brass bead.
- **Difficulty:** 1.

CONE HEAD RUBBER BUGGER

- **Size:** 4-8.
- **Thread:** Orange 6/0.
- **Hook:** 4X-long streamer.
- **Tail:** Pearl Krystal Flash, orange marabou, and brown marabou on top.
- **Body:** Orange Cactus Chenille.
- **Rib:** Orange rubber hackle.
- **Head:** Brass cone.
- **Difficulty:** 2.
- **Notes:** Also tied in black, brown, and olive.

HOT CONE WOOLLY BUGGER

- **Size:** 6-10.
- **Thread:** Black 6/0.
- **Hook:** 4X-long streamer.
- **Tail:** Black marabou and pearl Krystal Flash.
- **Body:** Black chenille with lateral stripes of pearl Krystal Flash.
- **Rib:** Black saddle hackle.
- **Head:** Hot orange metal cone.
- **Difficulty:** 2.
- **Notes:** Also tied in olive.

DOVER'S PEACH

- **Size:** 4-10.
- **Thread:** Orange 6/0.
- **Hook:** 4X-long streamer.
- **Tail:** Orange marabou and orange Krystal Flash.
- **Body:** Orange Cactus Chenille.
- **Head:** Brass cone.
- **Difficulty:** 1.

KRYSTAL BUGGER

- **Size:** 4-12.
- **Color Options:** Black, olive.
- **Hook:** 4X-long streamer.
- **Thread:** Black 6/0.
- **Tail:** Olive or black marabou with a few strands of pearl Krystal Flash.
- **Body:** Silver or pearl Ice Chenille or Sparkle Chenille.
- **Hackle:** Black or olive, palmered through body.
- **Difficulty:** 1.

MCGINNIS EXTRA STOUT

- **Size:** 4-8.
- **Thread:** Black 6/0.
- **Hook:** 4XL streamer
- **Tail:** Black and brown marabou.
- **Body:** Copper Laser Dub.
- **Collar:** Black Laser Dub with three groups of black rubber legs extending to sides.
- **Head:** Brass cone.
- **Difficulty:** 3.

TEQUEELY STREAMER

- **Size:** 2-6.
- **Hook:** 4X-long streamer.
- **Thread:** Black 6/0.
- **Tail:** Yellow and black marabou, mixed.
- **Body:** Brown Estaz or Sparkle Chenille.
- **Legs:** Three pairs of yellow rubber legs sticking out each side.
- **Head:** Gold bead.
- **Difficulty:** 3.

MEG A-EGG-SUCKING LEECH

- **Size:** 2-6.
- **Color Options:** Black/chartreuse, purple/pink.
- **Hook:** Salmon wet fly.
- **Thread:** Black 6/0.
- **Tail:** Purple or black marabou with pearl Krystal Flash.
- **Body:** Purple or black chenille.
- **Hackle:** Purple or black, palmered through body.
- **Head:** Pink or chartreuse Crystal Egg, slipped over point and glued to shank before tying fly.
- **Difficulty:** 2.

TUNGHEAD RUBBER LEGGED BUGGER

- **Size:** 4-10
- **Thread:** Brown 6/0.
- **Hook:** 4X-long streamer.
- **Tail:** Yellow and brown marabou.
- **Body:** Brown Cactus Chenille.
- **Rib:** Brown saddle hackle.
- **Collar:** Brown webby hackle and yellow Tentacle Legs.
- **Head:** Copper bead.
- **Difficulty:** 2.
- **Notes:** The rubber legs are tied in two groups in the thorax area for more movement. The fly is also tied in green or black.

TUNGHEAD WOOLLY BUGGER

- **Size:** 2-10.
- **Hook:** 4X-long streamer.
- **Thread:** Black 3/0.
- **Tail:** Marabou with four strands of Krystal Flash on each side.
- **Body:** Chenille.
- **Wing:** Black marabou.
- **Hackle:** Saddle, grizzly, or same color as body.
- **Head:** Tungsten bead.
- **Difficulty:** 1.

WOOLLY BUGGER

- **Size:** 4-14.
- **Color Options:** Black, tan, white, olive.
- **Hook:** 4X-long streamer.
- **Thread:** Black or white 6/0.
- **Tail:** Marabou to match pattern description.
- **Body:** Chenille to match pattern color.
- **Rib:** Grizzly hackle palmered through body or a hackle to match pattern color.
- **Difficulty:** 1.

General

TUNGSTEN JIG BUGGER

- **Size:** 6-12.
- **Thread:** Black 6/0.
- **Hook:** Heavy jig hook.
- **Tail:** Black marabou.
- **Body:** Black dubbing.
- **Rib:** Red wire.
- **Collar:** Black hackle and two black rubber legs.
- **Head:** Black tungsten slotted bead.
- **Difficulty:** 2.
- **Notes:** Also tied in tan and olive.

BEAD HEAD LITE BRITE ZONKER

- **Size:** 4-8.
- **Color Options:** White, olive, black.
- **Hook:** 4X-long streamer.
- **Thread:** 6/0 to match pattern color.
- **Tail:** Zonker strip cut so that it tapers to a point.
- **Rib:** Fine gold wire or copper wire (optional).
- **Wing:** Same Zonker strip used for the tail, continued to the hook eye.
- **Abdomen:** Lite Brite dubbing twisted in a dubbing loop.
- **Thorax:** Red Lite Brite dubbing twisted in a dubbing loop, picked out to simulate gills.
- **Head:** Brass or tungsten bead.
- **Difficulty:** 4.

BLACK GHOST

- **Size:** 6-12.
- **Hook:** 6X-long streamer.
- **Thread:** Black 3/0 or 6/0.
- **Tail:** Yellow hackle fibers.
- **Body:** Black floss.
- **Rib:** Flat silver tinsel.
- **Wing:** White saddle hackle or marabou.
- **Beard:** Yellow hackle fibers.
- **Difficulty:** 3.

BLACK NOSE DACE

- **Size:** 6-10.
- **Hook:** 4X-long streamer.
- **Thread:** Black 6/0.
- **Tail:** Short, stubby red wool (if using flat silver tinsel for body).
- **Body:** Flat silver tinsel or fine silver Mylar piping.
- **Rib:** Oval silver tinsel (if body is flat silver tinsel).
- **Wing:** Brown bucktail over dyed-black squirrel tail or bucktail over sparse white bucktail.
- **Tag:** Red 3/0 thread to secure end of Mylar-piping body.
- **Difficulty:** 3.

CONE HEAD MARABOU MUDDLER

- **Size:** 2-8.
- **Color Options:** Black, white, yellow.
- **Hook:** 4X-long streamer.
- **Thread:** Gray 6/0.
- **Tail:** Red hackle fibers.
- **Body:** Flat silver tinsel.
- **Wing:** Marabou, to match pattern topped with several strands of peacock herl.
- **Head:** Natural deer, clipped to shape with unclipped natural ends left pointing back toward the bend as a collar. Gold cone ahead of the deer-hair head.
- **Difficulty:** 4.

CONE HEAD MUDDLER MINNOW

- **Size:** 2-8.
- **Hook:** 4X-long streamer.
- **Thread:** Gray 3/0.
- **Tail:** Mottled turkey wing-quill segment.
- **Body:** Flat gold tinsel.
- **Rib:** Medium gold wire.
- **Wing:** Mottled turkey quill paired segments with underwing of gray squirrel tail.
- **Head:** Natural deer clipped to shape with unclipped natural ends left pointing back toward the bend as a collar. Gold cone ahead of the deer-hair head.
- **Difficulty:** 4.

CONE HEAD WOOLLY BUGGER

- **Size:** 2-10.
- **Color Options:** Olive, black.
- **Hook:** 4X-long streamer.
- **Thread:** Black 6/0.
- **Tail:** Black or olive marabou and pearl Krystal Flash.
- **Body:** Black or olive Vernille.
- **Rib:** Dark monofilament thread.
- **Hackle:** Black, palmered.
- **Head:** Brass cone.
- **Difficulty:** 2.

FRANKE SHINER

- **Size:** 4-10.
- **Hook:** 4X-long streamer.
- **Thread:** Olive 6/0.
- **Body:** Fluorescent white floss and pearlescent Mylar.
- **Wing:** Six to eight strands of olive Krystal Flash, light olive arctic fox or deer hair and dark olive arctic fox or deer hair.
- **Head:** Olive 6/0 thread with an eye painted on each side.
- **Difficulty:** 3.

DOUBLE BUNNY

- **Size:** 4-8.
- **Thread:** White 3/0.
- **Hook:** 4X-long streamer.
- **Body/Wing:** Olive rabbit strip on top and white rabbit underneath.
- **Eyes:** Red metal eyes with black pupils.
- **Difficulty:** 2.
- **Notes:** Puncture the olive rabbit strip before attaching so that it lays flat along the hook shank. The fly rides upside down so the darker strip, imitating the back of a baitfish, gets punctured. Glue the back ends of the hide strips together with a flexible glue.

FRESHWATER CLOUSER

- **Size:** 4-10.
- **Thread:** White 6/0.
- **Hook:** 2X-long nymph.
- **Wing:** White bucktail underneath, chartreuse bucktail and Krystal Flash on top.
- **Eyes:** Silver dumbbell eyes.
- **Difficulty:** 1.
- **Notes:** Can be tied in a wide variety of color combinations.

GRAY GHOST

- **Size:** 6-12.
- **Hook:** 6X-long streamer.
- **Thread:** Black 6/0.
- **Body:** Orange floss with a tag of flat silver tinsel.
- **Rib:** Flat silver tinsel.
- **Wing:** Four gray saddle hackles over golden pheasant crest curving downward.
- **Throat:** Three or four strands of peacock herl over sparse bunch of white bucktail over golden pheasant crest curving upward.
- **Shoulders:** Silver-pheasant body feathers.
- **Cheeks:** Jungle cock.
- **Difficulty:** 5.
- **Notes:** Most tiers leave off the expensive jungle cock.

HAWKINS' LITTLE RASCAL

- **Size:** 6-12.
- **Thread:** Black 6/0.
- **Hook:** 4X-long streamer.
- **Tail:** Black rabbit strip.
- **Body:** Black rabbit strip wound along shank and trimmed on the bottom.
- **Wing:** Red and pearl Flashabou.
- **Head:** Silver cone.
- **Difficulty:** 2.
- **Notes:** Also tied in white, tan, and olive and white.

HAWKINS' NUTCRACKER

- **Size:** 4-8.
- **Thread:** White 3/0.
- **Hook:** Ring-eye streamer hook.
- **Wing:** Long magnum Zonker strip.
- **Collar:** Tan marabou and mallard flank, topped with red and pearl Flashabou.
- **Head:** Deer hair, cut flat on the bottom and wedge-shaped on top. Leave fine ends of deer hair facing back to form a collar.
- **Difficulty:** 3.
- **Notes:** Also tied in yellow, olive, and black.

HAWKINS' HAT TRICK

- **Size:** 4-8.
- **Thread:** Black 6/0.
- **Hook:** Straight-eye streamer.
- **Tail:** Four black saddle hackles, splayed.
- **Body:** Black rabbit fur strip wound along hook shank.
- **Wing:** Orange Sili Legs.
- **Collar:** Black rabbit fur.
- **Eyes:** Silver dumbbell eyes.
- **Difficulty:** 2.
- **Notes:** Also tied in white, yellow, and olive.

HAWKINS' TRIPLE DOUBLE

- **Size:** 4-8.
- **Thread:** Olive 3/0.
- **Hook:** 4X-long streamer.
- **Tail:** Long olive magnum Zonker strip, tied over the top of the body Zonker-style.
- **Body:** Alternating bands of pink and white rabbit strip wound around shank.
- **Topping:** Olive Sili Legs and pearl Flashabou.
- **Eyes:** Gold-colored metal dumbbell eyes.
- **Difficulty:** 3.

IAN'S EPOXY MINNOW

- **Size:** 8-12.
- **Thread:** Monofilament.
- **Hook:** 4X-long streamer.
- **Tail:** Sparse fox squirrel tail over sparse white bucktail.
- **Body:** Small band of red thread at the tail. Body wound with pearl Diamond Braid.
- **Wing:** Fox squirrel from the tail pulled over the body and secured at head.
- **Eyes:** Stick-on.
- **Difficulty:** 2.
- **Notes:** Give the finished fly two or three coats of thin epoxy.

MARABOU MUDDLER

- **Size:** 4-8.
- **Color Options:** Gray/white, gray/black, gray/yellow.
- **Hook:** 4X-long streamer.
- **Thread:** Gray 3/0.
- **Tail:** Two red duck-quill sections.
- **Body:** Silver or gold (on yellow version) tinsel chenille or flat tinsel.
- **Wing:** White, black, or yellow marabou topped with several strands of peacock herl.
- **Head:** Spun natural gray deer hair, clipped to shape leaving untrimmed natural ends extending toward bend as a collar.
- **Difficulty:** 3.

MERLINO'S CRITTER

- **Size:** 1/0-4.
- **Thread:** Black 3/0.
- **Hook:** Gamakatsu B10S or other short-shank saltwater hook.
- **Tail:** Long blue-mottled magnum Zonker strip, topped with blue Mirror Flash.
- **Body:** Blue and white marabou wound around shank.
- **Collar:** Black arctic fox on top, red arctic fox below.
- **Eyes:** Red metal dumbbell eyes with black pupils.
- **Difficulty:** 3.
- **Notes:** Can be tied with varied colors of striped Zonker strips.

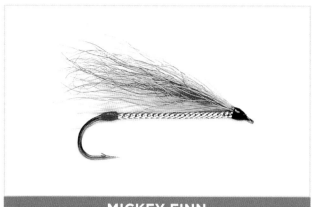

MICKEY FINN

- **Size:** 6-12.
- **Hook:** 4X-long streamer.
- **Thread:** Black 6/0.
- **Body:** Flat silver tinsel or fine silver Mylar piping.
- **Rib:** Oval silver tinsel (if body is flat silver tinsel).
- **Wing:** Yellow bucktail over red bucktail over sparse yellow bucktail.
- **Tag:** Red 3/0 thread to secure end of Mylar-piping body.
- **Difficulty:** 3.

ORANGE BLOSSOM SPECIAL

- **Size:** 4-8.
- **Hook:** 4X-long streamer.
- **Thread:** Brown 6/0.
- **Body:** Olive-brown Crystal Chenille.
- **Rib:** Gold wire.
- **Wing:** One orange, one yellow, and two brown webby neck hackles.
- **Hackle:** One yellow and one brown hackle tied as collar.
- **Head:** Brass cone with brown dubbed fur behind to hold it in place.
- **Difficulty:** 3.

SCHULTZY'S RED EYES LEECH

- **Size:** 2-4.
- **Thread:** Black 3/0.
- **Hook:** Standard saltwater.
- **Tail:** Black Zonker strip.
- **Body:** Zonker strip wound around shank.
- **Collar:** Mallard or wood duck flank mixed with strands from Amherst pheasant tail.
- **Topping:** Red and gold Mirror Flash.
- **Head:** Black rabbit fur cut from hide and wound in a dubbing loop.
- **Eyes:** Red metal dumbbell eyes.
- **Difficulty:** 3.
- **Notes:** Also tied in olive, tan, or brown.

SCHULTZY'S SINGLE FLY CRAY

- **Size:** 1/0-4.
- **Thread:** Red 3/0.
- **Hook:** Standard saltwater.
- **Tail:** Copper Flashabou, blue Flashabou, and orange Sili Legs. At each side of the tail, tie in a strip of tan-barred rabbit.
- **Body:** Tan-barred rabbit, wound around shank.
- **Collar:** Orange-dyed mallard flank.
- **Head:** Tan rabbit spun in dubbing loop and wound.
- **Eyes:** Red metal dumbbell eyes.
- **Difficulty:** 2.

SENYO'S TROUT PARR

- **Size:** 8-12.
- **Thread:** Olive 6/0.
- **Hook:** Standard wet fly.
- **Wing:** Short pearl Angel Hair, then pink Flash Blend, then green Flashabou.
- **Collar:** Olive rabbit wound in a dubbing loop.
- **Eyes:** Pearl eyes glued to side of collar.
- **Difficulty:** 2.

TACTICAL MASKED BANDIT

- **Size:** 8-12.
- **Thread:** White 6/0.
- **Hook:** Up-eyed short-shank grub hook.
- **Underwing:** Pearl Angel Hair or Ice Dub.
- **Wing:** Pine squirrel Zonker strip.
- **Collar:** Pine squirrel wound in dubbing loop.
- **Head:** Fish Skull.
- **Eyes:** Stick-on.
- **Difficulty:** 3.

SMACK EM SPEY

- **Size:** 6-10.
- **Thread:** White 6/0.
- **Hook:** 4X-long streamer.
- **Wing:** White marabou wound around shank, covered with sparse fox squirrel tail.
- **Eyes:** Stick-on.
- **Difficulty:** 2.
- **Notes:** Give the head two coats of clear epoxy or head cement.

TUNGHEAD & MARABOU MUDDLER

- **Size:** 4-10.
- **Color Options:** Black/gray, white/gray, gray/yellow.
- **Hook:** 4X-long streamer.
- **Thread:** White 3/0.
- **Tail:** Red hackle tips.
- **Body:** Flat gold or silver Mylar Tinsel.
- **Wing:** Marabou to match pattern description.
- **Topping:** 2-6 peacock swords.
- **Collar:** Deer body hair tips.
- **Head:** Spun deer body hair behind a brass or tungsten cone head.
- **Difficulty:** 4.

WILDWOOD'S 3M MINNOW

- **Size:** 1/0-4.
- **Thread:** White 3/0.
- **Tail:** White bucktail covered with white EP Fiber covered with copper Flashabou.
- **Body:** Long copper flashy chenille such as Senyo's Aqua Veil.
- **Eyes:** Stick-on.
- **Difficulty:** 2.
- **Notes:** Also tied in silver or green. Build up the head with two coats of clear epoxy.

ZONKER

- **Size:** 4-8.
- **Color Options:** Pearl, black, olive, Black Ghost.
- **Hook:** 4X-long streamer.
- **Thread:** 6/0 to match body color.
- **Tail:** Frayed ends of Mylar piping used for the body.
- **Body:** Mylar piping over cut plastic form.
- **Wing:** Zonker strip.

Mice

WILSON'S TREASURE

- **Size:** 6-12.
- **Thread:** Black 6/0.
- **Hook:** 4X-long or 6X-long streamer.
- **Tail:** Yellow hackle fibers.
- **Body:** Silver tinsel.
- **Rib:** Oval silver tinsel.
- **Wing:** Gray hackle feathers.
- **Cheeks:** Grizzly hackle feathers, imitation jungle cock, and wood duck flank.
- **Throat:** Sparse white bucktail, a few fibers of UV pearl flash, and a few peacock herls.
- **Difficulty:** 3.

CERMELE'S MASTER SPLINTER

- **Size:** 2-6.
- **Thread:** Brown 3/0.
- **Hook:** Straight-eye streamer.
- **Tail:** Brown Vernille.
- **Body:** Brown rabbit strip wound around hook shank.
- **Overlay:** Tan foam.
- **Head:** Foam folded over and secured.
- **Difficulty:** 2.

WHITE BELLIED MOUSE WAKER

- **Size:** 4 inches.
- **Thread:** Black 3/0.
- **Front Hook:** 40 mm shank.
- **Rear Hook:** Straight-eye streamer.
- **Connector:** 30-pound backing.
- **Rear Tail:** Leather strip.
- **Rear Body:** Trimmed white Zonker strip underneath the shank. Untrimmed gray Zonker strip on top.
- **Rear Legs:** Orange rubber.
- **Body:** White rabbit strip, then gray rabbit strip wound around hook.
- **Overlay:** Tan foam. Leave long in front, and trim to form a head.
- **Front Legs:** Pair of orange rubber legs.
- **Head:** Small amount of black sparkle dubbing.
- **Difficulty:** 4.

Sculpins

BUBBA'S NBK SCULPIN

- **Size:** 6-10.
- **Thread:** Olive 6/0.
- **Hook:** 4X-long or 6X-long streamer.
- **Tail:** Olive Zonker strip, punctured and continued over the belly of the fly (fly rides hook up).
- **Body:** Tan fur.
- **Rib:** Pearl Flashabou.
- **Wing:** Olive Sili Legs, pearl Flashabou, and pearl UV flash.
- **Collar:** Olive rabbit behind and in front of eyes.
- **Eyes:** Silver dumbbell eyes with small doll eyes glued to the ends.
- **Difficulty:** 3.
- **Notes:** Also tied in tan and rust.

FISH SKULL ZONKER

- **Size:** 4-8.
- **Thread:** Olive 6/0.
- **Hook:** 4X-long streamer.
- **Tail:** Copper Flashabou and olive Zonker strip continued over back of fly.
- **Body:** Olive sparkle dubbing.
- **Rib:** Olive wire.
- **Throat:** Olive rabbit.
- **Head:** Dark gray Fish Skull.
- **Eyes:** Pearl eyes.
- **Difficulty:** 3.
- **Notes:** Also tied in black or white.

GD SCULP SNACK

- **Size:** 6-10.
- **Thread:** Olive 6/0.
- **Hook:** 4X-long streamer.
- **Tail:** Tan marabou below, olive marabou on top. A few strands of copper Flashabou on the sides.
- **Body:** Olive Cactus Chenille.
- **Rib:** Gold wire.
- **Wing:** Brown-mottled Sili Legs.
- **Head:** Brass cone.
- **Difficulty:** 2.

MOTO'S MINNOW

- **Size:** 6-10.
- **Color Options:** Tan, brown.
- **Hook:** 3X-long nymph/streamer.
- **Thread:** Tan or brown 6/0.
- **Tail:** Gray marabou.
- **Body:** Mottled hen hackle palmered the full length of the body.
- **Collar:** Three to four turns of white hen hackle or a soft, webby saddle hackle.
- **Head:** Brass or tungsten cone head.
- **Difficulty:** 4.

MARTINEZ FRANKENSTEIN SCULPIN

- **Size:** 4-8.
- **Thread:** Olive 3/0.
- **Hook:** Straight-eye streamer.
- **Tail:** Tan-mottled marabou.
- **Body:** Tan Laser Dub.
- **Rib:** Mallard or wood duck flank and gold wire.
- **Wing:** Two bunches of tan-mottled marabou tied in at sides, two wood duck flanks or yellow-dyed mallard flanks tied flat on top.
- **Head:** Copper Fish Skull Sculpin Head.
- **Eyes:** Small pearl eyes glued into Fish Skull.
- **Difficulty:** 3.
- **Notes:** Also tied in olive.

MUDDLER MINNOW

- **Size:** 2-12.
- **Hook:** 4X-long streamer.
- **Thread:** Black 6/0.
- **Tail:** Mottled turkey-quill segment.
- **Body:** Flat gold tinsel.
- **Wing:** Mottled turkey-quill segments over gray squirrel tail.
- **Head:** Spun natural gray deer hair, clipped to shape leaving untrimmed natural ends extending toward bend as a collar.
- **Difficulty:** 4.

VILLWOCK'S OVER EASY SCULPIN

- **Size:** 3 inches.
- **Thread:** Olive 6/0.
- **Front Hook:** 40 mm shank.
- **Rear Hook:** Intruder hook.
- **Connector:** Silver wire.
- **Tail:** Olive-mottled Zonker strip continued over body Zonker-style.
- **Body:** Olive Cactus Chenille.
- **Rib:** Olive saddle hackle.
- **Wing:** Brown Laser Dub.
- **Pectoral Fins:** Olive-dyed partridge or mottled hen saddle.
- **Collar:** Orange guinea fowl hackle.
- **Eyes:** Black metal dumbbell eyes.
- **Difficulty:** 4.
- **Notes:** Also tied in tan.

STEELHEAD

Articulated

CHAIN REACTION LEECH

- **Size:** 5 inches.
- **Thread:** Fluorescent pink 3/0.
- **Front Hook:** 40 mm articulated shank.
- **Rear Hook:** Straight-shank saltwater.
- **Connector:** Connect rear hook directly to loop on shank.
- **Rear Tail:** Zonker strip.
- **Rear Body:** Cross-cut rabbit and silver Polar Chenille.
- **Body:** Cross-cut rabbit and silver Polar Chenille.
- **Bead:** Silver cone.
- **Difficulty:** 3.
- **Notes:** Popular colors are black, fuchsia, olive, white, and chartreuse.

INTRUDER

- **Size:** 2-3 inches.
- **Thread:** Black 6/0.
- **Front Hook:** Black 25 mm shank.
- **Rear Hook:** Intruder hook.
- **Connector:** Black wire.
- **Tail:** Black arctic fox and black ostrich distributed around shank. A few strands of purple Mirror Flash on top.
- **Body:** Pearlescent tinsel.
- **Wing:** Light blue arctic fox and black ostrich distributed around shank. A few strands of purple Mirror Flash on top.
- **Hackle:** Blue-dyed guinea fowl in front of eyes.
- **Eyes:** Blue metallic dumbbell eyes.
- **Difficulty:** 3.
- **Notes:** The Intruder is a style of tying as opposed to a specific pattern and can be tied in a wide variety of colors, with different materials. All materials should be chosen for their ability to move freely in the water.

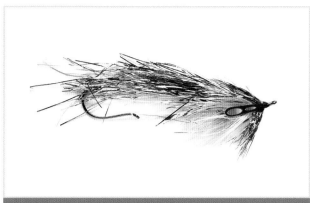

SENYO'S AI INTRUDER

- **Size:** 3 inches.
- **Thread:** Black 6/0.
- **Front Hook:** 25 mm black articulated shank.
- **Rear Hook:** Intruder hook or similar.
- **Connector:** Black wire.
- **Butt:** Chartreuse flash chenille.
- **Body:** Rear half silver Polar Chenille, front half white schlappen.
- **Wing:** Strands of Amherst pheasant tail covered with silver gray Iceabou covered with clear and rainbow Flashabou covered with silver black fleck Flashabou.
- **Hackle:** Guinea fowl.
- **Eyes:** Silver bead chain and imitation jungle cock.
- **Difficulty:** 3.

SENYO'S EGG RAIDER

- **Size:** 3.5 inches.
- **Thread:** Olive 6/0.
- **Front Hook:** 25 mm black articulated shank or hook with bend cut off.
- **Rear Hook:** Intruder style.
- **Connector:** White dacron backing, stiffened with flexible cement.
- **Tail:** Long olive Zonker strip, plus strips of orange and blue Holographic Flashabou.
- **Body:** Pearl Diamond Braid.

- **Rib:** Olive saddle hackle.
- **Wing:** Several olive Sili Legs.
- **Hackle:** Olive-dyed pheasant body feather and copper rubber hackle.
- **Eyes:** Green fluorescent plastic dumbbell eyes.
- **Head:** Large orange egg bead.
- **Difficulty:** 3.

SENYO'S GANGSTA INTRUDER

- **Size:** 3 inches.
- **Thread:** Black 6/0.
- **Front Hook:** 25 mm black articulated shank.
- **Rear Hook:** Intruder hook.
- **Connector:** Black wire.
- **Tail:** Slide a #0 nickel Indiana spinner blade on the loop of the shank. Surround the shank with pale olive Laser Dub, and tie several strands of green Amherst pheasant tail on each side.
- **Body:** Black Senyo's Aqua Veil chenille.
- **Hackle:** Black-dyed pheasant body feather.
- **Wing:** Black ostrich herl, purple and green Flashabou, and green Amherst pheasant tail.
- **Eyes:** Silver metallic dumbbell eyes with green iris and black pupil.
- **Throat:** Chartreuse rubber hackle behind the eyes, pink Laser Dub in front.
- **Topping:** Chartreuse Finn raccoon or arctic fox fur.
- **Difficulty:** 4.

Eggs

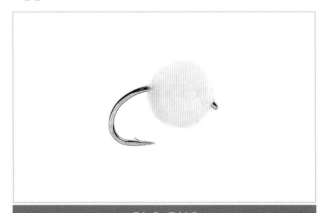

GLO-BUG

- **Size:** 8-14.
- **Color Options:** Chartreuse, pink, orange, white, blue, red, black.
- **Hook:** Short-shank curved nymph.
- **Thread:** To match yarn color.
- **Body:** Glo-Bug or egg yarn.
- **Difficulty:** 2.
- **Notes:** Tie about a hook-gape width of yarn firmly to the top of the hook in the center of the shank. Raise the yarn straight up, and take several circular turns of thread around its base. Then trim the yarn quickly with a sharp pair of serrated scissors while pulling the yarn straight up.

HAWKINS' CLOWN EGG

- **Size:** 8-14.
- **Hook:** Egg.
- **Thread:** Yellow 6/0.
- **Body/Wing:** Chartreuse, orange, and cream egg yarn.
- **Difficulty:** 2.
- **Notes:** Lay each color of egg yarn on top of the hook, and tie in with a figure-eight. Then raise them all up in a single bunch, and cut quickly and cleanly with a sharp pair of scissors.

LYNCH'S DOUBLE DOT EGG

- **Size:** 8-14.
- **Hook:** Egg.
- **Thread:** Yellow 6/0.
- **Body/Wing:** Pink and red egg yarn.
- **Difficulty:** 2.
- **Notes:** Tie one bunch of pink yarn under the hook. Then tie a small piece of red yarn on top of the hook and a larger pink piece on top. Pull the bottom yarn straight down, and trim. Then pull both top pieces up, and trim to the same length.

MEG A EGG

- **Size:** 8-14.
- **Hook:** Egg.
- **Thread:** Yellow 6/0.
- **Body/Wing:** Sparkle pom-pom threaded onto hook and glued in place.
- **Difficulty:** 1.

MICRO NUKE EGG

- **Size:** 8-14.
- **Hook:** Egg.
- **Thread:** Yellow 6/0.
- **Body:** Bright orange bug yarn.
- **Hackle:** Yellow bug yarn distributed around egg dot to form a veil.
- **Difficulty:** 2.
- **Notes:** Tie one small piece of orange yarn under the hook. Then tie a small piece on top of the hook. Pull the bottom yarn straight down and trim. Then pull the top piece up, and trim to the same length. Wrap yellow yarn with a distribution wrap around the entire hook shank. This pattern can be tied in any color combination.

STEAK-N-EGGS

- **Size:** 10-14.
- **Hook:** 2X-long nymph.
- **Thread:** Pink 6/0.
- **Tail:** Black biots.
- **Abdomen:** Black V-Rib.
- **Thorax:** Pink bug yarn.
- **Wing Case:** White bug yarn and pearl Midge Krystal Flash.
- **Legs:** Black biots.
- **Difficulty:** 3.
- **Notes:** Attach the pink bug yarn, a small piece of white bug yarn, and the Krystal Flash to the thorax. Pull the white yarn and Krystal Flash off to the side as you pull up on the pink yarn and trim it. Then bring the longer white yarn back to the center.

SCHULTZY'S STEECH

- **Size:** 8-14.
- **Hook:** Grub.
- **Thread:** Black 6/0.
- **Body:** Short black sparkle dubbing.
- **Wing:** Black arctic fox.
- **Hackle:** Black-dyed pheasant body feather.
- **Head:** Orange sparkle yarn.
- **Difficulty:** 2.

STEELIE OMELET

- **Size:** 8-14.
- **Hook:** Egg or grub.
- **Thread:** Yellow 6/0.
- **Body:** Pink Ice Dub Chenille or Estaz with yellow bank in center.
- **Difficulty:** 1.

TUNGHEAD EGGI JUAN KENOBI

- **Size:** 10-16.
- **Hook:** 2X-long nymph.
- **Thread:** Yellow 6/0.
- **Tail:** Red Vernille, burnt.
- **Abdomen:** Tail material looped over shank with the end left long and burnt.
- **Thorax:** Peach and hot orange bug yarn.
- **Bead:** Gold-colored tungsten.
- **Difficulty:** 3.

VITSO'S PSYCHO SPAWN

- **Size:** 8-14.
- **Hook:** Egg or grub.
- **Thread:** Yellow 6/0.
- **Body:** Orange yarn looped along both sides of hook with pearl Diamond Braid looped on top of the shank.
- **Difficulty:** 2.

Nymphs

CHICKEN HAWK

- **Size:** 10-16.
- **Hook:** Grub.
- **Thread:** Pink 6/0.
- **Abdomen:** Tan Midge Cactus Chenille.
- **Thorax/Head:** Orange bug yarn.
- **Legs:** Teal flank or gray partridge.
- **Difficulty:** 2.
- **Notes:** Other body colors include tan and chartreuse.

ROBINSON'S CHICKEN LITTLE

- **Size:** 10-16.
- **Hook:** 3X-long nymph.
- **Thread:** Pink 6/0.
- **Tail:** Tan-mottled marabou.
- **Abdomen:** Tan Midge Cactus Chenille.
- **Thorax/Head:** Orange bug yarn.
- **Legs:** Mallard flank dyed wood duck color.
- **Difficulty:** 2.

ROBINSON'S PSYCHEDELIC SMURF STONE

- **Size:** 12-14.
- **Hook:** 2X-long nymph.
- **Thread:** Yellow 6/0.
- **Tail:** Black biots.
- **Abdomen:** Hot yellow and blue Ultra-Wire wrapped together.
- **Thorax:** Chartreuse sparkle dubbing.
- **Wing Case:** Blue Antron yarn.
- **Legs:** White biots.
- **Bead:** Gold.
- **Difficulty:** 2.

RUSHER'S STEELHEAD FLIES

- **Size:** 6-10.
- **Color Options:** Black/blue, black/red, chartreuse, green, purple.
- **Hook:** 1X-long nymph.
- **Thread:** 6/0 to match pattern color.
- **Tail:** Goose biots, splayed.
- **Wing Case:** Flat-black or peacock metallic braid.
- **Abdomen:** Chenille in desired color.
- **Thorax:** Ice Chenille, Estaz, or Crystal Chenille.
- **Difficulty:** 2.

SCHULTZY'S FLESH NUG

- **Size:** 8-12.
- **Hook:** Heavy wet fly.
- **Thread:** Pink 6/0.
- **Tail:** Pink and white rabbit fur.
- **Body:** Tail materials wrapped forward.
- **Hackle:** Pink and white rabbit fur.
- **Difficulty:** 2.

SENYO'S WIGGLE STONE

- **Size:** 10-14.
- **Rear Hook:** Dry fly.
- **Front Hook:** Heavy wet fly.
- **Thread:** Black 6/0.
- **Tail:** Black biots.
- **Abdomen:** Black fur.
- **Rib:** Monofilament.
- **Thorax:** Sparkle dubbing.
- **Wing Case:** Pearlescent tinsel.
- **Legs:** Black biots.
- **Difficulty:** 3.
- **Notes:** The abdomen is tied on a separate dry-fly hook, and the bend is cut off close to the tails. It is then connected to the front hook (the thorax) with a loop of eight- to ten-pound monofilament.

STEELHEAD HAMMER

▎ **Size:** 8-14.
▎ **Hook:** Heavy wet fly.
▎ **Thread:** Black 6/0.
▎ **Tail:** Pheasant tail.
▎ **Abdomen:** Woven Antron yarn, dark color on top and lighter one on bottom.
▎ **Thorax:** Ice Chenille or Estaz.
▎ **Wing Case:** Black Antron yarn.
▎ **Difficulty:** 3.
▎ **Notes:** Can be tied in various color combinations depending on the mood of the tier—and the steelhead!

STEELHEAD STONE

▎ **Size:** 6-12.
▎ **Hook:** Scud.
▎ **Thread:** Red 6/0.
▎ **Tail:** Orange goose biots.
▎ **Abdomen:** Hare's-ear dubbing.
▎ **Thorax:** Orange sparkle dubbing.
▎ **Rib:** Oval gold tinsel.
▎ **Wing Case:** Orange Swiss Straw, in two sections.
▎ **Legs:** Brown partridge or speckled hen, in two sections.
▎ **Difficulty:** 3.
▎ **Notes:** Also tied with purple or red tails and thorax.

Traditional

FLESH FLY

▎ **Size:** 4-6.
▎ **Color Options:** Pink, tan.
▎ **Hook:** 3X-long nymph/streamer.
▎ **Thread:** Tan 3/0.
▎ **Tail:** Guard hairs from a cross-cut rabbit strip.
▎ **Body:** Cross-cut rabbit wrapped from hook bend to eye.
▎ **Difficulty:** 1.

SHOWGIRL

▎ **Size:** 2-6.
▎ **Hook:** Long-shank salmon hook.
▎ **Thread:** Hot orange 6/0.
▎ **Rear Hackle:** Red marabou.
▎ **Front Hackle:** Purple marabou.
▎ **Flash:** A few strands each of pearl Flashabou and pearl Krystal Flash tied on top, in between front and rear marabou.
▎ **Difficulty:** 2.

SALT WATER

Baitfish

BACK COUNTRY KINKY MUDDLER

- **Size:** 1/0-4.
- **Thread:** White 3/0.
- **Hook:** Short-shanked tarpon hook.
- **Wing:** Chartreuse over yellow Craft Fur or similar acrylic, banded with brown marker. Tie wing in the middle of the hook shank.
- **Head:** Top is reverse-tied chartreuse Kinky Fibre mixed with Angel Hair or Flash Blend, bottom is same material in yellow. Leave rear fibers long to blend into wing.
- **Eyes:** Medium-sized holographic.
- **Difficulty:** 2.
- **Notes:** Also tied in brown, black, and red/white.

BLUE WATER SOFTY MINNOW

- **Size:** 2/0-4.
- **Thread:** White 3/0.
- **Hook:** Standard saltwater.
- **Underbody:** Weighting wire covered with tying thread.

- **Wing:** Sili Skin cut to tapered shape and folded over hook, tied in three layers. Inner layer is silver, second layer is mother-of-pearl applied to the top only, and final layer is clear. Taper can be fine-tuned with scissors after skin is applied.
- **Eyes:** Stick-in prismatic, placed before outer layer is applied.
- **Difficulty:** 3.
- **Notes:** Although this fly looks simple, the material is tricky to work with and requires a deft hand and lots of practice.

BURKS HOT FLASH MINNOW

- **Size:** 2/0-4.
- **Thread:** White 3/0.
- **Hook:** Standard saltwater.
- **Wing:** Light blue Angel Hair over silver Angel Hair. Bars are made on the wing with black marker.
- **Throat:** White Angel Hair, slightly shorter than wing.
- **Eyes:** Prismatic.
- **Difficulty:** 2.

CLOUSER MINNOW

- **Size:** 2/0-6.
- **Color Options:** Olive/white, black/orange, chartreuse/white.
- **Hook:** Pre-sharpened saltwater.
- **Thread:** White 3/0.
- **Wing:** Bottom: White or orange (on black/orange pattern) bucktail tied down in front of eyes, pulled over them and tied down behind. Top: Rainbow Krystal Flash and olive, black, or chartreuse bucktail, tied down in front of eyes.
- **Head:** Dumbbell eyes.
- **Difficulty:** 1.
- **Notes:** Eyes are set back one-fourth the length of hook shank, on top of shank. Fly rides upside down.

COWEN'S ALBIE ANCHOVIE

- **Size:** 4-6.
- **Hook:** 3X-long pre-sharpened stainless.
- **Thread:** White 3/0.
- **Body:** Just behind the eye, tie in two equal bunches of fine pink synthetic hair on the top and bottom of the hook shank.
- **Belly:** Pearl Krystal Flash.
- **Overlay:** EZ Body braid tubing placed from the hook eye back to three-quarters the length of the fly.

- **Head:** Prismatic 2 mm or 3 mm eyes applied to the EZ Body Braid. A layer of clear epoxy is then applied to the braid, covering the eyes.
- **Other Materials:** Five-minute epoxy.
- **Difficulty:** 4.
- **Notes:** When preparing the EZ Body Braid, remove only the inner strings from one side of the tubing. When sliding the tubing in place, place the portion with the string so that it straddles the Gliss 'N Glow flash material on the belly.

COWEN'S BAITFISH

- **Size:** 2/0-2.
- **Color Options:** Chartreuse/white, olive/white, gray/white.
- **Hook:** Pre-sharpened stainless.
- **Thread:** White 3/0.
- **Tail:** White Polar Fibre.
- **Wing:** Bottom: White Slinky Fibre. Top: Chartreuse, olive, or gray Slinky Fibre.
- **Throat:** Pink Slinky Fibre, tied sparse.
- **Head:** 4 mm or 6 mm prismatic eyes.
- **Difficulty:** 3.

COWEN'S MAGNUM HERRING

▌ **Size:** 4/0.

▌ **Color Options:** Royal, blue/white (herring), olive/white (Bunker).

▌ **Hook:** Pre-sharpened stainless.

▌ **Thread:** White 3/0.

▌ **Body:** Underwing: White Icelandic sheep. Midwing: White bucktail tied at hook bend. Overwing: Olive or blue Icelandic sheep. Topping: Mixture of peacock Flashabou and peacock herl.

▌ **Head:** 6 mm or 7 mm prismatic eyes.

▌ **Other Materials:** A quick-drying epoxy is used to secure the eyes in place.

▌ **Difficulty:** 4.

▌ **Notes:** This fly is tied using the Brooks Hi-Tie method.

COWEN'S MULLET

▌ **Size:** 2/0-4.

▌ **Thread:** White 3/0.

▌ **Hook:** Standard saltwater.

▌ **Wing:** From bottom to top: White Fluoro Fiber or acrylic, small amount of gray Fluoro Fibre, small amount of pearl Krystal Flash, then four to six peacock herls.

▌ **Throat:** Small amount of white Fluoro Fibre.

▌ **Gills:** Red Krystal Flash.

▌ **Overlay:** Flex Tubing or similar tied forward and then pulled back so it extends to the back of the hook. Coat with Softex or thin epoxy.

▌ **Eyes:** Holographic, glued to sides of head.

▌ **Difficulty:** 3.

COWEN'S SILVERSIDE

▌ **Size:** 2-8.

▌ **Thread:** White 3/0.

▌ **Hook:** Standard saltwater.

▌ **Wing:** From bottom to top: white Fluoro Fiber or acrylic, then pale olive Fluoro Fibre. One piece of silver Mylar tinsel should be added along the sides after the wing is complete.

▌ **Overlay:** Flex Tubing or similar tied forward and then pulled back so it extends to the back of the hook. Coat with Softex or thin epoxy.

▌ **Eyes:** Holographic, glued to sides of head.

ENRICO'S FLOATING MINNOW

▌ **Size:** 2/0-4.

▌ **Thread:** Monofilament.

▌ **Hook:** Short-shank tarpon hook.

▌ **Tail:** White EP Fiber with Gray EP Fiber over. Red Flashabou over the top.

▌ **Body:** Continuation of gray and white EP Fibers.

▌ **Floating Tabs:** Tie in black rounded foam tabs on top of the hook right in front of tail and after second placement of body fibers.

▌ **Eyes:** Large 3-D eyes glued into holes made by burning slots into side of head.

▌ **Difficulty:** 3.

▌ **Notes:** Trim the fly to shape after tying. Apply a small amount of Super Glue on the top of the head, and work into the fibers to help the head hold its shape. This fly can be tied in many different combinations to imitate specific baitfish.

ENRICO'S PEANUT BUTTER FLY

- **Size:** 2/0-4.
- **Thread:** Monofilament.
- **Hook:** Short-shank tarpon hook.
- **Tail:** Purple EP Fiber with Black EP Fiber over. Red Flashabou over the top.
- **Body:** Continuation of black and purple EP Fibers, black on top and purple on the bottom.
- **Eyes:** Large 3-D eyes glued into holes made by burning slots into side of head.
- **Difficulty:** 3.
- **Notes:** Trim the fly to shape after tying. Apply a small amount of Super Glue on the top of the head, and work into the fibers to help the head hold its shape. This fly can be tied in many different combinations to imitate specific baitfish.

HALF AND HALF

- **Size:** 2/0-1.
- **Color Options:** Tan/white, black, olive/white, chartreuse/white.
- **Hook:** Pre-sharpened stainless.
- **Thread:** White 3/0.
- **Tail:** Four saddle hackles tied concave sides in at hook bend. Add Krystal Flash or Flashabou for accent.
- **Wing:** Lower Wing: White bucktail tied on each side of the hook shank. Upper Wing: Contrasting-color bucktail tied directly atop the lower wing on each side.
- **Topping:** Mixture of peacock herl and peacock Krystal Flash for accent.
- **Head:** Painted dumbbell eyes covered with epoxy.
- **Gills:** Red Krystal Flash, tied short.
- **Difficulty:** 3.

GIANT TREVALLY FLY

- **Size:** 4/0-2/0.
- **Thread:** Orange 3/0.
- **Hook:** Standard tarpon.
- **Wing:** White Ultra Hair with dark green Flashabou over the top.
- **Throat:** Red Ultra Hair, half the length of the wing.
- **Head:** Tying thread, long and coated with epoxy.
- **Eyes:** Very large stick-on prismatic eyes glued to sides of wing.
- **Difficulty:** 2.

KING'S HOO FLY

- **Size:** 2/0-6.
- **Thread:** White 3/0.
- **Hook:** Standard saltwater.
- **Tail:** Tan Craft Fur.
- **Wing:** Gray Laser Dub.
- **Throat:** Pink Laser Dub, slightly shorter than wing.
- **Head:** Coat Laser Dub with Liquid Fusion or similar semi-flexible cement back to the bend of the hook.
- **Eyes:** Holographic, glued to sides of head.
- **Difficulty:** 2.
- **Notes:** Can be tied in many different colors and can also be banded with vertical stripes using a permanent marker. The wing/body and throat are tied in segments, typically about three, along the shank. The first two segments are tied in a V-shape along both sides of the hook, and the final amount is not reversed but tied in a single bundle with the butt ends trimmed away.

KINKY MUDDLER

- **Size:** 2/0-2.
- **Thread:** Black 3/0.
- **Hook:** Short-shank saltwater.
- **Tail:** Purple bucktail with one pair of purple saddle hackles tied in first, then two pairs of black saddle hackles. The hackles should be oriented in an inverted V shape with the tops of the hackles touching but the bottom edges flared outward.
- **Body/Wing:** Black Flash Blend or a mix of Kinky Fibres and Angel Hair, tied in three segments along the shank.
- **Throat:** Purple Flash Blend or a mix of Kinky Fibres and Angel Hair, tied in three segments along the shank.
- **Eyes:** Large holographic, glued to sides of head.
- **Difficulty:** 3.
- **Notes:** The wing/body and throat are tied in segments, typically about three, along the shank. The first two segments are tied in a V-shape along both sides of the hook, and the final amount is not reversed but tied in a single bundle with the butt ends trimmed away. Also tied in white.

KIRK'S SPOON FLY

- **Size:** 2-6.
- **Color Options:** Silver/blue, gold/red, pearl/chartreuse.
- **Hook:** 3X-long pre-sharpened stainless.
- **Thread:** Black 3/0.
- **Body:** Extra-large Mylar tubing.
- **Other Materials:** Epoxy is used to coat the Mylar-tubing body and is painted with Pantone marking pens.
- **Difficulty:** 3.
- **Notes:** Underneath the Mylar tubing, put a precut flexible piece of metal such as aluminum foil. Bend it to shape prior to epoxying the body.

LEFTY' S DECEIVER

- **Size:** 2/0-1.
- **Color Options:** Black, white, yellow, olive/white, chartreuse, red/white, red/yellow, green/white.
- **Hook:** Pre-sharpened saltwater.
- **Thread:** White 3/0.
- **Tail:** Four to six saddle hackles, not splayed.
- **Body:** Silver Mylar tinsel.
- **Wing:** Bucktail tied in equal bunches on top of and below the shank; must extend beyond the bend of the hook.
- **Topping:** Peacock herl or Flashabou over the top bunch of bucktail.
- **Difficulty:** 3.

- **Notes:** If the fly is two-toned (e.g., olive/white), the darker color is tied on top of the shank, and the lighter color goes underneath.

MEGA CLOUSER

- **Size:** 4/0-2.
- **Thread:** White 3/0.
- **Hook:** Standard saltwater.
- **Wing:** Chartreuse bucktail.
- **Belly:** Pearl Krystal Flash, then white bucktail, then red bucktail.
- **Eyes:** Metal dumbbell eyes with red iris and black pupil.
- **Difficulty:** 1.

MIKKLESON'S EPOXY BAITFISH

- **Size:** 2-6.
- **Thread:** Clear monofilament.
- **Hook:** Standard saltwater.
- **Tail:** White bucktail with silver Krystal Flash.
- **Body:** Silver Krystal Flash wound around shank.
- **Rib:** Single strand of pearl Krystal Flash.
- **Wing:** Chartreuse bucktail.
- **Throat:** A few strands of red Krystal Flash.
- **Eyes:** Stick-on.
- **Difficulty:** 3.
- **Notes:** Coat the wing and body back to the bend of the hook with epoxy, and rotate while drying.

MONTAUK MONSTER

- **Size:** 6/0-2.
- **Thread:** White 3/0.
- **Hook:** Standard tarpon hook.
- **Tail:** Chartreuse bucktail.
- **Wing:** Large amount of chartreuse ostrich herl with pearl Krystal Flash and pearl Flashabou, covered with chartreuse marabou. Wing is tied in the middle of the hook shank.
- **Collar:** Chartreuse Finn raccoon Zonker followed by yellow Zonker strip, wound around hook. Then tie in three chartreuse Sili Legs on each side.
- **Head:** Spun from chartreuse deer hair, clipped flat on the bottom and in a V-shaped wedge on top.
- **Eyes:** Holographic, glued to sides of head.
- **Difficulty:** 4.
- **Notes:** Also tied in red/white and purple/black. Tie in a mono loop prior to tying the tail to keep the fly from fouling.

PREDATOR POUNDER

- **Size:** 4/0-2.
- **Thread:** Red 3/0.
- **Hook:** Standard tarpon.
- **Tail:** Four to six orange saddle hackles and a few strands of silver Flashabou.

- **Collar:** Short orange bucktail and long peacock herls on top; orange bucktail underneath.
- **Head:** Spun black deer hair on top, orange on bottom. Leave tips long to blend into the wing.
- **Eyes:** Metal dumbbell eyes with red iris and black pupil.
- **Difficulty:** 4.
- **Notes:** Also tied in chartreuse and white.

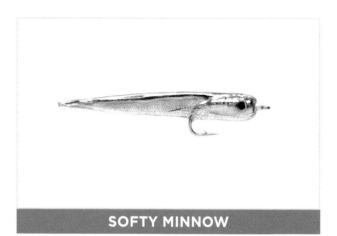

SOFTY MINNOW

- **Size:** 2-8.
- **Thread:** White 3/0.
- **Hook:** Standard saltwater.
- **Underbody:** Weighting wire covered with tying thread.
- **Wing:** Sili Skin cut to tapered shape and folded over hook, tied in three layers. Inner layer is silver, second layer is mother-of-pearl applied to the top only, and final layer is clear. Taper can be fine-tuned with scissors after skin is applied.
- **Eyes:** Stick-on prismatic, placed before outer layer is applied.
- **Difficulty:** 3.
- **Notes:** Although this fly looks simple, the material is tricky to work with and requires a deft hand and lots of practice.

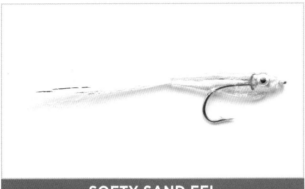

SOFTY SAND EEL

- **Size:** 2-8.
- **Thread:** White 3/0.
- **Hook:** Standard saltwater.
- **Underbody:** Weighting wire covered with tying thread.
- **Wing:** Chartreuse Ultra Hair over white Ultra Hair with a few strands of pearl Flashabou.
- **Body:** Sili Skin cut to tapered shape and folded over hook, tied in two layers. Inner layer is mother-of-pearl, and final layer is clear. Taper can be fine-tuned with scissors after skin is applied.
- **Eyes:** Stick-in prismatic, placed before outer layer is applied. Also add gill lines with red permanent marker before outer layer is applied.
- **Difficulty:** 3.
- **Notes:** Although this fly looks simple, the material is tricky to work with and requires a deft hand and lots of practice.

SOFTY SPOON FLY

- **Size:** 2/0-2.
- **Thread:** Hot orange 3/0.
- **Hook:** Long-shank saltwater, bent slightly.
- **Body:** Copper Sili Skin cut to shape and folded over hook shank horizontally.
- **Wing:** Pink Finn raccoon or arctic fox.
- **Difficulty:** 2.
- **Notes:** Also tied in gold.

SURF CANDY

- **Size:** 2-6.
- **Thread:** Clear monofilament.
- **Hook:** Long-shank saltwater.
- **Tail:** Long, thin silver Mylar tubing with trimmed badger saddle hackle glued into the end.
- **Body:** Continuation of tail.
- **Wing:** Olive Ultra Hair.
- **Throat:** White Ultra Hair.
- **Head:** Clear epoxy, two or three thin coats, over entire body to bend of hook.
- **Eyes:** Stick on eyes and red permanent marker gill slits, applied after first coat of epoxy.
- **Difficulty:** 3.
- **Notes:** Sometimes the extended body is left off. If so, the body of the fly is silver tinsel.

TURPIN'S MESSY MINNOW

- **Size:** 2-8.
- **Thread:** White 6/0.
- **Hook:** Standard saltwater.
- **Tail:** Gold Angel Hair.
- **Wing:** Gold Angel Hair topped with black Angel Hair.
- **Throat:** Gold Angel Hair.
- **Eyes:** Prismatic.
- **Difficulty:** 2.
- **Notes:** Also tied in silver.

VLAHOS' SANDBAR MULLET

- **Size:** 1/0-4.
- **Thread:** Tan 3/0.
- **Hook:** Standard tarpon.
- **Tail:** Four purple saddle hackles, with two smaller grizzly saddle hackles on each side.
- **Body:** Laser dub in three sections, purple then chartreuse then purple, tied on top and bottom and combed out.
- **Wing:** Red foam strips coated with red glitter, one in the middle of the hook shank, and one in front of the eyes. (Because this fly rides upside-down because of the heavy eyes, the wing should be tied on the bottom of the hook shank with the hook upside-down in the vise.)
- **Collar:** Purple Laser Dub on top and bottom.
- **Eyes:** Metal dumbbell eyes with red iris and black pupil.
- **Difficulty:** 4
- **Notes:** Also tied in tan, all-chartreuse, and black.

Bonefish

BONE CRUSHER

- **Size:** 4-6.
- **Hook:** Pre-sharpened stainless.
- **Thread:** White 3/0.
- **Body:** Twisted gold Krystal Flash, floss, or Flashabou.
- **Rib:** The body can be overwrapped with clear mono (optional).
- **Wing:** Tan calf tail.
- **Legs:** Mottled Living Rubber or Sili Legs.
- **Head:** Bead-chain eyes with pearl Ice Chenille, Estaz, or Krystal Chenille.
- **Difficulty:** 3.

BONEFISH BITTERS

- **Size:** 6-8.
- **Color Options:** Olive, amber, orange.
- **Hook:** Pre-sharpened saltwater.
- **Thread:** 6/0 to match body color.
- **Wing:** Sparse deer hair over Z-Lon underwing, same color as body.
- **Legs:** About eight legs made from grizzly rubber legs or Sili Legs, tied in middle of body.
- **Head:** Gold bead-chain eyes covered with colored epoxy or hot glue.
- **Difficulty:** 3.

BONEFISH CLOUSER FOXY RED

- **Size:** 4-6.
- **Hook:** 3X-long stainless.
- **Thread:** Tan 6/0.
- **Wing:** Underwing: Tan guard hairs from red-fox tail. Midwing: Gold and rust Flashabou.
- **Topping:** Black-tipped red-fox tail guard hairs.
- **Head:** Lead dumbbell eyes painted red with black pupils.
- **Difficulty:** 2.

BONE VOYAGE

- **Size:** 2-6.
- **Thread:** Tan 6/0.
- **Hook:** Standard saltwater.
- **Tail:** Tan Craft Fur barred with brown marker, two white Tentacle Legs, and a tuft of tan rabbit on the bottom.
- **Body:** Ball of orange yarn behind the eyes and three bunches of short, trimmed tan Flash Blend forward of the eyes (on the underside of the hook but top of the fly).
- **Underlay:** Tan Swiss Straw to cover the entire underbody.
- **Eyes:** Black painted dumbbell eyes or bead chain tied about three-quarters of the way back on the hook shank.
- **Difficulty:** 3.
- **Notes:** Eyes can be plastic, bead chain, or solid metal dumbbells, depending on depth required.

BORSKI'S BONEFISH SLIDER

- **Size:** 4-8.
- **Hook:** Pre-sharpened stainless.
- **Thread:** White 3/0.
- **Tail:** Tan Fly Fur striped medium brown with permanent marker.
- **Body:** Thread.
- **Hackle:** Grizzly, clipped on top and sides.
- **Head:** Tan deer hair, clipped to shape.
- **Sides:** Yellow Krystal Flash.
- **Collar:** Tan deer-hair tips, clipped on top and sides.
- **Eyes:** Yellow with black pupil.
- **Difficulty:** 2.

COWEN'S BONEFISH SCAMPI

- **Size:** 2-8.
- **Thread:** Pink 3/0.
- **Hook:** Standard saltwater.
- **Tail:** Pearl Flashabou, short.
- **Body:** Pearl Diamond Braid.
- **Body Overlay:** Tan Zonker strip bound in at tail and at head.
- **Wing:** Pink Craft Fur and pearl Krystal Flash.
- **Head:** Built up from tying thread.
- **Eyes:** Silver plastic, metal, or bead chain.
- **Difficulty:** 3.
- **Notes:** Eyes can be plastic, bead chain, or solid metal dumbbells, depending on depth required.

CRAZY CHARLIE

- **Size:** 4-8.
- **Color Options:** White, tan, yellow, pink.
- **Hook:** Pre-sharpened saltwater.
- **Thread:** White 6/0.
- **Body:** Pearlescent Mylar tinsel overwrapped with clear V-Rib.
- **Wing:** White, tan, yellow, or pink calf tail.
- **Head:** Silver bead chain.
- **Difficulty:** 1.
- **Notes:** Can be tied with bead-chain eyes, solid metal eyes, or plastic eyes, depending on depth required.

DOC HALL'S BONEFISH MINNOW

- **Size:** 4-8.
- **Thread:** Pink 3/0.
- **Hook:** Standard saltwater.
- **Wing:** White bucktail then pearl Flashabou then pale tan bucktail.
- **Eyes:** Silver plastic, metal, or bead chain.
- **Difficulty:** 1.
- **Notes:** Eyes can be plastic, bead chain, or solid metal dumbbells, depending on depth required.

ENRICO'S SPAWNING SHRIMP

- **Size:** 2-6.
- **Thread:** White 6/0.
- **Hook:** Standard saltwater.
- **Tail:** Orange Craft fur, two pearl and two black Krystal Flash fibers, black shrimp eyes, orange Sili Legs.
- **Body:** Pearl Angel Hair tied in a dubbing loop for a few turns against the tail, then tan Shrimp Dub.
- **Wing:** Tan EP Fibers tied over tail.
- **Weed Guard:** 20-pound monofilament.
- **Eyes:** Dumbbell eyes, bead chain, or plastic eyes depending on depth required.
- **Difficulty:** 3.
- **Notes:** Comb out body with a piece of male Velcro or fine-tooth comb.

FLATS KWABBIT

- **Size:** 2-6.
- **Thread:** Tan 6/0.
- **Hook:** Standard saltwater.
- **Tail:** Tan craft fur barred with brown marker.
- **Body:** Pieces of small tan Vernille or Ultra Chenille tied in across shank of hook, trimmed to form a crab-shaped body.
- **Wing:** Pale tan Sili Legs.
- **Throat:** Tuft of tan rabbit fur.
- **Eyes:** Silver metal dumbbell eyes.
- **Difficulty:** 3.

GOTCHA

- **Size:** 2-8.
- **Color Options:** Pink, chartreuse.
- **Hook:** Standard stainless.
- **Thread:** Pink or chartreuse 3/0.
- **Tail:** Frayed pearl Mylar tubing.
- **Body:** Clear V-Rib, Larva Lace, or pearl Diamond Braid over tapered tying thread.
- **Wing:** Fine beige synthetic hair with a half-dozen fibers of pearl Krystal Flash.
- **Head:** Bead chain.
- **Difficulty:** 2.

M2

- **Size:** 2-6.
- **Thread:** Pink 6/0.
- **Hook:** Standard saltwater.
- **Tail:** Burnt orange Craft Fur, pearl Krystal Flash, and a pair of burnt orange Sili Legs.
- **Body:** Brown dubbing.
- **Rib:** Trimmed brown hackle.
- **Eyes:** Black bead-chain eyes at bend of hook and silver-bead chain eyes at the head.
- **Difficulty:** 2.

HOT LEGS FOXY GOTCHA

- **Size:** 2-6.
- **Thread:** Pink 3/0.
- **Hook:** Standard saltwater.
- **Tail:** Pearl Flashabou, short.
- **Body:** Pearl Diamond Braid.
- **Wing:** Tan arctic fox, pearl Krystal Flash, and pink Hot-Tipped Crazy Legs.
- **Head:** Built up with tying thread.
- **Eyes:** Silver plastic, metal, or bead chain.
- **Difficulty:** 2.
- **Notes:** Eyes can be plastic, bead chain, or solid metal dumbbells, depending on depth required.

MEKO SPECIAL

- **Size:** 2-6.
- **Thread:** Pink 3/0.
- **Hook:** Standard saltwater.
- **Tail:** Tan Craft Fur and gold Krystal Flash.
- **Body:** Tan dubbing.
- **Rib:** Trimmed brown saddle hackle.
- **Head:** Built up with tying thread.
- **Eyes:** Silver plastic, metal, or bead chain.
- **Difficulty:** 2.
- **Notes:** Eyes can be plastic, bead chain, or solid metal dumbbells, depending on depth required.

MINKY SHRIMP

- **Size:** 2-6.
- **Thread:** Pink 6/0.
- **Hook:** Standard saltwater.
- **Tail:** Tan Craft Fur, black monofilament shrimp eyes, two burnt orange Sili Legs, and two long pieces of black Krystal Flash.
- **Body:** Pink dubbing with pair of burnt orange Sili Legs tied in the middle of the hook shank.
- **Wing:** Strip of tan mink fur tied down at bend and head.
- **Head:** Built up with tying thread.
- **Eyes:** Silver plastic, metal, or bead chain.
- **Difficulty:** 2.
- **Notes:** Eyes can be plastic, bead chain, or solid metal dumbbells, depending on depth required.

PETERSON'S SPAWNING SHRIMP

- **Size:** 1-6.
- **Hook:** Pre-sharpened stainless.
- **Thread:** Fluorescent pink 3/0.
- **Tail:** Light tan Antron.
- **Antennae:** Two long strands of pearl Krystal Flash under four short strands of pearl Krystal Flash.
- **Body:** Flat pearl ribbon, wrapped over rear one-third only.
- **Shellback:** Flat pearl ribbon, pulled over back and weight.
- **Wing:** Tan rabbit, tied in four segments.
- **Egg sac:** Bright orange rug yarn.
- **Legs:** Clear and black Sili Legs.
- **Head:** Pink thread.
- **Eyes:** Black glass beads glued onto mono posts. Silver dumbbell eyes.
- **Difficulty:** 4.
- **Antennae:** Twice shank length. Eye stalks: Gape width. Egg sac: Gape width. Body: One-third of shank. Shellback: One-third of shank. Wing: Twice shank length. Head: One-sixth of shank.

SCHULTZY'S BONEFISH SHRIMPISH

▌ **Size:** 2-6.

▌ **Thread:** Pink 3/0.

▌ **Hook:** Pre-sharpened stainless.

▌ **Tail:** Tan Craft Fur, black monofilament shrimp eyes, four Hot-Tipped Crazy Legs, and a few strands of pearl Krystal Flash.

▌ **Body:** Pink Laser Dub, with two sections of burnt orange Sili Legs.

▌ **Wing:** In three parts from the middle of the shank forward: First two are plain tan Craft Fur, last one is tan Craft Fur barred with black permanent marker.

▌ **Eyes:** Black dumbbell, bead chain, or plastic.

▌ **Difficulty:** 3.

▌ **Notes:** Eyes can be plastic, bead chain, or solid metal dumbbells, depending on depth required.

SIMRAM

▌ **Size:** 2-4.

▌ **Hook:** Pre-sharpened stainless.

▌ **Thread:** Hot pink 3/0.

▌ **Tail:** Light gold synthetic Fly Fur yellow Krystal Flash, twice shank length.

▌ **Body:** Rear half pearl Krystal Flash; front half tan crosscut rabbit strip, clipped top and sides.

▌ **Head:** Tied bigger than normal with tying thread.

▌ **Shellback:** Pearl Mylar piping tied flat over top of rabbit strip.

▌ **Eyes:** Silver dumbbell eyes tied on top of hook in the middle of the body.

▌ **Difficulty:** 3.

▌ **Notes:** This fly rides upside down, so what is referred to as the top here is actually the bottom of the fly when fished.

SKITTAL MANTIS SHRIMP

▌ **Size:** 2-4.

▌ **Thread:** Tan 3/0.

▌ **Hook:** Standard saltwater.

▌ **Tail:** Tan Craft Fur over white Craft Fur, black shrimp eyes, two tan Tentacle Legs, two strands of black Krystal Flash.

▌ **Body:** Single turn of hot orange Estaz or Ice Chenille, dubbed fur for underbody, with tan Zonker strips tied top and bottom at bend and secured at head.

▌ **Eyes:** Silver dumbbell, bead chain, or plastic.

▌ **Difficulty:** 3.

▌ **Notes:** Eyes can be plastic, bead chain, or solid metal dumbbells, depending on depth required.

SPAWNING GOTCHA

- **Size:** 2-8.
- **Hook:** Pre-sharpened stainless.
- **Thread:** Fluorescent pink 3/0.
- **Tail:** Hot orange hackle tips.
- **Body:** Pearl Poly Flash or wrapped Krystal Flash.
- **Wing:** Light gold Fly Fur with Pearl Krystal Flash on top.
- **Head:** Thread head.
- **Difficulty:** 2.

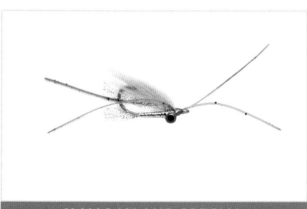

X-MAS ISLAND SPECIAL

- **Size:** 4-10.
- **Thread:** Hot orange 6/0.
- **Hook:** Standard saltwater.
- **Tail:** Orange Krystal Flash.
- **Body:** Pearlescent tinsel.
- **Wing:** Tan Craft Fur over orange Krystal Flash.
- **Legs:** Pink Sili Legs, tied to extend both forward over the eye and back along the wing.
- **Eyes:** Yellow metal dumbbell eyes with black pupil.
- **Difficulty:** 3.

Crabs

ADAMS' BASTARD CRAB

- **Size:** 2-6.
- **Thread:** Pink 3/0.
- **Hook:** Standard saltwater.
- **Tail:** Tan marabou.
- **Body:** Sections of tan EP Fiber tied in across shank with figure-eight. Three tan Sili Legs are tied in between sections.
- **Eyes:** Silver dumbbell, bead chain, or plastic.
- **Difficulty:** 3.
- **Notes:** Eyes can be plastic, bead chain, or solid metal dumbbells, depending on depth required. A mono weed guard from 20-pound tippet is usually added.

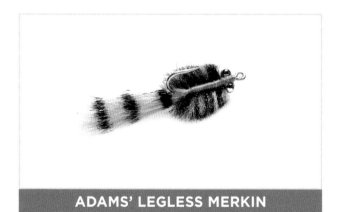

ADAMS' LEGLESS MERKIN

- **Size:** 2-6.
- **Thread:** Pink 3/0.
- **Hook:** Standard saltwater.
- **Tail:** Tan Craft Fur barred with black marker.
- **Body:** Alternating pieces of brown and tan EP Fiber, tied in across the shank with figure-eight.
- **Eyes:** Silver dumbbell, bead chain, or plastic.
- **Difficulty:** 2.
- **Notes:** Eyes can be plastic, bead chain, or solid metal dumbbells, depending on depth required. A mono weed guard from 20-pound tippet is usually added.

AVALON KEEL CRAB

- **Size:** 2-6.
- **Thread:** Pink 3/0.
- **Hook:** Standard saltwater.
- **Tail:** Orange Fluoro Fibre or Craft Fur, two orange Tentacle Legs, and two long black strands of Krystal Flash.
- **Body:** Pearl Diamond Braid.
- **Wing:** Two tan Zonker strip tied in on each side and not bound down at the bend.
- **Keel:** Four silver metal beads tied on a piece of 20-pound monofilament that is tied down at the bend and at the head.
- **Eyes:** Silver dumbbell eyes.
- **Difficulty:** 3.

HALL'S PERFECT CRAB

- **Size:** 2-6.
- **Thread:** Tan 6/0.
- **Hook:** Standard saltwater.
- **Tail:** Tan marabou banded with black marker, pink mono shrimp eyes, two strands of pearl Krystal Flash, and six brown Tentacle Legs.
- **Body:** Tan dubbing.
- **Rib:** Brown-dyed grizzly saddle, trimmed flat on the front underside.
- **Wing:** Brown deer hair, trimmed to shape.
- **Eyes:** Black dumbbell, bead chain, or plastic.
- **Difficulty:** 3.
- **Notes:** Eyes can be plastic, bead chain, or solid metal dumbbells, depending on depth required.

GRAND SLAM CRAB

- **Size:** 2-6.
- **Thread:** Tan 3/0.
- **Hook:** Standard saltwater.
- **Tail:** A small bunch of pearl Krystal Flash.
- **Claws:** Two grizzly large neck hackles, flared with center snipped out.
- **Body:** Tan EP Fiber, tied in flat and trimmed to shape.
- **Legs:** Three pairs of tan Sili Legs distributed along body.
- **Eyes:** Silver bead chain.
- **Keel:** Four silver beads threaded on 20-pound monofilament and tied in at head and tail.
- **Difficulty:** 4.

MERKIN

- **Size:** 2/0-6.
- **Hook:** Standard stainless.
- **Thread:** Fluorescent green 3/0.
- **Tail:** Pearl Flashabou with two splayed cree hackles on each side.
- **Body:** Alternating bands of tan and brown yarn, tied across the shank and brushed out.
- **Legs:** Three pairs of white rubber legs, distributed through the body. Tips of the legs are painted red.
- **Head:** Nickel-plated dumbbell.
- **Difficulty:** 3.

SIMON'S HOVER CRAB

- **Size:** 2-6.
- **Thread:** White 6/0.
- **Hook:** Standard saltwater.
- **Body:** Tan foam, tied to hook fore and aft, coated with clear glue mixed with tiny chopped up pieces of black Flashabou on top, coated with tan hot glue or colored epoxy on the bottom.
- **Legs:** On side opposite claws, set into glue, three sets of knotted grizzly Sili Legs at each end.
- **Claws:** Doubled and knotted Sili legs, one pair on same side as eyes.
- **Eyes:** Pearl plastic or glass eyes set into glue at both ends of body.
- **Difficulty:** 3.

VLAHOS' COMBO CRAB

- **Size:** 2-4.
- **Thread:** White 3/0.
- **Hook:** Standard saltwater.
- **Tail:** Shrimp-color Ice Dubbing, black mono shrimp eyes, pair of orange Crazy Legs on each side knotted together with ends snipped to form claws.
- **Body:** Alternating strands of tan and blue EP Fiber, with three pumpkin/blue silicone legs distributed along the body.

- **Wing:** Small amount of natural deer hair, then blue deer hair, then natural deer hair. Trim front to form head but leave rear tip fibers long. The hair should be allowed to flare but not spin around the hook.
- **Head:** Deer hair trimmed.
- **Eyes:** Silver dumbbell, bead chain, or plastic.
- **Difficulty:** 4.
- **Notes:** Eyes can be plastic, bead chain, or solid metal dumbbells, depending on depth required.

VLAHOS' MARBLED SAND FLEA

- **Size:** 2-4.
- **Thread:** Hot orange 3/0.
- **Hook:** Long-shank saltwater.
- **Tail:** Pearl Flashabou, short piece of soft orange yarn, and two chartreuse/orange Crazy Legs on each side.
- **Body:** Tan EP Fiber on top of hook only, tied in heavy and trimmed short. Distributed through the body are three pairs of tan Ultra Chenille or Vernille, tied short and burnt on the ends. After tying in marble the EP Fibers with a brown marker.
- **Eyes:** Black metal dumbbell eyes.
- **Difficulty:** 4.
- **Notes:** Coat the underside of the fly, which is bare tying thread, with epoxy.

Poppers

BANGER

- **Size:** 2/0-2.
- **Thread:** White 3/0.
- **Hook:** Kinked popper hook.
- **Tail:** Chartreuse bucktail.
- **Body:** Rear third is covered with chartreuse Ice Chenille, front two-thirds with chartreuse pearl Mylar sheeting glued over foam cylinder.
- **Eyes:** Large silver stick-on.
- **Difficulty:** 2.

BLADOS CREASE FLY

- **Size:** 2/0-2.
- **Thread:** White 3/0.
- **Hook:** Saltwater kinked shank popper hook.
- **Tail:** White bucktail and silver Flashabou.
- **Body:** Flat foam folded over hook and glued into place with Super Glue. The foam is covered entirely with a silver pearl Mylar sheet, with a blue piece across the top. The entire fly is coated with epoxy, sealing the bottom seam but with an opening in the front to produce air bubbles when the fly is stripped.
- **Eyes:** Large pearlescent stick-on.
- **Difficulty:** 3.

GURGLER

- **Size:** 2/0-6.
- **Thread:** Black 3/0.
- **Hook:** Long-shank saltwater.
- **Tail:** Black over white bucktail and a few strands of pearl Flashabou.
- **Body:** Black Ice Chenille.
- **Overlay:** Double strip of black foam, glued together and attached to hook at bend and eye. A slightly uplifted lip should be left at the front of the fly.
- **Throat:** Red Krystal Flash.
- **Difficulty:** 2.
- **Notes:** Also tied in white, yellow, or chartreuse.

MYLAR POPPER

- **Size:** 2/0-4.
- **Thread:** White 3/0.
- **Hook:** Saltwater popper.
- **Tail:** Chartreuse over white bucktail and a few strands of pearl Flashabou.
- **Underbody:** Cork, foam, or rigid plastic popper body. Top half should be colored with chartreuse marker or Mylar foil, then given blue slash marks.
- **Overlay:** Pearl Mylar tubing or Flex Tubing.
- **Head:** Paint front head of popper body red.
- **Eyes:** Large, stick-on.
- **Difficulty:** 3.

Notes: Tie in tail first, then stretch tubing over the popper body, and attach at bend and hook eye with tying thread. Coat the body with epoxy from the tail only to the front edge of the popper body. After the epoxy dries, trim the front flush with the edge of the popper, and leave a short collar of flash strands at the tail. Add the eyes and red paint to front of popper body, and add another coat of epoxy.

Snook, Redfish, and Sea Trout

BISSETT'S CRUSTACEAN SHALLOW

- **Size:** 2/0-4.
- **Thread:** Black 3/0.
- **Hook:** Standard saltwater.
- **Tail:** Long gray arctic fox and orange-speckled Sili Legs, with veil of shorter tan Laser Dub.
- **Body:** One band of olive, then tan EP Fibers tied in flat with figure-eights.
- **Eyes:** Small silver bead chain.
- **Difficulty:** 2.
- **Notes:** Run a bead of epoxy or head cement along the exposed thread under the body to ensure durability and to keep the body from rotating. Can also be tied with solid dumbbell eyes for deeper water.

BISSETT'S MUD BUG

- **Size:** 2/0-2.
- **Thread:** Chartreuse 3/0.
- **Hook:** Standard saltwater.
- **Tail:** Large bunch of yellow arctic fox, tied in the middle of the hook shank.
- **Wing:** Sparse chartreuse Laser Dub, veiling wing on all side.
- **Collar:** Tip ends of deer hair.
- **Head:** Purple deer hair, spun and trimmed.
- **Eyes:** Large metal dumbbell eyes, chartreuse with black pupils.
- **Difficulty:** 3.
- **Notes:** Also tied in orange and olive.

CALLAHAN'S STABILI SHRIMP

- **Size:** 2/0-4.
- **Thread:** White 3/0.
- **Hook:** Long-shank saltwater.
- **Tail:** Orange calf tail with long strands of root beer Krystal Flash.
- **Body:** Root beer Estaz or Ice Chenille.
- **Wing:** Long dark elk hair, extending to end of tail.
- **Weed Guard:** 30-pound monofilament, flecked with black nail polish to imitate legs.
- **Eyes:** Four connected bead chain, painted black and tied in next to tail.
- **Difficulty:** 2.
- **Notes:** Also tied in pink and olive.

CRAWSHRIMP

- **Size:** 2-4.
- **Thread:** Tan 3/0.
- **Hook:** Standard saltwater.
- **Tail:** Orange Laser Dub and several long black Krystal Flash strands.
- **Body:** Tan chenille, with eight tan Centipede Legs distributed around the read third of the body.
- **Wing/Overlay:** Strand of tan EP Shrimp Dub tied in at tail and at head.
- **Rear Eyes:** Black shrimp eyes.
- **Eyes:** Large metal dumbbell eyes tied in even with the hook point.
- **Difficulty:** 3.
- **Notes:** Also tied in rust or white.

GRASSETT'S DEEP FLATS BUNNY

- **Size:** 1/0-4.
- **Thread:** Red 3/0.
- **Hook:** Long-shank saltwater.
- **Tail:** Long chartreuse rabbit strip and pearl Krystal Flash, tied over a mono foul guard.
- **Tail Collar:** Sparse red Laser Dub tied to encircle tail.
- **Body:** Red Estaz or Ice Chenille.
- **Eyes:** Red dumbbell eyes with black pupils.
- **Difficulty:** 2.
- **Notes:** Usually tied with a mono weed guard. Also tied in tan and olive.

GRASSET'S SNOOK MINNOW

- **Size:** 2-6.
- **Thread:** Chartreuse 3/0.
- **Hook:** Standard saltwater.
- **Tail:** White Kinky Fibre or EP Fiber and a few strands of pearl Flashabou.
- **Body:** White Estaz or Ice Chenille.
- **Eyes:** Gold bead chain.
- **Difficulty:** 2.
- **Notes:** Usually tied with a mono weed guard.

GRASSETT'S FLATS MINNOW

- **Size:** 1/0-6.
- **Thread:** Chartreuse 3/0.
- **Hook:** Long-shank saltwater, eye bent down slightly to give it a curved shape.
- **Body:** Olive Estaz or Ice Chenille.
- **Wing:** Sparse olive over sparse white bucktail, topped with a few strands of peacock herl and pearl Krystal Flash.
- **Eyes:** Gold bead chain.
- **Difficulty:** 2.
- **Notes:** Usually tied with a mono weed guard. Also tied in all-white.

SCOF TAILER TRASH

- **Size:** 1.
- **Thread:** Chartreuse 3/0.
- **Hook:** Standard tarpon.
- **Tail:** Chartreuse Craft Fur and a few strands of UV flash.
- **Body:** Chartreuse Estaz or Ice Chenille with brown Sili Legs tied in regularly spaced intervals.
- **Overlay/Wing:** Tan foam tied in at tail, two-thirds of the shank forward, and at the head, forming two loops over the body.
- **Head:** Forward part of foam left extending over hook eye.
- **Eyes:** Chartreuse foam cylinder.
- **Difficulty:** 3.
- **Notes:** Also tied in cinnamon and tan.

Tarpon

FLOATING TARPON TOAD

- **Size:** 4/0-2.
- **Thread:** Red 3/0.
- **Hook:** Standard tarpon.
- **Tail:** Tan marabou, with orange marabou collar around it.
- **Body:** Alternating strips of orange and tan foam, trimmed to a crab shape.
- **Eyes:** Black plastic.

- **Difficulty:** 3.
- **Notes:** Also tied in chartreuse or purple. After the fly is tied and the body trimmed, lay a bead of cement or epoxy on the exposed thread underneath, and place a small dab between each of the foam strips to hold them in place.

MALZONE'S BLONDE

- **Size:** 4/0-1/0.
- **Color Options:** Light Blonde, Medium Blonde.
- **Hook:** Owner AKI Cutting Point.
- **Thread:** Light tan size A monocord or flat waxed nylon.
- **Tail:** Four honey cree or light badger saddles tied splayed at the bend, two on each side.
- **Body:** Bleached red squirrel.
- **Head:** Tan thread.
- **Difficulty:** 2.
- **Notes:** Matching the color of this pattern can be very difficult. The originator has found basic tan also to be effective.

MALZONE'S PURPLE DEMON

- **Size:** 4/0-1/0.
- **Hook:** Owner AKI Cutting Point.
- **Thread:** Black size A monocord.
- **Tail:** Four badger saddles dyed purple, splayed over eight to ten strands of black Flashabou.
- **Wing:** Gray squirrel dyed black.
- **Head:** Black size A monocord, tapered.
- **Difficulty:** 2.

MANGUM'S SLEEPING BEAUTY

- **Size:** 1/0-2.
- **Thread:** Red 3/0.
- **Hook:** Standard tarpon.
- **Tail:** Tan-mottled Zonker strip over mono foul guard.
- **Collar:** Tip ends of deer hair.
- **Body/Head:** Pale tan deer hair flared and trimmed on top of hook shank only (don't let it spin all the way around the shank).
- **Eyes:** Brown foam cylinder.
- **Difficulty:** 3.

ORVIS TARPON BUNNY

- **Size:** 2/0-2.
- **Thread:** Chartreuse 3/0.
- **Hook:** Standard tarpon.
- **Tail:** Tan rabbit strip and a few strands of red Krystal Flash. Tie in over a mono loop foul guard.
- **Collar:** Tan rabbit strip wound around hook.
- **Head:** Front half of hook shank covered with tying thread and epoxy.
- **Eyes:** Stick-on.
- **Difficulty:** 2.
- **Notes:** Also tied in black, red/black, chartreuse, and all-white.

TARPON TOAD

- **Size:** 2/0-2.
- **Thread:** Black 3/0.
- **Hook:** Standard tarpon.
- **Tail:** Purple rabbit strip and a few strands of purple Krystal Flash.
- **Collar:** Purple marabou wound at bend of hook.
- **Body:** Purple EP Fibers, tied in bunches along hook shank.
- **Eyes:** Black.
- **Difficulty:** 3.
- **Notes:** Also tied in red/black or purple.

Panfish

BIG EYED PANFISH BUG

- **Size:** 8-12.
- **Thread:** White 3/0.
- **Hook:** 3X-long nymph.
- **Tail:** White marabou.
- **Body:** Chartreuse sparkle dubbing.
- **Head:** Foam cylinder tied in with a figure-eight and colored with chartreuse marker.
- **Eyes:** Black paint.
- **Difficulty:** 2.
- **Notes:** Also tied in black or white.

BLUEGILL BUG

- **Size:** 12.
- **Color Options:** Yellow, black, white.
- **Hook:** 2X-long nymph.
- **Thread:** Black or white 3/0.
- **Tail:** Two wide saddle hackles, splayed apart.
- **Body:** Cork popper head with painted eyes.
- **Hackle:** Saddle hackle, same color as tail.
- **Difficulty:** 2.
- **Notes:** This kind of fly is easier if you buy pre-made bodies and paint and dress them yourself.

BULLY'S BLUEGILL SPIDER

- **Size:** 8-12.
- **Thread:** Yellow 3/0.
- **Hook:** 3X-long nymph.
- **Body:** Yellow chenille.
- **Wing:** Four round rubber legs.
- **Difficulty:** 1.
- **Notes:** Also tied in white, black, or olive.

MINI POP

- **Size:** 10.
- **Color Options:** Chartreuse, white scale.
- **Hook:** Mustad popper hook.
- **Thread:** White 6/0.
- **Tail:** A combination of floss, Living Rubber, and saddle hackles tied splayed; tail color to match body color.
- **Body:** Preformed popper body.
- **Head:** Painted on the preformed body.
- **Difficulty:** 2.

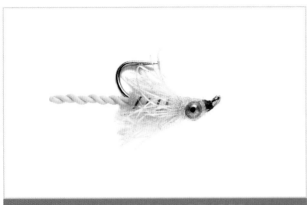

WILSON'S BRIM REAPER

- **Size:** 8-12.
- **Thread:** Yellow 6/0.
- **Hook:** 2X-long nymph.
- **Tail:** Yellow rubber leg, furled.
- **Body:** Wind tail material forward.
- **Rib:** Copper wire.
- **Collar:** Yellow Spanflex or Flexi Floss.
- **Head:** Yellow fur.
- **Eyes:** Gold bead chain.
- **Difficulty:** 2.
- **Notes:** Also tied in orange, olive, or black.

Bass

POPPERS

BASS POPPER

- **Size:** 1/0-6.
- **Color Options:** Frog, chartreuse/white, black/red.
- **Hook:** Bass bug.
- **Thread:** White 3/0.
- **Tail:** Grizzly saddle dyed to match head color.
- **Hackle:** Same as tail, wrapped tight to the back of the head.
- **Legs:** Living Rubber pulled through the head with a needle. Often epoxied in place.

- **Head:** Preformed balsa, foam, or plastic popper head. Often painted by the manufacturer.
- **Weed guard:** Heavy mono tied in a loop from the bend of the hook to the eye.
- **Difficulty:** 2.

CLASSIC FROG

- **Size:** 2-6.
- **Thread:** White 3/0.
- **Hook:** Stinger.
- **Tail:** Black over green bucktail, tied on bent needle, jointed with tying thread coated with epoxy, and then tied onto hook.
- **Body:** Made from spun and trimmed deer hair. White belly, with green top with narrow bands of black deer hair.
- **Eyes:** Red 3-D eyes with black pupils glued onto deer hair.
- **Weed Guard:** Monofilament looped from bend to eye.
- **Difficulty:** 5.

DANCING FROG

▌ **Size:** 2-4.
▌ **Thread:** White 3/0.
▌ **Hook:** Stinger.
▌ **Tail:** Large amount of yellow round rubber legs.
▌ **Body:** Mostly yellow spun and trimmed deer hair, with two concentric bands of green, brown, and black deer hair on top only.
▌ **Head:** Green deer hair with narrow wrist flared to hook eye, stiffened with glue on the front face.
▌ **Weed Guard:** Doubled monofilament looped from bend to eye.
▌ **Eyes:** Red 3-D eyes with black pupils glued onto deer hair.
▌ **Difficulty:** 5.

GULLEY FISH

▌ **Size:** 2/0-2.
▌ **Thread:** White 3/0.
▌ **Hook:** Long-shank saltwater.
▌ **Tail:** Blue over white marabou with pearl Flashabou in between.
▌ **Lip:** Clear hard plastic.
▌ **Body:** Oval-shaped white foam, with silver Flex Tubing pulled over the top, tied down at bend and eye. Put one coat of epoxy over the top half of the body only. Then trim the tubing from the underside of the body, add stick-on eyes, plus a black gill spot and a red throat colored with marker. Paint the top of the body with a blue marker. Finally, add two more coats of epoxy to the body.
▌ **Difficulty:** 4.

DRY RIND FROG

▌ **Size:** 2-6.
▌ **Hook:** Bass bug.
▌ **Thread:** Olive 3/0.
▌ **Tail:** Rawhide, cut to shape and colored with magic marker.
▌ **Body:** Yellow and olive spun and clipped deer hair in alternating segments. Flat on top and bottom, rounded on sides.
▌ **Other Materials:** Glued-on doll eyes. White rubber legs made from three pieces knotted together are tied on before last few segments of deer hair. V-shaped monofilament weed guard.
▌ **Difficulty:** 5.

HAIR BASS BUG

▌ **Size:** 2-4.
▌ **Thread:** Black 3/0.
▌ **Hook:** Stinger.
▌ **Tail:** Brown saddle hackles and black marabou.
▌ **Collar:** Tips of black deer hair immediately in front of tail.
▌ **Body:** White, then yellow, then white, then black, then white deer hair bands.
▌ **Legs:** Brown Tentacle Legs just in front of collar and in middle of body.
▌ **Eyes:** Doll eyes.
▌ **Difficulty:** 4.

PEEPER POPPER

- **Size:** 2-10.
- **Hook:** Kinked popper hook.
- **Thread:** Yellow 3/0.
- **Tail:** A pair of green and yellow hackle tips on each side.
- **Body:** Cork sanded to shape and painted yellow on bottom with green dots on top.
- **Hackle:** Green and yellow mixed.
- **Legs:** Living Rubber drawn through cork body.
- **Difficulty:** 2.
- **Notes:** Rubber legs may be pulled through cork body with a sewing needle.

SNEAKY PETE

- **Size:** 4-8.
- **Hook:** Bass bug.
- **Thread:** Black 3/0.
- **Tail:** Fluorescent green floss and white rubber legs.
- **Body:** Slider-type popper body painted chartreuse with black and white eyes.
- **Hackle:** Black.
- **Difficulty:** 2.
- **Notes:** This kind of fly is easier if you buy pre-made bodies and paint and dress them yourself.

RIVER RODENT

- **Size:** 2-6.
- **Thread:** Tan 3/0.
- **Hook:** Stinger.
- **Tail:** Tan Vernille or Ultra Chenille, burnt at end.
- **Body:** Natural deer hair, spun and trimmed.
- **Overlay:** Tan foam secured at back and front of hook shank.
- **Head:** Shaped deer hair with continuation of foam overlay.
- **Difficulty:** 3.

WHITLOCK MOUSERAT

- **Size:** 6.
- **Hook:** Bass bug.
- **Thread:** Black 3/0.
- **Tail:** Tan chamois.
- **Body:** Natural deer hair tied so natural ends are left long on top.
- **Head:** Deer hair trimmed into cone shape.
- **Ears:** Tan chamois.
- **Eyes:** Black paint or marker.
- **Whiskers:** Moose-mane fibers.
- **Weed guard:** Twenty-pound monofilament.
- **Difficulty:** 5.

BAILE'S OUT MINNOW

- **Size:** 2/0-4.
- **Thread:** Chartreuse 3/0.
- **Hook:** Stinger.
- **Tail:** Yellow marabou.
- **Body:** Yellow rabbit strip wound around body.
- **Overlay:** Chartreuse banded rabbit strip secured at bend and behind head.
- **Collar:** Yellow Laser Dub topped with chartreuse Craft Fur banded with brown marker, on top only. Draw a red gill line with a marker on the bottom of the yellow collar.
- **Head:** Epoxy over tying thread.
- **Eyes:** Large holographic.
- **Difficulty:** 3.

BASS BULLY

- **Size:** 2-6.
- **Thread:** Black 3/0.
- **Hook:** Stinger.
- **Tail:** Black rabbit strip.
- **Body:** Black Ice Chenille, then band of red Vernille.
- **Collar:** Black round rubber legs in front of Vernille.
- **Head:** Black wool, spun around hook and timed.
- **Eyes:** Red dumbbell eyes with black pupils.

- **Weed Guard:** Monofilament looped from bend to eye.
- **Difficulty:** 3.
- **Notes:** Also tied in rust and chartreuse.

COME AT ME CRAY

- **Size:** 2-6.
- **Thread:** Olive 3/0.
- **Hook:** Stinger.
- **Claws:** Olive rabbit strips with shaped olive foam glued to hide.
- **Rear Eyes:** Black plastic.
- **Body:** Olive Tarantula Hairy Legs Brush or Woolly Critter Brush or similar.
- **Overlay:** Olive Thin Skin coated with epoxy.
- **Rib:** Olive wire.
- **Collar:** Olive mottled Spanflex at tail area.
- **Head:** Thin Skin allowed to extend over eye to simulate a crayfish tail.
- **Eyes:** Silver bead chain at head; dumbbell eyes on shank opposite hook point.
- **Difficulty:** 4.
- **Notes:** Also tied in rust.

ENRICO'S DIVER

- **Size:** 2/0-4.
- **Thread:** Monofilament.
- **Hook:** Stinger.
- **Tail:** Red rabbit strip and red rubber legs.
- **Body:** Red Sparkle Brush with red rubber legs tied in two or three places in the middle of the body, underside of hook only.
- **Foam Tabs:** Three black egg-shaped foam discs tied on top of hook.
- **Difficulty:** 4.

GULLEY ULTRA CRAW

- **Size:** 2-6.
- **Thread:** Hot orange 3/0.
- **Hook:** Heavy jig hook.
- **Tail:** Trimmed section of suede tipped with orange fabric paint, plus a few strands of pearl Krystal Flash.
- **Body:** Wound with brown schlappen.
- **Collar:** Orange Sili Legs tied in at sides.
- **Head:** Tying thread covered with epoxy.
- **Eyes:** Two sets of silver dumbbell eyes.
- **Difficulty:** 3.

ENRICO'S BLUEGILL

- **Size:** 2/0-4.
- **Thread:** Monofilament.
- **Hook:** Stinger.
- **Tail:** Short red acrylic fibers like Craft Fur or EP Silky Fibers underneath, long pearl flash on top.
- **Body/Wing:** Olive 3D EP Fibers on top, tan EP Fibers below. Tie in stages, and halfway forward add strands of yellow EP Fibers on each side. At the head, continue the olive fibers on top but add orange fibers underneath for a throat. Add spots after trimming with black marker.
- **Eyes:** Large 3-D.
- **Difficulty:** 3.

GULLEY WORM

- **Size:** 1/0-2.
- **Thread:** White 3/0.
- **Hook:** Stinger.
- **Tail:** Three long strands of Estaz or Ice Chenille (two red and one black) braided together before attaching to the hook, with a foam tab coated with glue, sprinkled with sparkles, and then glued or tied to the end of the braid.
- **Body:** Red and black Estaz or Ice Chenille wound together.
- **Difficulty:** 3.

MAMA'S CORNBREAD

▎ **Size:** 1-4.
▎ **Thread:** Yellow 3/0.
▎ **Hook:** Daiichi 4660 or similar 90-degree jig hook.
▎ **Tail:** Yellow Flash Blend or Gliss N Glint, with white Craft Fur on top.
▎ **Tail Collar:** Tan alpaca or similar soft hair. Tie two yellow Centipede Legs along each side.
▎ **Body:** Tying thread.
▎ **Collar 1:** Brown raccoon tail.
▎ **Collar 2:** Yellow deer hair, on top side (same side as hook point) only.
▎ **Head:** Yellow fur.
▎ **Eyes:** Yellow dumbbell eyes with black pupils.
▎ **Difficulty:** 3.

MAY'S FULL MOTION CRAYFISH

▎ **Size:** 2-6.
▎ **Thread:** Red 3/0.
▎ **Hook:** 4X-long streamer.
▎ **Tail:** Yellow rabbit fur.
▎ **Body:** Brown wool, with a pair of black plastic eyes set just in front of the tail and about a dozen brown Sili Legs tied on bottom (opposite the hook point).
▎ **Collar:** Brown Zonker strip wound around hook shank in the middle of the body and then bound under toward the eyes.

▎ **Overlay:** Brown Furry Foam tied in at tail and head.
▎ **Eyes:** Unpainted dumbbell eyes.
▎ **Difficulty:** 3.

MINI FRANKENSTEIN SCULPIN

▎ **Most Popular Sizes.**
▎ **Thread:** Brown 3/0.
▎ **Hook:** Jig hook.
▎ **Tail:** Black and white barred marabou.
▎ **Body:** Brown Laser Dub palmered with brown webby hackle.
▎ **Collar:** Grizzly saddle hackle.
▎ **Head:** Brown Sculpin Helmet.
▎ **Eyes:** .3-D Eyes glued into head.
▎ **Difficulty:.2**

SCHULTZY'S LOW WATER CRAYFISH

▎ **Size:** 2-6.
▎ **Thread:** Olive 3/0.
▎ **Hook:** 3X-long nymph.
▎ **Tail:** Copper Flashabou and brown Sili Legs. Tie in an olive Zonker strip or Pine Squirrel Zonker strip on each side of the tail.
▎ **Body:** Olive grizzly marabou wound around hook shank.
▎ **Collar:** Orange grizzly marabou.
▎ **Head:** Brass cone.
▎ **Difficulty:** 2.

Pike

PIKE BUNNY

- **Size:** 6/0-1/0.
- **Thread:** Bright red 3/0.
- **Hook:** Pike and musky hook or long-shank saltwater.
- **Tail:** Long white Zonker strip and red Flashabou, over mono foul guard.
- **Body:** Red Magnum Zonker strip wound over hook shank.
- **Eyes:** Stick-on.
- **Difficulty:** 2.
- **Notes:** Also tied in black and yellow.

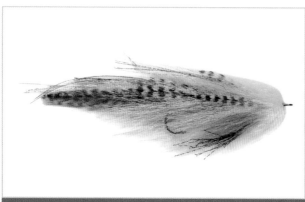

THE ROAMER

- **Size:** 4/0-1/0.
- **Thread:** Red 3/0.
- **Hook:** Pike and musky hook or Universal Predator for body; 40 mm shank for front.
- **Tail:** Two grizzly saddles inside two chartreuse saddles over white bucktail. A few strands of pearl Flashabou mixed in.
- **Body:** Chartreuse Polar Chenille.
- **Mid Wing:** Grizzly saddles over white bucktail (tie bucktail on top and bottom). Dark green Holographic Flashabou or similar over all.

- **Front Wing:** White bucktail covered with chartreuse bucktail (top and bottom) and dark green Holographic Flashabou, with grizzly saddle hackles over the top.
- **Throat:** Red Krystal Flash.
- **Collar:** Laser Dub, white on bottom and chartreuse on top.
- **Difficulty:** 3.
- **Notes:** Use either long deer body hair or bucktail from the base of the tail to get some flare to the hair. Also reverse-tie the hair (tips facing forward and then fold it back) to build up the profile of the fly.

RATTLIN BAITFISH

- **Size:** 2/0-2.
- **Thread:** White 3/0.
- **Hook:** Standard saltwater.
- **Wing:** Olive bucktail over pearl Krystal Flash over white saddle hackles tied flat over more white bucktail.
- **Rattle:** Glass rattle tied on top of hook shank, under wing.
- **Throat:** White bucktail.
- **Collar:** Deer hair tips from head.
- **Head:** Olive spun and trimmed deer hair on top. White deer hair, then a narrow band of red deer hair, then more white deer hair on bottom.
- **Eyes:** Red 3-D.
- **Difficulty:** 4.

Carp

HISE'S CARPNASTY

- **Size:** 4-8.
- **Thread:** Red 6/0.
- **Hook:** 2X-long nymph.
- **Tail:** Two brown partridge feathers and two tan Sili Legs.
- **Body:** Yellow sparkle dubbing palmered with brown partridge or speckled hen feather.
- **Collar:** Two tan Sili Legs tied on top.
- **Eyes:** Red dumbbell.
- **Difficulty:** 2.
- **Notes:** Also tied in gray.

JAN'S CARP TICKLER

- **Size:** 4-8.
- **Thread:** Red 6/0.
- **Hook:** Standard wet fly.
- **Tail:** Red Vernille with tuft of red marabou tied on the end.
- **Body:** Red Cactus Chenille or Estaz.
- **Legs:** Two red-tipped black rubber legs on each side.
- **Eyes:** Gold bead chain.
- **Difficulty:** 3.
- **Notes:** Also tied in rust or olive.

MAY'S CLEARWATER CRAYFISH

- **Size:** 2-6.
- **Thread:** Tan 6/0.
- **Hook:** Heavy jig.
- **Tail:** Long pheasant tail fibers, short bunch or orange fur, and two black plastic eyes.
- **Body:** Tan sparkle dubbing.
- **Legs:** Two tan Sili Legs tied in middle of body facing rearward.
- **Claws:** Two golden pheasant body feathers tied in middle of body facing rearward.
- **Overlay:** Natural deer hair, ribbed with copper wire forward of legs only. Leave butt ends trimmed short, facing up to imitate tail of crayfish.
- **Bead:** Copper slotted tungsten.
- **Difficulty:** 3.

MAY'S IDENTITY CRISIS

- **Size:** 4-8.
- **Thread:** Black 6/0.
- **Hook:** 4X-long Streamer.
- **Tail:** Brown marabou and two brown Sili Legs.
- **Body:** Brown sparkle dubbing.
- **Rib:** Copper wire over rear two-thirds of body only.
- **Overlay:** Brown mottled turkey quill.
- **Legs:** Four brown Sili Legs tied at front and back of thorax.
- **Gills:** A bunch of webby brown partridge fibers tied on both sides.
- **Eyes:** Bead chain painted black.
- **Difficulty:** 3.
- **Notes:** Also tied in tan and light olive.

MIKE'S GORGON CRAW

- **Size:** 8.
- **Thread:** Olive 6/0.
- **Hook:** Stinger.
- **Tail:** Olive rubber hackle and two olive Sili Legs.
- **Body:** Olive fur.
- **Wing:** Olive CDC.
- **Eyes:** Gold bead chain.
- **Difficulty:** 2.
- **Notes:** Also tied in tan.

SCOF SICK LITTLE MONKEY

- **Size:** 4-8.
- **Thread:** Red 6/0.
- **Hook:** 2X-long nymph.
- **Tail:** Brown marabou and copper Krystal Flash.
- **Body:** Tan fur ribbed with short olive-barred marabou or soft grizzly saddle hackle.
- **Legs:** Two brown Sili Legs on each side.
- **Head:** Olive Fish Skull Sculpin Head.
- **Eyes:** Holographic, glued to top of head.
- **Difficulty:** 3.
- **Notes:** Also tied in brown.

MIKE'S FUZZY NIBLET

- **Size:** 6-10.
- **Thread:** Tan 6/0.
- **Hook:** 2X-long nymph.
- **Tail:** Brown barred marabou.
- **Body:** Tan sparkle dubbing.
- **Throat:** Tan Laser Dub.
- **Collar:** Brown partridge.
- **Eyes:** Bead chain painted black.
- **Difficulty:** 2.
- **Notes:** Also tied in olive.

INDEX